HISTORICAL DICTIONARIES OF RELIGIONS, PHILOSOPHIES, AND MOVEMENTS
Jon Woronoff, Series Editor

1. *Buddhism,* by Charles S. Prebish, 1993
2. *Mormonism,* by Davis Bitton, 1994. *Out of print. See No. 32.*
3. *Ecumenical Christianity,* by Ans Joachim van der Bent, 1994
4. *Terrorism,* by Sean Anderson and Stephen Sloan, 1995. *Out of print. See No. 41.*
5. *Sikhism,* by W. H. McLeod, 1995
6. *Feminism,* by Janet K. Boles and Diane Long Hoeveler, 1995. *Out of print. See No. 52.*
7. *Olympic Movement,* by Ian Buchanan and Bill Mallon, 1995. *Out of print. See No. 39.*
8. *Methodism,* by Charles Yrigoyen Jr. and Susan E. Warrick, 1996. *Out of Print. See No. 57.*
9. *Orthodox Church,* by Michael Prokurat, Alexander Golitzin, and Michael D. Peterson, 1996
10. *Organized Labor,* by James C. Docherty, 1996. *Out of print. See No. 50.*
11. *Civil Rights Movement,* by Ralph E. Luker, 1997
12. *Catholicism,* by William J. Collinge, 1997
13. *Hinduism,* by Bruce M. Sullivan, 1997
14. *North American Environmentalism,* by Edward R. Wells and Alan M. Schwartz, 1997
15. *Welfare State,* by Bent Greve, 1998
16. *Socialism,* by James C. Docherty, 1997
17. *Bahá'í Faith,* by Hugh C. Adamson and Philip Hainsworth, 1998
18. *Taoism,* by Julian F. Pas in cooperation with Man Kam Leung, 1998
19. *Judaism,* by Norman Solomon, 1998
20. *Green Movement,* by Elim Papadakis, 1998
21. *Nietzscheanism,* by Carol Diethe, 1999
22. *Gay Liberation Movement,* by Ronald J. Hunt, 1999
23. *Islamic Fundamentalist Movements in the Arab World, Iran, and Turkey,* by Ahmad S. Moussalli, 1999
24. *Reformed Churches,* by Robert Benedetto, Darrell L. Guder, and Donald K. McKim, 1999
25. *Baptists,* by William H. Brackney, 1999
26. *Cooperative Movement,* by Jack Shaffer, 1999

27. *Reformation and Counter-Reformation,* by Hans J. Hillerbrand, 2000
28. *Shakers,* by Holley Gene Duffield, 2000
29. *United States Political Parties,* by Harold F. Bass Jr., 2000
30. *Heidegger's Philosophy,* by Alfred Denker, 2000
31. *Zionism,* by Rafael Medoff and Chaim I. Waxman, 2000
32. *Mormonism,* 2nd ed., by Davis Bitton, 2000
33. *Kierkegaard's Philosophy,* by Julia Watkin, 2001
34. *Hegelian Philosophy,* by John W. Burbidge, 2001
35. *Lutheranism,* by Günther Gassmann in cooperation with Duane H. Larson and Mark W. Oldenburg, 2001
36. *Holiness Movement,* by William Kostlevy, 2001
37. *Islam,* by Ludwig W. Adamec, 2001
38. *Shinto,* by Stuart D. B. Picken, 2002
39. *Olympic Movement,* 2nd ed., by Ian Buchanan and Bill Mallon, 2001
40. *Slavery and Abolition,* by Martin A. Klein, 2002
41. *Terrorism,* 2nd ed., by Sean Anderson and Stephen Sloan, 2002
42. *New Religious Movements,* by George D. Chryssides, 2001
43. *Prophets in Islam and Judaism,* by Scott B. Noegel and Brannon M. Wheeler, 2002
44. *The Friends (Quakers),* by Margery Post Abbott, Mary Ellen Chijioke, Pink Dandelion, and John William Oliver Jr., 2003
45. *Lesbian Liberation Movement: Still the Rage,* JoAnne Myers, 2003
46. *Descartes and Cartesian Philosophy,* by Roger Ariew, Dennis Des Chene, Douglas M. Jesseph, Tad M. Schmaltz, and Theo Verbeek, 2003
47. *Witchcraft,* by Michael D. Bailey, 2003
48. *Unitarian Universalism,* by Mark W. Harris, 2004
49. *New Age Movements,* by Michael York, 2004
50. *Organized Labor,* 2nd ed., by James C. Docherty, 2004
51. *Utopianism,* by James M. Morris and Andrea L. Kross, 2004
52. *Feminism,* 2nd ed., by Janet K. Boles and Diane Long Hoeveler, 2004
53. *Jainism,* by Kristi L. Wiley, 2004
54. *Wittgenstein's Philosophy,* by Duncan Richter, 2004
55. *Schopenhauer's Philosophy,* by David E. Cartwright, 2005
56. *Seventh-Day Adventists,* by Gary Land, 2005
57. *Methodism,* 2nd ed., by Charles Yrigoyen Jr. and Susan E. Warrick, 2005
58. *Sufism,* by John Renard, 2005

Historical Dictionary of Sufism

John Renard

Historical Dictionaries of Religions, Philosophies, and Movements, No. 58

The Scarecrow Press, Inc.
Lanham, Maryland • Toronto • Oxford
2005

SCARECROW PRESS, INC.

Published in the United States of America
by Scarecrow Press, Inc.
A wholly owned subsidiary of
The Rowman & Littlefield Publishing Group, Inc.
4501 Forbes Boulevard, Suite 200, Lanham, Maryland 20706
www.scarecrowpress.com

PO Box 317
Oxford
OX2 9RU, UK

British Library Cataloguing in Publication Information Available

Library of Congress Cataloging-in-Publication Data

Renard, John, 1944–
Historical dictionary of Sufism / John Renard.
p. cm. — (Historical dictionaries of religions, philosophies, and movements ; no. 58)
Includes bibliographical references.
ISBN 0-8108-5342-6 (hardcover : alk. paper)
1. Sufism—Dictionaries. I. Title. II. Series.

BP188.48.R46 2005
297'.09—dc22 2004026282

™ The paper used in this publication meets the minimum requirements of American National Standard for Information Sciences—Permanence of Paper for Printed Library Materials, ANSI/NISO Z39.48-1992.
Manufactured in the United States of America.

Contents

Editor's Foreword

Sufism, a term derived from the woolen garments of early ascetics, may not be the most exact expression to cover the mystical movements within Islam, but it is the best we have. And it would be hard to come up with another that is more precise, because the phenomenon itself has taken on such a variety of forms during the 1,200 or so years it has already existed. Under this heading come many different orders, established at many different times and in many different places, by many different spiritual directors. They did not always agree on all points—indeed, they occasionally quarreled and certainly rivaled one another—and this is still valid today. But their ultimate goals were the same, and they drew inspiration from the same holy Qur'ān and the awesome figure of the Prophet Muḥammad. It is this diversity that often confuses outsiders, and it is this diversity that makes a work of this sort so useful, since rather than trying to impose uniformity and order where none exist it can show the impressive variety of origins, structures and organizations, rules and creeds, and practices and concepts. It can also delve into the cultural wealth of art, music, dance, and literature.

This is facilitated by the format of a historical dictionary. First, the chronology traces the long and venerable list of spiritual directors, poets and philosophers, and also political leaders who created and enriched the movement. Then, the introduction, vital given the diversity, can bring the salient aspects together in a broad and ordered whole. But it is the dictionary that again allows a multitude of aspects, persons, places, events, institutions, and concepts to be considered individually. Since terminology is so important, and virtually all of it is in Arabic, Persian, and other languages unfamiliar to most English speakers, the glossary is particularly precious. For those who want to take the study of Sufism further, and there will be more and more with time, the bibliography points to other sources of information.

This *Historical Dictionary of Sufism* was written by John Renard, an eminent student and teacher of the subject. His doctoral dissertation dealt with the renowned Sufi Rūmī, and since then he has written a dozen books, mostly on Islam and Sufism. Since 1978, he has been teaching at the Department of Theological Studies at Saint Louis University. He is well aware of the diversity and variety, and, if anything, appreciates it, and over the past quarter century of writing and teaching he has become accustomed to explaining the many twists and turns, the highways and also the byways, the theological and legal aspects, and the rich culture that has grown up around it. Since Dr. Renard deals not only with scholars and initiates but also students and outsiders, he knows how to present Sufism to a more general public as well. So let us take advantage.

Jon Woronoff,
Series Editor

Acknowledgments and Credits

I gratefully acknowledge the kind assistance of the following colleagues in Islamic studies for their helpful comments on various drafts of several elements of this volume: Bruce Lawrence of Duke University; Ahmet Karamustafa of Washington University; Laury Silvers of Skidmore College; Hayrettin Yücesoy of Saint Louis University; and Qamar-ul Huda of Boston College. I wish to thank also series editor Jon Woronoff for his invitation to do this volume, his flexibility in the timing of its delivery, and for his ongoing comments as I hammered out the various pieces of the book. Special thanks to Matt Gilbertson and Inta Ivanovska of Saint Louis University for their able editorial assistance on various aspects of the project and in compiling the bibliography and chronology. My thanks go also to Saint Louis University for support in the form of a Mellon Summer Stipend and a Graduate School Summer Research Award.

I am grateful to the following institutions for permission to use their holdings as credited individually in the illustration section: The Saint Louis Art Museum, with special thanks to Pat Woods of Photographic Services and Permissions for help in securing the cover photo; the Los Angeles County Museum of Art; the Freer and Sackler Galleries of the Smithsonian Institution; the Fogg and Sackler collections of the Harvard University Art Museums; the Walters Museum in Baltimore; the Bawa Muhaiyaddeen Fellowship. I thank the University of California Press for permission to use the flyleaf map that appeared in my *Windows on the House of Islam* (1998). Lastly, I thank my wife, Mary Pat, for her loving support and unfailing good humor over the long haul.

PHOTO CREDITS

Cover Photo: Courtesy St. Louis Art Museum, 83.42

Map: Reprinted from John Renard, *Windows on the House of Islam*, copyright © 1998 by the Regents of the University of California, 1998, with permission of the University of California Press.

Fig. 1. Photo © John Renard.

Fig. 2. Photo © John Renard.

Fig. 3. Photo © John Renard.

Fig. 4. Photo © John Renard.

Fig. 5. Photo © John Renard.

Fig. 6. Photo © John Renard.

Fig. 7. Photo © John Renard.

Fig. 8. Material printed with the permission of the Bawa Muhaiyaddeen Fellowship, 5820 Overbrook Drive, Philadelphia, PA 19131.

Fig. 9. Thanks to Carl W. Ernst for supplying the calendar art.

Fig. 10. Courtesy of the Arthur M. Sackler Museum, Harvard University Art Museums, Sarah C. Sears Collection. 1936.28 Artist Unknown.

Fig. 11. Courtesy of the Walters Art Museum, Baltimore.

Fig. 12. Courtesy of the Arthur M. Sackler Museum, Harvard University Art Museums, Grace Nichols Strong, Francis H. Burr and Friends of the Fogg Art Museum Funds. 1950.135.

Fig. 13. Courtesy of the Arthur M. Sackler Museum, Harvard University Art Museums, Promised Gift of Mr. and Mrs. Stuart Cary Welch, Jr. Partially owned by the Metropolitan Museum and the Arthur M. Sackler Museum, HUAM 1988.460.3. Painted by Sultan Muhammad.

Fig. 14. Freer Gallery of Art, Smithsonian Institution, Washington, D.C.: Purchase, F 1946.12.

Fig. 15. Arthur M. Sackler Gallery, Smithsonian Institution, Washington, D.C.: Smithsonian Unrestricted Trust Funds, Smithsonian Collections Acquisition Program and Dr. Arthur M. Sackler, S1986.432.

Fig. 16. Arthur M. Sackler Gallery, Smithsonian Institution, Washington, D.C.: Smithsonian Unrestricted Trust Funds, Smithsonian Collections Acquisition Program and Dr. Arthur M. Sackler, S1986.35.

Fig. 17. Courtesy of the St. Louis Art Museum. Purchase 86:23.

Fig. 18. Courtesy of the St. Louis Art Museum. Purchase 386:1952.

Fig. 19. Courtesy Los Angeles County Museum of Art, Nasli M. Neeramaneech Collection, Gift of Joan Pavlevsky M.73.5.582.

Fig. 20. Photo © John Renard.

Reader's Note

The individual elements of this volume include a *map* showing major cities and regions from Spain to Indonesia; a *chronology* spanning some 14 centuries of Islamic history; a historical *introduction* that provides a quick overview of approaches to the history of Sufism; the A to Z entries of the *dictionary* proper; a *glossary* of technical terms; an extensive *bibliography* organized thematically; and a collection of *illustrations*, including photos of pertinent works of art and architecture as well as a few scenes of Sufi activities.

The Chronology

An extensive chronological table offers a running list of major events and persons in the history of Sufism as well as some other key events in Islamic history and beyond for purposes of broader contextualization. It provides a device that can suggest diachronic relationships among figures geographically distant, a relationship not otherwise easily shown. Here I have biased the dating toward the non-Islamic solar years (since most readers will look first for those dates) but have kept the Islamic lunar Hijrī dates as well; for example, 622/1.

The Illustrations

Photographs included here offer a blend of more contemporary "action" documentation, shots of relevant surviving medieval Sufi architecture, and representative works of art on Sufi themes in various media from the holdings of several American museums.

The Dictionary

A word about the structure and organization of the dictionary entries: My overall concern has been to balance the interests and needs of two general groups of potential readers. On the one hand, the entries in the dictionary are biased toward English, the better to serve readers not necessarily familiar with technical terminology of Islamic studies and the history of Sufism. On the other, I have included in the dictionary most of the foreign terms listed in the glossary, cross-referencing them to relevant entries linked to equivalent English terms and general concepts.

In general, I have maintained a bias toward Arabic terminology, since the vast majority of Sufi terms originated in Arabic. This overall bias has led to one unintended consequence resulting, in most cases, from morphological peculiarities of Arabic: I ask the reader's indulgence with the occasional blocks of cross-referenced technical Arabic and other non-English terms. Readers familiar with other volumes in this series will have encountered a similar organizational issue in Ahmad Moussalli's *Historical Dictionary of Islamic Fundamentalist Movements in the Arab World, Iran, and Turkey* (1999). Arabic and other technical terms that appear in various entries but do not have their own entries are not cross-referenced by bolding; for such terms, readers will find a quick reference in the glossary.

The present dictionary seeks to provide basic information on the considerable geographical breadth of Sufism's spread, with entries on most of the written and-nontextual sources mentioned here, as well as the major regions and cities of importance in the history of Sufism. Individual historical surveys of Sufism to date have in general not striven for the broadest possible geographical inclusiveness, typically scrimping on one or more regions, including China, Southeast Asia, Eastern Europe, and sub-Saharan Africa. Though the entries are in general not detailed enough to supply information for serious synchronic study, they will nevertheless give readers an idea of the vast possibilities awaiting further study along these lines.

The Glossary

Mostly in Arabic and Persian but including some Chinese and Turkish words, the glossary lists several hundred technical terms with very brief definitions for quick reference. These terms also appear in different contexts in the dictionary, typically cross-referenced from the original-language term to an article on a related topic.

The Bibliography

A reader's note that provides an introductory overview, highlighting key aspects of the literature, precedes the bibliography itself.

Transliteration

Authors of broad-ranging books in Islamic studies invariably confront the perplexing challenge of establishing a consistent protocol for transliterating non-English terminology. In the interest of technical precision (for the benefit of specialists), I have chosen a fairly comprehensive standard approach to transliterating names and technical terms. This includes indication of long vowels (ā, ī, ū) and consonants that require overstrike dots beneath them (ḥ, ṣ, ṭ, ḍ, ẓ). Again the bias is toward the largely Arabic origins of these terms, and I have opted for transliteration that reflects an Arabic pronunciation of many terms that have long been standard vocabulary in languages such as Persian, Turkish, and Malay. Attempting to acknowledge peculiarities of pronunciation in those and other languages would have resulted in a very confusing babble of conventions.

I have sought to maintain consistent transliteration of non-European vocabulary throughout the book, with the notable exception of the bibliography, because of the profusion of sources from which I drew the material (including lists that already showed titles and names modified from formats printed on the original works—works not readily available to me) and the bewildering variety of transliteration systems (or lack thereof) chosen by the original authors and publishers. The exception here is that I have attempted to give full transliteration of the names of the (generally Muslim) authors of works in the sections on primary-source editions and translations.

Within the dictionary entries I have opted for one minor, but consistent, variation: I have not incorporated diacriticals in the names of cities (such as Baghdad), regions (such as Khurasan), and nation-states (such as Iraq), except when those geographical designators are used adjectivally (e.g. Baghdādī, Khurāsānī, 'Irāqī), or when the place name merits its own entry, in which case the headword receives full transliteration (e.g., Ajmīr, Baṣra). Given the complexity of the whole business of transliteration, I ask the reader's indulgence with the numerous judgment calls the options demanded.

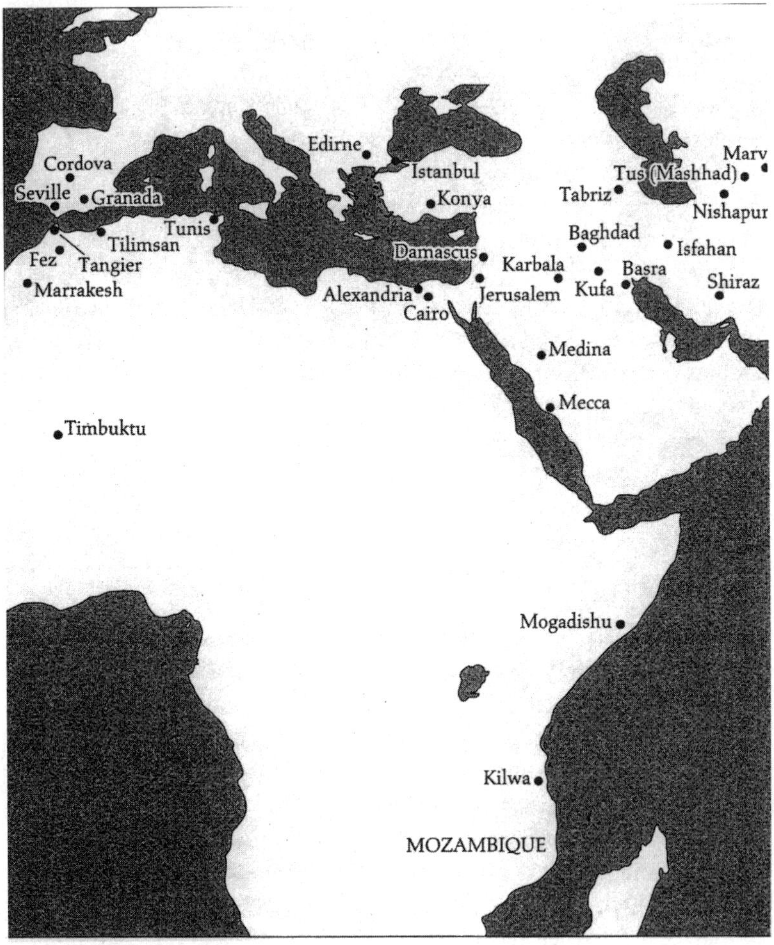

Cordova
Seville
Granada
Tunis
Tilimsan
Fez
Tangier
Marrakesh
Edirne
Istanbul
Konya
Damascus
Alexandria
Cairo
Jerusalem
Karbala
Baghdad
Kufa
Basra
Tabriz
Tus (Mashhad)
Marv
Nishapur
Isfahan
Shiraz
Medina
Mecca
Timbuktu
Mogadishu
Kilwa
MOZAMBIQUE

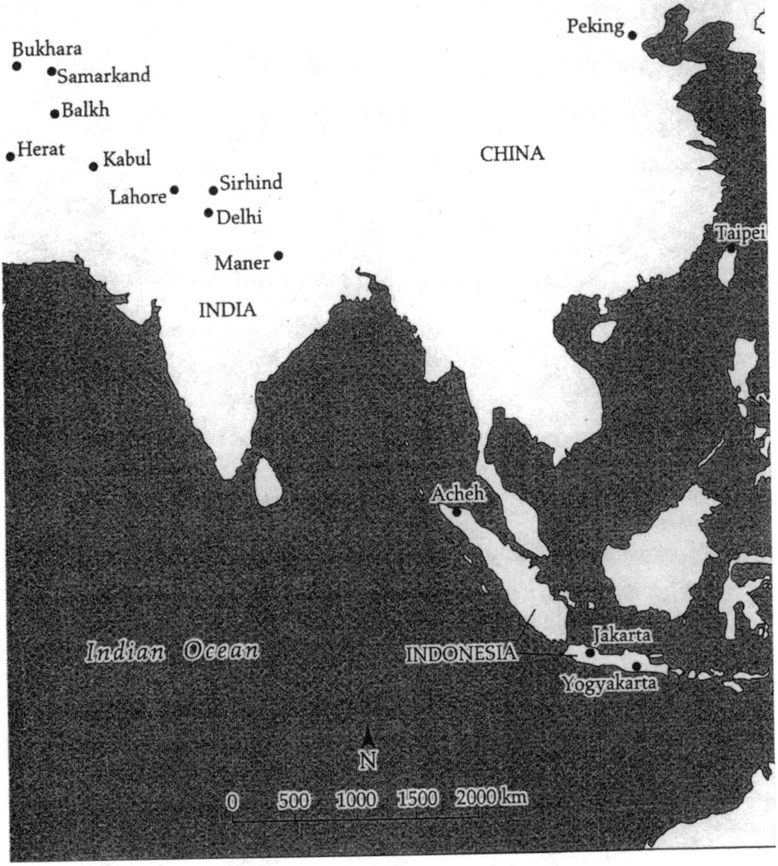

Bukhara
Samarkand
Balkh
Herat
Kabul
Lahore
Sirhind
Delhi
Maner
INDIA
Peking
CHINA
Taipei
Acheh
Indian Ocean
INDONESIA
Jakarta
Yogyakarta
N
0 500 1000 1500 2000 km

Chronology

Unless otherwise noted, a single date indicates an individual's year of death.

525 Dhū Nuwās, South Arabian Jewish king; south Arabia becomes an Abyssinian satrapy.

570 Ma'rib dam breaks for the third time (in Yemen); final disintegration of ancient south Arabian civilization.

570 Birth of the Prophet Muḥammad.

c. 595 Muḥammad marries Khadīja, first and only wife while she lived.

c. 595 End of the Lakhmid dynasty, which had served the Persians as a frontier guard in the city of Ḥirā and client state against the Byzantine Empire's Arab proxies, the Ghassānids.

610 Muḥammad's call and first experience of the Qur'ān.

615 "Little Hijra"—Muḥammad sends Muslims to seek refuge in Abyssinia.

619 Khadīja; and Muḥammad's protector and uncle Abū Ṭālib.

c. 621 Muḥammad's Night Journey (to Jerusalem) and Ascension the various levels of heaven and hell.

622/1 The *Hijra*: Muḥammad and followers travel from Mecca to Medina, and Muslim era begins.

624/2 Muslim victory over Meccans at Badr (March 13/17th Ramaḍān)

625/3 Muslim defeat at Uḥud (March, 15th Shawwāl)

630/9 Conquest of Mecca and integration of Ka'ba into Islamic practice.

630–631/9–10 Ja'far aṭ-Ṭayyār, Muḥammad's cousin, slain in early battle, called the "flyer" because he flew in spite of massive wounds; early paradigm of religious hero.

632/11 Prophet Muḥammad, succeeded by father-in-law, Abū Bakr.

632-634/11–13 Abū Bakr quells uprisings in Arabia (Wars of Apostasy, *ridda*) invades Mesopotamia and Palestine.

633/11 Fāṭima, daughter of Muḥammad and Khadīja, model for female spirituality.

634-644/13–24 Greatest conquests by early Muslim Arabs under Caliph 'Umar.

636-38/15-17 Capture of Damascus (December 636) and Jerusalem (Early 638).

639-640/18–19 Conquest of Egypt and Persia, end of Sasanian Zoroastrian empire.

641/20 or 21 Bilāl ibn Rabāḥ, black Abyssinian, first muezzin.

644/24 Second Caliph 'Umar ibn al-Khaṭṭāb, model of devout life.

c. 652/32 Abū 'd-Dardā', Companion of the Prophet in Medina and ḥadīth transmitter, considered by Sufis to be among the early Muslim ascetics dubbed the "People of the Bench."

653/32 Abū Dharr al-Ghifārī, a Companion of the Prophet, transmitter of ḥadīth, and ascetic model of devotion.

c. 653/33 Traditional date at which "canon" of the Qur'ān was established by 'Uthmān.

656/36 Salmān al-Fārisī (the barber), early Christian convert to Islam, model for later Sufis. Murder of 'Uthmān, the third caliph; 'Alī succeeds as caliph.

656/36–661/41 First *fitna*, internal struggles for Muslim leadership.

657/36 Uways al-Qaranī martyred in the Battle of Ṣiffīn on the side of 'Alī, the caliph. Kharijites "secede" from 'Alī, raising questions about who is "true Muslim" and the relationship of observable sin to membership in the community.

661/41 'Alī ibn Abī Ṭālib, first Shī'ī *Imām* and important figure in many Sufi lineages.

661/41–750/133 Umayyad dynasty founded, with capital at Damascus, important city in history of Sufism.

661/41–680/62 Mu'āwiya caliph; beginning of second great period of expansion.

662/42 Maximus the Confessor, first Christian mystic to articulate purgative, illuminative, and unitive phases of mystical path.

678/59 'Ā'isha, Muḥammad's youngest wife, daughter of Abū Bakr, responsible for transmitting important traditions.

680/61 Ḥusayn ibn 'Alī, grandson of Prophet, martyred at Karbalā' in southern Iraq; death commemorated on 10th of Muḥarram.

692/73 Completion of the Dome of the Rock, Jerusalem; traditional site of Prophet's Ascension.

8th century/1st–2nd century Jamīl, poet from tribe of 'Udhra, chaste love for Buthayna model for Sufi poets.

715/96–97 Completion of Al-Aqṣā Mosque, Jerusalem, traditionally identified as goal of Prophet's mystical Night Journey.

728/110 Ḥasan al-Baṣrī, community leader of Basra pietists, prototypical Sufi ascetic.

c. 748/131 Mālik ibn Dīnār, ascetic of Basra.

749/132 Farqad as-Sabakhī, ascetic of Basra.

750-1258/133–656 'Abbāsid dynasty, capital at newly founded city of Baghdad, early center of major ascetics and Sufi groups.

765/148 Ja'far aṣ-Ṣādiq, Shī'ī leader, sixth *Imām* (for most Shī'ī Muslims), major figure in history of mystical exegesis.

767/150 Abū Ḥanafa, jurist of Kufa, Ḥanafi School named for him. Muqātil ibn Sulaymān, major exegete of Iraq.

770/153 ʻUmar ibn ʻAbd al-ʻAzīz (ʻUmar II), Umayyad caliph, considered by Sufis and others as model of piety as ruler, less worldly than other Umayyads.

772/156 Ḥabīb al-ʻAjamī, important ascetic.

777/161 Ibrāhīm ibn Adham, Khurāsānī ascetic.

795/179 Mālik ibn Anas, Meccan founder of Sunnī law school that became dominant in Spain and North Africa.

750-850/133–236 Legal implications of the Qur'ān put into more systematic form by the scholars considered the founders of the four Sunnī law schools: Abū Ḥanīfa (d. 767), Mālik ibn Anas (d. 795), Ash-Shāfiʻī (d. 820), and Aḥmad ibn Ḥanbal (d. 855).

c. 800/184 Buhlul ibn ʻAmr, "wise fool" famed for his blunt social critique.

9th/2nd–3rd century Abū ʻAli as-Sindī, perhaps Bāyazīd al-Bisṭāmī's mystical master. Riḥāna al-Wāliḥa, saintly woman mystic. Rābiʻa ash-Shāmīya, Syrian wife of Ahmad ibn Abi'l-Ḥawārī, noted for her constantly changing mystical states.

c. 801/185 Rābiʻa al-ʻAdawīya, female poet, ascetic, mystic of Basra whom some consider the first true Muslim mystic in her desire to move beyond mere asceticism.

809/193 Hārūn ar-Rashīd, ʻAbbāsid caliph, "hero" of *1001 Nights*.

810/194 Shaqīq al-Balkhī, originated discussion of mystical "states."

815/200 Maʻrūf al-Karkhī, leading Sufi in Baghdad.

820/205 Ḥadīth scholar and jurist Muḥammad ibn Idrīs ash-Shāfiʻī, founder of Sunnī law school prominent in central Middle East, Indonesia. Shankara, Shaivite Hindu theologian and mystic.

824/208 Sayyida Nafīsa, female descendant of the Prophet, known for virtue and piety; tomb in Cairo still visited by devotees.

833/218 Ma'mūn, ʻAbbāsid caliph from 813–833, major sponsor of Arabic translations of Greek scientific and philosophical texts, preserving scholarship that influenced Western thought and science in the later

Middle Ages. Favored Mu'tazilite rationalist thought and recognized it as his 'state' creed.

841/227 Bishr ibn al-Ḥārith "Al-Ḥāfī," "The Barefoot," famous ascetic.

849/235 Fāṭima of Nishapur, Khurāsānī mystic, wife of Aḥmad Khiḍrūya, acquaintance of Bāyazīd and Dhū 'n-Nūn.

855/241 Aḥmad ibn Ḥanbal, founder of the fourth Sunnī school of law, currently dominant in the Arabian Peninsula.

857/243 Al-Ḥārith ibn Asad al-Muḥāsibī, 'Irāqī mystical teacher and theorist, author of *Observance of the Rights of God*.

860/245 Thawbān ibn Ibrāhīm Dhū 'n-Nūn, Egyptian Sufi considered to be creator of unique interpretation of experiential knowledge. Abū Turāb an-Nakhshabī, Central Asian ascetic and follower of Ḥātim al-Aṣamm.

861/246 Al-Mutawakkil, 'Abbāsid caliph who opposed Mu'tazilite theology and restored Ibn Ḥanbal's traditionalism to centrality.

c. 867/253 Sarī "as-Saqaṭī," Baghdad ascetic, controversial teaching on love.

870/256 Al-Buhkārī, Central Asian scholar whose collection of Ḥadīth became one of the two most important of the "Six" authoritative collections.

872/258 Yaḥyā ibn Mu'ādh ar-Rāzī, Sufi preacher of Nishapur.

873/259 Ḥunayn ibn Isḥāq, Scholar under whom Greek translation reached its height. Al-Kindī, first great Arab philosopher.

873/260 Twelfth *Imām* of the "Twelver Shī'a" goes into "Lesser Concealment." According to the Shī'ī belief, he works as Lord of Time from his concealment until his return.

875/261 Ṭayfūr ibn 'Īsā Abū Yazīd (Bāyazīd) al-Bisṭamī, Persian mystic known for his ecstatic utterances.

c. 878/265 Abū Ḥafṣ al-Ḥaddād, mystic/ascetic of Nishapur.

884/270–1 Ḥamdūn al-Qaṣṣār, Khurāsānī ascetic and leader of Malāmatīya.

888/275 Aḥmad Ghulām Khalīl, brought charges against Sufis of Baghdad and Nūrī in 885/272.

896/283 ‘Alī ibn ar-Rūmī, ‘Irāqī poet who described Sufi ascetical practices at Basra. Sahl at-Tustarī, early Sufi exegete and theorist, frequently cited by manualists, influenced the Sālimīya school of thought.

c. 898/285 Muḥammad ibn ‘Alī al-Ḥakīm at-Tirmidhī, Central Asian theorist.

899/286 Abū Sa‘īd al-Kharrāz, ‘Irāqī-born author of *Book of Authenticity*.

10th/3rd–4th century Period of major developments in Sufi literature: the first great manuals of spirituality by Makkī, Kālābādhī, and Sarrāj.

c. 904/291 Ibrāhīm al-Khawwāṣ, itinerant ascetic from Iraq.

907/295 Abū ’l-Ḥusayn an-Nūrī, Sufi in Baghdad, disciple of Sarī “as-Saqaṭī” and author of *The Stations of Hearts*.

909/296 Muḥammad ibn Dā’ūd, son of the founder of the Ẓāhirī school of law, denounced Ḥallāj and incited other scholars against him. Composed a book on the ideal of chaste love and stressed the martyrdom of chastity; denied the possibility of divine-human mutual love, excluding all human elements from mystical love. ‘Amr ibn ‘Uthmān al-Makkī.

910/298 Junayd, author, legal scholar, mystic in Baghdad, greatest of the “sober” mystics. Sumnūn ibn Ḥamza “Al-Muḥibb,” early Baghdad Sufi, follower of Sarī “as-Saqaṭī.” Abū ‘Uthmān al-Ḥīrī, Central Asian ascetic.

915/302–3 Ruwaym ibn Aḥmad, early Baghdad mystic, associate of Junayd.

c. 922/310 Abū ’l-‘Abbās ibn ‘Aṭā’ killed, supporter of Ḥallāj.

923/311 Abū Ja‘far aṭ-Ṭabarī, great historiographer and Qur’ān commentator.

931/319 Ibn Masarra, Iberian mystical author, philosopher, ascetic and leader of early Sufi school of Cordoba.

932/320 Muḥammad ibn ʻAlī al-Ḥakīm at-Tirmidhī, Central Asian theorist.

c. 932/320 Abū Bakr Muḥammad al-Wāsiṭī, Baghdad contemporary of Ḥallāj.

934/322 Abū Bakr al-Kattānī, early member of Baghdad school. Abū ʻAlī Aḥmad ar-Rūdhbārī, mystic of Shāfiʻī School of Law.

935/323 Al-Ashʻarī, leading theologian who introduced elements of Mu'tazilite methodology into mainstream theology.

945/333–4 Shiblī, ʻIrāqī Sufi and disciple of Junayd.

949-1022 Simeon the New Theologian, major Byzantine author on deification and mystical experience.

950/338–9 Al-Fārābī, major Islamic philosopher of Turkic descent.

959/348 Jaʻfar al-Khuldī, associate of Junayd in Baghdad.

965/354 or 976/366 ʻAbd al-Jabbār an-Niffarī, enigmatic ʻIrāqī author of *Book of Mystical Sayings* and *Mystical Adresses*.

965/354 Mutanabbī, great Arab Ḥamdānid court panegyrist.

969/358–1171/566 Fāṭimid dynasty rules central Middle East from newly founded capital of Cairo.

973/362 Azhar mosque founded in Cairo, becomes the center of Shīʻī intellectual life under Fāṭimid rule.

977/367 Abū 'l-Qāsim Ibrāhīm an-Naṣrābādhī, disciple of Shiblī.

982/371 Ibn Khafīf, major mystic of Shiraz, age of c. 100. Abū 'l-Ḥusayn al-Ḥuṣrī, ascetic of Basra.

988/378 Abū Naṣr as-Sarrāj, theorist of Khurasan and author of the influential manual, *Book of Light Flashes*.

990/380 Bishr Yā-Sīn, *shaykh* of Abū Saʻīd ibn Abī 'l-Khayr.

990/380 or 994/384 Abū Bakr Muḥammad al-Kalābādhī, historian and theorist of Sufism from Central Asia, wrote *Exploration of Sufi Teachings*.

995/385 Ibn an-Nadīm, wrote the *Fihrist* (major biographical dictionary) in which he mentions two of Dhū 'n-Nūn's works as alchemical writings; negative on Ḥallāj but comprehensive listing of works.

996/386 Abū Ṭālib al-Makkī, author of manual, *Sustenance of Hearts*.

997/387 or 1023/414 Abū 'l-Faḍl Muḥammad ibn Ḥasan Sarakhsī, Central Asian Khurāsānī *shaykh* and teacher of Abū Sa'īd ibn Abī 'l-Khayr.

c. 1000/391 Bābā Ṭāhir 'Uryān, author of early Persian Sufi quatrains.

c. 1010/400–401 Firdawsī finishes the Persian national epic *The Book of Kings,* first major landmark of "Islamicate" Persian literature.

1013/404 Al-Bāqillānī, jurist and major systematizer of Ash'arite theology.

c. 1021/412 Abū 'Ali ad-Daqqāq, mentor of Qushayrī.

1021/412 'Abd ar-Raḥmān as-Sulamī, exegete and hagiographer from Nīshīpūr, disciple of Naṣrābādhī.

1030/421 Maḥmūd of Ghazni, ruler of Afghanistan, conqueror of northwestern India.

1033/425 Abū 'l-Ḥasan 'Alī al-Kharaqānī, Persian mystic and *shaykh* of Anṣārī. Abū Isḥāq Ibrāhīm al-Kāzarūnī, Persian mystic and eponymous founder of Kāzarūnīya.

1037/428 Abū 'Alī ibn Sīnā (Avicenna), major Muslim philosopher from Central Asia, author of three "visionary recitals" and *Book of the Ascension*.

1038/430 Abū Nu'aym Al-Iṣfahānī, known for his famous hagiographic work *Ornament of the Friends of God*, completed 1031/422.

1048/439–40 Abū Rayḥān al-Birūnī, scholar of Indian philosophy and life.

1049/440–1 Abū Sa'īd ibn Abī 'l-Khayr, saintly poet of Khurasan.

1057/451 Abū 'l-'Alā' al-Ma'arrī, famed Syrian Arabic philosopher/poet.

1064/456 Ibn Ḥazm, Iberian politician, lawyer, religious polemicist.

c. 1072/465 ʻAlī ibn ʻUthmān Dātā Ganj Bakhsh Hujwīrī, Ḥanafī scholar and author of the manual *Revelation of Realities Veiled.*

1074/466–7 Abū 'l-Qāsim ʻAbd al-Karīm al-Qushayrī, Central Asian manualist and hagiographer who wrote *Treatise (on Sufism)*, a.k.a. *The Letter to the Sufis*, reconciles Sufism with Sunnī authorities.

1083/476 ʻAbd al-Mālik al-Juwaynī, central Asian theologian, teacher of Abū Ḥāmid al-Ghazālī.

1089/481 Khwāja ʻAbd Allāh Anṣārī, Khurāsānī scholar, author of *Hundred Fields* and *Dwelling Places of the Wayfarers.*

1092/485 Niẓām al-mulk, Saljūqid grand vizier who exiled Anṣārī from Herat in 1066, appointed Ghazālī professor at Niẓāmīya *madrasa* in Baghdad.

1096/490 First Crusade leads to Latin Kingdom of Jerusalem (1099–1189).

12th/6th century Al-Mukharrimī, built first Hanbalite *madrasa.*

1111/505 Abū Ḥāmid al-Ghazālī, professor in Baghdad and author of *The Revitalization of Religious Disciplines.*

1119/512–3 Ibn ʻAqīl, Hanbalite legal scholar.

1124/518 Ḥasan-i Ṣabāḥ, Persian Ismāʻīlī leader, militant branch of Shīʻa which gained a firm footing in parts of the Middle East.

1126/520 Aḥmad al-Ghazālī, younger brother of Abū Ḥāmid al-Ghazālī and author of *Sparks (Sawāniḥ)*. Rashīd ad-Dīn Maybudī, Persian scholar, exegete, and mystic, student of Anṣārī.

1131/525 Abū 'l-Majd Majdūd Sanā'ī, Persian Sufi poet, wrote classic didactic work entitled *The Hidden Garden of Ultimate Reality.*

1131/526 ʻAyn al-Quḍāt al-Hamadhānī, disciple of Aḥmad al-Ghazālī, persecuted in Baghdad and executed on the charge of aberrant views of sainthood and eschatology.

1132/526 "Umar Khayyām, Persian poet, used the image of the potter making beautiful things and then destroying them, implying God's role with the mystic, destroying the outward forms.

1140/534 Abū Qāsim Aḥmad as-Sam'ānī, Persian mystical poet who wrote *Refreshment of Spirits*, innovative for its blend of prose and poetry. Yūsuf Hamadhānī, Persian *shaykh* influential in Central Asia.

1141/536 Aḥmad of Jām, who authored several Persian works on spirituality. Ibn al-'Arīf, Iberian author of *The Beauties of Mystical Sessions*.

1153/548 Bernard of Clairvaux, reformer of Christian monasticism.

1157/556 Bahrāmshāh ibn Mas'ūd of Ghazni, sultan to whom Sanā'ī dedicated the 10th chapter of his *Hidden Garden of Ultimate Reality*.

1166/561 'Abd al-Qādir al-Jīlānī, famous Sufi preacher and eponym of the Qādirī order, considered the first formal Sufi order.

1168/563–4 Abū 'n-Najīb 'Abd al-Qāhir as-Suhrawardī, Persian *shaykh*, author, and scholar who taught Aḥmad al-Ghazālī, Najm ad-Dīn Kubrā and Abū Ḥafṣ 'Umar as-Suhrawardī. Wrote *Rules of Behavior for Sufi Seekers*.

1182/578 Aḥmad ar-Rifā'ī, 'Irāqī Shāfi'ī scholar and founder of the Rifā'īya.

1191/587 Shihāb ad-Dīn Yaḥyā as-Suhrawardī "Maqtūl," father of Illuminationist" school, influential in fields of theosophical and speculative Sufism.

1189/585–1192/588 Third Crusade, battle at Acre leads to truce, giving Christians access to Jerusalem.

1193/589 Ṣalāḥ ad-Dīn (Saladin), Kurdish sultan/founder of the Ayyūbid dynasty patron of Sufis, dervishes, hero of anti-Crusade against Richard the Lion-Hearted.

1197/594 Abū Madyan of Tlemcen, Sufi saint who gathered a following and was thought to be a disciple of 'Abd al-Qādir al-Jīlānī.

1198/594 Ibn Rushd (Averroes) of Cordoba, greatest Arabic commentator on Aristotle; refuted works of Ghazālī's polemics against philosophy; also court physician of the Moroccan Berber Almohad dynasty of Marrakesh.

Late 12th/6th century Fāṭima of Cordoba, female spiritual director of Ibn al-'Arabī. Ibn-i Munawwar, Persian hagiographer.

13th century/7th century A time of tremendous political changes, when Mongols swept across Asia and made deep inroads into Europe. Amid this destruction, the period produced a strong upsurge of mystical activity. The greatest mystical writers of the Islamic world came from this period. Orders established firmly in India and several originated in Egypt. Sari Ṣalṭūḳ, Turkish warrior dervish who fought against the Byzantines.

1200/596–7 Ibn al-Jawzī, theologian known for his cautious views and reservations about Sufism.

1204/601 Fourth Crusade, Latin armies sack Constantinople. Maimonides, great rabbi and theologian of Cordoba.

1206/602–1296/696 Slave dynasty of Delhi among early political regimes establishing Muslim power in northern India.

1206/602–3 Quṭb ad-Dīn Aybek of Delhi, patron of a Sufi shrine in Ajmer.

1209/606 Ilyās ibn Yūsuf Niẓāmī Ganjawī, Āzarbayjānī poet known for his mystical didactic anthology *The Quintet* (*Khamsa*).

1209/605–6 Rūzbihān Baqlī of Shiraz, major Persian author on mystical love.

1216/613 Al-Mālik aẓ-Ẓāhir, Ayyūbid ruler, patron of Sufis and scholars.

1219/616 Majd ad-Dīn Baghdādī, Kubrāwī *shaykh* and author.

1220/617 'Abd al-Khāliq Ghijduwānī, disciple of Hamadhani (?), propagated his teachings in Transoxania. Najm ad-Dīn Kubrā, Central Asian founder of Kubrāwīya.

1221/618 Farīd ad-Dīn 'Aṭṭār, poet and hagiographer from Nishapur, author of *The Conference of the Birds* (*Manṭiq aṭ-ṭayr*) and other works.

c. 1222/619 Jamāl ad-Dīn as-Sāwī, spread Qalandarīya to central Middle East.

c. 1225/622 Aḥmad Yasawī, Central Asian founder of the Yasawīya.

1225/622 An-Nāṣir, 'Abbāsid caliph who wanted to revive stagnant spiritual life of Islam and unite Islamic rulers against Mongol threat.

1226/623 Francis of Assisi, Italian Christian mystic, founder of Franciscans.

1227/626–7 Genghis Khan, infamous Mongol conqueror who ruled much of Central Asia and whose descendants went on to dominate much of the Middle East through the 15th/9th century.

1228/625 ʻAbd as-Salām ibn Mashīsh, Moroccan ascetic influential in the thought and practice of the Shādhilīya.

1231/628 Bahā' ad-Dīn Walad, Central Asian *shaykh* who fled westward with his family ahead of Genghis Khan's invasion; father of Rūmī.

1234/631–2 Abū Ḥafṣ ʻUmar as-Suhrawardī, Persian-born scholar, theorist and preacher who wrote *The Benefits of Intimate Knowledge* (*ʻAwārif al-maʻārif*).

1235/632 Ibn al-Fāriḍ, Egyptian Arabic mystical poet, wrote *Wine* ode and *Greater T-Rhyming Ode*.

1235/632–3 Quṭb ad-Dīn Bakhtīyār Kākī, saint revered by Iltutmish, first king of the Slave dynasty of Delhi.

1236/633 Muʻīn ad-Dīn Chishtī, Indian *shaykh* and major figure of early history of Chishtīya order. ʻAlā'ad-Dīn Kaykobad, Saljuqid Sultan of Rūm, patron of scholars, who built a magnificent mosque in Konya, where Rūmī's family settled.

1238/635 Awḥād ad-Dīn Kirmānī, Persian poet known for quatrains and acquaintance of Ibn al-ʻArabī.

1240/637–8 Muḥyī ad-Dīn ibn al-ʻArabī, Iberian-born mystical author who wrote *Meccan Revelations* and *Bezels of Wisdom*. Bābā Ilyās, mystic from Khurasan active in Anatolia.

c. 1241/639 Burhān ad-Dīn Muḥaqqiq, teacher of Rūmī.

1244/641–2 Jalāl ad-Dīn Tabrīzī, one of the first Suhrawardīs to go to India.

1247/645 Shams ad-Dīn Tabrīzī, dervish was associated with Rūmī and possibly the Kubrāwīya; inspiration for much of Rūmī's lyric.

1250/648–1517/923 Mamlūk dynasty ruled much of the central Middle East from its capital at Cairo after stopping the Mongol advance at

'Ayn Jalūt. Major patrons of the arts and architecture, and founders of many important Sufi institutions.

1252/649 Sa'd ad-Dīn Ḥammūya, Khurāsānī Shāf'ī scholar.

1256/654 Najm ad-Dīn Dāyā Rāzī, Persian Kubrāwī author and exegete, wrote *Path of the Godservants to the Starting Point and the Return* (*Mirṣād al-'ibād*).

1258/657 Abū 'l-Ḥasan ash-Shādhilī, Moroccan mystic, Friend of God, and founder of Shādhilīya. Ṣalāḥ ad-Dīn Zarkūb, mystical goldsmith influential on Rūmī; his daughter became Sulṭān Walad's wife.

1261/659 Sayf ad-Dīn Bākharzī, Central Asian pupil of Najm ad-Dīn Kubrā. Latin rule of Constantinople replaced by restored Byzantine rule.

1262/661 Bahā' ad-Dīn Zakarīya Multānī, began the Indian Suhrawardīya. Lāl Shāhbāz *qalandar*, Indian dervish of Suhrawardīya.

1265/664 Farīd ad-Dīn Ganj-i Shakar, a.k.a. Bābā Farīd, an Indian Chishtī *shaykh* and teacher of Niẓām ad-Dīn Awliyā'.

c. 1270–1/669 Ḥājjī Bektāsh Walī, Khurāsānī dervish, eponym of Bektāshīya.

1270/669 Ibn Sab'īn, Iberian Sufi and philosopher.

1273/672 Mawlānā Jalāl ad-Dīn Balkhī Rūmī, Persian mystical poet known as original "Whirling Dervish," author of *Spiritual Couplets* and other poetic works; inspiration for the Mawlawīya order.

1274/672–3 Qāḍī Ḥamīd ad-Dīn Nāgawrī, Indian Suhrawardī scholar. Ṣadr ad-Dīn al-Qūnawī, Anatolian scholar, stepson and disciple of Ibn al'Arabī, wrote commentary to Ibn al'Arabī's *Bezels of Wisdom*. Thomas Aquinas and Bonaventure, major Christian mystics and theologians, members of Dominican and Franciscan orders respectively.

1276/675 Sayyid Aḥmad al-Badawī, Egyptian dervish of the Rifā'īya.

1277/675–6 Mu'īn ad-Dīn Parwane, minister of the Saljūqid dynasty of Konya, major patron of Rūmī.

1278/677 Burhān ad-Dīn Ibrāhīm Dasūqī, Egyptian Sufi poet, founded Dasūqīya order.

1282/680 ‘Azīz ad-Dīn Nasafī, Central Asian Shī‘ī Sufi theorist and *shaykh* of the Kubrāwīya.

1284/683 Ḥusām ad-Dīn Çelebī, disciple of Rūmī and third leader of the Mawlawīya.

1287/686 Abū ’l-‘Abbās al-Mursī, successor of Abū ‘l-Ḥasan ash-Shādhilī.

1289/688 Fakhr ad-Dīn ‘Irāqī, Persian poet associated with both Rūmī and Ibn al‘Arabī and known for his *Divine Flashes* (*Lama‘āt*).

Late 13th/7th century Tapduq Emre, founder of a group of mystics in Anatolia.

1292/692 Muṣliḥ ad-Dīn Sa‘dī, Persian wisdom author and poet.

1296/695 Sharaf ad-Dīn al-Buṣīrī, Egyptian poet known for *Burda* in praise of the Prophet’s mystical status.

1309/709 Ibn ‘Aṭā’ Allāh of Alexandria, Egyptian author and hagiographer, member of Shādhilīya, credited with writing *Book of Aphoristic Wisdom*.

1312/712 Sulṭān Walad, Turkish poet and author, son of Rūmī, founder of Mawlawīya.

1316/716 Ramon Lull, Catalan (Spain) mystic and scholar influenced by Sufi literature.

1321/721 Yūnus Emre, major Turkish Sufi poet. Dante Alighieri, author of *The Divine Comedy*.

1324/724 Shāh Abū ‘Alī Qalandar of Pānīpāt, Indian Sufi who gave up theological study for a life of asceticism.

1325/725 Amīr Khusraw, best-known poet of early Muslim period in India; founder of Indo-Muslim musical tradition. Niẓām ad-Dīn Awliyā’, Indian scholar and leader, propagator of Chishtīya in India.

1327/728 Meister Eckhart, German Dominican mystic influenced by Maimonides, emphasized the divine ineffability.

1328/729 Amīr Ḥusaynī Harawī, Suhrawardī mystic and author. Ibn Taymīya, major medieval Hanbalī theologian, critic of Sufism.

1330/730 ‘Abd ar-Razzāq al-Kāshānī, author of important lexicon of Sufi terminology.

1334/735 Ṣāfī ad-Dīn Ardabīlī, Persian spiritual ancestor of Ṣafawid order.

1335/736 Abū ’l-Mafākhīr Yaḥyā Bākharzī, Kubrāwī *shaykh*.

1336/736–7 ‘Alā’ ad-Dawla Simnānī, Persian mystic and author. Ḥasan Sijzī Dihlawī, Chishtī hagiographer.

1337/737 Maḥmūd ash-Shabistarī, Persian author and poet who wrote *Rose Garden of Mystery* and *Treatise on (Mystical) Felicity*.

1337/738 Burhān ad-Dīn Gharīb, Indian scholar and successor of Niẓām ad-Dīn Awliyā’ in the Chishtī order.

1350/751 Ibn Qayyim al-Jawzīya, major theologian, wrote the *Mysteries of Ritual Prayer* in which he describes God as praising Himself through the mouth of the praiser. Ḍiyā’ ad-Dīn an-Nakhshabī, Persian author and poet associated with Chishtīya, author of *Book of the Parrot*.

1353/754 Muḥammad Ṭughlūq, powerful Indian dynastic ruler, forced many intellectuals/mystics to leave Delhi for the Deccan in 1327.

1356/757 Naṣīr ad-Dīn Maḥmūd Chirāgh-i Dihlī, Indian Chishtī scholar and successor to Niẓām ad-Dīn Awliyā’.

1357/758 Ḍiyā’ ad-Dīn Baranī, Indian historiographer who wrote about Niẓām ad-Dīn and his influence in the Chishtīya.

1368/770 Ming dynasty overthrows Mongol Yuan dynasty.

1371/772–3 Tāj ad-Dīn Subkī, classified 25 different types of miracles.

c.1377/779 Ibn Baṭṭūta, North African whose sweeping account of global travels provide much information on Sufi life and institutions.

1381/782 Sharaf ad-Dīn Manīrī, wrote letters, Indian leader of Firdawsīya.

1384/785 Jalāl ad-Dīn Ḥusayn al-Bukhārī (“Makhdūm-i Jahānīyān”), prolific writer in all religious fields, settled in Ucch, northeast of Multan.

1385/787 Mīr Sayyid ‘Alī Hamadhānī, active Kubrāwī founder in Kashmir.

1389/791 Muḥammad Shams ad-Dīn Ḥāfiẓ, major Persian mystical poet. Khwāja Bahā' ad-Dīn Naqshband, Central Asian Sufi and founder of Naqshbandīya, considered seventh *khwāja* in Abū Yūsuf's line.

1390/792 Ibn 'Abbād ar-Rundī, Ibero-Moroccan Shādhilī spiritual leader, famed for letters.

1391/794 Bahā' ad-Dīn Naqshband, Central Asian *shaykh*-eponym.

1394/796–7 Faḍl Allāh Astarābādī, founding leader of the Ḥurūfīya tradition.

Early 15th/9th century Kaygusūz Abdāl, Turkish mystical author and poet, Bektāshī.

1405/807–8 Timūr Lang, founder of Timūrid dynasty and reputed ancestor of Babur, who established beginning of Mughal dynastic rule over northwestern India in 1526. He and his line were major patrons of the arts and of Sufism.

1406/808–9 Ibn Khaldūn, major North African historian and philosopher of history whose *Introduction* offers much information about Sufism.

1408/810 Muḥammad Shīrīn Maghribī, Persian Kubrāwī author, poet.

1417/820 'Imād ad-Dīn Nesīmī, Ḥurūfī lyric poet inspired by Ḥallāj.

1419/822 Khwāja Muḥammad Parsā, early Naqshbandī master. Sulaymān Çelebī, major Turkish poet on the Prophet.

1422/825 Sayyid Muḥammad al-Ḥusaynī Gīsū Darāz, South Indian scholar, disciple of Chirāgh-i Dihlī, author in Chishtīya order.

c. 1425/829 Sayyid Ashraf Jahāngīr Simnānī, Persian saint, theorist and teacher who lived in India and was associated with many orders (mainly Chishtīya). 'Abd al-Karīm al-Jīlī, mystic of Iraq, author of *The Perfect Person.*

1431/834 Shāh Ni'mat Allāh Walī, Syrian-born author founded Ni'mat-Allāhīya and studied theology of Ibn al-'Arabī.

1453/857 Fall of Constantinople to Ottoman Turkish Sultan Mehmet I the Conqueror, continuation of dramatic expansion of the empire.

1459/863 Muḥammad Aq Shams ad-Dīn, mystic who influenced Mehmet the Conqueror.

c. 1465/869 Abū ʻAbd Allāh al-Jazūlī, Moroccan author of popular Sufi prayer book on trust in God and the Messenger.

c. 1470/874 Eshrefoğlu Rūmī, Turkish mystical poet.

1490/895 Khwāja ʻUbayd Allāh Aḥrār, Central Asian Naqshbandī *shaykh*. Abū ʻAbd Allāh Muḥammad as-Sanūsī, Maghribī author, scholar, and ascetic.

1492/897 Mawlāna ʻAbd ar-Raḥmān Jāmī, Persian poet and hagiographer, Naqshbandī, author of *The Seven Thrones* and *Warm Breezes of Intimacy*.

1492/898 Muslim rule in Spain ends with the expulsion of the Naṣrid dynasty from Granada.

1494/899 Aḥmad Zarrūq, Moroccan mystical author.

15th/9th–16th/10th century Period of the Walī Songo, "nine saints" of Indonesia. Balīm Sulṭān, second master of the Bektāshī order.

1501/906–1738/1151 Ṣafawid dynasty rules most of Persia, from Shāh Ismāʻīl's rise to power in 1501. Shiʻism became the official creed of Iran, and the Ṣafawid rulers were sometimes called *Sufi* or *Grand Sophi*. Major patron of Sufism and the arts, the dynasty ended with an Afghan invasion.

1501/906–7 Mīr ʻAlī Shīr Nawāʼī, Central Asian Naqshbandī who wrote a Chagatay version of the *Conference of the Birds*, greatest representative of Chagatay Turkish literature, accomplished artist.

1503/909 Ḥamd Allāh Ḥamdī, wrote Turkish version of Zulaykhā's love for Joseph, symbol of enrapturing power of love.

1505/911 Jalāl ad-Dīn as-Suyūtī, major religious scholar, exegete, administrator of large Shādhilī *khānqāh* in Cairo.

1506/912 Shams ad-Dīn Muḥammad Lāhijī, Persian poet and *shaykh* of Nūrbakhshīya.

1511/917 ʻAlī ibn Maymūn al-Fāsī spreads Shādhilīya into Syria.

1518/924 Kabīr, Indian Muslim mystical poet influential in the beginnings of Sikh tradition in connection with Gurū Nanak. Hindu Majapahit kingdom in Java overthrown by Muslim rule.

c. 1530/923 Muḥammad ibn ʿĪsā al-Mukhtārī, Moroccan founder of the ʿĪsāwīya order.

1524/930 Ismāʿīl, Ṣafawid Shāh whose victory in 1501 made Shīʿism the official creed of Persia.

1530/936–7 Bābūr, first ruler of Mughal dynasty which eventually ruled most of India and present-day Pakistan, descendent of the Timurid dynasty.

c. 1532/938 ʿAlī ibn Ḥusayn Wāʿiẓ Kāshifī, whose "Tricklings from the Fountain of Life" is a main source of knowledge about Khwāja Aḥrār.

1536/942 Jamālī Kanbōh, Iskandar Lodi's mystical court poet.

1537/944 ʿAbd al-Quddūs Gangōhī, Indian Chistī poet and Ibn alʿArabī apologist.

1556/963 Hamayun, second great Mughal emperor, father of Akbar. Ignatius of Loyola, Spanish mystic, founder of Jesuits order.

1560/968 Ḥamza Fanṣūrī, Indonesian mystical author and poet, popularizer of Malay *syair* poetic genre.

1562/969–70 Muḥammad Ghawth Gwāliyārī, Indian Sufi of Shaṭṭārīya.

1565/973 ʿAbd al-Wahhāb ash-Shaʿrānī, Egyptian mystical hagiographer.

1566/974 Sulaymān the Magnificent, Ottoman ruler responsible for dramatic expansion of the empire, major patron of Sufis.

1567/975 Shaykh ʿAlī al-Muṭṭaqī, Indian leader of the Chishtīya, associated with other orders after settling in Mecca.

1572/980 Shaykh Salīm Chishtī, spiritual guide of Emperor Akbar.

1582/990 Theresa of Avila, Christian mystic of Spain, author of *Interior Castle*, with its metaphor of seven mansions of the soul.

1585/993 Bāyazīd Anṣārī (Pīr-i Rawshan or "Radiant Master"), founder of Rawshanīya movement, applied Persian metrics to Pashto.

1591/999–1000 Muḥammad ash-Shīrāzī 'Urfī, one of Akbar's court poets, lamented degeneration of Sufism. John of the Cross, Spanish Christian mystic, author of *Ascent of Mount Carmel*.

1592/1001 Wang Daiyu, early translator of Sufi concepts into Chinese.

17th/11th century Bābā Lāl Das, Hindu sage, had disputations with Dārā Shikūh. Sayyid Sulṭān, taught even Iblīs should be honored since he once held a high position, and one should honor and obey one's *shaykh* even if he is a Satan. Sunbul Efendi, Shaykh of Khalwatīya order in Istanbul. Merkez Efendi, successor of Sunbul Efendi. Lāl Udero, saint claimed by both Hindus and Muslims, defender of the unity of being. Adam Olearius, translated Sa'dī's *Gulistān* into German, making it a favorite of European intellectuals. Ḥajji Muḥammad, wrote *The Book of Light*, important Sufi work in Bengālī.

1603/1012 Khwāja Bāqī Bi-'llāh, Afghan Naqshbandī scholar and author, teacher of Aḥmad Sirhindī.

1605/1014 Akbar, Mogul emperor, Babur's grandson, tried to establish a religious eclecticism containing the best elements of all the religions he knew, frequented Sufi *shaykhs*.

1621/1031 'Abd ar-Ra'ūf al-Munāwī, Egyptian hagiographer. Bahā' ad-Dīn Āmilī, Persian Shī'ī Sufi poet.

1624/1034 Aḥmad Sirhindī, Naqshbandī reformer.

1627/1036–7 Jahāngīr, Mughal emperor, adorned Ajmer, Mu'īn ad-Dīn Chishtī's city, with beautiful marble buildings. Aḥmad Bābā, legal scholar influential on Sufism in Niger.

1630/1039 Shams ad-Dīn as-Samaṭrānī, a.k.a. Shams ad-Dīn of Pasai, Indonesian Sufi scholar involved in the *wujūdī* controversy.

1631/1040–1 Ismā'īl Rusīhī Anqarāwī, Turkish mystic who wrote fine commentary on Rūmī's *Mathnawī*. Mumtaz Mahal, wife of Shāh Jahān, who built the Tāj Mahal as a monumental tomb for her.

1633/1042–3 Muḥammad Ghawthī, member of the Shaṭṭarīya order, composed hagiography of 575 Indo-Muslim saints.

1635/1044–5 Miyān Mīr, nickname of Shaykh Muḥammad Mīr of Sind, an Indian Qādirī Sufi and spiritual counselor to certain Mughal rulers.

1640/1050 Ṣadr ad-Dīn Shīrāzī (Mulla Ṣadrā), major philosopher deeply influenced by Suhrawardian thought.

1642/1052 Muḥaddith ʻAbd al-Ḥaqq Dihlawī, famous Indian Ḥadīth scholar and hagiographer.

1646/1056 Madhō Lāl Ḥusayn, Panjabi Qādirī poet.

1647/1057 Bībī Jamāl Khatūn, Indian mystic, sister of Miyān Mīr, and member of Qādirīya.

1653/1063 Jaʻfar al-ʻAydarūs, translated *Safīnat al-awliyā'* (*Biographies of the Saints*) into Arabic.

1658/1068 Nūr ad-Dīn Rānīrī, Indian Rifāʻī Sufi scholar in Mecca, opponent of Ḥamza Fanṣūrī and Shams ad-Dīn as-Samaṭrānī.

1659/1069 Dārā Shikūh, Indian member of Qādirīya known for the treatise *The Confluence of the Two Seas*.

1659/1069–70 Shāh Jahān, father of Dārā Shikūh, Mughal builder of Tāj Mahal.

1661/1071–2 Sarmad, Jewish convert to Sufism, executed in Mughal India; shocked listeners by calling people to imitate Satan.

1661/1072 Mullā Shāh Badakhshī, Indian mystic and poet, Qādirī, disciple and successor of Miyān Mīr.

1668/1078–9 Pīr Muḥammad Maʻṣūm, son of Aḥmad Sirhindī, who claimed Muḥammad Maʻsūm was second after him in ranks of four men selected by God.

1669/1079–80 Mirān Ḥusayn Shāh, saint of Bijapur, translated Hamadhānī's *Tamhīdāt* into Dakhnī Urdū.

1670/1081 Birth of Liu Chih, Chinese scholar and hagiographer who translated Sufi texts into Chinese.

1677/1088 Angelus Silesius, German Christian mystic.

1678/1088 Sīdī Maḥmūd al-Baghdādī, West African Sufi *shaykh* thought to be a martyr and namesake of Maḥmūdīya.

1681/1092 Jahānārā, Mogul princess and student of Mullā Shāh, sister of Awrangzeb and Dārā Shikūh.

1683/1094 Shaykh ʻAbd ar-Raḥmān Chishtī, Indian leader of Chishtīya. Ottoman dynasty's second siege of Vienna unsuccessful.

1689/1100 Khushḥāl Khān Khattak, translated works of Saʻdī and Jāmī into Pashto from Persian.

1689/1100 Zīb an-Nisā', daughter of Mughal Awrangzeb, talented poetess.

1690/1102 Ibrāhīm ibn Ḥasan al-Kuranī, Kurdish mystic.

1691/1102 Edward Pocock, British scholar who misrepresented Ḥallāj's image in his writings. Sulṭān Bāhū, major Panjābī mystical poet.

1693/1104 ʻAbd ar-Ra'ūf as-Sinkilī, Indonesian Shāfiʻī scholar, member of Shaṭṭārīya, credited with bringing Islam to Acheh in Sumatra.

1694/1105 Niyāzī Miṣrī Efendi, Turkish poet, spiritual leader who used traditional methods of interpretation in his commentary.

1697/1108–9 Nasir ʻAli Sirhindī, Indian Naqshbandī, poet, compatriot of Bedil.

Early 18th/12th century Mīrzā Khān Anṣāri, descendent of Bāyazīd Anṣārī, a leading mystical poet of the later days of Awrangzīb's reign.

18th/12th century Badr al-Hijāzī, Arabian who wrote satiric material on the decline of Sufism. Ibrāhīm Ḥaqqī Erzerumlu, Turkish Sufi writer. Hāshim Shāh, contemporary of Bullhe Shāh, used folk tales for mystical expression. Khwāja Muḥammad Banqash, expressed mystical teachings in Pashto, poet and member of the Chishtī order.

1700/1111–2 ʻAbd al-Aḥad Gul, Indian master/teacher of Saʻd Allāh Gulshān. Fl. ʻAbd al-ʻAzīz ad-Dabbāgh, Moroccan neo-Sufi.

c. 1707/1119 Walī Deccanī, great mystical poet of south India.

1717/1130 Maḥmūd Baḥrī, Indian Chishtī Persian and Urdu poet.

1718/1130 Shāh ʻInāyat Shahīd, mystical leader who attracted a large number of Sufi aspirants.

1719/1132 Hilāl ad-Dīn Qi Jingyi, founder of Chinese branch of Qādirīya.

1721/1133 Mīrzā 'Abd al-Qādir Bīdil, poet who criticized Sufis who constantly mentioned food.

1724/1136–7 Ismā'īl Haqqī Bursali, Turkish mystical poet who wrote a commentary on Rūmī's *Mathnawī*.

1728/1140–1 Sa'd Allāh Gulshān, prolific Persian poet, fond of music and part of the musical society of Delhi.

1731/1143 'Abd al-Ghanī an-Nābulusī, Syrian scholar of the Shāfi'ī school, poet and Sufi commentator on Ibn al-Fāriḍ, member of Naqshbandī and Qādirī orders.

1738/1151 Sulaymān Nahīfī, translated commentary on the *Mathnawī* of Rūmī into Turkish.

1740/1153 Pīr Muḥammad Zubayr, fourth and last Indian Mujaddidī Naqshbandī *qayyūm.*

Mid-18th/12th century Dīwān Gidumal, British minister of Sindh, gave invading Nādir Shāh some dust of the city's saints.

1747/1160 Nādir Shāh, Afghan military leader who conquered Persia in 1722.

1752/1165 Shāh 'Abd Al-Laṭīf Bhitā'ī, mystic/poet from Hyderabad-Sindh.

1754/1167 Jān Allāh Rizwī, outstanding Persian poet from Sind.

1759/1172 Nāṣir Muḥammad, Indian Mujaddidī Naqshbandī, father of Mīr Dard, wrote Urdu poetry under name 'Andalīb ("Nightingale").

1760/1173–4 Makhdūm Muḥammad Hāshim, sober mystic who attacked Sufis who defended the emotional side of religion, such as dancing in Makli Hill's cemeteries.

1762/1175–6 Shāh Walī Allāh of Delhī, Indian scholar and reformer, translated Qur'ān into Persian, member of both Naqshbandī and Qādirī.

1766/1180 Ma Laichi, major Chinese Naqshbandī leader.

1767/1181 Bulhe Shāh, greatest Panjābī Sufi poet.

1778/1192 'Abd ar-Rahīm Girhori, Suhrawardī mystic and missionary.

1781/1195 Maẓhar Jān-i Janān, Mujaddidī Naqshbandī, militant adversary of Indian Shī'a. Ma Mingxin, major figure in Chinese Sufism.

1785/1199 Khwāja Mīr Dard, major Indian Naqshbandī poet and author. Fl. 'Abd aṣ-Ṣamad of Palembang (Sumatra).

Late 18th/early 13th century Wārith Shāh, Panjābī poet.

1792/1207 Muḥammad ibn 'Abd al-Wahhāb, major modern critic of Sufism.

1799/1213–4 Ghālib Dede, classical Turkish poet, member of the Mawlawīya and *shaykh* of the Galata *tekke* in Istanbul.

1809/1224 Aḥmad ibn 'Ajība, Moroccan scholar known for commentaries on the works of earlier Sufis and his autobiography.

1810/1225 Mīr Taqī Mīr, poet who wrote mystical verse in Urdu, though he was not formally part of a Sufi community.

1811/1226 Sīdī Mukhtār al-Kuntī, West African Sufi tribal leader.

1815/1230 Aḥmad ibn Muḥammad at-Tījānī, North African Sufi founder.

1823/1239 Mulay al-'Arabī ad-Darqāwī, North African Sufi reformer and founder of Darqāwīya branch of Shādhilīya.

1824/1239 Shāh 'Abd al-Azīz, Indian Naqshbandī legal scholar and exegete.

1826/1242 'Abd al-Wahhāb Sachal Sarmast, Sindhī Sufi poet.

1831/1246 Sayyid Aḥmad Brelwī, an Indian Sufi reformer who sought to rid Islam of elements of Shī'ī and Hindu syncretism. Shāh Ismā'īl Shahīd, Indian scholar and reformer.

1838/1253 Aḥmad Ibn Idrīs, Moroccan reformer and Sufi author.

1838/1254 Silvestre de Sacy, early master of Arabic studies and Orientalist translator.

1843/1259 Dāwūd al-Fatānī, Malay participant in *wujūdī* controversy.

1851/1267–8 Mu'min, important early modern Urdu poet.

Mid-19th/13th century Especially in North and Central Africa, Sufi organizations play important roles in fighting against colonial rulers.

1856/1272–3 Joseph von Hammer-Purgstall, German who translated Sufi poetry.

1858/1274 Engku Muda Rāja 'Abd Allāh, Malay ruler who was also a Naqshbandī *shaykh*.

1859/1276 Muḥammad ibn 'Ali as-Sanūsī, North African scholar who founded the Sanūsīya.

1864/1281 Al-Ḥajj 'Umar ibn Sa'īd Tall, West African Tījānī leader.

1866/1282–3 Friedrich Rückert, major German scholar of Sufism.

1869/1286 Mīrzā Asad Allāh Ghālib, major poet in Urdū, one of whose major themes was that only death expresses true mystical love.

1871/1288 Ma Hualong, Chinese Sufi martyr.

1874/1291 Ma Fuchu, Chinese scholar of Yunnan, translated Sufi texts into Chinese.

1877/1294 F. A. D. Tholuck, German author of the first comprehensive book on Sufism, published in 1821.

1882/1300 Edward Henry Palmer, author of *Oriental Mysticism* (1867).

1883/1300 Amīr 'Abd al-Qādir ibn Muḥyī ad-Dīn al-Ḥasanī, Algerian Sufi who fought against the French colonials, eventually being sent into exile.

1885/1302-3 Ernest Trumpp, German missionary who published the collection *The Book of Shah* in 1866.

1892/1309–10 Sir James W. Redhouse, British orientalist who studied Rūmī.

1898/1315 Sir Sayyid Aḥmad Khān, reformer of Naqshbandīya and Indian Islam.

20th/14th–15th century Sufi orders begin to be established in Europe and the Americas.

1914/1332 Shiblī Nu‘mānī, wrote Urdū biography of Rūmī (1903). Ma Qixi, Chinese Sufi reformer.

1925/1344 Mustafa Kemal Atatürk, founder of the Turkish Republic, after declaring a secularized state, outlaws all dervish orders lest they agitate against his reforms.

1927/1346 Amadu Bamba Mbacké, Qādirī *shaykh* of Senegal.

1933/1351 Sayyid Aḥmad Sanūsī, North African mystic and third *shaykh* of the Sanūsīya.

1934/1353 Abū ’l-‘Abbās Aḥmad Al-‘Alawī, Darqāwī saint who then began his own order focusing on spiritual retreat.

1938/1357 Sir Muḥammad Iqbāl, Indian Sufi scholar, philosopher, author.

1943/1362 Muḥammad Ashraf ‘Alī Thanvī, Indian Sufi leader.

1946/1366 Amīr Ḥamza, author of mystical poetry in Malay.

Mid-20th/14th century Predominantly Muslim nations from Morocco to Malaysia gain independence from European colonial rule.

1951/1371 Sayyid Zawqī Shāh, Indian Chishtī *shaykh*.

1958/1378 Ma Zhenwu, Chinese Sufi leader of Hui rebellion.

1978/1399 Shahīd Allāh Farīdī.

1986/1407 Bawa Muhaiyaddeen, Sri Lankan leader of major American Sufi group headquartered in Pennsylvania.

2003/1424 Annemarie Schimmel, German scholar who made many major contributions to the understanding of Sufi thought and literature.

Introduction

"Sufism was once a reality without a name, and now it has become a name without a reality,"[1] lamented a revered Sufi of nearly a millennium ago, already pining for the "good old days." That ancient observer was talking about a rich, complex religious and cultural phenomenon, an aspect of the tradition known as Islam, that he and his contemporary Sufis had already long understood to be rooted in the very beginnings of the Islamic faith. An insight into what he meant will unfold in the next few pages, and the remainder of the present volume is devoted to providing a wide range of details to fill out this more general initial impression.

OVERVIEW OF THE HISTORY OF SUFISM

The history of Sufism is not the story of some aberrant sect or cult, no mere chronicle of a motley collection of wayward Muslims. It is integral to the history of the global faith community of Islam. Wherever Muslims have traveled over nearly 14 centuries, there Sufis have gone. Today, virtually wherever there are Muslims, one also finds Sufis—with the sole notable exception, perhaps, of parts of Saudi Arabia. Spanning, as it does, such vast expanses of time, space, and cultural diversity, the history of Sufism is understandably complex and full of twists and turns. Beginning with disparate individuals known for outstanding piety and later identified as the earliest Sufis, Sufism came to develop a host of social, ritual, artistic, institutional, and political manifestations.

Orders spread from the central Middle East across North Africa and Western and Central Asia, and eventually into parts of Africa and South and Southeast Asia. Sufism and its organizations have fallen on hard times off and on during this long history, especially the 18th and 19th centuries, when they were subject to the stresses of Western colonialism. But Sufism has also proven amazingly durable. During the Soviet era, Sufism was a major factor in the survival of Islam in the so-called Five Stans—the former southern Soviet republics of Central Asia, such as Kazakhstan and Uzbekistan. In more recent times, even the less-than-devout Saddam Hussein cultivated relationships with the leaders of important Sufi groups in Iraq, such as the Qādirīya order. (This suggests only that Hussein was eager to take advantage of their influence with segments of the population, not that he shared their religious views.) Today in the United States, one of the best-selling poets in English (translation) is Jalāl ad-Dīn Rūmī, the original "Whirling Dervish" and perhaps the most celebrated Sufi of all. Here is a brief overview of how this fascinating history unfolded, starting from the beginning.

From the Sufi perspective, at the heart of religious faith is a distinctive and intensely relational kind of religious experience embodied most strikingly in God's choosing, mentoring, and sending prophetic messengers to deliver the divine communication to humankind. The revelatory succession begins with Adam and proceeds through a long list that includes such biblical figures as Abraham, Moses, David, Solomon, and Jesus and non-Biblical Arabian prophets such as Ṣāliḥ and Hūd, culminating in Muḥammad. Sufi authors see a number of common features in the religious experiences of these individuals, including intimate relationships with God, occasional manifestations of miraculous power, and the willingness to be led on a journey of discovery requiring complete trust in the divine guide. The prophets are, in a word, the prime models for every Sufi seeker on the spiritual path.

Prophets are specially chosen human beings and represent a level of experience far beyond what the average spiritual seeker could expect to attain. Nevertheless, Sufis have long regarded the last Prophet as a paragon of devotion, simplicity of life, mystical attainment, and spiritual authority. In addition, Sufi sources regard various individuals who lived during Muḥammadís lifetime—part of the first generation of Muslims called the Companions—as exemplars of a more accessible level of spiritual commitment. They single out the Prophet's barber, Salmān the Persian, for the blessing of his being so close to the Prophet; the "Weepers," a group of ascetics who embodied compunction for their sins; the "People of the Bench (or Portico)" who gave up worldly comfort for the privilege of living near the Prophet; and people like the first successors to Muḥammad, Abū Bakr and 'Umar, as models of absolute commitment and devotion to the Messenger of God.

After the Prophet's death in 11/632 and on into the late second/eighth century, individuals most noted for the quality of their religious commitment were generally those most inclined to self-discipline and an ascetical life. People like the great preacher Ḥasan of Basra (in southern Iraq) gave voice to the need for constant vigilance and austerity, after the model of the Prophet, who had dressed in rough clothing, led his own donkey around, ate from a rough wooden bowl while seated on the ground, and refused to stand on ceremony. But by the end of the second/eighth century, a new voice was being heard with a startling new message. Rābi'a, a woman also of Basra, dared to suggest that human beings could speak of how God's love for them—perhaps even a mutual love—trumped all other concerns and banished both fear of hellfire and hope for reward. It is often said that the love she preached is precisely the difference between asceticism and true mysticism, and some scholars consider this the beginning of Sufism strictly so-called. Ḥasan lived during the era of the first major Islamic dynasty, the Umayyad, which expanded Islamdom all the way to Spain in the West and to the Indus River in the East. Rābi'a's life spanned the transition from the Umayyads, with their capital in Damascus, to the beginning of the 'Abbāsid dynasty, which founded a new capital at Baghdad in the heart of Iraq in 145/762.

Rābi'a's bold insights were in the vanguard of dramatic new developments to unfold during the third/ninth century. Intriguing characters like Dhū 'n-Nūn of Egypt, Bāyazīd of Bistam (in Iran), and Ḥallāj of Baghdad fairly blurted out their deepest insights into their relationships with God, unable to restrain themselves. The result was strikingly exuberant assertions that seemed to many observers to suggest that these characters were, at best, mad, and, at worst, heretics. All three thus ran afoul of certain religious and political authorities, who, to say the least, took a jaundiced view of their claims. But it was Ḥallāj who paid with his life and was executed, ostensibly on the charge of blasphemy, for saying "I am the Truth." Sufis sympathetic to him interpret his utterance as the uncontrollable response to a divine intimacy that annihilates the human personality, leaving nothing but the reality of God behind.

At the same time, Sufism's earliest "theorists" began to reflect on the often rough-hewn expressions of their contemporary mystics. Authors like Junayd and Muḥāsibī of Baghdad opted for a more theologically cautious approach, one often referred to as "sober" mysticism, as a counter to the "intoxicated" outbursts of their less circumspect contemporaries. Scholars today often refer to these first three centuries or so in the history of Sufism—from the Prophet's time up to about 339/950—as the "formative" period, focusing on the development of an emerging sensitivity to the various manifestations of interior spiritual experience.[2] Others have seen the rise of individualized religion as a reaction against formalist, authority-based institutional religion as a key characteristic of the period.[3]

Beginning around the later fourth/10th century, both the history of Sufism as written by Sufis and systematic analysis of Sufi thought emerged in the form of the first of a number of major compendia of spirituality. Paul Nwyia calls this second period that of "elucidation," Annemarie Schimmel that of "consolidation."[4] It runs from about 339/950 to 494/1100 and is characterized by the evolution of a more or less standard array of Sufi practices and technical terminology, especially as recorded in the classical "manuals" or compendia of spirituality by authors already mentioned. The authors of the earliest of these handbooks—Sarrāj, Kalābādhī, and Abū Ṭālib al-Makkī—all had among their purposes in writing the need to defend Sufism against a growing chorus of criticism from religious officialdom. They were at pains to demonstrate that, far from playing fast and loose with the Islamic faith tradition and its sources, the Sufis represented the highest values in the quest for religious knowledge. Turning the arguments of their critics back against them, they asserted that it was in fact only the Sufis who were qualified to build on the traditional acquired religious sciences and move beyond them toward experiential knowledge. In addition to explaining key concepts and central ritual practices, these compendia also analyze the elements of spiritual experience systematically and lay them out in typological structures designed to allow seekers to monitor their progress with the guidance of a *shaykh* knowledgeable in the "science of hearts."

One common concern of the manualists and other "theorists" of Sufism was an attempt to define Sufism. Some of the more ancient explicit and generally positive statements about Sufism, as well as some more recent explorations, have focused on the origins of the name. Perhaps the most broadly accepted explanation was the etymological derivation of the term from the Arabic for "wool," *ṣūf*, associating practitioners with a preference for poor, rough clothing. This explanation clearly identifies Sufism with ascetical practice and the importance of manifesting spiritual poverty through material poverty. In fact, some of the earliest Western descriptions of individuals now widely associated with the larger phenomenon of Sufism identified them with the Arabic term *faqīr*, mendicant, or its most common Persian equivalent, *darwīsh*.

Historically important written sources by Sufi authors, however, pay far more attention to sayings of early spiritual masters who defined *taṣawwuf* (the Arabic term commonly translated as "Sufism") variously in terms of interior attitudes rather than exterior practices. Many of these definitions also turned on etymological derivations, most often associating Sufism with the Arabic for "purity," *ṣafā'*, with its connotations of elite spiritual and moral development. Authors of classical handbooks of Sufi thought and practice often produce lists of definitions of Sufism in the form of responses of famous early teachers to inquiries from their followers about the meaning of Sufism or about the qualities of "the true Sufi."[5]

The fifth/11th century witnessed a second wave of influential Sufi works, including major Arabic manuals by Qushayrī and Abū Ḥāmid al-Ghazālī, as well as the first manual in Persian, by Hujwīrī. There were also new works on the history of Sufism itself by 'Abd ar-Raḥmān as-Sulamī and 'Abd Allāh Anṣārī, demonstrating a growing sense of Sufism as an integral part of the Islamic tradition. An important theme was the systematic establishment of sainthood as a parallel to prophethood. Just as Muslims had traditionally spoken of Muḥammad as the "seal" of the prophets, Sufis now spoke of leading Friends of God as contenders for the title "seal" of the saints. Sufi authors also further elaborated distinctively mystical ways of reading and interpreting the Qur'ān, shoring up what would become an important foundation for Sufi exegesis. And all the while, Sufis found new ways and venues in which to gather in greater numbers around *shaykhs* reputed for their spiritual acumen. Men like Ghazālī sometimes gained notoriety through their professorial positions at *madrasas*, institutions of higher learning, which were sponsored by highly placed officials in various dynasties.

By the end of this second period, the 'Abbāsid dynasty was already experiencing serious difficulties maintaining central control of a far-flung empire. At the fringes, from Spain eastward along North Africa as well as from Iran eastward to the edges of what is now India, independent principalities were declaring themselves free of Baghdad. More ominously still, the new Islamized Saljūqid Turkish dynasty had swept in from Central Asia in 447/1055 and reduced the Caliphate to a shadow of its former self by setting up the parallel institutions of the Sultanate as the real power in Baghdad.

From about 494/1100 until the late eighth/14th century, the three hallmarks of Sufism were developments in institutionalization, intellectualization, and the refinement of various literary and artistic forms as vehicles for the expression of Sufi values. The first trend manifested itself in the formalization of the earliest Sufi orders, with their normative understandings of the relationships between aspirant and *shaykh*, and set requirements for membership and training. Though tradition accords the distinction of founding the first order to ʻAbd al-Qādir al-Jīlānī, there were likely other "intentional communities" before him (such as that associated with Kāzarūnī in southwestern Iran). What is new in this "institutionalization" is the beginning of the growth of well-endowed stable foundations, with their own dedicated facilities for community living, spiritual formation, and ritual practice. Major orders that came into being during this period include the Mawlawīya in Turkey, better known as the Whirling Dervishes because of the paraliturgical dance that imitates the movements of the spheres in search of their center; the Suhrawardīya farther east in Iran, whose principal handbook proved to be the last of the "classical" manuals and was adopted by a number of other orders as well; and the Chishtīya, which became a dominant order in South Asia.

What some scholars call "intellectualization" was manifest in the "speculative" Sufism of authors like Rūzbihān Baqlī from Shiraz, Iran, and Ibn al-ʻArabī, who was born in Spain but was a longtime resident of Damascus and other parts of the central Middle East. These and other writers developed often elaborate systems of psychology and cosmology to explain the larger meanings of Sufi spiritual experience. Ibn al-ʻArabī's influence was so pervasive that countless major Sufi theorists after his time continued to process his thought, either to support or refute it, concerning the nature of mystical union.

Surely one of the greatest of Sufism's contributions to Islam, and to the larger world as well, has been its wealth of creative imagination in literature and the arts. Some of the world's greatest religious poets and prose stylists have been members of Sufi orders, and they have left literary monuments in Arabic, Persian, Turkish, and a dozen other major Islamicate languages. Ibn al-Fārid, Farīd ad-Dīn 'Aṭṭār, and Rūmī are but a few major seventh/13th century masters. Calligraphers, too, were well-represented among the ranks of the Sufi orders. Then, as now, the arts cost money to produce, and to sustain themselves Sufi institutions needed the support of endowments funded by royal and other wealthy patrons.

All of these developments within Sufism took place in a variety of changing political contexts during this period. The Umayyad caliphate of Spain collapsed in 423/1031 and was supplanted by the theologically conservative Almoravid and Almohad dynasties of Moroccan origin. Eastward across North Africa, the Ismā'īlī (Shī'ī) Fātimids rose to power and founded the new capital of Cairo in 359/969, developing that city into a major Mediterranean center of culture and the arts. When the Crusaders began to threaten, the Fātimid rulers called on the Kurdish Sunni military hero Saladin for assistance. He responded and soon replaced the Fātimids with his own Ayyūbid dynasty in 567/1171, under which Cairo was gradually transformed into a center of Sunni Islam and of major patronage of Sufi individuals and organizations. By 648/1250, a revolt by the Turkic palace guard, known as the Mamlūks, resulted in yet another political transition. For the next two and a half centuries, the Mamlūks would rule much of the central Middle East, including Syria and Palestine. Mamlūk sultans offered considerable support for Sufi orders and institutions, endowing numerous major residential facilities and architectural complexes.

Meanwhile, farther east, the Saljūqids, who had taken Baghdad in 447/1055, had continued their push northward through Syria and into Anatolia, where a branch of the dynasty established its capital at Konya in the center of what is now Turkey. Under Saljūqid patronage, the Mawlawīya order of Rūmī began and prospered. But the turn of the eighth/14th century saw the rise of the early Ottoman dynasty, which quickly gained control of most of Anatolia in its drive to bring down the Byzantine Empire. By the end of this period, the Ottomans were poised to land a decisive blow in the conquest of Constantinople in 857/1453. Still further to the east, the Mongols, led by a grandson of Genghis Khan, sacked Baghdad in 656/1258, effectively putting an end to the caliphate. Sufi orders managed to do more than survive these cataclysmic changes, expanding and spreading across the central Middle East and Iran. In South Asia, this was the age of several great sultanates. Under their patronage, Sufi orders took root and thrived in Pakistan and India.

From about 803/1400 to the mid-12th/18th century, Sufi institutions from Iberia to Indonesia enjoyed varied fortunes. While it has not been uncommon to characterize this period as one of stagnation or, worse, of simple deterioration across the board in the history of Sufism, recent research has begun to reveal more in the way of strength and even growth than was previously acknowledged. This is certainly the case of the Chishtīya in India and beyond, and further research will likely prompt similar conclusions about other orders as well, especially in parts of Africa. Whatever value judgment one chooses to apply to a given order or region, it seems clear that Sufi orders in many regional contexts remained influential and vigorous during this "precolonial" period.

On the Islamic political front, the major story during this period is that of the rise and fall of the three so-called Gunpowder Empires of early modern times. In the west, the Sunni Ottoman dynasty expanded to control an expanse of North Africa and the Middle East greater than that of the Byzantine Empire at its height. Ottoman sultans, such as Sulayman the Magnificent, were often avid patrons of Sufism, and a number of orders benefited from royal funding. In Iran, the Ṣafawid dynasty took power in 907/1501, establishing Shīʿī Islam as the state creed. It was under their rule that the most important Shīʿī Sufi orders developed. Around the same time, the Sunnī Mughal dynasty began to take control of parts of Afghanistan, Pakistan, and northern India. Mughal sovereigns like Akbar and his son Shāh Jahān were major patrons of various Sufi orders, especially the Chishtīya. Not long after the Ṣafawids succumbed to an Afghan invasion in the early 12th/18th century, the Mughal dynasty went into political decline and soon gave way to British power.

In general, however, many orders did not fare so well during the peak era of Western colonialization, whether in North Africa, the central Middle East, or South Asia. The health of Sufism's institutions suffered, not surprisingly, along with other indigenous institutions that languished under colonial regimes. The ability to maintain levels of education and spiritual formation more typical (as the historical sources would have us believe) of earlier times suffered in some cases from the drive to mobilize Sufis as anticolonialist military forces.

Today, Sufism remains surprisingly well represented in many different forms and in many regions. It has survived a variety of forces and changes that have threatened to reduce it to a museum piece. A number of the smaller suborders have fallen by the wayside due to attrition, poverty, and other social and cultural vicissitudes. Even some of the once-larger orders have suffered as a result of political intervention, as in the case of the Mawlawīya after it was officially outlawed by Atatürk early in the 14th/20th century. Sufism has continued to attract a wide variety of attention, from an idealized understanding of its role as a phenomenon of spiritual quest that transcends confessional allegiance to outright condemnation of Sufism as the root of all corruption within the realm of things Islamic.[6] Not long ago, the educational attaché of a major Middle Eastern embassy in Washington, D.C., declared in no uncertain terms that Sufism was "the ruination of Islam." Such categorical dismissals of a complex phenomenon whose history is intertwined in so many important ways with the greater history of the Islamic tradition are, unfortunately, not uncommon. They are typically based on either truncated views of Islamic history or just plain lack of information about Sufism—or both. Early modern and contemporary condemnations of Sufism as "un-Islamic" have often cited such practices as visitation to the tombs of holy persons, miracle-mongering, and various rituals and concepts that seem to accord unacceptable mediatorial status to human beings.

Enmity to Sufism goes back nearly as far as Sufism itself, and, not surprisingly, has a great deal to do with how one defines the phenomenon. Sufism's earliest critics articulated a wide spectrum of concerns about the social, political, and religious implications of the example of individual ascetics and teachers and of the groups that began to coalesce around them from the first/seventh century on. A widespread criticism of religious authorities arose out of concern that Sufis were setting themselves above and beyond the fundamental requirements of Revealed Law, the *Sharī'a*. These include not only adherence to the basic meanings of the confession of faith (*shahāda*), faithful observance of the five daily ritual prayers, fasting during the ninth lunar month of Ramaḍān, almsgiving, and pilgrimage to Mecca (the "Five Pillars") but also to a host of details regulating acceptable behavior and social relations. Early critics pointed to a dangerous elitism inherent, they believed, in presumptuous Sufi ideas about the possibility of intimate relationships between human beings and God. Some authorities took the early ascetics and Sufis to task for their quietistic tendencies, arguing that such a preference for withdrawal from society suggested an unwillingness to accept ethical responsibilities.

Nevertheless, one can still find active Sufi groups nearly everywhere across the globe. And although few of the orders manage to maintain the extensive institutions and facilities they once commanded in great numbers, Sufis still come together to engage in many traditional practices. Moroccan, Turkish, and Egyptian Sufi groups still gather for communal *dhikr* ceremonies, complete with vocal and instrumental ensembles that execute complex musical settings. In Iran, the major Shīʿī orders attract members from all walks of life, and several Sufi groups are convened by and for Iranian women. Chinese, Central Asian, Pakistani, and Indian Sufis still celebrate the birthdays of famous holy persons. *Shaykhs* still offer spiritual guidance, both to groups and to individuals. Seekers still avail themselves of the various spiritual disciplines, including the rigorous forty-day retreat and diverse types of fasting. And Sufi organizations continue to appear in various forms in the United States and Canada. All in all, the phenomenon of Sufism is still very much alive.

SCOPE AND SOURCES

This historical dictionary cuts a wide swath for Sufism, including some figures and concepts that might not find a place under a narrower definition of Sufism. For example, some sources would exclude "fringe" groups such as the Malāmatīya, Qalandarīya, and Ḥaydarīya and would argue that early ascetics and other "pre-Sufi" figures have no place in the history of Sufism. An overriding concern has been to extend the coverage of an already expansive topic in the hope of suggesting Sufism's broader social, political, cultural, and religious contexts. Sufism, as presented here, therefore embraces a host of ritual, institutional, psychological, hermeneutical, artistic, literary, ethical, and epistemological features. Primary sources for the history of Sufism cover a broad spectrum of literary and nontextual material.

Two large types of "documentation" provide a wide range of data about the history of Sufism. First and foremost, of course, are written sources represented by a host of genres in both prose and poetry. But in addition, a vast array of nontextual material reveals a great deal about Sufism that verbal communication alone cannot convey. Recent scholarship has made increasingly available for our interpretation a full spectrum of architectural monuments with an array of functions and forms, and visual arts in numerous media and degrees of sophistication. Here the most important examples of textual and nontextual documentation across this broad spectrum will be described briefly.

Beginning as early as the third/ninth century, Sufi authors composed important prose works essential to our knowledge of the history of Sufism. The variety of texts is considerable. Principal extant prose genres include manuals or compendia (such as those by authors already mentioned), more theoretical treatises, hagiographical texts, diaries and accounts of an autobiographical nature, letters, discourses, prayer books, and pilgrim guides.

Manuals or compendia, such as those by the authors mentioned above, provide comprehensive coverage of Sufi thought and practice, often in the context of defending Sufism against its critics among the religious "establishment." Treatises differ from the manuals in that they tend to offer more focused analyses of concepts and practices, while attending less pointedly to questions of Sufism's relationship to the broader Islamic tradition. Literary genres with affinities to the treatise include letters and discourses. Writing to a wide variety of correspondents, Sufi masters from at least the third/ninth century on have discussed a host of practical and theoretical concerns. Some epistles are addressed to individuals who inquired about their personal problems in the spiritual quest, while others are "letters" in a more generic sense and are meant for a wider readership among spiritual seekers. Discourses constitute a sizable body of written material. Typically cast in the form of a *shaykh*'s responses to queries of members of a Sufi order assembled to hear the leader's teaching, most discourses attributed to a particular master were collected and edited by disciples. These sources provide indispensable data about the lives and times of major Sufi spiritual guides as well as about the orders with which they were affiliated.

Another group of literary genres includes a vast corpus of works in the categories of hagiography and history. Authors of several of the great classic manuals developed an already long-standing practice, begun in the earliest collections of Ḥadīth, of showcasing the "excellences" or virtues (*faḍā'il*) of the Prophet and his Companions, the first generation of Muslims. They thus inaugurated a Sufi tradition of acknowledging the exemplary character of a spiritual elite that subsequent hagiographers elaborated further in the genre called "generations." These works were, in effect, anthologies of holy lives, typically short on continuous narrative and long on disparate anecdotes and sayings of the various leading Sufis. Before long, other authors began to craft life stories of individual saintly characters, freestanding works that varied in length from a few pages to several hundred. Study of such hagiographical works is still in its relative infancy, and further scholarship promises to expand our knowledge of the history of Sufism considerably.

In addition, one can garner a great deal of information, especially on Sufi orders and institutions, from two other genres of "historical" literature. During medieval times, guidebooks for pilgrims assisted spiritual sojourners with detailed accounts of major sacred sites, along with instructions on how to survive the rigors of negotiating foreign lands and cultures. Pilgrim guides came to include not only the ritual precincts of Mecca and Medina but countless tombs and shrines associated with famous Sufis as well. Though they tended to be more concerned with the logistics of getting to the goal and the etiquette of ritual at the site, these sources also provide valuable details on the history of the holy places and their relationship to Sufi orders. Travel accounts penned by such legendary globetrotters as Ibn Jubayr (d. 614/1217) and Ibn Battūta (d. 770/1368) supply supplementary information on Sufi institutions through often detailed descriptions of the inhabitants and practices of Sufi institutions.

Over and above such narrative accounts, there is also an immense wealth of devotional material and poetic works. Prayer books and collections of exhortatory preaching offer important insights into the spiritual tone of major Sufi leaders and their constituencies in diverse cultural and social settings. Poetic works span a considerable spectrum of genres in the two broad categories of didactic and lyric poetry. Lyric genres—*ghazal*, *qaṣīda* and *rubā'iyāt*—developed as significant vehicles for the communication of intense spiritual longing from as early as the second/eighth century. Didactic genres evolved from the sixth/12th century on, most notably in Persian and especially in the form of mystical epic and romances in rhyming couplets (*mathnawī*).

Possibilities of comparative synchronic studies on the basis of these highly developed literary resources are enormous but still rather sparsely explored. First and foremost, scholars of Sufism require more comparative studies of literary genres across cultural and linguistic boundaries. One excellent example of such an investigation is *Qasīda Poetry in Islamic Asia and Africa*, edited by Stefan Sperl and Christopher Shackle.[7] Studies of this kind open up new perspectives on the history of Sufism by facilitating analysis of similarities and differences in the ways Sufis in different linguistic and cultural contexts developed a single literary form as a major vehicle for expressing complex themes.

Significant written materials also include what one might call "archival" sources. Among the more important works in this category are foundational texts and court histories.

A vast lode of historical information has only begun to be mined from the largely undervalued documentation of Islamic traditions of "pious endowment." Many important institutional developments would have been impossible without the extensive funding made available to Sufi organizations through both royal and middle-class patronage. Records of such bequests are preserved in *waqf* (pl. *awqāf*), documents drawn up by wealthy donors that provide invaluable information about the structure and day-to-day operations of many Sufi-related institutions. They tell us, for example, what types of facilities were designed for Sufi orders and their administrations within larger royal architectural complexes; what kinds of activities were prescribed for the Sufis in a given institution; and what material resources, such as food and clothing, were designated for the institution's Sufis. In the case of the largest complexes, which housed a variety of functions in addition to Sufi residential facilities (tombs, law colleges, libraries, medical facilities), one can also get a sense of the role of Sufism in relation to other facets of society: *waqf* texts allow us to follow the money trail in most instructive ways.

Sovereigns of many major dynasties have been major patrons of Sufi leaders and their orders, as endowment records indicate. Court histories offer a window on the history of Sufism very different from the view afforded by texts written from a uniquely Sufi perspective. Royal archives typically evaluate the role of Sufism in the life of the ruler and his realm that suggest a broader context than Sufi hagiographical sources do, and in some instances give an invaluable sense of the ruler's personal connection to "his" Sufis. Like endowment texts, such histories offer a critically important perspective in that they tend to be written from outside Sufi organizations as such.

Written works are by no means the only important sources for the history of Sufism. Architecture and the visual arts offer an indispensable, but often overlooked, trove of nontextual data. Textual sources tend to be privileged because of the entrenched, but questionable, assumption that they are easier to interpret unambiguously. Architectural sources that supply invaluable information are monuments that serve a variety of functions and take various shapes. The earliest Sufi institutions known to us largely from written sources were typically either residential (the *zāwiya* and the *ribāṭ*) or ritual spaces, or a combination of these. Some of the oldest extant buildings are tombs and shrines (*qubba*, *imāmzādā*, *türbe*) many of which have continued to function as pilgrim goals or centers of expanded Sufi activity. Institutions on which solid archaeological data is available, or of which significant large structures are extant, tend to be those endowed by royal or extremely wealthy patrons (although there are many examples of "middle-class" patronage as well). These "complexes" typically combine several functions, including residential, ritual, funerary, and social (such as medical facilities, libraries, and educational facilities).

Sufis have created, and been the subject of, a wide range of visual arts as well. A number of accomplished calligraphers have been members of Sufi orders, as have several important painters. Calligraphic compositions created by and for Sufis and their institutions reveal, subtly but significantly, recurring themes in Sufi spirituality and imagery. Sufi artists have been responsible for some of the more creative calligraphic visual metaphors, fashioning symbolic images out of calligraphic forms at once legible and pictorial. Illustrated manuscripts of important prose and poetic works by Sufis afford us a window into the interpretative choices of both patrons and artists, and those in turn inform us about the key themes of Sufi life contemporary with the manuscripts. In addition, many album pages devoid of text have taken many aspects of Sufi life as their subjects.ṭ

NOTES

1. See, for example, Kalābādhī's remarks in *The Doctrine of the Sufis*, trans. A. J. Arberry (Cambridge: Cambridge UP, 1978 repr.), 2–3.

2. Paul Nwyia, *Ibn 'Aṭā' Allāh et la naissance de la confrérie Šādhilite* (Beirut: Dar el-Machreq, 1972), 4–18; Annemarie Schimmel, *Mystical Dimensions of Islam* (Chapel Hill: U of North Carolina P, 1975), 23–98.

3. J. Spencer Trimingham, *The Sufi Orders in Islam* (New York: Oxford UP, 1998), 70–71.

4. Nwyia, *Ibn 'Aṭā' Allāh et la naissance de la confrérie Šādhilite*, 4–18; Schimmel, *Mystical Dimensions of Islam*, 23–98.

5. For an excellent survey of this large subject of the meaning of Sufism, see Carl W. Ernst, *The Shambhala Guide to Sufism* (Boston: Shambhala, 1997), 1–31.

6. For an expansive approach to the history of negative assessments of Sufism, see Frederick de Jong and Bernd Radtke, *Islamic Mysticism Contested: Thirteen Centuries of Controversies and Polemics* (Leiden: Brill, 1999).

7. Stefan Sperl and Christopher Shackle, eds. *Qasīda Poetry in Islamic Asia and Africa*. 2 vols. (Leiden: Brill, 1996).

The Dictionary

– A –

ĀBĀD. *See* ABODE.

'ABBĀSID DYNASTY. Second of many Islamicate dynastic political regimes, nominally ruling from 133/750–656/1258 after supplanting the **Umayyad dynasty**. Claiming legitimacy as descendants of the **Prophet's** uncle 'Abbās, the 'Abbāsids made an important symbolic political statement by moving the capital from **Damascus** to the newly founded city of **Baghdad** in 145/762. The rulers asserted their claim to universal caliphal dominion over all of Islamdom, from Spain to the Indus River, but it was little more than 50 years before provincial governors, first in **Central Asia** and the **Maghrib** and eventually across the **Middle East**, began asserting their de facto independence of the central authority in Baghdad. The caliph's authority was increasingly contested by regional rulers, some of whom even arrogated caliphal legitimacy to themselves. The first major assault on Baghdad itself was effected by the **Saljūqid dynasty** in 447/1055, but the 'Abbāsids suffered the definitive blow when Mongol descendants of Genghis Khan sacked the capital in 656/1258. It was especially during the middle years of the dynasty that **political** patronage of major Sufis supported major **institutional** developments in Sufi **organizations**.

'ABD AL-AḤAD GUL (d. c. 1112/1700). South Asian Sufi ***shaykh*** and relative of **Aḥmad Sirhindī**. Known as "Gul" or "rose," the nickname connected him with the common Sufi **metaphor** of the **Lover** (**nightingale**) hopelessly enamored of the **Beloved** (rose).

'ABD AL-'AZĪZ, SHĀH (1159/1746–1239/1824). Indian Naqshbandī, exegete, traditionist and legal scholar, son of **Shāh Walī Allāh of Delhī**. He was on generally good terms with the British and weighed in against Sufis he regarded as tilting toward innovation, issuing *fatwās* denouncing, for example, animal sacrifice at saints' **tombs**. Theologically, however, he espoused a variety of the theory of *waḥdat al-wujūd* (**unity** of being), explaining that it differed from the less controversial *waḥdat ash-shuhūd* (unity of experience) largely as a matter of emphasis and ought not be interpreted as theologically dangerous. The former position, he argued, emphasized that God's unity is in no way compromised by human participation in the divine being, whereas the latter limited that participation to a more distant kind of witnessing.

'ABD AL-GHANĪ AN-NĀBULUSĪ (1050/1641–1143/1731). Syrian religious scholar of the Shāfi'ī **Law** school, **poet**, and mystic perhaps best known for his **Arabic** commentaries on the works of earlier Sufis, such as the *Dīwān* of **Ibn al-Fāriḍ** and Muḥyī ad-Dīn **Ibn al-'Arabī**'s mystical **prophetology**, *Bezels of Wisdom* (*Fuṣūṣ al-ḥikam*). His commentarial work is known for its imaginative exegesis and heavy influence of Ibn 'Arabī. He was a prolific author said to have penned over 200 works. He was a member of both the **Naqshbandī** and **Qādirī orders** and is an important source of information on these and other Sufi institutions, especially the **Mawlawīya**. Based in **Damascus**, he also spent some years in **Baghdad**, and documented many of his extensive travels through the Middle East in highly personal recollections on a number of sacred **places**.

'ABD AL-ḤAQQ DIHLAWĪ, MUḤADDITH (958/1551–1052/1642). Persian and **Arabic**-writing Indian Sufi, religious scholar and commentator who spent much of his long life in Delhi, where he enjoyed the patronage of **Mughal** rulers Jahāngīr and Shāh Jahān in particular. As his title suggests, he was a specialist in prophetic tradition (**Ḥadīth**) and is considered a pioneer in Indian Ḥadīth criticism. A member of the **Qādirī order**, he made a significant contribution to Sufi **hagiography** in a work entitled *Accounts of the Chosen Ones and Secrets of the Devout* (*Akhbār al-akhyār wa asrār al-abḥār*) dedicated mostly to Indian figures, and a biography of his order's founder, **'Abd al-Qādir al-Jīlānī**, on one of whose works he also wrote a commentary. He was at odds with the **Naqshbandī** leader **Aḥmad Sirhindī** concerning the nature of religious reform.

'ABD AL-KARĪM AL-JĪLĪ. *See* JĪLĪ.

'ABD AL-LAṬĪF BHITĀ'Ī, SHĀH (1102/1690–1165/1752). Mystic and poet of Hyderabad-Sindh in present-day **Pakistan**. He composed literary works known in **Sindhī** as *risālō,* portions of which he named after traditional musical modes and which are still sung in those musical forms by devotees at his **tomb** in Bhit. Themes of many of his poems derive from Sindhi and **Panjābī** folklore, and he was clearly very fond of the works of **Rūmī**. He then recast the romances in the Sufi idiom of the lover's relentless quest for the beloved, often making explicitly theological glosses on the tales. From the Sufi perspective, it was the varying aspects of inner experience the **poet** discerned in his characters that rendered the stories mystically instructive. Particularly noteworthy is the artist's penchant for especially refined development of the interior lives of his characters who were **women**.

'ABD AL-QĀDIR AL-JĪLĀNĪ (470/1077–561/1166). Celebrated as a Sufi **preacher**, father of 49 children, and eponymous ancestor of the **Qādirī order**, from the Persian region of Jīlān. During his youth he studied Ḥanbalī **law** in **Baghdad**, and there he became a disciple of the Sufi ***shaykh*** Abū 'l-Khayr ad-Dabbās (d. 525/1131). After many years as an itinerant hermit, he began his career as a preacher in 521/1127, apparently as a result of anxious dreams about his mission in life. Stories abound of his charismatic performances in Baghdad, which drew such crowds it was difficult to find adequately spacious venues. Most of the extant material attributed to him has survived in the form of some 200 sermons recorded by disciples. He expressed himself in direct, nontechnical language appealing to a broad public that included Christians and Jews as well as Muslims. He was also a noted scholar of **Qur'ān**, **Ḥadīth**, and religious **Law**. Some regarded him as the spiritual **pole** of his age. Among Sufi **Friends of God**, none has sustained such universal popular appeal across cultural and ethnic lines for so long as this worker of **wonders**. Today one can find countless examples of illustrated tales of this Sufi, from **painted** glass images to children's readers and coloring books, from Morocco to Malaysia. The order that bears his name is traditionally considered the first formally constituted *ṭarīqa* and is among the most influential and widespread. According to critics, the order's popularity came at the price of excessive openness to folk practices and the resultant dilution of authentic Muslim values.

'ABD AL-QĀDIR IBN MUḤYĪ AD-DĪN AL-ḤASANĪ, AMĪR (1223/1808–1300/1883). Widely known as an Algerian patriot and fighter who led resistance to the establishment of French colonial rule from 1248/1832–1264/1847, he was perhaps even more important as a Sufi. He was deeply influenced by the thought of **Niffarī**, especially as interpreted by **Ibn al-'Arabī**, and wrote a major work called *The Book of* ***Standings*** (*Kitāb al-mawāqif*) that outlines his view of the **stations** and **states** of the spiritual **journey**. After his capitulation to the French, he went into exile, first to **Turkey** and eventually to **Damascus**, where he died.

'ABD AL-QUDDŪS GANGŌHĪ (c. 860/1456–944/1537). Indian Sufi poet, author of treatises in Hindi, **Arabic** and **Persian**. From a family of religious scholars of the Ḥanafī school, he joined a branch of the **Chishtī order**. He lived during the reigns of the earliest **Mughal** rulers. His theology was characterized by the centrality of the concept of "**unity** of being" (*waḥdat al-wujūd*) and by his staunch defense of the thought of **Ibn 'Arabī**. Some of his writings suggest the influence of **Hindu**/yogic spiritual practices.

'ABD AR-RAḤMĀN CHISHTĪ, SHAYKH (d. 1094/1683). Indian religious scholar, **hagiographer** and leader of the **Chishtīya** during the later **Mughal** period. His *Mirror of Secrets* (*Mir'at al-asrār*) is a landmark of Chishtī historiography in the literary **genre** of **generations**, interpreting all of Indo-Persian Sufism as a monument to divine providence as implemented through the leaders of successive generations who functioned as cosmic **poles**.

'ABD AR-RA'ŪF AS-SINKILĪ (c. 1030/1620–c. 1105/1693). Sumatran (**Indonesia**) Shāfi'ī **Law** scholar and Sufi, member of the **Shaṭṭārīya order**. He wrote several **Malay**-language treatises, along with some **Arabic** works, and a Malay rendering of the **Qur'ān**. Local tradition reveres him (less than accurately) as the man who planted Islam in the Sumatran region of Acheh.

'ABD AR-RAZZĀQ AL-KĀSHĀNĪ. *See* KĀSHĀNĪ.

'ABD AṢ-ṢAMAD OF PALEMBANG (d. c. 1203/1789). Indonesian religious scholar from Sumatra who dedicated a great deal of effort to translating Abū Ḥāmid al-**Ghazālī's** *Revitalization of the Religious Disciplines* into **Malay**. He lived for many years in Arabia as a student in **Mecca**, and was a follower of Muḥammad as-Sammān, eponym of the **Sammānīya** order. His thought shows affinities with that of **Ibn al-'Arabī** even though he generally criticized Sufis who taught ontological **unity**, tilting toward the side of the ***wujūdī*** **controversy** that he and like-minded thinkers characterized as "distorted" or "corrupt."

'ABD AL-WAHHĀB, MUḤAMMAD IBN. *See* WAHHĀB.

ABDĀL. *See* SUBSTITUTES.

ABIDING. Arabic term for one of many important concepts developed to describe subtle aspects of mystical **experience**, typically paired with its polar opposite, **annihilation** (*fanā'*). Abiding (*baqā'*) refers to the paradoxical experience of surviving an encounter with the divine, a meeting that, according to some theorists, means the destruction of the "self" or individual personality and at the very least means the cessation of self-awareness. Others adopt an ethical interpretation, suggesting that abiding refers to the perdurance or survival of praiseworthy attributes in an individual once the negative qualities have vanished. The term appears in some listings of **stations** and **states**, but theorists who emphasize the more generalized aspects of this pair of concepts (abiding and annihilation) do not so categorize them.

ABODE. Persian term (*ābād*) often used as a suffix to refer generally to various aspects of the notion of spiritual place. On the **journey** or quest, the seeker's progress is marked by arrival at various waystations, habitations, or stopping places, which are further characterized by a host of technical terms for spiritual **experience**. *See also* STATE; STATION.

ABRAHAM. The **prophet** Ibrāhīm often mentioned in the **Qur'ān** and to whom **Muḥammad** is often likened. Islamic tradition identifies Abraham as the first *ḥanīf*, seeker after the One **God**, in whose footsteps the **Prophet** would later follow. Sufis focus on several features of the Abraham story. He models the quest for divine **unity**, his scriptural words "I love not things that set" (referring to God's revealing the divine ultimacy) in contrast to the contingency of the heavenly lights often cited by Sufi poets. Abraham's willingness to sacrifice his son Ismā'īl (Ishmael) betokens the mystic's slaying the **ego** as well as the ultimate generosity; and the willing son symbolizes mystical **annihilation**. As the Intimate Friend of the Merciful, *Khalīl ar-raḥmān*, Abraham declined even the assistance of Gabriel after the evil Nimrod had catapulted the prophet into a fire. As the "man who sighed often," Abraham was the epitome of **prayerfulness**, for one could hear from afar his heart "bubble" with longing for God.

ABRĀR. *See* FRIEND OF GOD.

ABSENCE. Arabic term often paired with its polar opposite, **presence**, to describe aspects of spiritual **experience**. In its positive aspect, *ghayba* often refers to lack of awareness of undesirable qualities or elements of "ordinary" experience—such as is meant by the phrase "taking leave of one's senses"—as a result of total preoccupation with input from a higher source. As such the concept is related to **annihilation** as well as to the principal term for "unseen/noncorporeal world" (*ghayb*).

ABŪ 'ALĪ QALANDAR OF PĀNĪPĀT, SHĀH (d. 724/1324). Major **Indian** Friend of God who renounced theological scholarship for the rootless **ascetical** life of a ***qalandar***. He is credited with composing a body of sophisticated **Persian** poetry that includes a work in the "spiritual **couplets**" (*mathnawī*) genre and a poem on the Prophet **Muḥammad**'s nativity.

ABŪ BAKR AṢ-ṢIDDĪQ (c. 570–13/634). First Muslim caliph (according to Sunni reckoning), father-in-law of the Prophet **Muḥam-**

mad. Sufi poets often describe him as the "Friend of the Cave," referring to an episode in which he accompanied the **Prophet** on the dangerous journey from **Mecca** to **Medina** in 1/622. According to tradition, as they sought refuge in a cave from the pursuing Quraysh forces of Mecca, God caused a spider to spin its web across the mouth of the cave with miraculous speed, thus leading the pursuers to assume no one had crossed the threshold recently. As the Prophet's companion in time of danger, the "Friend of the Cave" became a model of dedication and love of the Prophet, a spiritual state prized by many Sufis. Sufis also underscore the spiritual significance of the first caliph's ancient title, the "Authentic or Trustworthy One" (*aṣ-Ṣiddīq*).

ABŪ 'D-DARDĀ' (d. c. 32/652). Medinan Companion of the **Prophet**, transmitter of Prophetic traditions, one of the "Helpers" (*anṣār*), assigned by the Prophet as "brother" of **Salmān al-Fārisī**. Sufis regard him as a member of the early group of ascetics known as the "people of the **bench**."

ABŪ DHARR AL-GHIFĀRĪ (d. c. 32/653). Companion of the **Prophet**, **ascetic**, transmitter of Prophetic **traditions**, possibly one of the Helpers in **Medina**. His humility and simplicity were such that Sufis liken him to **Jesus**, who relied entirely on **God**. Tradition has it that a central theme in his public discourse was that those who have great wealth—indeed, any wealth at all—and refuse to spend it in the cause of God will be punished for their lack of generosity. His piety was such that he was said to have engaged in the ritual **prayer** several years before he even met the Prophet. Some sources emphasize his personal intimacy with the Prophet, and that relationship together with his **renunciation** of wealth commended him to Sufis as a model of piety.

ABŪ MADYAN OF TLEMCEN (520/1126–594/1197). Andalusian saint who left home in his youth for Fez, Morocco, traveled extensively in the **Middle East**, and died near Tlemcen, Algeria, while en route from his home base in Bijaya to Marrakesh at the behest of the Sultan. According to tradition, **'Abd al-Qādir al-Jīlānī** was one of his *shaykhs*. His disciples attributed marvels to him and regarded him as the paragon of **ascetical** virtue and the **pole** of the age. His **tomb** near Tlemcen was severely damaged in recent times by radical Islamists, but the site remains a pilgrimage goal for devotees from all across **North Africa**.

ABŪ NU'AYM AL-IṢFAHĀNĪ (336/948–430/1038). Persian-born religious scholar best known for his multivolume Arabic **hagiographic** anthology, *Ornament of the Friends of God* (*Ḥilyat al-awliyā'*). He includes brief bio-sketches of some 649 devout Sufis, tracing their lineage (often spuriously and imaginatively) back to the **Prophet** via the first caliphs, offering more in the way of narrative than the hagiographic work of his contemporary, **Sulamī**. His work provided much data for a major hagiography by **'Aṭṭār**.

ABŪ SA'ĪD IBN ABĪ 'L-KHAYR (357/967–440/1049). Khurāsānī mystical poet and **ascetic**, student of Shāfi'ī **Law** and Sufi thought. Tradition has it that he formally began his life as a Sufi at the age of **forty**. He was initiated into Sufism by **Sulamī** in Nishapur, and dedicated himself for some years to an austere life of serving the poorest. He was known, however, to go to the other extreme on occasion, hosting sumptuous gatherings funded by well-heeled friends, all by way of demonstrating the virtue of detachment. Among the critics of his sometimes extravagant style was 'Abd Allāh **Anṣārī**. He was noted for his powers of clairvoyance (*firāsa*), and is credited with promulgating the earliest equivalent of disciplinary requirements for life in the **khānqāh**.

ABŪ ṬĀLIB AL-MAKKĪ (d. 386/996). Sufi author from the **Arabian Peninsula**, who spent much of his adult life in **Mecca**, **Basra**, and **Baghdad**, and is most noted for his widely influential **manual** of spirituality and Sufi life, *The Sustenance of Hearts* (*Qūt al-qulūb*). This extensive work treats, as the fuller title indicates, a broad range of aspects of "one's conduct toward the Beloved, and a description of the **Path** of the seeker toward Divine Unity" and is heavily slanted toward questions of practice. He studied the religious **law** of three of the four principal Sunni schools, the Shāfi'ī, Mālikī, and Ḥanbalī, and insisted that genuine Sufism was in no way at odds with mainstream tradition and practice. Authentic spirituality consists in interiorizing the full significance of the deeds required of all Muslims. Unlike the authors of several other major manuals of Sufism, he does not describe the spiritual quest in terms of an ascending order of spiritual stations and states as though the Path were some sort of parallel track for Sufis. He prefers to build his entire understanding squarely on the profound inner meanings of the Five **Pillars of Islam** incumbent on every Muslim.

ABŪ YAZĪD AL-BISṬĀMĪ. *See* BĀYAZĪD.

ACCEPTANCE. *See* CONTENTMENT.

ADAB. *See* BEHAVIOR.

ADAM. The first of God's "caliphs" (vice-gerent) on earth and the first of a long line of **prophets**. Sufis associate him especially with mystical **knowledge**, for God infused in Adam knowledge of the names of all things and commissioned him to teach all humankind. The **forty** days it took God to knead Adam's clay into a finished product, and Adam's forty years in sorrowful exile from the Garden, symbolize the **formative** experience of the **retreat**. Sufis associate the Day of the **Covenant** with the creation of Adam. As the first ***shaykh*** of the human race, his role is to help seekers recover their lost memory of their divine source and the goal of the spiritual **journey**. It was because of his refusal of God's command that he bow to the newly created body of Adam that the **angel** Iblīs became **Satan**.

AESTHETICS. Some scholars have argued that there is a distinctively "Islamic aesthetic" and that one can discern in **art** created by Muslims various characteristics (dematerialization, abstraction, modular composition, repetition—all features of the general category of "arabesque") that imply the divine attributes of **unity** and transcendence (*tawḥīd*). Others have gone so far as to suggest that the use of specific **symbolic** colors and shapes is based on an underlying, if never explicitly articulated, set of uniquely Sufi aesthetic principles. Neither approach has proven quite satisfactory, for they fail to account adequately for historical context. One can nevertheless suggest credibly that Sufis who have communicated through **literature** and the visual arts have been very much aware of earthly beauty as a reflection of the divine magnificence. The traditional saying "God is beautiful and He loves beauty" has been a Sufi favorite that implicitly validates the cultivation of highly refined creativity in verbal and visual expression. Among Sufi authors who developed sophisticated aesthetic hermeneutics, **Shabistarī** stands out.

AFFILIATION. *See* ORGANIZATION.

AFLĀKĪ, SHAMS AD-DĪN (c. 685/1286–761/1360). Major **hagiographer** of the **Mawlawīya** who lived in Konya during the generation after **Rūmī**. His most famous Sufi work is *The Feats of the Mystics* (*Manāqib al-'ārifīn*), written in **Persian**, including life stories of Rūmī's father, Rūmī himself, and his **successors**.

AFRICA, EAST. *See* EAST AFRICA.

AFRICA, WEST. *See* WEST AFRICA.

AFRICA, NORTH. *See* NORTH AFRICA.

'AHD**.** *See* INITIATION.

AHL AṢ-ṢUFFA**.** *See* BENCH, PEOPLE OF THE.

AḤMAD BRELWĪ, SAYYID (a.k.a. Sayyid Aḥmad of Rae-Bareilly) (1201/1786–1246/1831). Indian reformer, disciple of Shāh **'Abd al-'Azīz**, who **initiated** him into three **orders**: the **Naqshbandīya**, **Chishtīya**, and **Qādirīya**. His overriding concern was to cleanse Islam of spurious beliefs and practices introduced as a result of intermingling with **Shī'īs** as well as Hindus and other non-Muslims. He named his movement the "Order of **Muḥammad**" (*ṭarīqa-yi muḥammadīya*). Perhaps emboldened by the Arabian **Wahhābī** movement, he was active in the resistance against the British, and died in battle with the Sikhs, who were prominent in **Panjab**.

AḤMAD IBN IDRĪS (1200/1785–1253/1838). Moroccan reformer and author of Sufi **treatises**. Though he himself did not found a distinct **order**, several of his most prominent disciples—especially **Sanūsī** and Mīrghānī—spread his work through their own organizations. His indirect influence is thus still felt in Eritrea, Somalia, and parts of **East Africa** as well as Niger, Chad, and Libya. Ironically, perhaps, he himself gravitated to the prayer traditions of the **North African Shādhilīya** order, but toward the end of the 19th century, some members of his family did constitute an order and named it the Idrīsīya.

AḤMAD-I JĀM (440/1049–536/1141). Author of several **Persian** works on spirituality, born in **Khurasan**. Tradition has it that he experienced a dramatic conversion from a life of hard drinking, and that at age **forty** he moved to the Afghan town of Jām where he set up a *khānqāh* and a mosque and in effect founded his own **order**. Stories of his life seek to confer on him the aura of institutional authority, by connecting him spuriously with **Abū Sa'īd ibn Abī 'l-Khayr**, as well as underscoring his divine connection, by insisting that he was theologically illiterate and that the learning he demonstrated in his writings was miraculously infused. His mystical **theology** is generally consistent with those of mainstream Sufi **theorists**.

AḤMAD KHĀN, SIR SAYYID (1232/1817–1316/1898). Indian reformer and activist from a family long affiliated with the Mujaddidī **Naqshbandī order**. He was very involved in political affairs and worked for reconciliation between the British and Muslim communities. He founded the famed educational institution at Aligarh and worked to spread Muslim education on the model of Oxford and Cambridge universities, thereby running afoul of more tradition-minded Muslim religious scholars.

AḤMAD SIRHINDĪ. *See* SIRHINDĪ, AḤMAD.

AḤMAD YASAWĪ. *See* YASAWĪ, AḤMAD.

AḤRĀR, KHWĀJA 'UBAYD ALLĀH (806/1404–896/1490). Central Asian Naqshbandī ***shaykh*** who spent most of his adult life in Tashkent and Samarkand, in present-day Uzbekistan. His public authority, probably not as broad as his **hagiographers** would have us believe, was enhanced by his own family's considerable mercantile wealth and extensive property holdings. Some of the most important documents about his role are those governing foundational **endowments** called *waqfs*. His extant Persian works include a text on Sufi ethics as well as a collection of **letters**.

AJMĪR (Ajmer). North-central **Indian** city that grew in importance as a pilgrimage center, largely due to high-profile annual visits (until c. 988/1580) by the **Mughal** emperor Akbar to the **tomb** of Shaykh **Mu'īn ad-dīn Chishtī**. Akbar's sons Jahāngīr and Shāh Jahān later built more magnificent additional monuments there. The city has remained inextricably linked to the origins of the **Chishtīya**.

AKHĪ. From the Arabic for "my brother," a reference especially to medieval **Turkish** groups associated with **chivalric** organizations.

AKHLĀQ. *See* ETHICS.

AKHYĀR. *See* CHOSEN ONES.

'ALAM. *See* STANDARD.

'ĀLAM. *See* REALMS; *See also* COSMOLOGY.

ALAST, RŪZ-I. *See* COVENANT, DAY OF.

'ALAWĪ, ABŪ 'L-'ABBĀS AḤMAD AL- (a.k.a. Ibn 'Alīwa) (1286/1869–1353/1934). Algerian saint, author of **treatises** and **poet**. He began his Sufi life after joining the 'Īsawīya, but soon abandoned that order's preference for the spectacular (such as snake-charming) for the somewhat more studious and reflective way of the **Darqāwīya**. He rose in the ranks of that order and succeeded his own ***shaykh*** as its leader in 1327/1909, eventually breaking away to form an order whose method of **retreat** was more systematic and supervised. His order spread rapidly across **North Africa**, his followers establishing *zāwiyas* in various parts of the central Middle East and Europe as well. Many have regarded him as the major **reformer** (*mujaddid*) of his age. His poetry and theoretical treatises, still relatively little studied, are among the most substantial of modern Sufi writings.

ALEXANDRIA. Egypt's "second city," over a thousand years older than Cairo, on the Mediterranean shore near the northern end of the Nile. Named *al-Iskandarīya* after "founder" Alexander the Great (al-Iskandar in Arabic), the city played an important role in the history of Sufism as the eventual home of **Shādhilī** himself, who also died there, and of the famed **Shādhilīya** Sufi **Ibn 'Aṭā' Allāh** and the poet **Buṣīrī**.

'ALĪ HAMADHĀNĪ, MĪR SAYYID (d. 787/1385). Kubrāwī *shaykh* and author who established the order in Kashmir after settling there with (a reputed) 700 disciples in 783/1381. He wrote dozens of (mostly brief) treatises and translated **Ibn al-'Arabī's** prophetological work *Bezels of Wisdom* into **Persian**.

'ALĪ IBN ABĪ ṬĀLIB (598–40/ 661). Cousin and son-in-law of the Prophet, fourth caliph (by Sunni reckoning) and first Imām (in **Shī 'ī** thought). As husband of the Prophet's daughter **Fāṭima**, he became the model of the family man, and Sufis revere him as a paragon of intimacy with the Prophet that made him uniquely capable of transmitting mystical **knowledge**, just as he is said to have passed on the mantle conferred on him by the Prophet. He is considered among the highest **Friends of God** (who possess attributes identical with those of Shī'ī Imāms) and a model of **asceticism**. Most Sufi **lineages** (with the notable exception of the **Naqshbandīya**) trace their origins to the Prophet through 'Alī. He is also closely linked with organizations identified with the movement called *futūwa* (**chivalric** organizations), and is known as the quintessential *fatā* (young man, heroic youth) or epitome of virtue. He is particularly important for the **Bektāshīya**, whose idiosyncratic (often called extremist) doctrine makes him part of a trinity along with God and the Prophet.

'ALĪ AL-MUṬṬAQĪ, SHAYKH (885/1480–975/1567). Indian religious scholar, leader of the **Chishtīya,** and widely traveled author who settled in Mecca (then under Ottoman rule) and there became affiliated with the **Qādirīya**, Madyanīya, and **Shādhilīya** orders. He had a reputation for giving to the poor most of what donors gave him and leaving very meager pickings for those who came to live in his *khānqāh*. So austere was he that he even declined to bestow the patched **cloak** on his disciples. Tradition attributes some 100 works to him.

'ALĪ SHĪR NAWĀ'Ī, MĪR (d. 907/1501). Central Asian vizier, patron of the arts, poet, **hagiographer**, member of the **Naqshbandīya**, foremost author in Chagatay **Turkish**. He penned a Chagatay mystical work in **couplets**, *The Tongue of the Birds* (*Lisān aṭ-ṭayr*) based on **'Aṭṭār's** *Conference of the Birds*; and an anthology of Sufi biographies entitled *Breaths of Love* (*Nasā'im al-maḥabba*), which is inspired by and elaborates on **Jāmī's** *Warm Breezes of Intimacy*.

ALLĀH. *See* GOD.

ALLEGORY. A literary **genre** as well as a method of **exegesis**, allegory involves an extended set of **metaphors**, somewhat the way a **parable** consists of an extended set of similes. Countless Sufi authors have made use of allegory both as a **hermeneutica**l principle in Qur'ānic **exegesis** and as a pedagogical device. Shihāb ad-Dīn Yaḥyā as-**Suhrawardī** wrote a remarkable series of allegorical treatises. His *Treatise on the Reality of* ***Love*** retells the scriptural tale of **Joseph** (Sura 12) by showing the relationships among Beauty (Joseph), Love (the power that moves **Zulaykhā**, the wife of Pharaoh's minister who is smitten with Joseph), and Grief (Joseph's father who weeps himself blind at the loss of his son), as attributes of God's first creation, Intellect. **'Aṭṭār's** *Conference of the Birds*, for example, allegorizes the various species of birds and the seven valleys through which they must journey in their quest for the Divine. *See* also LITERATURE; SYMBOLISM.

ALLUSION. A technical **term** referring to a kind of usually brief mystical statement, *ishāra* (pl. *-at*), that discloses insights accessible only to more advanced seekers. According to an early definition of the term, the form communicates an intimate **knowledge** that slips further into obscurity the more insistently one attempts to analyze it. In this sense the mystical allusion shares an important quality of paradox or **ecstatic** utterance. Two masters of the mystical allusion are Aḥmad al-**Ghazālī** and **Niffarī**. Another related form of cryptic mystical expression is the **aphorism**.

ALPHABET. Known as *abjad*, a combination of the first four basic consonant forms (a, b, j, d), the **Arabic** alphabet consists of 28 consonants. The Arabic consonants have long been used numerically (a = 1, b = 2, j = 3, d = 4, and so on). Popular use of numbers to refer to important religious phrases remains common; so for example, the number 786 that appears often on everything from calendars to doorways is the numerical value of the phrase "In the name of God." But it is the wider symbolism of the letters that is especially relevant here. Sufi **poets**, writing in many **languages**, and **calligraphers** in particular, have delighted in fashioning literary and visual puns using the Arabic alphabet. Mystical interpretation of the various letters began early in the history of Sufism with sophisticated symbolic **exegesis** of the sacred text, including elaborate analyses of the so-called mysterious letters with which several of the **Qur'ān's** *sūras* begin. Later developments ranged from elaborate plays on certain letters singled out because they form names or references to God, to playful explanations based on the alleged likeness of certain letters to the eyes, lips, or other features of the Beloved, for example.

AMERICA, UNITED STATES OF. Sufism began to develop noticeably in the United States during the 20th century, as a result of both immigration and conversion. Various groups have settled in different parts of the country, in many instances around the tomb of a foundational figure. For example, the followers of Bawa **Muhaiyaddeen** are centered in eastern Pennsylvania, while those of Murshid Samuel Lewis look to Abiquiu, New Mexico, as the spiritual center of their organization, known as the Sufi Islamia Ruhaniat Society. Some groups identify themselves as branches of major **orders** "transplanted" here from the lands of their origins. For example, representatives of the **Naqshbandīya**, **Halvetī-Jerrāhī**, and **Ni'mat-allāhīya** have centers in various places. One group identify themselves as members of the "Sufi Order in the West," following the tutelage of Pīr Ḥaẓrat Ināyat Khān, who established a development of the Niẓāmī branch of the **Chishtīya** in 1910. The Ṣābirī branch of the Chishtīya is also represented in the United States. A Moroccan-based branch of the **Shādhilīya** arrived in 1973. A number of organizations have assumed variant forms in the United States, including the New Mexico–based Sufi Foundation of America, the Zahra Trust in Texas; the

School of Islamic Sufism headquartered in San Rafael, California; and an organization (but not precisely an order) called Zaytuna, representing a more "conservative" Sufi approach to the religious disciplines.

AMĪR ḤAMZA. *See* ḤAMZA, AMĪR.

'AMR IBN 'UTHMĀN AL-MAKKĪ (d. c. 296/909). Mystic of **Baghdad**, disciple of **Junayd**, author of perhaps the first treatise on mystical **love** and **intimacy**. He was among those who advised their flamboyant disciple **Ḥallāj** against giving public expression to his mystical **experiences**.

ANATOLIA. Known under Roman imperial rule as Asia Minor, Anatolia was once the heartland of the Byzantine Empire and now constitutes the bulk of the modern nation-state of **Turkey**. Sufism's most celebrated development in Anatolia is the rise of the **Mawlawīya** in Konya during the second half of the seventh/13th century under the leadership of **Rūmī** and his descendants. Other major **orders** of particular historical importance in Turkey have been the **Bayrāmīya**, **Bektāshīya**, **Khalwatīya**, **Naqshbandīya**, and **Qādarīya**.

ANDALUSIA. Known in Arabic as *al-Andalus*, Andalusia generally refers to approximately the southern two-thirds of the **Iberian** Peninsula (i.e., Spain and Portugal), conquered by Arab-led Muslim forces in the decades following their crossing from **North Africa** to Gibraltar in 93/711. Many important Sufis were born in Andalusia, including **Ibn 'Abbād**, **Ibn al-'Arabī**, **Ibn al-'Arīf**, and **Ibn Sab'īn**. Quite a few migrated to North Africa and the **Middle East**, but some remained to make significant contributions in Andalusia.

ANECDOTE. A short **genre** of **storytelling** called the *laṭīfa* that communicates in very condensed form episodes in the lives of famous holy persons. A more expanded form of story narrative is called the *ḥikāya* and occurs often in various kinds of **didactic** Sufi **literature**, such as certain works of **'Aṭṭār** and **Sa'dī**, as well as in **hagiographic** literature.

ANGELS. Creatures of light who mediate between the divine and human **realms**, the unseen and the seen. As the name suggests, angels are primarily "messengers" entrusted with delivering God's word to **prophets** who then relay the message to humankind. Paradoxically perhaps, angels rank lower than human beings in the sense that angels are not capable of knowing God with the intimacy allowed to human beings. When Gabriel guided the Prophet on his **Ascension**, the angel had to take leave of the Prophet as they neared the Throne, for in God's presence even a mighty angel is no greater than a finch. In addition, angels are inferior to human beings in **knowledge**, for God taught **Adam** what no angel ever knew. Belief in angels is an article of faith for Muslims, and tradition distinguishes among various individual angels—Gabriel (bringer of revelation), Michael (tender of souls), Isrāfīl (sounder of the last trumpet), 'Azrā'īl (angel of death), for example; as well as among several classes of angelic beings—including those who bear the Throne, guardian angels, those assigned to each of the heavens, and the cherubim. Sufis have had much to say especially about the chief fallen angel Iblīs, because of the intriguing questions his case raises about the origins of evil. (Many sources argue that this first **devil** was actually a *jinn*, a creature of smokeless fire, rather than an angel as such.) But angels also play a broader role in Sufi thought, for angels suffuse the cosmos and participate in every aspect of human life. Some authors have suggested that individual angels represent specific human faculties on the macrocosmic level.

ANNIHILATION. Generally paired with **abiding**, annihilation (*fanā'*) or "passing away" refers to a fundamental aspect of spiritual **experience**. Sufis have interpreted the experience in various ways. At one end of the spectrum, the individual is said to lose all traces of individual personality. If **God** is the only reality, and nothing else possesses authentic existence, the full realization of this ultimate truth constitutes "loss" of self in the One. So-called **ecstatic** utterances (*shaṭḥīyāt*) such as "I am the Truth" (attributed to **Ḥallāj**) seem to suggest such a radical loss of self. Other sources, however, explain that such expressions are open to two dangerous interpretations. One is that they can imply that if God is everything, then all things are God (a form of monism). The other is that God has descended into the individual human being in a form of "indwelling," a heretical notion related to "incarnationalism." As a result, some Sufis have deemphasized the notion of the union of the human self with the Divine and underscored the need for the "passing away of passing away," so that the mystic is unaware of a transformation of individual status and thus is not moved to give utterance to the unutterable. Some **orders** also developed the concept of "annihilation in the *shaykh*" and "annihilation in the Messenger of God" as steps toward annihilation in God.

ANṢĀRĪ, KHWĀJA ʻABD ALLĀH (396/1006–481/1089). Khurāsānī teacher, **exegete**, **hagiographer**, and polemicist, from Herat (in present-day Afghanistan). Schooled in Ḥanbalī methodology in **Law** and **traditionist** studies from his youth, he engaged in ongoing debate with both Ashʻarī and Muʻtazilī scholars who generally enjoyed the patronage of the sultan, and whom he regarded as straying too far from the core meaning of the sacred texts. He claimed that his most formative influence in Sufism was that of Abū 'l-Ḥasan **Kharaqānī**. At Gazurgāh, near Herat, the shaykh had established a *khānqāh*. There he continued to receive and teach students during the latter years of his life, even after he lost his sight in 473/1081, and it was during that period that he dictated the works for which he is most renowned. His extant output includes works in various **genres**, in both **Persian** and **Arabic**. His Persian *Hundred Fields* (*Ṣad maydān*) lays out the spiritual itinerary in a series of stages, a schema he later developed further in the Arabic *Dwelling Places of the Wayfarers* (*Manāzil as-sā'irīn*). For pedagogical purposes he clusters the essential aspects of experience along the journey in 10 groups of 10, making them easier to memorize. His treatment of these psycho-spiritual **typologies** is therefore much more streamlined than those developed in the **manuals** of some of his predecessors, such as **Kalābādhī**, **Sarrāj**, and **Makkī**. Perhaps his most popular work of all is the brief collection of *Intimate Conversations* (*Munājāt*), beautiful and intensely personal **prayers** in the Persian dialect of Herat.

APHORISM. A literary **genre**, belonging to the larger category of "**wisdom literature**," made famous especially by **Ibn ʻAṭā' Allāh of Alexandria's** *Book of Aphoristic Wisdom* (*Kitāb al-ḥikam*). Sufi aphorisms tend to be short, pithy, generally paradoxical statements describing myriad aspects of the divine-human relationship. With their apparent contradictions, aphorisms spur reflection on virtually every imaginable type of inward **experience**, allowing the seeker to move toward ever deeper self-knowledge. Aphorisms have been a popular genre of mystical expression into modern times, as in the work of the Algerian Aḥmad al-**'Alawī**.

APOPHATIC. From the Greek compound *apo-phasis*, "speaking against," hence "denial," the opposite of **kataphatic**. Authors in virtually all mystical traditions have attempted to come to terms with the impossibility of speaking about ineffable realities. One avenue of approach has been a kind of negative path (*via negativa*) in which one limits oneself to speaking of what the ultimate reality, and the experience thereof, is *not*. Some Sufi authors have recommended not attempting to speak of such things at all, while others have often resorted to starkly paradoxical language in efforts to say, without actually saying, the unsayable.

'AQL. *See* KNOWLEDGE, DISCURSIVE.

ARABIAN PENINSULA. A largely desert region bounded by the Persian Gulf on the northeast, the Red Sea and Gulf of Aden along the west and southwest, and the Arabian Sea along the south and southeast. To the north lie the modern nation-states of Iraq and Jordan. Located in the northwestern quarter of the peninsula, known as the Hijaz, **Mecca** is the site of the birth and early life of **Muḥammad**. Some 250 miles to the north, **Medina** (formerly known as Yathrib) became the center of the Islamic community after the **Hijra** in the year 1/622. Sufi tradition counts among its Arabian ancestors a number of **Companions** of the **Prophet** as well as major figures from medieval times who studied and taught in the two great Prophetic cities. Today there are almost no traces of Sufism in the peninsula as a result of the reforming policies of the **Wahhābī** movement, and in this respect the region is virtually unique.

ARABIC. The most widely spoken of the living Semitic **languages**, classified historically as one of the Southwest Semitic tongues. During the pre-Islamic period, Arabic had become a highly refined poetic medium, but it was not until Islamic times that it became widely used as a written language. Like languages of its family generally, Arabic is based on triliteral consonantal roots (the Arabic **alphabet** has 28 consonants) modified by the addition of prefixes, infixes, and suffixes, and changing vocalization. Arabic is the only Semitic language essential to the study of Sufism. Much Islamicate **literature** of importance for Sufism is written in Arabic, beginning with the **Qur'ān** and **Ḥadīth**, early Sufi **exegetical** works, theoretical treatises or **manuals** of spirituality, **hagiographical** works, and religious **poetry**.

ARBA'ĪNĪYA. *See* RETREAT.

ARCHITECTURE. Sufism's initial impact on developments in architecture occurred in response to the need for more ample, serviceable spaces for gatherings of devotees around individuals noted for their piety and religious learning. At first, followers of a particular ***shaykh*** or *shaykha* would seek their teacher's company in his or her own residence, in small groups. The name *zāwiya* or "corner" was one of the technical terms for such a dwelling-with-meeting space. As devotees multiplied, Sufis expanded the venues for teaching, spiritual direction, and paraliturgical rituals. Some **residential facilities**, such as the *ribāṭ*, provided accommodations for travelers, and eventually the *khānqāh* or *tekke* developed into a complex that included residential quarters for members and administrators of Sufi **orders**, along with prayer and, often, social service facilities. In addition, **tombs** and related funerary structures have figured prominently in Sufi history, whether as freestanding structures or integrated into larger residential and/or ritual complexes. On the whole, Sufism's influence on architectural developments has had more to do with function than with form, though there are some examples of distinctively Sufi spatial arrangements and decorative programs.

'ĀRIF, 'ARĪF. *See* KNOWLEDGE, MYSTICAL.

ARKĀN. *See* PILLARS; REALMS.

ART FORMS. A wide range of visual arts have been associated with Sufism, and Sufis have been among the most accomplished artists in many Muslim societies. **Calligraphy** has been a primary art because of its obvious connection with the divine word of the **Qur'ān**, and some first-rate calligraphers have been Sufis. This is so not only because of the inherently devotional nature of inscribing the sacred text, but also because of a host of **symbolic** associations Sufis have discerned in calligraphic imagery, from the Arabic **alphabet** itself to the countless allusions they find in the very elements of calligraphy to beauty and the face of the **Beloved**. For example, some have associated the word for "writing" with the "down on the Beloved's cheek," or seen a metaphoric connection between ink and love. Mystical ideas have been expressed through countless examples of visual **metaphor** and **allegory**, particularly in the form of illustrations to **lyric** and **didactic poetry**. Miniature paintings as well as images on ceramic objects and in other media have often depicted individual Sufis or more generic scenes of Sufi life, either as direct illustration of a literary text or as a discrete reminder of the spiritual dimension of life. Creators of unusual objects, such as oil lamps shaped like candlesticks, have often inscribed their works with Sufi **poetry** that confers on the object a metaphorical message: just as the candle weeps its tears of wax, so the **Lover** pines for the absent Beloved. *See also* LITERATURE; MANUSCRIPT ARTS; PAINTING.

ASCENSION. Muslim tradition, beginning with **Qur'ān** 17:1, teaches that God granted the **Prophet Muḥammad** unique access to the unseen realm through a twofold experience that has been interpreted in various ways. According to the scriptural text, God "caused His servant to travel by night from the *masjid* of the sanctuary to the farther *masjid*." Long-standing tradition identifies the former site with the **Ka'ba** in **Mecca** and the latter with the southern end of the platform believed to have been the site of Solomon's temple, where now stands the early eighth century Al-aqṣā **mosque**. According to several extended **Ḥadīths**, after this "**Night Journey**" (*isrā'*), the Prophet then ascended (in the *mi'rāj*) through the seven heavens even to the very throne of God, and was also shown the punishments of the damned in Hell. Nearly all Sufis have accorded the experience great significance, typically interpreting it as a spiritual journey rather than a matter of physical locomotion. Some, such as **Bāyazīd al-Bisṭāmi**, have gone so far as to interpret their own experience according to the Prophetic paradigm, identifying their own inward journeys by using the Ascension of Muḥammad as a pattern. Even some have of the more "sober" Sufis have likened the departure and return to **annihilation** and **abiding**. Chronologies vary somewhat, but many traditional sources date the experience to the year 621, and Muslims in various regions still celebrate the occasion on the 27th of the lunar month of Rajab.

ASCETICISM. Self-discipline and renunciation (*zuhd* and *nusk*) in Sufism has run the gamut from an abiding concern for simplicity of life as an expression of deep **trust** in **God** as the source that supplies all one's needs, to a severe regimen of the most extreme self-denial and even self-inflicted violence and mutilation. Several of the major **manuals** list ascetical renunciation among the earlier **stations** on the **Path**, typically in proximity to **repentance** and **poverty**. Paradoxically, some Sufis have rejected renunciation itself on the grounds that it represents just one more thing to grasp at, so that even asceticism can raise a veil between the seeker and God. None other than **Jesus** and the **Prophet Muḥammad** stand as prime examples of the ascetical life, modeling as they did consistent self-discipline characterized by the rejection of luxury and privilege in favor of a simple, ordinary mode of living. Ascetical practices include, for example, **fasting**, various forms of interior **struggle** (*jihād*) and **retreat**, and a range of other methods of self-imposed hardship and solitude. Ascetics are usually referred to with the terms *nāsik/nussāk* and *zāhid/zuhhād*, individuals who lead an abstemious (and perhaps reclusive) life.

'ĀSHIQ. *See* LOVE.

ASIA, CENTRAL. *See* CENTRAL ASIA.

ASIA, EAST. *See* EAST ASIA.

ASIA, SOUTH. *See* SOUTH ASIA.

ASIA, SOUTHEAST. *See* SOUTHEAST ASIA.

ASIA, WESTERN. *See* MIDDLE EAST.

ĀSITĀNE. *See* INSTITUTIONS.

'AṬṬĀR, FARĪD AD-DĪN (c. 540/1145–618/1221). Khurāsānī poet and **hagiographer** from Nishapur. He appears not to have been formally affiliated with any particular **order** or teacher. Best known for his didactic **mathnawī** *The Conference of the* ***Birds*** (*Manṭiq aṭ-ṭayr*) he also wrote three other narrative **didactic** poems, a **lyric** *dīwān*, and biographical dictionary of famous Sufis called *Recollections of the Friends of God* (*Tadhkirat al-awliyā'*), modeled partly on similar works by **Abū Nu'aym** and **Sulamī**. The first work, the most celebrated of his three "mystical epics," tells the story of how all the members of the kingdom of birds assemble to go in search of their absent king. Many of the birds are fearful of this perilous quest and excuse themselves, so that finally a much reduced contingent set off for the distant mountains. En route, they pass through seven valleys, each representing an aspect of inner spiritual **experience**: quest, love, understanding, detachment, acknowledgment of God's transcendent **unity**, bewilderment, and, finally, **poverty** and death to self (or **annihilation**). By the time they arrive at the castle of the Sīmurgh (a fantastic bird, mystical **symbol** of the divine), only 30 birds have survived. They ask to see their king and are ushered into a room where the chamberlain draws back a veil, leaving the bedraggled travelers looking at a mirror. There they see in their own reflection the *sī murgh*, "30 birds," the poet's ingenious if tantalizingly ambiguous suggestion of divine immanence. In his anthology of lyric poetry, 'Aṭṭār develops his mystical themes largely in the *ghazal* **genre**; and in his hagiographical work he adds a great deal of personal anecdotal detail about individual Sufis not found in Sulamī's accounts.

ATTENDANCE. An aspect of **experience** that **Qushayrī** clusters together with **unveiling** and **witnessing**, thus suggesting the tenor of being in the presence of divine disclosure. In this instance, the one, "presence of the **heart**" (*muḥāḍara*), is prerequisite to the next, with the second and third representing greater levels of clarity and certitude.

AUDITION. A category of Sufi **ritual** much contested because it involves the use of **music**, which mainstream Muslim tradition has generally condemned because of its emotional power and soul-altering properties. Audition (*samā'*) often also incorporates the recitation of sacred text and **poetry** as well as various forms of ritual movement or **dance**. While some Sufis have argued against the practice, many Sufi organizations have regarded audition as an essential ingredient of spiritual practice and have evolved their own distinctive forms. Perhaps the best known is the whirling dance of the **Mawlawīya**, set to the **music** of an instrumental group with the reed flute (*ney*) as its lead voice. Some Sufis have considered audition as a re-living of the Day of **Covenant.**

AUTHENTICITY. A major, inclusive concept in Abū Sa'īd al-**Kharrāz's** analysis of the spiritual life in his *Book of Authenticity* (*Kitāb aṣ-ṣidq*). He discusses authenticity as an essential quality or virtue as it applies to a series of 16 progressive stages on the **path**. Similar to (and sometimes even translated as) sincerity, the term *ṣidq* means absolute reliability and genuineness, so that one's word and intention are exactly what they claim to be. **Qushayrī** locates authenticity as the fifth **state** (subsequent to his list of 20 **stations**), after **sincerity** and before **shame**. **Anṣārī** locates it after shame and before altruism. The **Prophet's** first successor, Abū Bakr, was given the honorific title "The Authentic One" (*aṣ-Ṣiddīq*) and it was largely for this reason that he became a paragon of this virtue for Sufis.

AUTHORITY. God is the ultimate source of all authority. From a religious perspective, therefore, any authority human beings claim must be shown to have been conferred from on high, and the **Prophet** is the paradigmatic human authority figure. **Hagiographic** traditions often go to great lengths to demonstrate that individual Sufis—even those to whom sophisticated writings are attributed—were uneducated, suggesting that their evident learning can only have come from God directly. As a result of the need to maintain this connection to divine **authority**, Sufi **organizations** generally developed **hierarchical** structures of **governance**. Authority devolved virtually undiminished upon duly appointed **successors** to founding figures. Sufis have typically demonstrated that unbroken heritage through the **chain** (*silsila*) and the genealogical **tree** (*shajara*), tracing the present leader back to the wellsprings of the organization's authority. One of the more important **symbols** of authority is the prayer **carpet** (*sajjāda*) and the current leader of an order was known (in Persian-speaking circles, at least) as the "one who sits on the prayer carpet" of the founder. The sheepskin (*pōstakī* [T]) plays a similar role in some orders. Various **ranks** in the structure of many orders are based on a division of labor, with specific aspects of governance handled by individual officers. Mechanisms of delegation of authority included conferring various forms of "license." For example, the *ijāzat at-tabarruk* testified that a disciple of ***shaykh*** rightly claimed a connection via **blessing** to an **order's** foundational figure. *Shaykhs* in some orders also delegate authority to a *muqaddam(a)* who leads sections and sometimes has power to **initiate**. The term most often used to refer in general to the office of the *shaykh* is the Arabic *mashyakha*.

AUTOBIOGRAPHY. A **genre** in which some Sufi authors have reflected in the first-person on their personal spiritual **experiences**. No one technical term in Sufi traditional jargon refers specifically to this type of **literature**. Some (such as those of **Rūzbihān** and **Tirmidhī**) take the form of diaries, including dream and visionary accounts; some (such as those of **Bāyazīd** and **Ibn 'Ajība**) adopt an overtly mystical structure such as that of the multi-level "**ascension**"; and others (such as those of **Ghazālī** and **Hamadhānī**) are couched in terms of the writer's intellectual and spiritual search for true belief. Some examples of the genre called the **discourse**, such as a work of **Shams** of Tabriz, are notably autobiographical in tone and content.

ĀWARD BURD. *See* BREATH CONTROL.

'AWĀRIF AL-MA'ĀRIF. By Abū Ḥafṣ 'Umar as-**Suhrawardī**, one of the most influential **manuals** of Sufi spirituality and thought. Written in Arabic, the work was soon translated into Persian and became essential reading for Sufis of various **South Asian** organizations. A blend of theoretical discussion and practical concerns, the work's 63 chapters begin with an extended analysis of the epistemological foundations of the Sufi way and progress through a thorough description of various aspects of Sufi institutional life and practice. Among the work's most distinctive and important contributions are its latter chapters, on the refined art of spiritual **discernment** and the role of the ***shaykh*** in spiritual direction, and on the subtler aspects of mystical **experience**.

AWE. An aspect of **experience** that **Qushayrī**, for example, pairs with **intimacy**, so that the two represent the paradoxical blending of reticence and fascination in the divine presence. Awe (*hayba*) and intimacy (*uns*) mark a progress beyond **constriction** and **expansion** as these latter represent an advance beyond **fear** and **hope**.

AWLĀD AṬ-ṬARĪQA. See ORGANIZATION.

AWLIYĀ'. *See* FRIEND OF GOD.

AWRĀD. *See* LITANIES.

AWTĀD. *See* SUPPORTS.

AXIS. *See* POLE.

'AYN. *See* ESSENCE.

'AYN AL-QUḌĀT AL-HAMADHĀNĪ (492/1098–526/1131). Mystical teacher, author, and **martyr** from western Persia, disciple of **Aḥmad Ghazālī**. His **Persian** writings betray significant influence of the thought of the earlier Sufi martyr **Ḥallāj**. He ran afoul of the religious authorities in **Baghdad** who interpreted his **theology** as monistic. They also objected to his views on sainthood as encroaching on the uniqueness of **prophethood** and took exception to his reduction of the "last things" (death, judgment, heaven and hell; i.e., **eschatology**) to microcosmic rather than macrocosmic realities (i.e., occurring in the individual rather than on a global scale at the end of time). He was brutally tortured and executed in Hamadhān. His most influential work is the Persian *Tamhīdāt* (*Preludes*), which explore in 10 thematic segments various aspects of the mystical life, often embodying controversial interpretations of scriptural and earlier Sufi texts.

'AZĪZĀN. *See* ORGANIZATION.

– B –

BĀBĀ. *See* HONORIFICS.

BĀBĀ, AḤMAD (d. 1037/1627). West African scholar of religious **law** from Timbuktu (Mali) who is an important source on Sufism in Niger. His work on the role of the *mujaddid* (renewer/**reformer** of each age promised by **God**) especially sheds light on the teaching and work of Sīdī **Maḥmūd al-Baghdādī.** In his scathing critique, Aḥmad Bābā argues that the ***shaykh's*** importing of ecstatic and other antinomian practices from further east renders him guilty of innovation. He goes so far as to encourage *jihād* against the "Baghdādī heretic."

BĀBĀ ILYĀS (d. 638/1240). Khurāsānī mystic who traveled to **Anatolia** during the early seventh/13th century. **Hagiographic** accounts say that after one of his disciples engaged in a disastrous battle against the forces of the **Saljūqid** sultan, he **ascended** to the heavens on a white horse, never to be seen again.

BĀBĀ ṬĀHIR 'URYĀN (d. early fifth/11th century). Persian **dervish** from Hamadhān who composed **poetry** mostly in a variation on the standard **quatrain** genre, some of which have been set to **music** in recent times. He also produced a collection of some 400 Arabic **aphorisms**, many on the theme of **knowledge**, on which later famous Sufis have commented. Called a **qalandar** in Persian literary sources, he is said to have confronted the **Saljūqid** Sultan Tughril, insisting that God wanted the ruler to establish a just society. In several accounts that represent a kind of topos designed to give religious **authority** precedence over temporal power, the ruler does homage to the Sufi. In exchange for this acknowledgment of the mystic's divinely originated authority, the Sufi gives the sultan a simple ring as a symbol of the religious conferral of **political** authority.

BADAL. *See* SUBSTITUTES.

BADAWĪ, SAYYID AḤMAD AL- (c. 596/1200–675/1276). Egyptian dervish known as the **pole** of his age, celebrated for many **wonders**, and author of a collection of prayers and a "spiritual testament" addressed to his successor to the leadership of his **order**. The saint is noted especially for his ability to find the lost and release prisoners. His family may have moved from Arabia to Fez (Morocco), where he was born. Celebrated in his youth for bold equestrian deeds, he experienced a kind of conversion in his mid-30s. He became reclusive and devoted himself to prayer and scriptural studies. In response to a series of visions, he traveled to **Iraq** to visit the graves of various great saints. There he was **initiated** into the **Rifā'īya** order and it was as a representative of that order that he returned to Ṭanṭā in Egypt, where he spent the rest of life. His mosque-**tomb** remains a goal of **visitation** for regional pilgrims. Tradition has it that several **Mamlūk** rulers were openly devoted to him and his memory, and his **birthday** celebration is still a popular occasion in spite of sporadic disapproval over the centuries by political authorities opposed to Sufism in general. His tradition is maintained by a Sufi order called variously the Aḥmadīya or **Badawīya**, **symbolized** by a red banner or **standard**.

BADAWĪYA. **Egyptian** Sufi **order** (not to be confused with a 13th/19th century Moroccan order of the same name) who are the spiritual descendants of **Aḥmad al-Badawī**, also known as the Aḥmadīya. It is one of the most popular orders in Egypt but is not well represented elsewhere. The order's beliefs and practices suggest the influence of the **Shādhilīya** as well as the perdurance of some pre-Islamic traditions.

BAGHDĀD. **'Irāqī** city founded on the Tigris River in 145/762 by the first 'Abbasid caliph, al-Manṣūr. Originally designed as a circular enclosure, it was meant to symbolize the unity of all Muslims. This was the center of one of the earliest "schools" of Sufism, whose leader is generally identified as **Junayd**, but whose origins may be traced back further to **Ma'rūf al-Karkhī**. It was also the adopted home of many famous Sufis including **Bishr ibn al-Ḥārith al-Ḥāfī**, Abū Ḥāmid al-**Ghazālī**, **Ḥallāj**, Abū Sa'īd Aḥmad al-**Kharrāz**, **Rābi'a**, and **Sarī as-Saqaṭī**. The city remained, at least nominally, the capital of the caliphate until it was destroyed in 656/1258 by a Mongol invasion led by a descendant of Genghis Khan named Hülegü.

BAGHDĀDĪ, MAJD AD-DĪN (554/1159–616/1219). Khurāsānī successor to Najm ad-Dīn **Kubrā**, author of Persian **treatises** and **poetry**, and teacher of **Najm ad-Dīn Dāyā Rāzī** and (likely also) **'Aṭṭār**. In addition to a lovely short **Persian** treatise on the spiritual life as a **journey**, the *Treatise on Journeying* (*Risāla dar safar*), he also wrote on **symbolism** in the interpretation of **dreams** and **visions**.

BAHĀ' AD-DĪN MUḤAMMAD WALAD (546/1151–628/1231). Khurāsānī religious scholar, **ascetic**, and **preacher** of Balkh (in present-day Afghanistan), father of **Rūmī**. He moved his family westward—perhaps at the approach of the Mongol Genghis Khan and likely also as a result of negative reactions to his outspoken criticism of the political establishment in Balkh—and eventually settled in the **Anatolian** city of **Konya**, then under **Saljūqid** Turkish rule, in around 626/1229. For the remaining two years of his life he enjoyed royal patronage as a celebrated intellectual, and when he died his position went to his son Jalīl ad-Dīn. Tradition connects him to Sufi **lineages** that link him with both Aḥmad **Ghazālī** and **Kubrā**, though there is little evidence to support the second affiliation. His only extant written legacy, a collection of **discourses** entitled *Aspects of Mystical Knowledge* (*Ma'ārif*), are heavily **exegetical** and **theological**.

BAHĀ' AD-DĪN NAQSHBAND (718/1318–791/1391). Central Asian dervish after whom the **Naqshbandīya** order takes its name. According to tradition, he was an **Uwaysī** by virtue of a "spirit **initiation**" that he experienced in a **vision**. He was for a time a footloose wanderer and espoused a spiritual style that eschewed external display of any kind. After settling down in his home town again, he began to accept followers as initiates in his **path**, emphasizing silent or "hidden" **recollection** and rejecting the practices of **audition** and **retreat**. Not unlike the founder of the **Shādhilīya**, he preferred that his followers avoid the outward trappings typically associated with membership in an **order**. He therefore refused to establish **khānqāhs**, deprecated the use of formal **garb** and listing one's Sufi credentials, and denied the significance of saintly **wonders**.

BAHĀ' AD-DĪN ZAKARĪYA MULṬĀNĪ (578/1182–661/1262). Indian religious scholar, ***shaykh***, and in effect the founder, of the Indian branch of the **Suhrawardīya**. He traveled widely through the **Middle East** and while in **Baghdad** studied with Shihāb ad-Dīn Abū Ḥafṣ ʻUmar as-**Suhrawardī**, who in very short order commissioned him to launch the organization in India. He established a pattern of a rather well-to-do, elite style of life for the **order** and maintained broad connections with **political** authorities, and generally did not cultivate relations with the rival **Chishtīya**.

BAḤR. *See* OCEAN.

BAḤRĪ, MAḤMŪD (895/1490–1130/1717). Indian member of the **Chishtīya**, author of didactic and lyric **poetry** in **Persian** and Dakhni **Urdu**, from the Deccan region. After he moved to the kingdom's capital of Bijapur, he became a hermit who gave literary expression to his negative opinion of both the religious and **political** establishment.

BĀKHARZĪ, ABŪ 'L-MAFĀKHĪR YAḤYĀ (d. 736/1335–6). Persian author of a large two-part **manual** entitled *Litanies of the Most Beloved Friends and Gem-settings of Proper Behavior* (*Awrād al-aḥbāb wa fuṣāṣ al-ādāb*), major ***shaykh*** of the **Kubrāwīya**. Like a number of earlier classic works of the **genre**, this compendium is valuable particularly for its contribution to Sufi **lexicography** and the subtle interpretation of technical **terminology**. The work's 60 chapters cover the full range of topics that became more or less standard beginning with the great manuals from the fourth/10th century on. The *shaykh's* records are particularly useful in that they include specific reference to major Sufi works that had especially influenced his thinking, including several by **Abū Ṭālib al-Makkī**, **Ibn ʻArabī**, and Abū 'n-Najīb and Abū Ḥafṣ ʻUmar as-**Suhrawardī**.

BĀKHARZĪ, SAYF AD-DĪN (d. 659/1261). Khurāsānī *shaykh* who was among the chief disciples of Najm ad-Dīn **Kubrā** in **Transoxiana**, religious scholar and grandfather of Abū 'l-Mafākhīr **Bākharzī**. He authored a number of Sufi works in **Arabic** and **Persian**, including a **treatise** on mystical love and an analysis of the experience of **retreat**.

BAKKĀ'ŪN. *See* WEEPERS.

BALĪ'. *See* TRIAL.

BALKANS. The geographical region generally situated between the eastern shore of the Adriatic Sea and the western end of the Black Sea, including the nation-states of the former Yugoslavia (Slovenia, Croatia, Bosnia-Herzegovina, Serbia, Kosovo, Montenegro) along with Macedonia, Albania, Bulgaria, and Rumania. Under the influence of the **Ottoman** Empire from the eighth/14th century well into modern times, the region has had significant Muslim populations, particularly in Albania, Bulgaria, Kosovo, and Bosnia-Herzegovina. In addition to the **Bektāshīya** and **Naqshbandīya**, the **Malāmatīya** (especially in Bosnia) and the **Shādhilīya** have also had a significant presence in the region at various times. Branches of the Sha'bānīya sub-**order** of the **Khalwatīya** enjoyed a brief but noteworthy flowering during the 13th/19th century.

BAMBA MBACKÉ, AḤMAD or AMADU (d. 1346/1927). West African Wolof founder of the Murīdīya, a kind of offshoot of the **Qādirīya**, in Senegal. In the long run, after he had returned in 1331/1912 from exile in Gabon and Mauritania, he counseled a cooperative approach to working with the French colonial authorities. His **order**, which he founded in 1323/1905, is noteworthy for the prominence of **women** leadership as spiritual guides during the later 14th/20th century especially.

BANNER. A cloth wall hanging traditionally displayed wherever a particular Sufi **order** is located or performing a **ritual** ceremony for a special occasion. Each order typically has its distinctive **color**. Like the **standard**, the banner is one of the more important public **symbols** of Sufi identity and affiliation.

BAQĀ'. *See* ABIDING.

BĀQĪ BI-'LLĀH, KHWĀJA (971/1563–1012/1603). Afghan religious scholar, mystical author, and **Naqshbandī** Sufi. Born in Kabul, he traveled north to Transoxiana, and after a sojourn in Lahore he returned to Central Asia and was initiated as a Naqshbandī in the **lineage** of **Aḥrār**. He was eventually commissioned to set up a *khānqāh* of the **order** in **Delhi**, and identified as the essentials of life in the order as **repentance**, **renunciation**, **trust** in God, resignation, seclusion, and **patience**. He wrote extensively in **Persian**, in a variety of **genres**, including **treatises**, **poetry**, and **letters**. There, as well as in his collected **discourses** (*malfūẓāt*) he expressed an abiding interest in the often-controversial views of **Ibn al-'Arabī** and 'Alā' ad-Dawla **Simnānī**. Perhaps his most famous disciple was Aḥmad **Sirhindī**. *See also WUJŪDĪ* CONTROVERSY.

BAQLĪ, RŪZBIHĀN. *See* RŪZBIHĀN BAQLĪ.

BARAKA. *See* BLESSING.

BARANĪ, ḌIYĀ' AD-DĪN (684/1285–758/1357). Indian historian and author of two works in the **genre** known as the "mirror for princes." His views of the religious life in general were much influenced by his Sufi role as *khādim* (attendant, servant) to the great **Chishtī *shaykh* Niẓām ad-Dīn Awliyā'**. His "mirrors" are fine examples of the literary interface between religion, Sufism, and **political** life: they measure current rulers against the standard of the **Prophet** and the first four caliphs, who embodied the qualities of Sufi saints.

BAṢRA. City in southern **Iraq**, now second in size only to **Baghdad**, that grew from a military garrison during early Islamic conquests into an important center of early Sufi activity. One of the earliest communities of **ascetics** is believed to have been established there in the mid-to-late eighth century by Aḥmad al-Hujaymī. The city was the adopted home of **Ḥasan al-Baṣrī** and place of origin of some of his ascetical followers, as well as of **Muḥāsibī** and **Rābi'a**.

BAṢRĪ, ḤASAN AL-. *See* ḤASAN AL-BAṢRĪ.

BASṬ. *See* EXPANSION.

BĀṬIN. *See* INWARD.

BAY'A. *See* INITIATION.

BĀYAZĪD AL-BISṬĀMĪ, ṬAYFŪR IBN ʻĪSĀ (d. c. 261/875). Persian mystic and onetime student of Ḥanafī **Law**, most famous for **ecstatic** utterances, such as "Glory be to me! How great is my majesty!" Some say it was he who first articulated the concept of **annihilation**, though he may have learned that from a certain Abū ʻAlī of Sindh (now in **Pakistan**), leading some scholars to suspect the influence of **Indian** thought. Some 500 of his sayings have been preserved only in the works of later historians, commentators, and theorists. He was one of the Sufis who most famously regarded the **Prophet's Ascension** as a template for his own spiritual **journey**. Among the other famous early Sufis with whom he was acquainted are **Junayd** and **Dhū 'n-Nūn**. Few early Sufis communicate a more profound sense of **awe** in the presence of God as he grapples with the mystery of the divine-human relationship.

BAYRĀMĪYA. Order founded by Ḥajjī Bayrām al-Anṣārī (d. c. 833/1430) in **Turkey**. An **Egyptian** branch was begun in the late 10th/16th century by a Bosnian member of the order. Some scholars link the origins and spirit of the organization to the **Malāmatīya**, and some see affinities with the **Khalwatīya** and **Naqshbandīya**.

BEAUTY. Sufi authors of many **genres** have addressed the significance of beauty (*jamāl*) from various perspectives. Beginning with the traditional saying, "**God** is beautiful and loves beauty," they have sought to plumb the meaning of how God communicates His beauty, how it is that God loves beauty, and how human beings can survive an experience of the divine comeliness. For mystical **poets**, the challenge has been to express the ineffable in human language, and they have crafted countless narratives and **allegories** around the longing of the human lover for the bewilderingly beautiful countenance of the divine **Beloved**. They dwell in great detail on every **metaphorical** aspect of that loveliness, exploring each minute feature of the **Face**. *See also* AESTHETICS.

BEGGING BOWL. Called the *kashkūl* (literally, "beggar") in Persian, the begging bowl was as much a **symbol** of Sufi **poverty** (like some items of **headgear** and **clothing**) as a practical **implement** to be used in daily life. Eventually the bowl was transformed, ironically, into an **art form** often so sumptuous as to be unrecognizable as a reminder of poverty. Many are carved from coconut, but elegantly carved and polished, but there are numerous examples of high art as well. Made of copper, cast bronze, or even the much more expensive cut steel, the bowls were sometimes shaped like a boat, inlaid with gold and silver, and inscribed with poetic texts in exquisite **calligraphy**. Artists chose the texts with a view to underscoring the spiritual wealth and nobility of the person who possessed the object, though the more refined artistic versions were of course meant for people of considerable means.

BEHAVIOR. All of the requirements of Sufi etiquette and discipline. *Adab* is an Arabic term used to refer to proper demeanor or "courtesy" as well as to the broader categories of refined **literature** and culture. Each of the Sufi **orders** has had its own distinctive brand of *adab*, calling for varying emphases on such things as practices governing **initiation**, elements of **ritual**, means of **livelihood**, degree of involvement in public life and **politics**, attitudes toward marriage and **celibacy**, and matters of internal **governance**. Sufi authors have produced many texts outlining the details of the *adab* of their respective organizations, from relatively brief charterlike documents providing numbered lists of essentials to lengthy sections of larger **manuals** of spirituality to separate **treatises**. Although in general modes of behavior tend to be predominantly ordinary and often mundane, the category encompasses a wide range of practices, including such peculiar features as *tamzīq*, the ecstatic tearing of one's **clothing**.

BEING. Ontological reality (*wujūd*), a status ultimately belonging only to **God**, a concept of particular importance in **theoretical** and **theosophical Sufism**. If God alone is "the really real," all things beside God have no independent claims to existence. Mystical **theologies** vary as to precisely how they define the concept in relation to the human being who seeks union with the divine, a debate prominently exemplified in the ***wujūdī* controversy**.

BEKTĀSH WALĪ, ḤĀJJĪ (d. c. 669/1270–71). Khurāsānī dervish said to have been the founder of the **order** that bears his name. He may have moved to the west around the time that the family of **Rūmī**

left home in advance of the Mongol invasion. Rich **hagiographical** accounts assert that he died in the year 738/1338, but 738 turns out to be the numerical equivalent of the letters of the Arabic **alphabet** in the name **Bektāshīya**. His mentor may have been a certain Bābā Rasūl (a.k.a. Ilyās or Isḥāq), whose name has been attached to a rebellion against the **Saljūqid** rulers in 638/1240. Tradition also traces the saint's spiritual pedigree to the Central Asian ***shaykh*** Aḥmad **Yasawī**. Some scholars suggest that Bektāsh ought to be numbered among the ***qalandars*** because of his relaxed approach to ritual obligations. What is beyond dispute is that this character remains among a small handful of "signature" Sufi saints of modern Turkey, along with, for example, Rūmī and **Yūnus Emre**, and he appears to have been a patron saint of the Janissary Corps in **Ottoman** times.

BEKTĀSHĪYA. Sufi **order** of **Anatolian** origin that arose after the seventh/13th century Bābā'ī rebellion. A certain Bālim Sulṭān is often identified as the actual founder of the movement. The order eventually spread to the **Balkans** and was transplanted to parts of the central **Middle East** and **Iran**. Later **Shī'ī** elements influenced the **hagiographic** traditions connecting the order's spiritual lineage to the line of *imāms*. Much influenced by Anatolian **Qalandarī** practice, the order's ritual gradually became quite elaborate and colorful. Strong elements of Shī'ī ritual were also incorporated into the order's liturgical calendar, especially observance of the martyrdom of Ḥusayn. By the 10th/16th century the order had split into **celibate** and non-celibate branches, with all major foundations under the jurisdiction of a celibate leader in Anatolia. Another significant later development was the influence of the esoteric **Ḥurūfī** movement. Devotion to **'Alī** (some go so far as to call it deification) and a curious, trinity-like association of 'Alī with the Prophet and God are among the idiosyncratic features of the order. Some scholars suggest that they continued some practices and teachings of the **Ḥaydarīya**.

BELOVED. One of many ways of naming the object of the mystical quest. Sufi **poets** frequently leave draped in tantalizing ambiguity whether the beloved is human or divine, but in general, even a human **love** interest (*maḥbūb*) is at the very least a reflection of the divine.

BENCH, PEOPLE OF THE. A group of early Muslim devotees known as *ahl* (or *aṣḥāb*, "companions") *aṣ-ṣuffa*, traditionally said to have lived in poverty in a portico attached to the **Prophet's** mosque in Medina. They thus modeled simplicity of life and utter dedication to the Prophet. Some traditional sources have seen in the Arabic word for bench (*ṣuffa*) a possible etymological origin of the term *ṣūfī*.

BENGAL. Region in the northeast of **India**, eventually divided into east and west sections, the former segment now the nation-state of Bangladesh, itself separated from **Pakistan** as an independent nation in 1391/1971. Sufism was first introduced formally to Bengal during the eighth/14th century, with further developments in the following century. The two **orders** most influential there have been the **Chishtīya** and the **Shaṭṭārīya**. The **poet Bīdil** is one of the most famous of Bengal's Sufi literary figures. An important group of Bengali figures often identified as mystical are the Bauls (the name meaning mad, off-center, deviant). They bear some features similar to those of the **Qalandarīya**, but appear to have been influenced by Vaishnava Hinduism.

BĪBĪ JAMĀL KHATŪN (d. 1057/1647). Indian woman ascetic and mystic, younger sister of **Miyān Mīr**. She was initiated into the **Qādirīya** by one of her brothers. **Dārā Shikūh** called her the "**Rābi'a** of the Age," and tradition credits her with a number of saintly **wonders**.

BĪDIL (BEDIL), MĪRZĀ 'ABD AL-QĀDIR (1054/1644–1133/1721). Indian poet of **Bengal** who wrote largely in **Persian**. His work shows considerable influence of Sufi tradition. This is especially true of his shorter **lyric ghazals** and his four **didactic mathnawīs**. The latter works pick up large themes from such earlier figures as **Ibn al-'Arabī** (especially the seminal concept of *waḥdat al-wujūd*) and Farīd ad-Dīn **'Aṭṭar**, and devotes two entire poems to the theme of mystical **knowledge**. He was a major figure in Indian intellectual history, for he explored his mystical themes within the context of the great philosophical questions and against the expansive backdrop of the broader Indian religious and cultural heritage.

BILĀL IBN RABĀḤ (d. c. 20/641). An Abyssinian slave and **Companion** of the **Prophet** chosen to be the Muslim community's first *mu'adhdhin* (a *muezzin*; i.e., the one who makes the call to prayer). Sufis emphasize his intimacy with the Prophet as the model of a devotion so pure that the Prophet easily overlooked Bilāl's faulty **Arabic** pronunciation. They tell of how the Prophet redeemed the slave from his former owner, who had treated the slave as disdainfully as **Joseph's** brothers had treated Joseph. The call to prayer from Bilāl's lips was a summons to the spiritual journey.

BIRD. An important **symbol** that occurs in a variety of forms in Sufi **literature**. Among the more important specific species of bird are the **falcon** and **nightingale**. Over all the members of the bird kingdom rules the extraordinary mythical being called the **Sīmurgh**. In addition, and in a more generic way, birds frequently play an instrumental role in **anecdotes** about **Friends of God**, sometimes speaking, sometimes guiding. Finally, Sufi authors often speak of the **soul** as a bird.

BIRTHDAY. *Mawlid* (also *mawlūd*; pl. *mawālid*) is the Arabic term used to refer to celebrations of the birth-anniversaries of the **Prophet** and numerous holy persons. The term also refers to panegyric texts recited at the Prophet's birthday celebrations. The nearly universal popularity of observance of the Prophet's birthday, never entirely without varying degrees of official government and other types of opposition, has been due in large measure to Sufi influence. Debate concerning whether the practice constitutes an innovation and, if so, of an acceptable kind or not, has been ongoing through Islamic history. Celebrations typically include recitation of **Qur'ān**, processions, special forms of **recollection** and **audition**, and public meals. In a related development, pious folk have long made **visitations** to the birthplaces, as well as to the **tombs**, of the Prophet and countless Friends of God to avail themselves of the **blessings** of the place's patron. In some regions, *mawlid* **poems** are recited on occasions other than the actual birthday, including the **wedding**. During the 13th/19th and 14th/20th centuries especially, proponents of the **Wahhābī** ideology have sought to eradicate the practice as heretical. A particularly important aspect of such observances for Sufis has been a strong sense of the **presence** of the Prophet.

BISHR IBN AL-ḤĀRITH "AL-ḤĀFĪ" (c. 150/767–227/841). Khurāsānī traditionist of Merv who may have studied with Mālik ibn Anas, nicknamed "The Barefoot." He became noted for his particularly austere practice of poverty. After an apparently undisciplined early life, he pursued formal religious studies and later experienced a **conversion** whose details are unclear. At some point he decided to cease teaching and transmitting **Ḥadīth** because he saw in even such an evidently pious pursuit the danger of becoming attached to being acclaimed as an authority in religious matters. A key principle of his spirituality was avoidance of publicity for one's deeds of devotion and kindness. Nevertheless, later Sufi sources have cited extensively his observations on the quiet life of self-denial. He lived much of his adult life rather reclusively and died in **Baghdad**.

BLAME. Proof that an individual is truly dedicated to a life of piety. Some Sufis have held the view that if a person is authentically attached only to God, his or her beliefs and actions will inevitably cause others to respond with condemnation, insults, and indignities (blame, *malāma*). The underlying principle is that one should avoid religious display at all costs, even if that means seeming not to observe the fundamental requirements of the Islamic faith. Hence, those associated with the **Malāmatīya** often went to the other extreme so as to be sure they would inspire in others the contempt they felt they needed to keep their intentions pure. Ironically, this might include the pursuit of conspicuous wealth, since many regarded evident **poverty** as a sign of devotion. Beneath whatever external circumstances the individual might cultivate, the idea was to leave one's spiritual **state** purely a matter between God and the servant. Although this tradition exhibits some similarity with ***qalandar*** tradition, the two remain significantly different in many ways.

BLESSING. A beneficial spiritual force accessible through the power and proximity of **Friends of God** to the source of grace. Called *baraka* all over the world, the concept of "blessing" has become a broadly inclusive way of describing the desired result of all popular devotion and interaction between devotees and the various personalities that embody holiness preeminently in any given local or regional context. Of course, all blessing derives ultimately from God, and sincere seekers of blessing know that one ought not take it for granted. For many Muslims, **visitation** to the **tombs** of holy persons remains one of the favorite modes of benefiting from blessing.

BREATH CONTROL. One of the widespread practices associated with Sufi **recollection**, **ritual**, and **prayer**, designed to assist the individual toward greater concentration, often referred to with the **Persian** expression *ḥabs-i dam* or *āward-burd*. One of the earliest Sufis (**Shiblī**) identified Sufism with sense-control and awareness of breathing. A critical distinction is that between breath associated with the **ego** (or material soul, *nafs*) that comes from the lower body and out the mouth, and breath of the **spirit** (*rūḥ*) that originates in the brain and emanates through the nose. Breath control naturally played an important role in practices that involved speaking or singing, and in some cases has been associated with altered consciousness resulting in effect from hyperventilation. Expelling a great deal of breath while chanting a specific repetitive *dhikr* formula (such as the word *Allāh*), for example, eventually affects one's balance and awareness. Some forms of recollection involve a quieter and simpler observation of breathing in and out in which the practitioner simply focuses on parts of one phrase (such as "there is no god" while exhaling, and "except God" while inhaling).

BU'D. *See* DISTANCE.

BUKHĀRA. Central Asian city in present-day Uzbekistan particularly prominent in medieval times as a center of religious studies, philosophy, and culture. Two of the "six" authoritative collections of **Ḥadīth** originated there, and the city was home to the great philosopher **Ibn Sīnā**, author of important "visionary **recitals**."

BULHE SHĀH, MĪR (d. after 1181/1767). Member of both the **Shaṭṭārīya** and **Qādirīya orders**, considered by many the greatest **Panjābī** Sufi **poet.** He became a ***shaykh*** and initiated disciples into a variety of orders, including the **Chishtīya** and **Suhrawardīya**.

BURĀQ. Human-headed, winged quadruped traditionally identified as the **Prophet's** means of conveyance during the **Night Journey** prior to, and during, his **Ascension**. Though early sources generally describe the mount in generic terms as a horse or quadruped, later authors embellished both on the creature's appearance and capabilities. Eventually the steed took on a human visage (in miniature **paintings** especially) and the ability to fly with enormous speed. It was in fact the visual **arts** that accounted for most of the once-humble mount's aggrandizement in popular tradition. Burāq has remained a frequent subject for depiction in various media, from underglass painting to decorative designs on trucks and taxis. For many Sufi **poets**, the steed represents not only a being intimate with the Prophet privileged to travel into the environs of the divine Throne, but a **metaphor** for the soul's conveyance on its heavenward trajectory and a **symbol** of love as well as of the victory of spirit over materiality.

BURDA**.** "Mantle" of the **Prophet** and title of a **poem** by al-**Buṣīrī** in praise of **Muḥammad**. It is among the most famous poems in the **Arabic** language and is still recited in many parts of the **Middle East** on the occasion of the Prophet's **birthday**.

BURHĀN AD-DĪN GHARĪB (654/1256–738/1337). Indian religious scholar and successor to **Chishtī** shaykh **Niẓām ad-Dīn Awliyā'**. He spent much of his career (well-documented in *malfūẓāt*) in Delhi, moving to the newly established Tughluqid capital to the south at Deogir toward the end of his life. His spiritual way was marked by the vigorous practice of **audition**, and he is a crucial link in the history of the Chishtīya in India. His **tomb** at Khuldābād, surrounded by the graves of many other saints, remains an important center of devotional **visitation**.

BURHĀN AD-DĪN MUḤAQQIQ (d. c. 639/1241). Anatolian dervish who became a principal teacher of **Rūmī** after the death of the latter's father in 628/1231, who had earlier taught Burhān ad-Dīn. He introduced Rūmī to the works of **Sanā'ī** and for nearly a decade schooled him in the finer theoretical points of the Sufi path. Around 638/1240, he departed **Konya** for Kayseri, where he died and was buried.

BUṢĪRĪ, SHARAF AD-DĪN AL- (610/1213–695/1296). Egyptian Berber **poet** most celebrated for his ***Burda*** in praise of the **Prophet**.

He was a student of the **Shādhilī** *shaykh* Abū 'l-'Abbās al-**Mursī** but little else is known of his Sufi affiliations. Tradition has it that the Prophet appeared to him in a **dream** and spread his mantle over him, healing him of a paralysis.

– C –

CALLIGRAPHY. "Beautiful writing," predominantly in **languages** using the **Arabic alphabet**. Strictly speaking, the term applies only to writing with pen or brush on paper or similar media, as distinguished from **epigraphy**, which refers to the application of inscriptions on works of stone, marble, stucco, wood, ceramics, fabric, and metal. In Sufi circles, as among most Muslims historically, the calligraphic **arts** have been important, rather generically, for creating beautiful **Qur'āns** and decorative texts of **Ḥadīth**. But Sufis have used many of the dozens of alluring calligraphic styles for distinctively Sufi purposes as well. A favorite decorative practice has been to fashion a stylized face, symbolic animal, or other object in outline (sometimes in right-left mirror technique) from the name of an important religious figure or a prayer. Sufis have employed calligraphy particularly for producing texts of mystical **poetry**, and some of the most prominent calligraphers have been Sufis as well.

CARPET. Principally a **ritual** object used for the daily liturgical **prayer**, the *sajjāda* (on which one performs ritual prostration, *sujūd*) typically depicts a niche, recalling the visually focal architectural feature on the **Mecca**-ward wall of every **mosque**. The carpet's niche design is often highly geometric in design, but some still depict some sort of lamp hanging from the arch, a vivid reminder of the Qur'ānic "Verse of Light" (24:35) with its evocation of the niche illumined by an eternal, cosmic sacred beacon. But in addition, the *sajjāda* functions as a symbol of **authority** and leadership in Sufi **orders**. A common **Persian** title for the superior of an order is *sajjāda-neshin*, the one who "sits on the carpet."

CAUCASUS. Region to the northwest of Iran, between the Black Sea and the Caspian Sea, currently encompassing the former Soviet republics and regions of Azerbaijan, Armenia, Chechnya, Dagestan, Ingushetia, and Georgia. The region is extraordinarily rich in ethnic diversity, and Sufis have been active in recent times in various ethnically based independence/secessionist movements. Estimates as to Sufi numbers include, for example, as many as 95,000 active in the small region of Dagestan alone during the late Soviet era. The most significant **orders** there have been the **Naqshbandīya** and **Qādirīya**.

ÇELEBĪ. **Turkish** term of respect and nobility (meaning "sage" and "man of letters," among other things) that became the title for the chief **authority** in an **order**, principally the **Mawlawīya**.

CELIBACY. Religiously motivated choice to remain unmarried and to refrain from sexual activity. Various Sufi **orders** have practiced celibacy either mandatorily (very exceptional) or as a discipline to be observed by one or other subgroup within the organization. In some instances, individual branches of a given organization (such as the **Qalandarīya**) made celibacy mandatory. Some married Sufis have in effect practiced celibacy temporarily, living without family in **residential** facilities where **women** were typically not allowed. But the **Bektashīya** set aside separate residential facilities for celibate women as well as men. Among the more famous Sufis who opted for lifelong celibacy are **Ibn 'Abbād ar-Rundī** and **Niẓām ad-Dīn Awliyā'**. *See also* GENDER; SEXUALITY.

CENTRAL ASIA. Now generally identified as the five largely Muslim nations, mostly **Turkic** ethnically and linguistically, formerly republics of the Soviet Union: Kazakhstan, Tajikistan, Uzbekistan, Turkmenistan, and Kyrgyzstan (or Kirgiz Republic). A further traditional geographical distinction identifies the area east of the Oxus River as **Transoxiana**, and some descriptions include Afghanistan as part of Central Asia. The region known as **Khurasan** crosses current boundaries between **Iran** and the Central Asian states. Major **orders** in the region have included the **Kubrāwīya**, **Naqshbandīya**, **Qādirīya**, and **Yasawīya**. Elements of the **Qalandarīya** were also historically important, especially in the environs of the Uzbek city of Samarkand. However, the formal structures of the classic orders generally gave way during a century or so prior to the Soviet era, and

Sufi groups were more loosely organized around ***shaykhs*** sometimes referred to with the respectful third-person plural Persian pronoun *īshān*, "they." The phenomenon is sometimes called "Ishanism," and Sufism is often credited with an important role in the survival of Islam through the Soviet era.

CERTITUDE. A critical, multifaceted concept associated with the relationship between faith and **experience**. In general it means knowledge without admixture of doubt, but the Sufis agree almost unanimously that there are three significantly different degrees of certitude (*yaqīn*). Beyond certain discursive knowledge there is the "essence of certitude" and the "truth of certitude."

CHAIN OF SUCCESSION. Spiritual **lineage** by which Sufis traced their line of initiation back to the **Prophet** or other early paradigmatic Muslim figure. The *silsila* represents a major symbol of **authority** claimed by members of an **order**. Sufis have designated various ways of tracing lineage using this image, referring variously to chains of **blessing**, **initiation**, and **formation**. The **Naqshbandīya** speak of a "chain of gold," which the poet **Jāmī**, a member of that order, appropriated as the title of one of his **didactic** works, *Silsilat adh-dhahab*.

CHIEF. Also rendered "lieutenant," the Arabic terms *naqīb* (pl. *nuqabā'*) and *najīb (nujabā')* refer to a cluster of three generally unnamed figures who rank (in some schemes) just below the **Pole** in the cosmic **hierarchy** of **Friends of God**.

CHILLA. *See* RETREAT.

CHINA. Largest and most ethnically diverse of the nations of **East Asia**, where Islam is said to have taken root as early as the seventh century. Most Chinese Muslims identify themselves as Hui people, many are ethnically and linguistically **Turkic**. The largest concentrations are in the western province of Xinjiang, formerly known as Eastern Turkistan, which is contiguous with the Turkic republics of **Central Asia**. Sufi teachers and missionaries have been among those most responsible for the spread, and maintenance, of Islam in China over the centuries, and have been among the most active translators of **Persian**-language texts into Chinese. Sufi proselytism was a major factor in the "second wave" of Islamization in China during the ninth/15th and 10th/16th centuries (Ming Dynasty). During the 12th/18th and 13th/19th centuries (Qing Dynasty), Sufis were instrumental in a third wave of growth, this time especially in reform movements such as the **Qādirīya**, **Shādhilīya**, **Naqshbandīya**, and **Khalwatīya**.

Sufism in China has often been viewed in juxtaposition (or even outright opposition) to *gedimu* Islam (from the Arabic *qadīm*, ancient or long-standing). In general, Sufi **terminology** shows a bias toward key concepts of the Daoist tradition as points of reference in choosing analogous concepts with which to describe Islamic mystical ideas. Sufism became a more broadly influential presence in China around the latter half of the 11th/17th century.

Sufi **organizations** in China are known principally as *menhuan*, descent groups or **lineages** of holy persons or leading figures. Although the bulk of the Muslim population is centered in the northwest, it was in the east-central Linxia region that the *menhuan* system took root. The **orders** most influential in China have been the Qādirīya (C. Gadelinye), the Jahrīya (C. Zheherenye) and Khafīya (C. Hufuye) branches of the Naqshbandīya, and, to a somewhat lesser extent, the **Kubrāwīya** (C. Kuburenye). These four organizations trace their genealogies, respectively, to the four Rightly Guided Caliphs: **'Alī**, **'Uthmān**, **Abū Bakr**, and 'Umar. Though there are relatively few Chinese **Shī'ī** Muslims, some adherents of the Kubrāwīya associate their origins with the **Prophet's** daughter **Fāṭima**. Likely the earliest firmly established was the Qādirīya, founded by **Qi Jingyi**. The Khafīya *menhuan* was founded by **Ma Laichi**, and the Jahrīya by **Ma Mingxin**. Both of the latter suborders further developed their own sub-groups. Other important Chinese Sufis include **Ma Fuchu**, **Ma Hualong**, **Ma Qixi**, **Ma Zhenwu**, and **Wang Daiyu**.

CHINESE. East Asian language spoken in dozens of dialects, principally in the People's Republic of China and Taiwan. Although even the full **Qur'ān** was not rendered into Chinese until 1346/1927, S. Murata has shown that a number of major Sufi works were translated into Chinese over several centuries, particularly in early modern times. Among those are **Najm ad-Dīn Dāyā Rāzī**'s *Path of God's Servants*; 'Aziz ad-Dīn **Nasafī**'s *Farthest Goal*; **Jāmī**'s commentary on **'Irāqī**'s *Flashes*, entitled *Rays from the Flashes*; and Jāmī's *Spiritual Gleams*.

CHIRĀGH-I DIHLĪ, NAṢĪR AD-DĪN MAḤMŪD (675/1276–757/1356). Indian religious scholar and **Chishtī** shaykh known as the "Lamp of Delhi," successor to **Niẓām ad-Dīn Awliyā'**. Leaving home at 25, he opted for the rigorously **ascetical** life of a quasi-solitary dervish, and at 43 he moved to Delhi where he joined the **Chishtīya**. For several years in the late 740s/1340s, he reluctantly became involved in **politics** as part of a concerted and successful effort to fend off a potential Mongol takeover of northern India. He insisted on sound adherence to religious legal requirements as the foundation of Sufi life and was a major proponent of a critical approach to the **order's hagiographic** traditions. His **successorship** to top rank in the order was contested by some, since there were several contenders for the post whose legitimacy was acclaimed by their own followers. Among his principal disciples were **Mīr Khurd** and **Gīsū Darāz**.

CHISHTĪYA. Major Sufi **order**, founded by **Mu'īn ad-Dīn Chishtī** in **Ajmīr**, particularly influential in **India**. Chishtī ***shaykhs*** founded numerous *khānqāhs* throughout northern India during the seventh/13th and eighth/14th centuries, and members generally remained aloof from **political** affairs. But during the subsequent two centuries, the highly centralized administration of the order weakened, quasi-independent *khānqāhs* began to spring up, and considerably greater political activism became generally acceptable. This naturally marked a significant change in means and level of **livelihood**, and the order came to be known for its cordial relations with the rulers of the **Mughal** dynasty, beginning with Babur. From the ninth/15th and 12th/18th centuries on, respectively, two large branches, the Ṣābirīya and Niẓāmīya, developed, and the organization enjoyed significant advances beyond the borders of India. Concern for the poor and socially marginalized has historically been a hallmark of the order.

Theologically the order leaned toward the concept of ontological **unity**, and in principle they preferred material simplicity and emphasized the centrality of love of God. Ritual practices included audible (as opposed to silent) **recollection**, **breath control** exercises, and the **forty**-day **retreat**. Some of the organization's ritual practices have suggested the influence of Yogic traditions. Two of the earlier **treatises** most formative of the order's path were those of **Hujwīrī** and Abū Ḥafṣ 'Umar as-**Suhrawardī**. What is known of the order and its most famous members comes in large part from the **discourses** attributed to leading *shaykhs*, a **genre** developed to a high art in this order. Among the most famous Chishtīs have been **'Abd al-Quddūs Gangōhī**, **'Abd ar-Raḥmān Chishtī**, **Burhān ad-Dīn Gharīb**, **Farīd ad-Dīn Ganj-i Shakar**, **Gīsū Darāz**, and **Niẓām ad-Dīn Awliyā'**.

CHIVALRY. Generic term used to refer to the spirit that characterized **organizations** called *futūwa* groups, sometimes associated with Sufism. The term derives from the Arabic word *fatā*, meaning noble youth, a kind of heroic figure. During the period of the Crusades especially, *futūwa* organizations arose in some numbers under the official leadership of the **'Abbāsid** caliph. These groups typically traced their **lineages** back to **'Alī**, the paradigm of chivalry traditionally said to have been the noblest *fatā* of them all. Unlike Sufi **orders,** these organizations tended to be more social than spiritual in orientation. **Sulamī** and **Kāshānī** wrote important sources on this phenomenon. The **virtues** regarded essential to members in these organizations include **repentance**, generosity, humility, tranquility, **authenticity**, guidance, advice, and fidelity.

CHOSEN ONES. A **rank** in the **cosmological** Sufi **hierarchy** that also includes, for example, **Chiefs**, **Pole**, **Supports**, and **Substitutes**. Among the **Friends of God**, the *akhyār* are numbered variously (as are some of the other hierarchical categories) at seven, 300, or simply unlimited at any given time. Their function is sometimes described as that of a kind of divine emissary dispatched wherever a spiritual disruption requires healing at the highest level.

CLAIRVOYANCE. A type of saintly **wonder**, including the ability to read the thoughts of others and have knowledge of events occurring at a great distance. Usually called *firāsa*, it is a gift given to many **Friends of God** as described in **hagiographic** sources.

CLOAK. Also called the "patched frock," the *khirqa* ("rag") or *muraqqa'a* ("assembled from pieces") is an article of **clothing symbolic** of **initiation** into Sufi life through the **oath** of obedience to the ***shaykh***. Though most Sufis have typically been invested with the cloak as part of formal ceremonies in institutional settings, some have claimed that they received the garment directly from **Khiḍr** or some other "spirit-*shaykh*" in **dreams** or **visions**. Some distinguish between spiritual and material cloaks. In any case, the garment represents **authoritative** incorporation into a Sufi **lineage**, and sources as early as the third/eighth century spoke of donning the cloak as an indicator that an individual traveled a distinctive spiritual path. Eventually various **orders** may have used different kinds of cloaks to distinguish different ranks within the organization. Many Sufis trace the origins of the symbolic conferral of a cloak to the experience of the **Prophet** himself, upon whom God, and later Gabriel, bestowed the cloak of poverty. The concept of the hereditary symbolism associated with the cloak applies also to other **implements** and items of clothing. Some orders also considered the cloak as a reminder of the burial cloth, symbolic of the individual's awareness of mortality and death to self. **'Abbāsid** caliphs and rulers in **Egypt** and **Syria** after them also conferred a special cloak as symbol of membership in **chivalric** organizations.

CLOTHING. A wide range of **symbolic** and utilitarian accoutrements, from **headgear** to footwear, that often came to be distinctive of individual **orders**. In addition to the **cloak** that many Sufi orders wear, important articles of clothing include various types of hats and jackets in a range of **colors**, depending on the tradition of the order. For example, a **Turkish** order called the **Mawlawīya** wear close-wrapped pants (for the liturgical dance only), then a skirted tunic without sleeves, then a long-sleeved waist-length garment called a *destegül* beneath an outer cloak. Specific items of clothing typically varied depending on one's **rank** in the **organization**. Verses from scripture or sayings of the **Prophet** might be embroidered on very special items.

COLORS. Many Sufi authors have developed **symbolic** systems in which various colors are connected to specific aspects of spiritual **experience**. An early **Kubrāwī** Sufi named **Najm ad-Dīn Dāyā** associated white with Islam, yellow with faith, dark blue with doing good spiritually, red with experiential knowledge, black with **ecstasy**, and green with tranquility. **Simnānī**, a later member of the same **order**, associated the seven "inner prophets" with seven spiritual faculties and seven colors: **Adam** with the flat black of exteriority; Noah with the blue of the ego-soul; **Abraham** with the red of the heart; **Moses** with the white of the inmost secret; **David** with the yellow of the spirit; **Jesus** with the shiny black of the hidden center; and **Muḥammad** with the green of ultimate reality.

COMMENTARY. An important **genre** of Sufi **literature**, mostly in prose, in which disciples and later students produce elaborations (*sharḥ*) of seminal works of earlier Sufis. Commentary ranges from brief glosses on selected sayings or **aphorisms** to extensive **treatises** on complete works. Among the authors whose works have inspired numerous commentaries are **Ibn 'Aṭā' Allāh** and **Ibn al-'Arabī**.

COMPANIONS. The first generation of Muslims, those who lived with and knew **Muḥammad** personally. These represent an unsurpassed level of spiritual experience in that respect alone, but some of them stand out still further for their additional personal qualities. The latter include **Abū Bakr**, 'Umar ibn al-Khaṭṭāb, and **'Alī**.

COMPANIONSHIP. From the Arabic *suḥba*, the term refers to the establishment of a relationship with some individual noted for holiness, beginning with the **Prophet** and including also **Friends of God**. By extension it can also be synonymous with discipleship to a ***shaykh*** and membership in a community of Sufis, sharing common life (*mu'āshara*). Concern with establishing at least minimal norms concerning the kind of **behavior** essential to fostering companionship in community led to the development of **treatises** on *adab*. Some forms of **visualization** facilitate the experience of companionship.

COMPETITIVENESS. One of many manifestations of ego-centricity to which the seeker must learn to be attuned. Called *mubāha*, it shows itself in every form of adversarial relationship and one-upmanship, from name-dropping to belittling one's companions in public to succumbing to the temptation to act violently.

CONCEIT. A serious obstacle to spiritual growth in that it betokens excessive focus on the delusions of the ego-soul. Conceit (*riyā'*) in all its forms is inauthenticity, the diametric opposite to **sincerity**. According to **Muḥāsibī**, it is manifest in such spiritual aberrations as desire for recognition and power, envy, and **competitiveness**.

CONCERT. *See* AUDITION.

CONSTRICTION. An aspect of advanced spiritual **experience** typically paired with its opposite, **expansion**. The pair might be said to describe intensified levels of, and presuppose the experience of, fear and hope, respectively. Constriction (*qabḍ*) applies to one's present **state** whereas **fear** is future-oriented. It is generally understood to be a state and therefore transitory and gratuitous.

CONTEMPLATION. Variously referring to method and/or content of various forms of interior **prayer**. A Sufi might "contemplate" using the method of focusing on a particular mental image, a kind of **visualization** technique. The goal of the process is to achieve communion (*murāqaba*) with the object of contemplation, whether that is an image of the mystical **Beloved** or one's ***shaykh*** or the spirit of a deceased holy person, including the **Prophet**. Another aspect of the theme is represented by the term *mushāhada*, which suggests a form of "witnessing"—an interior vision or experiential encounter with the object of contemplation. Some would argue that witnessing is a higher level of contemplative concentration and that it can be the end result of **recollection**. Still another form is *tawahhum*, reflection on the occurrences to be expected on **Judgment** Day, and *tawajjuh*, a form of concentration or "confrontation" of a spiritual reality.

CONTENTMENT. Also translated as satisfaction or acceptance (from the Arabic *qanā'a*, *riḍā*), an elevated level of ability to see the good in whatever condition God has seen fit to bestow on the individual. It suggests the resolution of the states of **patience** and **gratitude** and presupposes a high level of **trust**.

CONTEST. Competition (*munāqara*) among saints in **hagiographical** accounts. Questions of religious **authority** have occasionally led to arguments as to whose patron **Friend of God** had greater access to spiritual power. Elements of saintly competition sometimes insinuated themselves into Sufi sources even when Sufi leaders strenuously repudiated them, not least because reliance on **wonders** is unworthy of serious spiritual seekers.

CONVENT. *See* RESIDENTIAL FACILITY.

CONVERSION. *See* REPENTANCE.

COSMOLOGY. Systematic conceptualization of the structure of the universe, in this instance particularly concerning its spiritual dimensions and meaning. Sufi theorists have developed several ways of understanding the cosmos beyond its empirical or phenomenal aspects. They are especially concerned with explaining and describing the various arenas of **experience** beyond the traditional division of "created reality" (*khalq*) into the seen and the unseen, or the transient (this world) and the hereafter. The former encompasses the physical earth and "heavens," the latter **Heaven** and **Hell** and their respective topographies. Sufi **hermeneutics** generally makes the fundamental distinction between the dimensions of appearance and meaning. In the latter category, some Sufi theorists describe five areas, all in relation to the divine reality: God's being, names, attributes, deeds, and the products of those deeds. Along with philosophers and some Ismā'īlī thinkers, they have developed varying views on the interrelationships of a number of **realms** complete with a **hierarchy** of spiritual beings. Although Sufi authors do not always use their terminology consistently, their universal concern is to analyze the multiple aspects of the suprasensory world in which authentic spiritual **journeyers** travel.

COUPLETS. Important **poetic** structure used extensively in Sufi **didactic** works. Many of the greatest Sufi poets employed the **genre** of *mathnawī* ("doubled"), with each verse composed of hemistichs that rhyme with each other. Unlike so-called mono-rhyming forms, each line can end in a different syllable. Among poets who penned major works in the form are **'Aṭṭār**, **Rūmī**, and **Sanā'ī**.

COVENANT, DAY OF. The moment at the dawn of creation of humankind at which God asked all unborn souls "Am I not your Lord?" and they replied "Yes, we testify to that" (Qur'ān 7:171). The day is therefore called in Persian as *rūz-i alast*, "The Day (when God asked) "Am I not [your Lord]?" (*alastu [bi-rabbikum]*). The most common Arabic expression is *yawm al-mīthāq*, "The Day of Affirmation," on which humankind assented to and confirmed its essential relationship to God. *A* classic goal for the Sufi is described as returning spiritually to that time "when one was before one was"; that is, when the individual existed only in God. The experience is related to that of **annihilation**.

CREED. Known as the "testimony" or "witnessing" (*shahāda* in Arabic), the assertion "There is no deity but Allah and **Muḥammad** is the Messenger of **God**." Sufi **poets** and other authors have developed distinctively mystical interpretations of the statement. These have ranged from relatively simple, straightforward glosses, to elaborate **exegeses** based on **alphabetic** and **number symbolism**, to more philosophical discussions of necessary and contingent **being**.

CUPBEARER. From the **Persian** term *sāqī,* one who provides drink, a **metaphor** dear to Sufi **poets** for speaking of the **intoxication** of divine, mystical **love**. Typically the poet calls upon the cupbearer to bring on the **wine** of love that in turn yields the salutary bewilderment the mystic experiences in the presence of the **Beloved**.

– D –

DABBĀGH, 'ABD AL-'AZĪZ AD- (fl. c. 1112/1700). Moroccan **neo-Sufi** to whom tradition attributes the founding of the Khaḍirīya **order** in 1173/1760 after he himself experienced spirit **initiation** from **Khiḍr**. He left no written legacy and is known largely through the work of his disciple Aḥmad ibn al-Mubārak al-Lamaṭī (d. 1155/1742), which constitutes a major source for our knowledge of neo-Sufism generally. Central to that written work is an account of Dabbāgh's commentary on **Ibn al-'Arabī's** *Bezels of Wisdom*.

DĀ'IRA. *See* RITUAL.

DALĀ'IL AL-KHAYRĀT. *See* JAZŪLĪ.

DAMASCUS. Ancient **Syrian** city that was the capital of the **Umayyad** caliphate from 41/661 to 133/750. It was home to many prominent Sufis from the eighth century on, beginning with several prominent **ascetics,** and an important center of Sufi activity and organizations throughout the medieval period. Among the city's more famous Sufi citizens was **Ibn al-'Arabī**, who called Damascus home for the last 14 years of his life, and whose **tomb** there remains a major local holy site and goal for pilgrim **visitation**.

DANCE. Rhythmic movement (commonly called *raqṣ*), whether elaborately choreographed or allowing for spontaneity, that is an element in the paraliturgical **ritual** of many **orders**. Although the whirling dance that has become the hallmark of the **Mawlawīya** is by far the best known example of Sufi dance, there are other important examples as well. Many involve some form of circle formation with oscillating, swaying movement, around, into and out of the circle. Occasionally an individual participant will step into the middle of the circle. It may be that, for example, a member of the Mawlawīya attends an **audition** of, say, the Halvetī-Jerrāhī order and performs his whirling in the middle while the members of the host group form concentric circles around him. Simpler forms may involve little more than rhythmic lilting back and forth, or from side to side, while chanting a *dhikr* text or syllable. Sacred movement has been an important medium in which Sufis have sought to involve themselves more fully in the **experience** of **prayer**, and it has in some cases been employed explicitly as a means to altered consciousness or **ecstasy**. *See also* MUSIC; RECOLLECTION.

DAQQĀQ, ABŪ 'ABD ALLĀH (d. last quarter of 6th/12th century). Moroccan Sufi who spent time in **Fez** and apparently met **Abū Madyan** there and became his ***shaykh***.

DAQQĀQ, ABŪ 'ALĪ AD- (d. 405/1015 or 412/1021). Khurāsānī Sufi teacher, father-in-law and ***shaykh*** of **Qushayrī** whose views figure prominently in the latter's *Treatise*. He was one of the most important formative influences in the career of Qushayrī, steering him into religious studies and introducing him to major traditionists, Shāfi'ī jurists, and Ash'arī theologians at **Nishapur**. His daughter, Kadbanū Fāṭima, was also a noted traditionist and renowned for learning and holiness.

DĀRĀ SHIKŪH (1024/1615–1069/1659). Indian mystic, member of the **Qādirīya**, son of **Mughal** ruler Shāh Jahān (builder of the Tāj Maḥal. He is perhaps best known for a short **treatise** called *The Confluence of the Two Seas* (*Majma' al-baḥrayn*), an esoteric reading of Sura 18 intended to bridge the gap between Islamic and **Hindu** spirituality. Following up on his great-grandfather Akbar's openness to Hinduism, he translated the Upanishads into **Persian**. In addition he authored several important Sufi texts, including **hagiographical** accounts of his own ***shaykh*** **Miyān Mīr** as well as of earlier prominent Sufis. His openness to other spiritual traditions and emphasis on **experience** over unquestioning imitation in religious matters roused the ire of religious authorities and his own brother Awrangzīb had him executed, ostensibly for heresy, but more importantly in order to seize the throne from the heir apparent. His sister **Jahānārā** was also a noteworthy Sufi author.

DARAJĀT. *See* RANKS.

DĀRĀNĪ, ABŪ SULAYMĀN AD- (d. 215/830). Syrian ascetic in the **Baṣran** tradition of **Ḥasan**, whose numerous pithy **aphoristic** sayings are known only from the writings of Sufi theorists and **hagiographers**. His claim to have had **angelic visionary** experience got him exiled from Syria.

ḌARB. *See* RECOLLECTION.

DARD, KHWĀJA MĪR (1133/1720–1199/1785). Indian mystical author in **Persian**, **Urdu**, and **Arabic**, ***shaykh*** of both **Chishtī** and **Naqshbandī** groups in Delhi, and famous patron and proponent of **music**. His spiritual path blended Naqshbandī **ritual** and technique with a fairly fundamental reading of the sacred sources. As an author, he is most noted for personal accounts of his spiritual quest, one in which his father played a crucial role. Theologically he was opposed to proponents of the concept of ontological **unity** (or unity of ecstatic being, *waḥdat al-wujūd*) and preferred the **metaphor** of divine **light** to which the seeker gains access through rigorous spiritual discipline. His Urdu lyric **poems** are acknowledged to be some of the finest in that language.

DARGĀH. *See* INSTITUTIONS.

DARQĀWĪ, MULAY AL-'ARABĪ AD- (1150/1737–1239/1823). **North African** Sufi reformer, **pole** of his age, ***shaykh*** in the **Shādhilī** tradition and posthumous eponym of its **Darqāwīya** branch. We know of him directly only through a collection of **letters**, but his influence on Moroccan Sufi life was considerable. He injected an element of heightened affective engagement into the otherwise somewhat staid Shādhilī style. He discouraged teaching the public to seek **blessing** through the **order**. Though he insisted that his disciples keep their distance from **politics**, he and the order eventually changed direction and became identified with early 14th/19th century militant movements associated with resistance to **Ottoman Turkish** rule and nascent French colonialism.

DARQĀWĪYA (a.k.a. DARQĀWA). Sufi **order** founded in Morocco during the late 13th/18th century and established predominantly in Morocco and Algeria. With the exception of some participation in the early 14th/19th century Berber rebellion and French takeover of Algeria, members of this order have generally eschewed **political** activism in favor of a relatively reclusive life. Their **residential facilities** and spiritual centers are generally known as *zāwiyas*. They have a tradition of elaborate **recollection** sessions, complete with **music**, **dance**, and **poetry**. As many as 10 suborders are said to have been founded, especially in the **Maghrib** but further east as well, by individuals once associated with this order. These offshoots were largely independent and not subject to any centralized **authority**. **Women** apparently were free to exercise notable authority in the order, at least in Morocco, where a 13th–14th/20th century report counted eight women functioning as "circle leaders" (*muqaddamāt*). One of the most influential offshoots was that founded by Aḥmad al-**'Alawī**.

DARWĪSH. *See* DERVISH.

DASŪQĪ, BURHĀN AD-DĪN IBRĀHĪM (633/1235–677/1278). **Egyptian** Sufi author, from a family of Sufis famous as a conduit of **blessing**, founder of the **Dasūqīya**. His writings include **poetry**, instructional material concerning proper **behavior**, personal **prayers**, and auto-**hagiographical** accounts of his **wonders**. Although he was initiated into the **Badawīya**, **Rifā'īya**, and **Suhrawardīya**, he emphasized the inward nature of all spiritual action, for the Sufi lives truly in the *zāwiya* of the heart. He is perhaps the most prominent Sufi memorialized in the hagiographic work of **Sha'rānī**.

DASŪQĪYA. Originally called the Burhānīya or Ibrāhīmīya after founder Burhān ad-Dīn Ibrāhīm **Dasūqī**, the **order** began in **Egypt** but was eventually transplanted into parts of the central **Middle East**, especially **Syria** and the **Arabian** peninsula. The order experienced something of a renewal in later medieval and early modern times.

DĀTĀ GANJ BAKHSH. *See* HUJWĪRĪ.

DAVID. Prophet, father of the prophet **Solomon**, celebrated in Sufi **literature** as musician, judge, and model of the ***shaykh***. **Rūmī**, for example, tells a story of how, in response to a poor man's prayer for sustenance, a cow entered the man's house and allowed him to kill it for food. When the cow's owner sought David's judgment in his favor, David ordered the owner to give all his wealth to the poor man! David's judgment arose out of his miraculous discernment that the cow's owner had once murdered his own master. Here the cow symbolizes the **ego** that the seeker must be willing to sacrifice. As a **musician**, David's heart-beguiling song represents the power of divine love, and his ability as a smith to melt steel is the image of God's own power to soften the hardest heart.

DĀWŪD AL-FATĀNĪ (d. 1259/1843). Malay Sufi scholar of South Thai origin who was of a reformist bent and shared the views of **'Abd aṣ-Ṣamad of Palembang** concerning the **wujūdī controversy**. He argued that genuine Sufis emphasized divine transcendence and downplayed speculation about ontological **unity**. He composed a major

theoretical work on these theological issues, criticizing as charlatans all who made mystical union the centerpiece of their teachings. He spent his latter years in **Mecca**.

DAY OF JUDGMENT. The moment of final accountability in which all will be held responsible for their deeds in life. This looms especially large for **ascetics**, for whom compunction for sin takes precedence in some ways over divine love. Sufis generally have expressed varying views of the place of final judgment, and **repentance** in view of that, in their spiritual theories and practices. Some go so far as to take God to task for holding Judgment over their heads as an unnecessary threat. Most insist that ultimately it is only love of God, not fear of accountability, that matters. *See also* ESCHATOLOGY.

DAYLAMĪ, ABŪ 'L-ḤASAN (c. late fourth/10th century). Persian Shirāzī Sufi scholar in the tradition of **Ibn Khafīf**, author of an influential **treatise** on mystical **love**. He schematized 10 **stations** of love, running from familiarity, intimacy, and affection upward through recklessness, ravishing, and bewilderment and culminating in the 11th station of complete devotion. **Rūzbihān** later incorporated important aspects of his work.

DAYLAMĪ, SHAMS AD-DĪN (d. c. 593/1197). Exegete, mystical author, and theologian known particularly for his Sufi commentary on scripture. He apparently underwent a serious change of mind about Sufism, moving away from the highly critical view suggested in his earlier work. He referred to Sufism as a "school" of religious thought equivalent in authority to any of the major schools of **law**. In addition to his exegetical work, he wrote important works on Sufi **ethics**, **cosmology**, and mystical **theology**.

DEDE. *See* HONORIFICS.

DELHI. Present-day capital of **India** and earlier capital of various Muslim ruling dynasties, beginning in medieval times and culminating in the **Mughal** dynasty from the 10th/16th and into the 12th/18th century. It was home to a number of major Sufi **organizations** and leaders, particularly of the **Chishtīya** and **Suhrawardīya**, and there were as many as 2,000 Sufi **institutions** in the city under Mughal rule. *See also* DIHLAWĪ.

DEOBANDĪS. A name given to **reformist** scholars of the *Dār al-'ulūm* (Academy of Religious Disciplines) founded in 1284/1867 in the **Indian** city of Deoband. These scholars were critical of some aspects of popular piety widely associated with Sufism in **South Asia**, but generally maintained relationships with their students that had much in common with those of ***shaykhs*** with their disciples. The Deobandis discouraged such practices as **audition**, seeking **intercession**, and **visitation**, and had distinctive views on questions of **authority** and spiritual **direction**. On these matters they disagreed notably with the views of the reform-minded Sufis of **Rae Bareilly**. One major difference involved approaches to Sufi training: whereas the Deobandis preferred a model in which the *shaykh* **instructed** seekers, leaving much of the ethical struggle to the initiative of the disciple, the Brelwīs opted for a more comprehensive approach to Sufi **formation**.

DERVISH. From a Persian compound meaning "door-seeker" (*darwīsh*), suggesting itinerant mendicancy. Technically correct usage generally leans toward restricting the term to individual Sufis not connected with specific **orders**, or those affiliated with **organizations** whose members tended to be less attached to stable **institutional** life. In more colloquial usage, however, the term has come to refer more loosely to the generality of Sufis. In **North Africa**, dervishes are referred to as "brothers" (*ikhwān*), and in Arabic generally the equivalent is "poor one" (*faqīr*).

DESIRE. A concept (known in Arabic as *shawq*) originally associated with longing to see the **face** of **God** and later incorporated by Sufi **theorists** as a waystation on the spiritual path. Since according to a Sufi tradition, the Prophet possessed 99 of the 100 parts of desire (the remaining part distributed among the rest of humankind), he became the model of the seeker yearning for the **Beloved**. Sufi authors accorded desire varying roles in their systematic analyses of spirituality, depending on their views of its relationship to **love** and the degree to which they considered active longing for God an appropriate goal.

DESTEGÜL. *See* CLOTHING.

DEVIL. *See* SATAN.

DHĀT. *See* ESSENCE.

DHAWQ. *See* TASTE.

DHIKR. *See* INVOCATION; RECOLLECTION.

DHŪ 'N-NŪN, THAWBĀN IBN IBRĀHĪM (c. 180/796–245/860). **Egyptian** Sufi best known for his unusual behavior and generally acknowledged as the originator of a distinctively Sufi interpretation of experiential knowledge. He identified a higher form of infused, mystical knowledge (*ma'rifa*) with **ecstasy** and a divinely bestowed **light**. And he was among the earlier Sufis to employ the **metaphors** of **cup[bearer]** and **wine**. Some sources acknowledge him as a **pole** of his time. He ran afoul of **'Abbāsid** religious authorities and was imprisoned for a time in Baghdad when some people denounced him as a heretic or "free-thinker"—and he explicitly disagreed with the Mu'tazilī doctrine of the createdness of the **Qur'ān**—but he was released and returned to Egypt. Stories tell how some of his friends regarded him as mentally unfit and had him committed, but later Sufis interpret such accounts as proof only that he possessed a higher form of **knowledge**. He left no mystical writings as such, but numerous sayings and **prayers** attributed to him are preserved by **theorists** and **historians** of Sufism.

DIARY. *See* AUTOBIOGRAPHY.

DIDACTIC POETRY. One of the two most important large categories of Sufi verse (along with **lyric poetry**), developed by authors such as **'Aṭṭār**, **Rūmī**, **Sa'dī**, and **Sanā'ī**. The preferred structure of the **literary form** is that of the **couplet**. Narrative is the principal method of didactic poetry, though the greatest poets frequently interject more "theoretical" reflections among the exemplary anecdotes.

DIHLAWĪ ("From Delhi"). *See* 'ABD AL-ḤAQQ DIHLAWĪ, MUḤADDITH; CHIRĀGH-I DILHĪ, NAṢĪR AD-DĪN; ḤASAN SIJZĪ DIHLAWĪ; SHĀH WALĪ ALLĀH.

DIL. *See* HEART.

DIRECTION, SPIRITUAL. *See* SCIENCE OF HEARTS.

DIRECTOR, SPIRITUAL. *See SHAYKH.*

DISCERNMENT. The ability to see beneath appearances, to understand the secrets of the **heart**, in ways that sometimes approximate a kind of **clairvoyance**. Often expressed with the Arabic term *tafṣīl*, discernment is especially important in Sufi thought because of its implications for the "**science of hearts**," or spiritual direction. It is based on the conviction that ultimately human beings cannot hide what is within them from everyone. Discernment therefore implies a unique insight into human nature with which certain people are gifted. But whereas the traditional science of discernment means extrapolating how an individual might act on the basis of body language, for example, the Sufi science of hearts requires the ability to "see" the seeker's inner states and assess the quality of the individual's spiritual commitment and progress. Some authors refer to the quest for, and possession of, the "philosopher's stone" (*al-kibrīt al-aḥmar*, lit., "the red sulphur") as a **metaphor** for the ultimate in spiritual discernment.

DISCIPLE. Follower of a ***shaykh***, student of a Sufi teacher; aspirant or seeker along the mystical **path**. Sufi texts use the Arabic terms *ṭālib*, a "student-seeker," generally in relation to traditional religious studies, and *tilmīdh*, "probationer, apprentice, trainee." But the most important technical term, *murīd*, refers to an "aspirant-seeker" understood to be a member of an **order** in the initial phases of training (i.e., a "novice"). An aspirant becomes subject to the guidance of a spiritual **director** (*murshid*) or teacher by agreeing to be totally docile to whatever instruction is given. In traditional Islamic education, disciples receive a credential or "license" (*ijāza*) authorizing them to pass on a certain category of **knowledge**, and in some instances Sufi disciples receive a similar approval to establish an extension of an order or hand on the master's teaching. *See also* ORGANIZATION.

DISCOURSE. Literary record of the public or semiprivate utterances of a Sufi ***shaykh***. A major Sufi literary **genre**, known in Arabic as *malfūẓ(āt)* the discourse was typically the outcome of publishing the copious notes taken by **disciples** at a *shaykh*'s teaching sessions. One of the common features of the genre is a question-answer format, in which the teacher provides an often lengthy response to a generally brief query of someone in the audience. Many of the leading *shaykhs* have discourses attributed to them, and the genre is one of the most important sources of information available about both individual figures and their central ideas and methods. An **order** whose *shaykhs* have been among the most prolific authors of discourses is the **Chishtīya**. Other major Sufis whose discourses are extant include **Manīrī**, **Rūmī**, and **Shams** of Tabriz. Occasionally collections of a holy person's sayings are referred to by the term *majlis*, "assembly" or "circle."

DISPENSATION. A category in Islamic **Law** that allows for flexibility in the implementation of specific requirements under certain extenuating circumstances. For example, if the strict application of some rule might endanger someone's life, it may be permissible to alter the rule accordingly. Sufi **orders** have adapted the concept of *rukhṣa* (pl. *rukhaṣ*) to the **ethical** demands of **behavior** required of members in a given **organization**. For example, some orders consider allowing individual members to marry and pursue means of **livelihood** outside the confines of the community forms of dispensation. According to some sources, even the use of **audition** and **dance** falls under the heading of exceptional (and implicitly less than laudable) practice and is questionably justified under the rubric of dispensation. But some Sufis make a point of refraining from all dispensations, even if all four Sunnī schools of Law support them.

DISTANCE. A dimension of mystical **experience** expressed with the Arabic term *bu'd* and typically juxtaposed to proximity (*qurb*). It is often described as the result of the seeker's obstinacy and refusal to surrender in obedience to God.

DĪWĀN. A collection of **poetry**, often including two or more **genres**, such as the love lyric or *ghazal*, the lengthier ode or *qaṣīda*, and the brief quatrain or *rubā'ī* form. Many important Sufi poets have such collections to their credit, including, for example, Farīd ad-

Dīn **'Aṭṭār**, **Ḥāfiẓ**, **Ibn al-Fāriḍ**, **Rūmī**, and **Sanā'ī**. The collection is typically of shorter **lyric** forms as distinguished from longer, free-standing **didactic** works such as the "**couplets**" or *mathnawī* genre.

DOME OF THE ROCK. Major **architectural** monument in **Jerusalem** completed under the **Umayyad** dynasty in 73/692. The octagonal structure, approximately 180 feet across, is crowned by a prominent gold dome about 60 feet in diameter. Very ancient **Middle Eastern** traditions identify the location as the spot on which **Solomon** built his temple (and the site of the eventual "Second Temple"). Islamic tradition from as early as the second/eighth century identified the site of the Dome as the place from which the **Prophet** experienced his **Ascension**. Throughout medieval and early modern times, Europeans generally identified the Dome as the "temple of Solomon," ironically identifying a place of symbolic importance to Jews and Christians with images of a major Muslim monument.

DREAMS. The communication of some special spiritual message while one is in the sleeping state, as distinct from **visions**, which occur in the waking state (though occasionally the same technical terms are used for both). Sufi texts, both brief anecdotal narratives and more extended **hagiographical** accounts, frequently include dream (*manām*) descriptions in which the subject encounters either the **Prophet** or some important Sufi. The purpose of such accounts is often either to corroborate a choice the subject has made, to correct a less than happy decision, to initiate a Sufi spiritually outside of the usual course of things, or to underscore the subject's own spiritual authority. An extensive science of dream interpretation has spawned a **literature** of its own, as in the celebrated work of Ibn Sīrīn. Basic distinctions are between true and false dreams; those of **prophets**, **Friends of God**, and ordinary believers; those that require the science of interpretation, and those of no particular **symbolic** importance.

DRESS. *See* CLOTHING.

DROWNING. Widely used **metaphor** for mystical **union** or **annihilation**. God and his various attributes (such as love and mercy) are often likened to the **ocean** in which the **lover** is lost.

DRUGS. Some groups identifying themselves as Sufis have sought mystical **ecstasy** through the agency of intoxicants of various kinds, including wine and hashish. **Behavior** of this sort has generally elicited scathing criticism from Sufis and non-Sufi authorities alike, who have labeled practitioners of deviant, manipulative conduct as pseudo-Sufis at best. Recourse to such means is totally contrary to the generally **ascetical** regime adopted by major **orders**.

DU'Ā'. *See* PRAYER, PERSONAL; SUPPLICATION.

DUWAYRA. *See* RESIDENTIAL FACILITY.

– E –

EAST AFRICA. Coastal regions along and south of the Red Sea, as well as those immediately inland of those areas, including here (for the sake of convenience) Sudan and the states of the "Horn of Africa" (Eritrea, Ethiopia, Somalia), along with Kenya, Tanzania, Mozambique, Uganda, and the island of Zanzibar. Among the major **orders** in the region are the **Khalwatīya**, **Qādirīya**, Ṣāliḥīya, **Sammānīya**, and the **Shādhilīya**. East African Sufis associated themselves genealogically with certain scholarly lineages particularly from **Egypt** and the **Arabian** region of the Hijāz (in which **Mecca** and **Medina** are located). Formal associations with Sufi orders developed especially during the 13th/19th century, though individual connections with ***shaykhs*** of the Qādirīya and Shādhilīya were in evidence as early as the 10th/16th (possibly even as early as the ninth/mid-15th, according to some sources).

EAST ASIA. Principally the modern nation-states of **China**, Taiwan, Korea, and Japan. Of these, only China has ever had a sizeable Muslim population, currently estimated diversely as anywhere from 40 million to 120 million. Most of the Muslims, called the Hui people, live in the eastern segment of a large transnational area called Turkistan, part of which constitutes a major portion of eastern Central Asia.

ECSTASY. The **experience** of loss of self, of "standing out" of one's being, in the human encounter with the divine. Sufis most often refer to ecstasy with the multivalent term ***wajd*** (consonantal radicals in bold) and various cognates, from a root that means "to find." Ecstasy is thus paradoxically an experience of both "finding" and "being found" that is related to "being ecstatic" (***wujūd***). One must be wary of trying too hard to fabricate the condition through one's own effort, as described by the pejorative term "inducing ecstasy" (*ta**wāj**u**d***). Sufi authors use a variety of **metaphors** to hint at the elusive complexity of ecstatic experience. Some of their most famous, indeed notorious, verbal attempts to capture the meaning of ecstasy are called *shaṭḥ*, from a root that suggests the overflowing that occurs when one tries to sift flour and has put too much into the sieve. Ecstasy runs the gamut from the feeling of the ultimate bewilderment and perplexity to perfect **annihilation** in the Beloved. In order to find one's Lord, one must lose oneself, and only in that process can the seeker be truly "found" and only in that condition does the seeker truly "exist." Theologically speaking, ecstasy is the condition in which one fully acknowledges and realizes the divine transcendent unity (*tawḥīd*), since in ecstasy all that is not God recedes into nothingness. Finally, ecstasy presupposes that one has been "drawn" (*majdhūb*); that is, that the experience is a gift rather than precisely the result of human effort.

EDUCATION. *See* FORMATION.

EFFACEMENT. An aspect of spiritual **experience** typically paired with, and the opposite of, "affirmation." Certain of the seeker's negative qualities must be effaced so that positive traits can be confirmed. Effacement (*maḥw*) does not represent complete loss of self, as in **annihilation**, for some "trace" of the individual must remain in which positive qualities can be affirmed.

EGO. The sum of natural human tendencies whose centrifugal effects continually threaten to distance the individual from the true center, God. One's "lower self" or "ego-soul" (*nafs*, also rendered as **soul**), often symbolized by the dog or the ass, is described in the **Qur'ān** as functioning in various ways: inciting to evil (12:53); blaming or admonishing, serving as a kind of conscience (75:2); and bringing about a peaceful condition resulting from its purification (89:27). Sufi **theorists** incorporated this scriptural typology into their systems of spiritual **formation** in different ways, differing somewhat from one **order** to another. But underlying almost all Sufi thought on spiritual discipline is the fundamental notion that the "greater *jihād*" is the **struggle** with one's ego. Some theorists devised elaborate **typologies** in which the various conditions of the ego represented up to seven **stages** in ethical rather than mystical development, moving from inciting to evil, to blameworthy (rather than admonishing), to inspired toward more positive inner deeds, to peaceful, to **contented**, to accepted (by God), and finally perfected or fully purified. Whatever the specific system or typology, the ego constitutes, along with **Satan** and the material world with all its blandishments, one of the critical sources of misguidance for seekers.

EGYPT. Easternmost of the **North African** states with northern borders along the Mediterranean, with Libya to the west, Sudan to the south, and the **Arabian Peninsula** to the east across the Red Sea. **Alexandria** is its oldest major Islamic city, and Cairo, though much larger and historically more important as the capital of several major dynasties, was founded only in 359/969. Among the most influential **orders** have been the **Badawīya**, Bayyūmīya, Dimirdāshīya, **Khalwatīya**, and **Shādhilīya**.

ENDOWMENT. Generally known by the Arabic term *waqf*, the provision of funds, ostensibly out of pious motives, for the foundation and upkeep of major **institutions**. Countless Sufi **residential** and related structures and complexes from Morocco to Malaysia have been made possible through the generosity of wealthy patrons of individual Sufi leaders as well as **orders**. Much of what is known about important historic Sufi foundations is available to us in documents detailing the genesis and stipulations of the endowment. They provide information about the benefactor and his or her (many endowments originated with **women**) express motives, but a great deal more that is essential in reconstructing the history of Sufism. Endowment documentation describes, for example, the kinds of facilities the foundation brought together (**mosque**, **tomb**, ***madrasa***, social services such as kitchens for the poor, libraries); specific arrangements for the housing of Sufis, including the number to be accommodated as well as the offices to be provided for the order's local administrative **organization** and **authority** structure; and the amount of money and the various kinds of clothing and sustenance to be provided annually to the various ranks within the organization. Sometimes these invaluable documents even provide a glimpse into the daily order to be maintained by residents of the foundation.

ENEMY. *See* SATAN.

ENNEAGRAM. Nine-part personality **typology** often popularly, but not convincingly, identified as the "Sufi Enneagram." Popular in the United States for several decades, the typology is said by some to have been invented and popularized by Bolivian Oscar Ichazo and Chilean Claudio Naranjo; others say that Georgy **Gurdjieff** "rediscovered" the typology while traveling among the **Naqshbandīya** in **Central Asia**. Each of the nine positions on the typology is associated symbolically with an animal (such as the fox), and the teachers of the Enneagram identify the origins of the associations with Sufi teaching fables. Proponents of the Sufi connection insist that the reason the typology's Sufi roots are so hard to discern in primary sources is that it represents an arcane, secret teaching that should never have been allowed to gain such popularity in the first place.

EPIGRAPHY. Use of inscriptions and often monumental **calligraphy** on buildings and various **ritual implements** and, in general, on material other than paper. Sufis have emblazoned many works of **art** and **architecture** with **symbolic** and thematically apposite texts chosen especially from **Qur'ān**, **Ḥadīth**, and mystical **poetry** to communicate more fully the meaning and function of the structure or object in question. Techniques vary according to the medium, ranging from low relief carving to engraving to painting, gilding, and glazing, or combinations of these.

ESCHATOLOGY. Religious beliefs and theories about the "last things," including death, **judgment**, **resurrection**, **heaven**, and **hell**. In the Islamic tradition this also encompasses various distinctive features such as the *barzakh* and the "bridge" over which individuals much cross to negotiate the passage to the next world. Sufi interpretations of eschatological themes further introduce distinctive **cosmological** features and typically add a **metaphorical** element through their understandings of **annihilation, abiding**, **ecstasy**, and **union**. For example, they speak of death as the "little resurrection," thereby underscoring the importance of the **Ḥadīth** "Die before you die," and generally regard every feature of macro-eschatology as having a counterpart in the daily spiritual **experience** of each seeker.

ESHREFOĞLU RŪMĪ (d. 874/1470 or 899/1493). Turkish mystical **poet** of Iznik and member of the **Qādirīya**, whose lyrics of **wine** and **love** were set to music and sung.

ESOTERIC. Inward (*bāṭin*), hidden, and relating to the life of the spirit, as distinct from the **exoteric** or **outward** (*ẓāhir*), apparent, and relating primarily to legal and ritual obligations. Sufi **theorists** have generally insisted on the need to recognize the coexistence of both dimensions of religious life, for one presupposes the other. Their overriding concern has been to point out the subtleties of inward experience and as a result their **hermeneutical** methods have typically emphasized the esoteric. This emphasis has, in turn, often been a major target of their critics over the centuries.

ESSENCE. Common translation of two terms Sufis have used to refer to the kernel of reality or the penultimate state, level, or expression of some condition. One term, *dhāt*, is feminine and functions for **Ibn al-'Arabī** as a way of referring to a feminine dimension of the divine. The other, ***'ayn*** or "eye," is more commonly used to denote the middle of three levels of a condition, such as **certitude**. So for example, the "essence of certitude" is a step above knowledge of certitude and a step below the "truth of certitude."

ETHICS. Underlying principles governing the specific requirements of Sufi **behavior** as elaborated by the various **orders**. As a philosophical category, Muslim authors have generally referred to ethical concerns with the Arabic term *akhlāq*, the study of **virtue** and character. Sufis have focused primarily on spiritual development and related psycho-spiritual categories, but they have not lost sight of the ethical implications. Spiritual growth in fact presupposes awareness of one's moral obligations and moral action presupposes purity of intention, as the early Sufi **ascetics** insisted. There is, therefore, an inherently ethical quality to all the various levels or **stages** on the spiritual path even when the focus of Sufi analysis is clearly on inner rather than outer deeds. The Persian term *jawānmardī* ("young-manly virtue") with its connotations of courtly, gentlemanly conduct, has sometimes been used to refer to Sufi **chivalric** codes of behavior. Some groups, such as **Malāmatī's** and **Qalandarīs'**, made a point of appearing to flout conventions of ethical conduct under some circumstances.

EXEGESIS. Interpretation of sacred sources, especially **Qur'ān** and **Ḥadīth**, employing specially developed **hermeneutical** principles to "draw out" (from the Greek compound *ex hēgeomai*) the text's meaning(s). Sufi authors speak of the need to command the tools of *tafsīr*, the term most commonly used to refer to fundamental interpretation or "elaboration" (*sharḥ*) of a text. But they also frequently employ the terms *ta'wīl* ("going back to the origin") and *istinbāṭ* ("deriving deeper meanings," from a root that suggests discovering an overflowing hidden source) to characterize their distinctive exegetical methods. Their approach often roused the suspicions of religious authorities, not least of all because Qur'ān 3:7 explicitly states that "none knows the *ta'wīl* (of the sacred text's ambiguous verses) except God." *See also* COMMENTARY.

Sufi exegesis, featuring especially seminal works under the names of **Sahl at-Tustarī** and **Sulamī**, for example, developed elaborate systems of **symbolic** correspondences and cross-references between key scriptural terms and major ingredients in their psycho-spiritual typologies. Scripture thus becomes the foundational warrant for Sufi analyses of the intricacies of mystical **experience**. G. Böwering suggests a four-phase developmental schema for understanding the history of Sufi exegesis. Phase one encompasses about 300 years, beginning with fragmentary works by several second/eighth century figures (especially, **Ḥasan al-Baṣrī**, **Ja'far aṣ-Ṣādiq**), and followed by citations from seven others from the following two centuries (**Dhū 'n-Nūn**, Abū 'l-'Abbās **Ibn 'Aṭā'**, **Junayd**, **Kharrāz**, **Sahl**, **Shiblī**, and **Wāsiṭī**).

Stage two begins with Sulamī's compendium of glosses and includes both Arabic and Persian works from the fifth/11th to the seventh/13th centuries, by such figures as **Anṣārī**, Abū Ḥāmid al-**Ghazālī**, **Rūzbihān Baqlī**, and Abū Ḥafṣ 'Umar as-**Suhrawardī**. From the early seventh/13th to the mid-eighth/14th century, various schools of Sufi exegesis evolved under the inspiration of **Ibn al-'Arabī** and Najm ad-Dīn **Kubrā**. Finally, from the ninth/15th to 12th/18th century, scholars in Ottoman lands dominated the genre, as in the work of **Niyāzī Mişrī**.

EXERCISES, SPIRITUAL. The full range of both outward **ritual** and inward spiritual activities called in Arabic *riyāḍāt*, though some sources suggest the term refers only to **ascetical** disciplines. These include, for example, **audition**, **contemplation**, **dancing**, **invocation**, **retreat**, as well as a host of lesser daily **ascetical** and devotional practices.

EXOTERIC. Outward, apparent (*ẓāhir*), related generally to the understanding and implementation of the requirements of religious **law**, the **hermeneutical** complement of **esoteric**. **Theorists** and historians have often defended Sufism against what they regarded as baseless accusations of disregard for the Islamic tradition's most fundamental **ritual** and **ethical** obligations. **Exegesis** of sacred texts must begin, they argue, with an awareness of their exoteric meanings and only then delve into the less obvious, **symbolic** levels of meaning.

EXPANSION. Called *basṭ* in Arabic, an aspect of spiritual **experience** typically juxtaposed with **constriction**. It is a **state** that represents a refinement or advanced form of **hope**. Although its immediate effect might be similar to a form of elation, Sufi teachers caution that one ought not succumb to its appeal, for it can be a detour on the **path** and a distraction from the ultimate goal.

EXPERIENCE, SPIRITUAL. The entire complex of the many facets of the spiritual **journey**, including **knowledge** of self, perceptions of the "world" and one's place in it, and awareness of one's responses to the perceived action of God in one's life. Sufi theorists have analyzed in detail countless aspects of experience, pointing out the affective subtleties and refinements of hidden motivation to which the seeker must learn to be attuned. Through their **science of hearts**, they have identified varying numbers and combinations of **states** and **stations** as well as gradations or **ranks** among the spiritually accomplished, who are by definition those most aware of their inner lives. This requires a lifetime of disciplined sensitivity to the subtlest movements of the spirit and an ability to evaluate and sort out the various causes of spiritual change on the basis of their origins: God, the world, **Satan**.

EYES. A major feature in the symbolism of mystical love **poetry**. The eye is inherently fascinating and attractive, but more importantly, it is through the eye that the **Beloved** both reveals and conceals. Poets speak often, not only of eyes as such, but of the eyebrows and eyelashes, which express the Beloved's intentions. Most of all, Sufi poets long for a favorable arch of the brow, but because the lover is desperate, even a dismissive flick of the eyebrow is preferable to utter inattentiveness from the Beloved.

– F –

FACE. Major **metaphor** for the **Beloved** and for the presence of **God**. According to the **Qur'ān**, "Everything is perishing save (God's) face (*wajh*)" (28:88, and similarly 55:26–27). The scripture often exhorts believers to "seek God's face," and Sufis have been particularly fond of the scriptural notion that "wherever one turns, there is the face of God" (2:115). **Poets** write often of the **beauty** of the Beloved's countenance, remarking on the attractiveness of individual features (downy cheeks [*rukh*], a mole, the shape of **eyes**, nose, lips). Their language is highly **symbolic**, but still got them into difficulty with religious authorities often enough.

FAḌL ALLĀH ASTARĀBĀDĪ (740/1340–796/1394). Persian religious scholar, **poet**, and mystic who spent significant years of his life in western **Iran** and is often identified as the founder of the **Ḥurūfī** sect. He was known for an abiding interest in **dream** interpretation. He is said to have foretold the circumstances of his coming death and became a martyr to his followers when he was executed in Azerbaijan. His followers venerated the site of his death as a new "**Ka'ba**" and the center of unique **pilgrimage** practices modeled in part on the *Ḥajj*.

FAKHR AD-DĪN 'ĪRĀQĪ (610/1213–688/1289). Persian mystical **poet** and author, onetime ***qalandar*** and associate of the **Suhrawardīya**. He traveled widely, from India, where he married the daughter of **Bahā' ad-Dīn Zakarīya**, to **Anatolia**, where he participated in **Rūmī's** sessions and studied with **Qūnawī**, a major protégé of **Ibn al-'Arabī**. He is best known for his *Divine Flashes* (*Lama'āt*), a blend of **poetry** and prose in which he expands on a series of **allusive** statements ("flashes") focused on the theme of divine love. He died and was buried in **Damascus**.

FALCON. A **metaphor** for the **prophet** or **Friend** as lover of God, related to the larger category of **bird** imagery often employed to speak of the **soul** of the seeker. The hunting bird flies from the king's hand and stoops toward its natural prey. But its dedication to the king is so complete that when it hears the drum calling "return," it will pull up from an all-out dive, return to the king's forearm, and nuzzle its crown on the king's cheek. Here the **Persian** poets are punning on the sound of the words for "falcon" (*bāẓ*) and "return" (*bāz āmadan*). Sometimes the falcon plays the role of **ecstasy** or **love** itself.

FANĀ'. *See* ANNIHILATION.

FANṢŪRĪ, ḤAMZA. *See* ḤAMZA FANṢŪRĪ.

FAQĪR. *See* DERVISH.

FAQR. *See* POVERTY.

FARD. *See* FRIEND OF GOD.

FARĪD AD-DĪN GANJ-I SHAKAR (a.k.a. Bābā Farīd) (c. 570/1175–664/1265). Indian ascetic and **Chishtī *shaykh***. Nicknamed "Treasury of Sugar," he spent some years in **Delhi** under the tutelage of Quṭb ad-Dīn Bakhtīyār **Kākī**, then moved west to spend the remainder of his life in the **Punjab** where he accepted disciples in his *khānqāh*. He emphasized the practices of **fasting**, **audition**, and the "suspended" **retreat**. Among his more famous pupils was **Niẓām ad-Dīn Awliyā'**.

FARQ. *See* SEPARATION.

FARQAD AS-SABAKHĪ (d. 132/749). Austere **ascetic** of **Basra**, contemporary and associate of **Ḥasan al-Baṣrī**, and a convert from Armenian Christianity to Islam. He was known for his **preaching** and **storytelling**, and may have mentored **Ma'rūf al-Karkhī**.

FĀSĪ, 'ALĪ IBN MAYMŪN AL- (854/1450–917/1511). Moroccan mystical author who commented on the work of **Ibn al-'Arabī**. He spent the last 16 years of his life traveling in the **Middle East** and died in **Damascus**. There he had persuaded Sultan Selim I to construct a grand monument over the grave of Ibn al-'Arabī, which had previously remained virtually unidentifiable.

FASTING. One of the five **pillars** of Islamic religious practice (known as *ṣawm*), developed in several different forms as part of Sufi **ascetical** discipline. All Muslims are enjoined (assuming good health and absence of other extenuating circumstances) to refrain from food and drink from sunrise to sundown during the 28–30 days of the ninth lunar month, Ramaḍān. Sufis of the different **orders** have added several variations on the practice to their regimen of spiritual **exercises**. One widespread practice is the "Fast of **David**," in which one refrains from food on alternate days so as to avoid becoming accustomed either to deprivation or satiety. More extreme practices include extending the prescribed fast to as much as seventy days, or full fasting during the **forty**-day **retreat**. Many Sufi groups have paid particular attention to food intake even when not specifically engaged in full-fledged fasting, since they regard hunger as an essential aspect of **experience** on the spiritual path. Some orders, such as the **Naqshbandīya**, have opted for a more **symbolic** approach in which fasting means most of all refraining from sinful thoughts.

FATĀ. *See* CHIVALRY; MYSTIC; ORGANIZATION.

FĀṬIMA BINT MUḤAMMAD (d. 11/633). Most famous daughter of the **Prophet**, wife of **'Alī**, mother of **Ḥasan** and **Ḥusayn**. She has been regarded as one of the four "ideal" women of Paradise (along with Āsiya wife of Pharaoh; Mary, Mother of **Jesus**; and Khadīja, the Prophet's first wife). Tradition attributes a number of **marvels** to her, and she has been an important model of female piety and sanctity for many of the **women** of Sufism.

FĀṬIMA OF CORDOBA (late sixth/12th century). One of the two **women** whom **Ibn al-'Arabī** identifies as his own ***shaykhas*** while he lived in **Iberia**. In his short biographical sketch of her, Ibn al-'Arabī observes that even at the age of 95, her beauty was that of a very young woman, so replenished was she by the love of God.

FĀṬIMA OF NISHAPUR (d. 235/849). Khurāsānī mystic, wife and ***shaykha*** of Aḥmad Khiḍrūya. Traditional accounts say that she was acquainted with **Bāyazīd** and **Dhū 'n-Nūn**, and stories of her dealings with these two paragons of spiritual achievement underscore an important dimension of the contribution of Sufi **women**. The anecdotes, part of a **genre** of **hagiographical** accounts, suggest that even these two men had to learn from her that their inability to avoid focusing on her feminine attributes—or simply on the fact that she was a woman—betrayed a flaw in their devotion to God.

FAYḌĪYA. *See* SAMMĀNĪYA.

FEAR. An important aspect of **experience**, generally paired with **hope**. Fear (as expressed in both *khawf* and *taqwā*) is a necessary and salutary experience in that it prevents one from nonchalance in the presence of God and forgetting one's frailty and sinfulness. As with many other key elements in their psycho-spiritual **typologies**, Sufi authors further analyzed fear into various subcomponents and varieties.

FEZ (Fās). Ancient religious and intellectual center of Morocco, home of important Sufis, such as **Ibn 'Abbād of Ronda**, and a major center of the **Shādhilīya** and **Darqāwīya**. It is perhaps most famous as the environs of a holy man named Mawlay Idrīs (d. 175/791), acclaimed by some as the ancestor of **North African** Sufism. According to tradition, it was he who founded Fez, and his **tomb** some distance outside the city remains the region's most revered site.

FĪHI MĀ FĪHI. *See* RŪMĪ, JALĀL AD-DĪN.

FIRĀSA. *See* CLAIRVOYANCE.

FIRDAWSĪYA. Important **Indian order** that branched off from the **Kubrāwīya** initially under the leadership of Badr ad-Dīn as-Samarqandī, a student of Sayf ad-Dīn **Bākharzī**, in **Delhi**. Samarqandī's successor, Najīb ad-Dīn Firdawsī, was the eponym of the organization. It was most influential in what is now the Indian state of Bihar, where its leading figure in medieval times was Sharaf ad-Dīn **Manīrī**, a direct disciple and **successor** of Firdawsī.

FIRE. A favorite Sufi poetic **metaphor** for suffering, purification, and even authentic life itself, as in **Rūmī's** image of the reed **flute**. It is the candle's fire of **annihilation** that draws the moth to its death. Amid the flames of Nimrod's bonfire, **Abraham** enjoys the divine comfort of a garden. In the fire of the burning bush, **Moses** recognizes a divine **manifestation**. Sharing the red glow of **wine** and the **rose's** hue, fire is the power of love's intoxication.

FIXITY. A facet of spiritual **experience** featured in various catalogues of **stations** and **states**. Sometimes paired with its apparent opposite, metamorphosis (*talwīn*), *tamkīn* represents a fairly advanced degree of spiritual maturity. **Qushayrī**, for example, underscores the paradoxical nature of this mystical stability, explaining that the most accomplished mystics move from one experience of immutability to another.

FLUTE. Most famously fashioned into a **metaphor** for the human **heart** and **soul** by **Rūmī** in the prologue of his *Spiritual* ***Couplets***. Torn from its bed of rushes, the reed flute complains longingly of its desire to return to its origin in God. Its sound is not wind, but **fire**, and one who does not know that fire of longing may as well not exist.

FORM. A critical concept in Sufi **hermeneutics**, typically juxtaposed with **meaning**, much as the **exoteric** complements the **esoteric** and **outward** is the opposite of **inward**. Many people spend their lives addicted to the attractive superficialities of form (*ṣūra*) alone, without ever getting beneath the surface. But although ordinary human **knowledge** cannot occur without form, spiritual seekers cannot allow it to stop there. Only infused or experiential knowledge circumvents form and connects immediately with meaning, but that presupposes a high level in which the **heart** well-polished enjoys direct access to the unseen world.

FORMATION. An ingredient in Sufi spiritual formation typically expressed with the terms *tarbīya* and *tadrīb*, and distinguished from the complementary category of **instruction** (*ta'līm*). According to a classic functional distinction, there are several kinds of ***shaykh***, each with slightly different roles in the formation of Sufi seekers and adepts. The "formative *shaykh*" teaches by example rather than by more conventional pedagogical methods, and is responsible for the ongoing guidance of the seeker in spiritual exercises and disciplines. From this *shaykh* the seeker receives a specially assigned **invocation**, daily direction through an extended **retreat**, specific requirements of a daily order (including times assigned for sleeping, silence, eating, and manual labor), and individually tailored **ritual** requirements. While an individual could study simultaneously under more than one instructional *shaykh*, one could follow the guidance of only one formation *shaykh* at a time.

FORTY. One of the more frequently used **numbers** in the Sufi repertoire of **symbolism**. God kneaded the clay of **Adam** for 40 days, leading Persian Sufis to identify the discipline of the spiritual **retreat** simply as "the 40" (*chilla*) days, the time the seeker needs to be fashioned into a spiritually mature being. It was at the age of 40 that the **Prophet** is traditionally believed to have received his inaugural **revelations**, and 40 is the most commonly mentioned number of the **Substitutes**.

FRIEND OF GOD. Ordinary designation of a category in the **hierarchy** of spiritually advanced individuals, second only to **prophets**. The **Arabic** *walī*, is from a root meaning "close to, near," thus suggesting in this usage divine protection or patronage; it is related to the terms often used for "sainthood" and "saintly (or religious) authority," *walāya* and *wilāya.* As a category, they are known in the plural as *awliyā' Allāh*. The term is roughly parallel to the term "saint" often used in Christian parlance. A major difference is that Friends of God are so designated through a process similar to popular acclaim rather than through the elaborate institutionally dictated course of investigation, testing and validation in use by the Roman Catholic Church. In addition to being regarded as conduits of **blessing**, Friends of God are often attributed with powers of healing, walking on water, clairvoyance, and other **wonders**, whereas the extraordinary powers bestowed on prophets are known as evidentiary **miracles**. Friends are sometimes referred to as *abrār*, "pious ones," emphasizing their devotion.

Some Sufi **theorists** have elaborated a detailed system of sainthood to parallel that of prophethood, so that there is also a **seal** of the Friends of God. Many Friends of God have also been prominent Sufis in life, and their **tombs** have often become goals of devotional **visitation**. Friends of God belong to the comprehensive **cosmological** designation "people of the Unseen World" (*ahl al-ghayb*), and some Friends are further identified by other titles that locate them in the spiritual universe of Sufi cosmology. These include, for example, **Chiefs**, **Chosen Ones**, **Pole**, **Substitutes**, and **Supports**, in addition to a designation for the lowest rank, the "singular/unique ones" (*fard/afrād*). Although some Friends have assumed virtually global significance, many are important only in local contexts. A regionally important cluster of Friends are the **Walī Songo** of **Indonesia**.

FRIENDSHIP. *See* COMPANIONSHIP.

FU'ĀD. *See* HEART.

FUḌAYL IBN 'IYĀḌ (d. 187/803). Central Asian ascetic and traditionist said to have experienced a dramatic conversion from a youthful career as a bandit. His often arresting sayings are frequently cited by Sufi **manualists** and **hagiographers**.

FURŪZANFĀR, BADĪ' AZ-ZAMĀN (15th/20th century). Major **Iranian** scholar, noted for his editions, translations, literary analysis, and commentary on a wide range of Sufi works, particularly those of Jalīl ad-Dīn **Rūmī**.

FUTŪḤ. *See* LIVELIHOOD.

FUTŪWA. *See* CHIVALRY.

– G –

GABRIEL. The **angel** principally responsible for delivering divine **revelation** to **prophets** throughout human history. Known in **Arabic** as Jibrīl (or Jabrā'īl), from a Hebrew term appropriately rendered "strong man of God," he is typically said to appear in otherwise unremarkable human form. The **Qur'ān** calls him by name three times but more often alludes to him as "the spirit" who mediates between the divine and human **realms**. The **Prophet** is said to have received two **visions** of the angel, who under these most mysterious circumstances is manifest in superhuman form propelled by 600 world-filling wings. And it is Gabriel who serves as the Prophet's guide during his **Night Journey** and **Ascension**. Sufi **poets** allude often to Gabriel's role in this paradigm of mystical **experience**, some even referring to the angel as the "celestial **bird**" who bore the Prophet aloft. As the teacher and guide of prophets, Gabriel is like a ***shaykh***; but since the Prophet is at home in "the kitchen where angels are cooked" (**Rūmī**), Gabriel must end his journey so that the Prophet proceeds to God's Throne alone. Just as the Prophet sees Gabriel where ordinary people see only a human being, so mystics see beneath the **form** to the true **meanings** of things.

GENDER. Questions relating to distinctions, or lack thereof, between male and female or masculine and feminine roles and attributes. Gender as such is a more inclusive category than **sexuality**, and in Sufi **literature** is often used to communicate a host of **metaphorical** and **symbolic** themes. Some authors comment favorably on the symbolism of the feminine gender of certain Arabic terms (such as *rūḥ*, **spirit**; and *dhāt*, **essence**), suggesting the need to think about the divine reality as beyond gender; or negatively as in the case of a term like *nafs* (also feminine), **ego**-soul. Poets occasionally allude to the potential of all human beings to be "pregnant" with the "**Jesus** of the spirit," as Mary was with that **prophet**. Other related issues are the social and religious status and roles of **women** in Sufi life.

GENERATIONS. Classification used in various ways to structure Sufi **hagiographical** texts; by extension, the name of a sub-**genre** of hagiography, the biographical dictionary or anthology. From an Arabic term that can also be rendered "categories" (*ṭabaqāt*), the underlying concept is that one can best understand the history of Sufism by grouping major figures using models based on chronology, lineage, or similarity of views. Sometimes the term is used more loosely to mean simply "biographical notices." A number of major Sufi authors have written important works with the term in their title (most prominently **Abū Nu'aym al-Iṣfāhānī**, **Anṣārī**, and **Sulamī**). Still others (including **'Aṭṭār** and **Jāmī**) have authored works in the genre under different titles (most importantly, **Remembrances**). In addition, several of the major Sufi **manuals** (such as those of **Hujwīrī** and **Qushayrī**) include sections belonging to this genre.

GENRE. A wide range of types and forms of **literature**, both in **poetry** and prose. The major genres include **lyrical** love songs, **didactic** romances and epics, **panegyrics** of the **Prophet** and **Friends of God**, devotional songs of **supplication** and **repentance**. Falling under the general category of literary forms, but not as clearly creative and artistic as the various **poetic** genres, are the mainly prose genres associated with **exegesis** and other forms of **commentary**, whatever the original text; **manuals** and works of mystical theory, including **lexicons**; **discourses** of teachers recorded for posterity by their students; and **hagiography**. Genres that are primarily prose often cite copious amounts of poetry and are sometimes our only sources for the now-fragmentary work of a number of famous Sufis who expressed themselves poetically. Along with **aphorisms** and other typically brief forms of ethical, inspirational, or "wisdom" literature, one could also locate the **anecdote** and two types of compact, mystically dense forms: the **allusion** and the **ecstatic** utterance (*shaṭḥ*).

GHĀLIB, MĪRZĀ ASAD ALLĀH (d. 1286/1869). Indian Sufi-influenced **poet** who wrote in **Persian** and **Urdu**. His most important contributions to the development of **genres** and imagery about the Prophet include **praise** poems as well as longer **didactic** works.

GHĀLIB DEDE (or Shaykh Ghālib) (d. 1214/1799). Turkish poet and ***shaykh*** of the **Mawlawīya**, called the last truly classical Turkish mystical poet. He wrote of the spiritual power behind the whirling **dance** characteristic of his **order**.

GHAWTH. *See* POLE.

GHAYB. *See* MYSTERY.

GHAZAL. A **genre** of **lyric poetry**, generally of 14 or fewer monorhyming verses. Composed especially in **Arabic**, **Persian**, **Turkish**, and **Urdu**, as well as other **languages**, ghazals focus on themes of love and loss, **union** and **separation** and often function as **prayer** texts. Many classic poems are still being set to **music** as popular song-forms, especially in the **Middle East** and **South Asia**.

GHAZĀLĪ, ABŪ ḤĀMID AL- (450/1058–505/1111). Major religious scholar and **theorist**, mystical and pastoral **theologian**, author. He was born and raised in **Khurasan**, where he studied Shāfi'ī **Law** and Ash'arī theology. At the insistence of the **Saljūqid** vizier, he moved to **Baghdad** in 484/1091 to serve as professor at the vizier's newly founded ***madrasa***. In his "**autobiography**," he reports that, after several years of teaching, he experienced psychosomatic difficulties that caused him to reexamine his most deeply held values. He forsook his teaching position in 488/1095 and spent the next 11 years in Syria and parts of the central **Middle East** before returning to Nishapur. During these years he composed his masterwork, *The Revitalization of Religious Disciplines* (*Iḥyā' 'ulūm ad-dīn*), in which he lays out the spiritual path both systematically and pastorally. The compendium represents the fruit of in-depth reflection on both traditional sources and his own spiritual **experience**. During subsequent years, he returned to teaching in northeastern **Iran**, wrote his autobiographical *Deliverance from Error* (*Al-Munqidh min aḍ-ḍalāl*), and finally left the academic life again to return home to Ṭūs. There he founded a *khānqāh*, accepted aspirants for Sufi **formation**, and lived his last days. He is one of the most influential authors in the history of Islamic religious studies. Two other works of major significance for the history of Sufism include the Arabic *Niche for Lights* (*Mishkāt al-anwār*), and extended **exegesis** of the scriptural "Verse of **Light**" and the Persian *Alchemy of Happiness* (*Kīmiyā-yi sa'ādat*).

GHAZĀLĪ, AḤMAD AL- (d. 520/1126). Sufi author and popular **preacher**, younger brother of Abū Ḥāmid al-**Ghazālī**. His most important work is a Persian text called *Adversions* (*Sawāniḥ*), a treatise on mystical love using the **genre** of the **aphorism**. He was also known for his sympathetic view of **Satan's** plight, regarding him as a creature caught in an impossible dilemma: God had ordered him to bow to none but God, and then required all the **angels** to pay homage to the newly created **Adam**. Among his most famous students was **'Ayn al-Quḍāt al-Hamadhānī**.

GHIJDUWĀNĪ, 'ABD AL-KHĀLIQ (d. 617/1220). May have been a central member of an early group of Khwājagān who went on to form the nucleus of the **Naqshbandīya**. **Naqshbandīs** situate him in the **lineage** of their founder, Bahā' ad-Dīn **Naqshband**, whom Ghijduwānī was said to have **initiated** in a **vision**. Tradition credits 'Abd al-Khāliq with formulating the eight essential spiritual **exercises** that came to be among the hallmarks of the Naqshbandīya.

GHULĀM KHALĪL, AḤMAD (d. 275/888). An early opponent of Sufism in **Baghdad**, who was among the first to level formal accusations of heresy against **Nūrī** and other associates of **Junayd**.

***GINĀN*.** A **genre** of mystical **poetry** especially popular in **South** and **Southeast Asia**, whose name derives from the Arabic *ghinā'* (**singing**). Composed in a wide variety of regional **languages**, these poems often focused on the theme of yearning for the **Beloved**.

GĪSŪ DARĀZ, SAYYID MUḤAMMAD AL-ḤUSAYNĪ (721/1321–825/1422). South **Indian** religious scholar, **exegete**, disciple of **Chirāgh-i Dihlī**, and most prolific mystical author of the **Chishtīya**. Most of his works are in **Persian** but he wrote several important texts in **Arabic** as well. As a ***shaykh*** and spokesperson of the Chishtī **order**, he promoted the writings of the **Suhrawardīs** and defended traditional practices of the order against the misgivings of regional religious authorities. His **tomb** in Gulbarga remains a goal of annual **visitation** for large numbers of regional pilgrims.

GOD *(Allāh)*. The one, transcendent Being who is creator, sustainer, and disposer of all things, as described in the "99 Most Beautiful Names." Uppermost in the religious concerns of every Muslim is the affirmation of the divine transcendent **unity** (*tawḥīd*). Sufi **theology** develops fundamental Muslim notions of the deity and of the relationships of the deity to creation and humanity, beginning with the conception of human beings as servants of God. Early **ascetics** focused on the attributes of divine majesty and power, especially God's judgeship before which human beings can rightly think only of accountability for sin. In later theological developments, Sufi **exegetes** and mystical authors have often gravitated toward the Names that suggest divine care and even intimacy with creation. But they are speaking of a closeness born wholly of God's largesse and in no way merited or deserved.

GOLCONDA. A southeastern **Indian** pre-Mughal sultanate with a major city of the same name, important in the history of Sufism especially during the **Mughal** period. Part of the region known as the Deccan, Golconda was just to the east of another major sultanate in which Sufism was a prominent feature, Bijapur.

GOVERNANCE. The overall administration of Sufi **organizations**, including theories and structures of **authority** and a host of **institutional** concerns. Sufi orders run the gamut from very loosely structured to intricately hierarchical, resulting in a wide range of structures and methods of governance. Those with the most detailed and complex "flowcharts" reflect the greatest degree of internal division of labor, with varying degrees of authority delegated to assistants by the overall superior. Most organizations developed stable procedures for establishing **successorship** to a founder and subsequent ***shaykhs***. Some orders sought to maintain a high level of centralization even after new branches or suborders had been authorized, while in others new foundations began and remained quite independent. Many orders evolved distinctive **ranks** and titles, such as those of *nā'ib* (deputy *shaykh*), *khādim* (servant, assistant), *qayyūm* (high-ranking **Naqshbandī**), and *muqaddam* (leader of a group within a local organization).

GRACE. A **theological** category referring to perfectly gratuitous divine assistance of any sort, expressed by such **Arabic** terms as *luṭf*, *ni'ma*, by association, *baraka* (**blessing**). Grace is an expression of

God's intimate involvement with creation, and nothing occurs apart from grace. Although human beings are incapable of earning divine aid as such, they are in no way excused from striving to be worthy of it. Indeed, even the latter condition is itself strictly speaking not attainable by human effort alone and comes about only as a result of grace.

GRATITUDE. The quintessential religious virtue for Muslims, the opposite of attributing to what is not **God** qualities that belong only to God. Sufi **poets** like to pun on the **Arabic** words for gratitude (***sh**u**kr***—here the consonantal radicals are in boldface type) and idolatry (***sh**i**rk***) to underscore the differences as well as the paradoxical and dangerous proximity of the two. Only a full realization of the centrality of divine **grace** can lead one to constant gratitude. *See also* PATIENCE.

GREEN. The **color** often said to be **symbolic** of the **Prophet**, or of prophets as a group in some cases, and, by extension, of Islam itself. Some Sufis have associated green with the authority of a spiritual director, and in some **cosmological** schemes it is the color of the emerald mountain that is the goal of spiritual **pilgrimage**. It is thus also the color of Paradise itself, where everyone will wear green. **Khiḍr** is inextricably linked with greenness, and some Sufi poets refer to the down on the Beloved's cheek as freshly verdant. In some **orders**, green worn on items of **clothing** or **headgear** has designated a particular **rank**.

GUIDEBOOKS. A subset of the genre of geographical literature, works dedicated to assisting travelers intent on formal **pilgrimage** to **Mecca** as well as **visitation** to local and regional holy places. Sometimes referred to with the Perso-Arabic term *ziyāratnāma*, they were produced in considerable numbers especially during the later medieval period (sixth/12th–10th/16th centuries). These books spotlight religious institutions of all kinds, including considerable information about Sufi **tombs**, **residential facilities**, and other architectural complexes associated with various **orders**. The annotated travelogues have often been illustrated with images of the holy sites described in their texts.

GUJDAWĀNĪ, 'ABD AL-KHĀLIQ. *See* GHIJDUWĀNĪ.

GULSHAN, SA'D ALLĀH (d. 1204/1728). Major figure in the evolution of **Urdu** as a language of mystical poetry. Associated with the **Naqshbandīya**, he became the ***shaykh*** of Muḥammad Naṣīr 'Andalīb (1109/1697–1172/1758), the father of Mīr **Dard**.

GURDJIEFF, GEORGY IVANOVICH (c. 1294/1877–1369/1949). Russian-born religious figure sometimes popularly associated with developments in Sufism's adaptation to "western" contexts. His work on religious movement, or **dance**, attracted a following in the United States during the 1920s, 1930s, and 1940s. Although he does not appear to have associated himself explicitly with Sufism, some accounts of "Sufism in the West" identify him, along with P. D. **Ouspensky**, as a figure in the spread of the "Tradition" in Europe and the United States. Some Sufis now repudiate any such association on the grounds that neither of these individuals had the **authority** to teach Sufism, although some **Naqshbandīs** have gone so far as to list him in their **lineage**.

GWĀLIYĀRĪ, MUḤAMMAD GHAWTH (906/1500–970/1562). Indian mystical author and leading member of the **Shaṭṭārīya**. He spent part of his adult life in the state of Gujarat before developing a brief relationship with the **Mughal** Akbar in Agra. Like a number of prominent Sufi authors before him, he developed the theme of **Ascension** as a paradigm of spiritual **experience**. He was influential in the growing importance of the Shaṭṭārīya, and Akbar recognized his significance by building him a splendid **tomb** in Gwāliyār.

– H –

ḤABS-I DAM (P). *See* BREATH CONTROL.

ḤABĪB AL-'AJAMĪ (d. 156/772). An **ascetic** whose nickname meant "foreigner," indicating that he was a non-Arab. **Manualists** have preserved a number of his sayings, such as that he recommended praying only for two things: not to have reason for shame at the **Resurrection**, and to be gifted with a happy and prosperous life.

ḤAḌĀRA. *See* PRESENCE.

ḤADDĀD, ABŪ ḤAFṢ AL- (d. c. 265/878–79). A former blacksmith, **ascetic** and mystic of **Nishapur**, frequently quoted in **manuals** and **hagiography**. He left no written works of his own but was acknowledged as a Sufi whose spiritual authority in **Khurasan** was equivalent to that of **Junayd** in **Baghdad**. His occasionally bizarre behavior may have been related to his association with the **Malāmatīya**.

ḤADĪQAT AL-ḤAQĪQA. *See* SANĀ'Ī.

ḤADĪTH. Saying, tradition, record of the words and deeds of the **Prophet Muḥammad**, consisting of a chain of transmitters and a "body" or text (*matn*). Originally committed to memory by **Companions** and transmitted only orally from one generation to the next, the Prophet's legacy spread across the length and breadth of lands under Muslim rule. By around the mid-eighth century, religious scholars expressed concern that the corpus of this sacred patrimony was too expansive and precious to continue to entrust to fallible human memory. They began a far-flung "quest for Ḥadīth" in which specialists sought to retrieve and record in writing as many of the remembered traditions as possible.

A critical ingredient in the methodology of the search was establishing the authenticity of each saying. After first ascertaining the names of every individual known to have passed along a given tradition, scholars then classified those individuals according to degree of credibility. By the end of the ninth century, six major written collections had been published, each offering thousands of sayings with their chains of "supports" (*isnād*) and an evaluation of the soundness or weakness of each saying. Dozens of additional anthologies have been published over the centuries, but these six remain the most authoritative. Countless major Sufis have been traditionists—specialists in the sayings of the Prophet—and Sufi texts cite this material extensively.

As with scriptural **exegesis**, Sufi use of prophetic traditions is colored by a particularly intense interest in those texts that highlight the Prophet's relationship with **God** and emphasize his role as paragon of spiritual values. In addition to the sayings of the Prophet, Muslim tradition has also preserved in a place of honor a large number of *ḥadīths* attributed to God Himself. Known as "sacred sayings" (*aḥādīth qudsīya*), these form an amazing treasure trove in which Sufis over the centuries have found insights into the essential features of the divine-human relationship. For the mystics, these sacred traditions reveal God's very heart, so to speak, one that is immanently accessible and desirous of being known.

Finally, following this model of gathering authoritative utterances and exemplary anecdotes, Sufis have also developed collections of sayings and deeds of famous Sufis, complete with chains of transmitters. This **genre** of Sufi **literature** thus parallels the broader phenomenon of Islamic documentation of the **Prophetic Example**.

ḤAḌRA. *See* RECOLLECTION.

ḤĀFIẒ, MUḤAMMAD SHAMS AD-DĪN (726/1325–791/1389). **Persian** lyric and panegyric **poet** from Shiraz in southwestern **Iran**. Although he is not known for significant connections to a given **order**, his ***ghazals*** especially have often been interpreted mystically. Perhaps most importantly, this poet has been most influential through his elaboration and refinement of many **metaphors** often adopted by Sufi poets.

HAGIOGRAPHY. Writing about holy persons, distinguished from the more modern **genre** of "**history**" because of the tendency to elevate its subjects beyond the merely human through the inclusion of elements of miracle and magic. Hagiography constitutes a major type of Sufi **literature** in itself, and encompasses a variety of genres. Hagiographical works can take the form of larger accounts of a single individual (*sīra*, a term that applies preeminently to the life story of **Muḥammad**, but has also been used to refer to saintly figures) as well as of biographical dictionaries or anthologies such as works in the genre called "**generations**" (*ṭabaqāt*). Some such works are entitled "memorial" or "**remembrances**" (*tadhkira*) while others are known as *siyar* (life story, the pl. of *sīra*). A special type of sacred biography that focuses on the extraordinary deeds of **Friends of God** is known by the term *manāqib*. Still another distinctive genre, sometimes called the *maqtal*, specializes in the stories of **martyrs** and their families and supporters. But hagiographical elements, generally in the form of anecdotes, appear in many other literary genres, beginning with the **Ḥadīth** and including a range of Sufi **poetry** and prose. In the former case, the subgenre recounts the "virtues" (*faḍā'il*) of important individuals, beginning with the **Companions** of the **Prophet**. Much of what we know about hundreds of Sufis derives from hagiographical sources. Critical analysis of this vast corpus of material, still a relatively fresh enterprise, reveals the particular biases of the works' authors and provides invaluable insights into the character of the Sufi **organizations** that supported the production of such works. Analysis thereby also provides clues as to a particular document's "factual" reliability. One could also argue that **autobiography** belongs in the category of hagiography.

ḤĀL. *See* STATE.

ḤALLĀJ, ḤUSAYN IBN MANṢŪR AL- (244/857–309/922). Persian-born mystical author and **poet** who spent much of his life traveling throughout the central **Middle East** as well as central and parts of **South Asia**, and was brutally executed in **Baghdad** as a heretic. Known as the "Carder [of Consciences]" because of his trade as a wool-carder, he was **initiated** into Sufism in **Basra** by **'Amr ibn 'Uthmān al-Makkī**. He later came to know **Junayd** in Baghdad, traveled back to Iran and opted for a less formal Sufism by forsaking the **cloak** in favor of lay garb. Eventually he again assumed a more **ascetical** public demeanor and clothing and returned to Baghdad, where his wife and family had been living.

During his latter years Ḥallāj articulated his intense spiritual **experience** in original, elegantly simple **lyric** poetry as well as highly controversial **ecstatic** utterances. His theologically motivated sympathy for **Satan** became one of his hallmarks. Nearly as important as his poetry, Ḥallāj's most influential work is his short *Book of Ṭā-Sīns* (*Kitāb aṭ-ṭawāsīn*), a densely **allusive** reflection on his own mystical experience. After hotly contested and politicized legal proceedings, his gruesome death made him the paradigmatic mystical **martyr**. Sufi theorists and **hagiographers** cite him with great frequency and reverence, as do many poets, and Ḥallāj is acknowledged as a cornerstone in the mystical **theology** founded on the concept of "ontological **unity**" (*waḥdat al-wujūd*). Although he himself did not originate a formal order, groups of his followers have been identified as the Ḥallājīya. During his lifetime, Junayd was among his staunchest critics, and three centuries later, **Ibn al-'Arabī** criticized him from his unique perspective.

ḤALQA. *See* RITUAL.

HALVETĪ-JERRĀHĪ. *See* KHALWATĪYA.

HAMADHĀNĪ. *See* 'ALĪ HAMADHĀNĪ, MĪR SAYYID; 'AYN AL-QUḌĀT AL-HAMADHĀNĪ; YŪSUF HAMADHĀNĪ.

ḤAMDĪ, ḤAMD ALLĀH (853/1449–909/1503). Turkish didactic and **lyric poet** most famous for his mystically oriented romances about **Joseph** and **Zulaykhā** and the star-crossed lovers, Laylā and Majnūn. His father had been ***shaykh*** of the Bayrāmīya, and the son, whose writing is suffused with Sufi concepts, eventually became the disciple of one of his father's successors to the leadership of the **order**.

ḤAMDŪN AL-QAṢṢĀR, ABŪ ṢĀLIḤ (d. 271/884). Khurāsānī ascetic most noted as a leader of the **Malāmatīya** movement. His most famous associates included **Nakhshabī** and **Naṣrābādhī**.

ḤAMĪD AD-DĪN NĀGAWRĪ (d. 673/1274). Indian religious scholar, mystical author, **successor** to **Mu'īn ad-Dīn Chishtī** and ***shaykh*** of the **Suhrawardīya**. Arguably Indian Sufism's first major writer, he penned a number of theoretical works as well as some **Persian poetry**.

ḤAMMŪYA, SA'D AD-DĪN (c. 586/1191–649/1252). Khurāsānī Shāfi'ī religious scholar, disciple of **Kubrā**, ***shaykh*** of 'Azīz ad-Dīn **Nasafī**. He was **initiated** into Sufism in **Damascus** and is said to have met Shihāb ad-Dīn Abū Ḥafṣ 'Umar as-**Suhrawardī** in **Mecca**. During later travels through the central **Middle East** he met Ṣadr ad-Dīn al-**Qūnawī**, became a proponent of *waḥdat al-wujūd*, and was influenced by **Ḥurūfī** thought.

ḤAMZA, AMĪR (1329/1911–1366/1946). Malay son of a Sufi, wrote mystically inspired **poetry** influenced by the likes of **Rūmī**. His story is a reminder that Sufism's extent both chronologically and geographically is ongoing.

ḤAMZA FANṢŪRĪ (fl. c. 968/1560). Sumatran (**Indonesian**) author and **poet**. He was influenced by the thought of **Ibn al-'Arabī** and advanced the theory of *waḥdat al-wujūd*. He created some of the earliest examples of the **Malay** *syair*, a variation on the **quatrain genre** using an a-a-a-a rhyme scheme (rather than the **Persian** a-a-b-a scheme), typically stringing from 10 to 20 of the quatrains together to develop a theme at greater length. Though the quatrain is formally closer to **lyric**, his use of the form transformed it into more of a **didactic** genre. Many of his 32 poems are homiletical in tone, and he invariably gives traditional scriptural themes a mystical interpretation. Little is known of his personal life or explicit affiliation with any particular **order**.

ḤAQĪQA. *See* REALITY, ULTIMATE.

ḤAQQ. *See* TRUTH.

HARAWĪ, AMĪR ḤUSAYNĪ (d. after 729/1328). Mystical author in **Persian**, from Herat (present-day Afghanistan), member of the **Suhrawardīya**. He wrote several theoretical works as well as a collection of **poetry**, most of which were lost during the Mongol invasion.

ḤASAN AL-BAṢRĪ (21/110–642/728). Medinan-born religious scholar and **preacher** who moved to **Basra** and is most famous as an **ascetic** and was claimed by later Sufis as one of the earliest Sufis. He was reportedly of such dour demeanor and dwelt so much on ethical responsibility that one would have thought Hell had been created just for him. Since he was old enough to have been personally acquainted with a number of the **Prophet's Companions**, Sufis have often seen him as a crucial link to the Prophet and have thus typically included him in their **lineages**. **Hagiographical** sources often place him in a chronologically unlikely relationship to **Rābi'a**.

ḤASAN SIJZĪ DIHLAWĪ (652/1254–737/1336). Major **Indian Chishtī hagiographer** and **poet** of Delhi. He is best known for his compilation of the **discourses** of his ***shaykh***, **Niẓām ad-Dīn Awliyā'**, but he also composed hundreds of **lyric ghazals** in **Persian** and a book of **aphorisms**.

ḤAWLĪYA. *See* WEDDING.

ḤAYDARĪYA. A movement of mendicant **dervishes**, founded in **Iran** by Quṭb ad-Dīn Ḥaydar (d. c. 618/1221–22). His name means "Lion," a symbol largely associated with **'Alī**. Bearing noteworthy similarities to the **Qalandarīya**, they spread quickly to **Turkey** and **India**, and the **Bektāshīya** were responsible for spreading some of their traditions as well. Like the ***qalandars***, they typically practiced **celibacy**, wore distinctive clothing and headgear, and sported prominent moustaches. Among their more extreme practices was wearing iron rings from various parts of their bodies, including genitals.

ḤAYRA. *See* PERPLEXITY.

HEADGEAR. A wide variety of hats and decorative trim, often called a "crown" (*tāj*) and used to distinguish one **order** from another as well as to designate **ranks** within a given **organization**. Like the **cloak**, the hat functions as a **symbol** of **initiation** into an order. Distinguishing features include material as well as shape and **color**. The two most widely used types are the turban or similar wrapped arrangements (such as the **Turkish** *qāwuk*) and the one-piece cap of various sizes and shapes (such as the Persian *qalansuwa*). Among the orders that preferred turbans, the **Qādirīya** wound theirs with six folds while the **Bektāshīya** used 12. Some orders, such as the **Mawlawīya** and **Naqshbandīya,** use the *kulāh* or *sikke* ("seal"), a conical pointed or cylindrical domed hat (also called the *ṭarṭūr*) of woolen felt, sometimes adorned with outer wrapping. A common item of this type is the skullcap called the *ṭāqīya*. Some **Chinese** Sufis wear a six-cornered hat.

In the practice of some orders, the hat has born special significance not only as a symbol of **poverty**, but as a hereditary link with the **Prophet** and his **Companions** and to previous **prophets**. God originally gave **Adam**, and later Noah, **Abraham** and **Muḥammad**, hats of poverty said to have been marked with four folds or slashes symbolic of various levels of abandonment. In addition to the association with spiritual poverty, hats symbolized **virtues**, each of which was characteristic of a particular prophet: Adam's command, Noah's vision, Abraham's generosity, and the Prophet's munificence. All but the last of these hats was lost or borne to heaven by a prophet who inherited it from a predecessor. According to Naqshbandī traditions, Sufi hats connect their wearers spiritually to the Prophet, since he passed his own hat to **Abū Bakr**. In some regions, such as Turkey, a version of a dead Sufi leader's headgear is attached to the upper end of the sarcophagus in the **tomb**, and many tombstones bear likenesses of the hats worn in life by those buried there.

HEART. Both a physical organ essential to life and the human faculty at the center of all spiritual **experience**. It is therefore the focus of Sufi discernment and spiritual direction, known as the **science of hearts**, a term first used by **Ḥasan al-Baṣrī**. A seeker's lifelong project is "polishing the mirror of the heart" through the various **ascetical** and **contemplative** disciplines, which burnish away the rust and corrosion of self-deceit and all the **ego**-soul's considerable powers of obfuscation. Sufis are fond of a Sacred Ḥadīth in which God says that though the heavens and earth are too small for Him, in the human heart there is ample room. The most important **Arabic** term for heart is *qalb*, from a root that means to turn or rotate (i.e., fluctuate or vacillate), because the heart is susceptible to the attractions of the ego-soul as well as the **spirit** (*rūḥ*). (The most common Persian term is *dil*.) The "greater *jihād*" is therefore analogous to a kind of tug-of-war between ego and spirit to win the heart's attentiveness. This is a tripartite model devised by **Ja'far aṣ-Ṣādiq** and further developed by **Kharrāz**, and it ranks among the earliest models of Sufi **psychology**.

Some theorists explain that at the center of the heart is the "innermost secret" or **mystery** (*sirr*), which some describe as analogous to conscience. According to **'Amr al-Makkī**, for example, the *qalb* represents love, within which is contained the *rūḥ* of **proximity**, which is in turn the dwelling place of the *sirr* of **union** with God. In a somewhat more elaborate four-part model, **Nūrī** explains that the locus of surrender (*islām*) is the center of one's being (the *ṣadr*, a kind of spiritual pericardium), which requires one to overcome the ego (*nafs*). Enclosed within that is *qalb*, the locus of faith (*īmān*), with its requirements of self-denial. At the next level inward, the *fu'ād* contains mystical **knowledge** (*ma'rifa*), which requires **self-scrutiny**. At the innermost center of the "heart" is the *lubb* (kernel, marrow, pith), home of the acknowledgment of the divine transcendent **unity**, which requires absolute fidelity to God. **Tirmidhī** developed a similar four-part model, further identifying each of the four elements with one of the four aspects of the **soul**/self: commanding evil (*ṣadr*), inspiring (*qalb*), blaming (*fu'ād*), and resting in tranquility (*lubb*). Most important, the heart is the seat not only of **ethical virtue** but of **knowledge**. Sufi **poets** and other authors describe the heart also as the locus of the **vision** of the Beloved. Common related expressions used to describe spiritually advanced individuals include "people of . . ." (*ahl-i dil*), "owner of . . ." (*ṣāḥibdil*), "masters of . . ." (*arbāb al-qulūb*) and "possessors of . . ." (*ūlū 'l-albāb*) hearts. *See also* COLOR.

HEAVEN. The supraterrestrial **realms**, the various levels of firmament "above" earth, and the state and/or place of eternal happiness awaiting the faithful who die in **grace**. The Heavens (*as-samā'*), taken in the first sense here, are traditionally said to have seven levels, each sometimes associated with one of the seven major **prophets**, and through which the Prophet arose during his **Ascension**. Early apocalyptic texts in the **Qur'ān** describe how at the end of time these "heavens" will be rolled up like a scroll and be no more. Muslim tradition generally uses the scriptural designation of the "Garden" (*al-janna*), or **Paradise**, to refer to the realm of final reward for the righteous. For Sufis generally, the Garden of Paradise represents pure **intimacy** with **God**, and many have insisted that if **Hell** were the place of intimacy they would prefer to be there. Even desire for Heaven can be an obstacle to one's relationship with God. **Rābi'a**, for example, insisted that love alone—not hope of reward or fear of punishment—was a worthy spiritual motive.

HELL. The state or **realm** in which unrepentant sinners will be punished for consistently choosing what is "other than **God**." The **Qur'ān** speaks of "the **Fire**" (*an-nār*), "the Flaming" reality (*al-jaḥīm* or *as-saqar* or *aṣ-ṣa'īr*), "the Pressure" (*al-ḥuṭama*), or "the

Abyss" (*al-hāwiya*). Many Muslims consider Hell a physical as well as spiritual reality. Mainstream Muslim tradition has long allowed for the possibility that God might forgive the most heinous sins of a person bound for Hell, and that Hell functions for some individuals much as Purgatory does in Christian **theology**: a temporary abode whose purpose is to cleanse and make possible a heavenly reward after all. In their poems and prayers, many Sufis have insisted that **fear** of Hell is an unacceptable motive for good **behavior**. Some have discussed the tradition that says the "believer sees by the **light** of God," explaining that the light of faith alone can extinguish the fires of Hell and show them for the utter darkness that they represent. *See also* ESCHATOLOGY; HEAVEN.

HERMENEUTICS. Principles and methods of interpretation of sacred texts, including most prominently scriptural **exegesis**. One of the earliest major Sufi exegetes, **Sahl at-Tustarī**, laid out a number of important hermeneutical guidelines that exerted a profound influence on subsequent generations of Sufi **Qur'ān**ic commentators. A fundamental principle is the understanding that **outward** expression, or **form**, conceals the **inward** substance of **meaning.** Combining that with the Qur'ān's own suggestion (3:7) that there are verses whose meaning is "categorical" (*muḥkamāt*) and thus not subject to interpretation, as well as verses whose significance is (according to some translators) "in need of further elaboration" (*mutashābihāt*, referring to the so-called ambiguous verses), the interpretative possibilities begin to multiply.

Sahl and his successors were careful to note that the exoteric or outward meanings must be understood as a foundation (a level of exegesis called *tafsīr*), before one could proceed to the inward meanings through esoteric interpretation known as *ta'wīl*. In Sahl's view, the Sufi reads the sacred text for a kind inspiration through the imaginative power stirred by the text, a "keynote" (to use G. Böwering's term) that elicits "mental associations." Everything depends on the Sufi exegete's basic assumptions about the function of the Qur'ān: it is, to be sure, a source of guidance concerning specific matters governing the pursuit of a religious life on the outward level; but it is, more importantly, guidance, light, and knowledge inwardly.

Sahl and subsequent Sufi exegetes further elaborated on the possibilities for interpreting each scriptural text, adding to outward and inward meanings the much-debated levels of ethical (*ḥadd*) and mystical (*maṭla'*) significance. In addition, the concept of progressive **revelation** implied in the principle of *naskh* (abrogation) is particularly important: because human beings are not capable of absorbing the full divine truth at a stroke, God has seen fit to reveal it piecemeal, making it necessary to supersede some earlier revelations with subsequent disclosures. Finally, one of the more important terms Sufis use to describe the whole hermeneutical endeavor is *istinbāṭ* (deeper understanding), from a root that suggests the discovery of a hidden source that overflows inexhaustibly.

HIERARCHY. An **organizational** feature both on the level of **cosmological** structures and in the **institutional** frameworks of many **orders** and, in a broader way, within Muslim religious communities in general. As for the overall sociological structures of Muslim religious communities, the ancient distinction among the **Companions**, Followers (second generation among the earliest Muslims), and Followers of the Followers, along with various generalized rankings within each of those categories according to spiritual qualities and **knowledge**, set an important pattern. **Shī'ī** tradition has institutionalized more obviously hierarchical structures than the Sunnī majority. This is evident both in the **theologies** of history that led to belief in a succession of spiritual leaders in the family of the **Prophet** known as *imāms*, and in the hierarchical structures of religious **authority** and **law** in which two ranks of *āyatullāh* (sign of God), and two of *ḥujjat-al-islām* (proof of Islam) exercise priority over the lower orders of *thiqqat-al-islām* (trustee of Islam) and *mullā*.

To a lesser degree, the history of Sunnī communities also evidence varying degrees of at least implicit hierarchical ranks among the community. One could either earn various titles through practice or accomplishment (such as **martyr**, pilgrim, warrior for the faith, professional religious scholar) or have a title bestowed or attributed (such as ***shaykh***, *sayyid* [descendant of the Prophet], or *mujaddid* [renewer promised by God at the turn of each new Islamic century]). It is in the latter category especially that Sufi hierarchical rankings generally fall. A cosmic spiritual hierarchy consists of several ranks of figures known as the "Men of the Unseen World" (*rijāl al-ghayb*), including **Chiefs**, **Chosen Ones, Pole**, **Substitutes**, and **Supports**. Finally, structures of **governance** within the orders manifest an often high degree of hierarchical organization.

ḤIFẒ' AL-QUR'ĀN. *See* QUR'ĀN, MEMORIZING.

HIJRA. "Migration," the technical term that refers to the journey of the young Muslim community from **Mecca** to **Medina** in 1/622. For Sufis, *hijra* also refers **metaphorically** to the journeys away from the security of home and into the unknown upon which **God** told all the **prophets** to embark, trusting only in their Creator. By extension, each seeker of God must set out on his or her own *hijra* "toward God and His Messenger" that is the spiritual quest.

ḤIKAM. *See* APHORISM.

ḤILYAT AL-AWLIYĀ'. *Ornament of the Friends of God*, major **hagiographical** work of **Abū Nu'aym al-Iṣfahānī**. Published in modern **Arabic** editions in as many as 10 or 12 volumes, the work was completed around 422/1031 with the express purpose of defending Sufism against its detractors. It includes records of some 649 famous Sufis whom it calls specifically "**ascetics**" (*nussāk*). It parallels in a general way the work of the contemporary **Sulamī** but includes far more anecdotal material, and it served in part as a model for the **Persian** hagiographical work of Farīd ad-Dīn **'Aṭṭār**.

HINDUISM. The dominant family of religious traditions indigenous to **India**, where Islam and Hinduism first encountered each other seriously from the sixth/12th century on. Sufism's contacts and mutual interaction with Hinduism have been numerous and significant, especially since individual holy persons invested with spiritual teaching authority have been accorded special roles in both traditions. As a result, influential Indian Muslims have sometimes consulted not only with Sufi ***shaykhs***, but with Hindu gurus as well. And Hindu devotees still visit the **tombs** of Sufi saints, such as **Mu'īn ad-Dīn Chishtī**, in considerable numbers. Several major Sufi authors have engaged elements of Hindu thought and practice from a more theoretical perspective. Perhaps the most influential of these is **Dārā Shikūh**, whose *Confluence of the Two Seas* was a comparative study of major concepts in

Sufism and Vedanta thought; and whose translation of 52 Upanishads into **Persian** remains a landmark in interreligious relations in India.

ḤĪRĪ, ABŪ 'UTHMĀN AL- (d. 298/910). Khurāsānī ascetic widely considered responsible for the beginnings of Sufism in Nishapur and credited with establishing one of the first formal regimens of **formation**. A follower of **Yaḥyā ibn Mu'ādh** and maternal grandfather of **Sulamī**, he is sometimes identified as an important figure in the early history of the **Malāmatīya**. Many of his sayings are preserved in the major **manuals**.

HISTORIOGRAPHY. Traditions in the documentation and analysis of the **history** of Sufism and its **institutions**. Major examples of the Sufi adaptation of methods of historical recording date from at least the fourth/10th century, in the early **manuals**. Certain recurring themes in these and later sources suggest the evolution of at least some general principles of historical interpretation, often woven tightly with **hagiographical** concerns. Such themes include, for example, divergence of opinion between Sufis and the generality of religious scholars concerning the nature and scope of the religious disciplines; **hermeneutical** issues in **exegesis**; the identification of "schools" or **generations** within Sufism; the relationship between more "settled" or institutional Sufism and the socially and ideologically marginal elements represented by ***qalandars***, for example; and the appropriate role of Sufis in public life generally and relationships between Sufis and **political** authorities in particular. An overriding issue in Islamicate historiography generally that has also influenced Sufi sources is the conviction that the era of the **Prophet** and his **Companions** constituted the apex of human history, and that a process of spiritual entropy set in at the time of his death.

HISTORY, SUFI INTERPRETATIONS OF. The record of tradition, the story of the relationship between present and past, and the thread by which one remains connected with the sources of spiritual **authority**. For Sufi authors generally, history is composed of the example of the **Prophet** and the narratives and sayings of great Sufis of the past who have embodied that example. As a whole, **hagiographical** sources construe history on the framework of **generations**, forming a complex network of relationships that build on each other over the centuries. *See* the Introduction for a survey of the history of Sufism.

ḤIZB. *See* LITANIES.

HONORIFICS. Names and titles bestowed as acknowledgments of public esteem and affection as well as more informal spiritual **authority**. In addition to the official designations devised to distinguish the various **ranks** in Sufi **governance** and other **hierarchical** structures, popular usage in different cultures has conferred on individuals known for piety and learning such terms of respect and endearment as *bābā* (papa) and *dede* (elder), some of which have also become designations of formal leadership in **orders**.

HOPE. An important aspect of spiritual **experience**, typically paired with its essential complement, **fear**. Abū Ḥāmid al-**Ghazālī**, along with earlier Sufis, speaks of hope and fear as the "two wings of a **bird**" that is incapable of level flight without both and is grounded altogether without either. **Qushayrī** identifies hope as the "**heart's** attachment to an object of **love**" that it believes will occur or become available in the future.

ḤUBB. *See* LOVE.

ḤUḌŪR. *See* PRESENCE.

HUJWĪRĪ, 'ALĪ IBN 'UTHMĀN DĀTĀ GANJ BAKHSH (d. c. 465/1072). Mystical **theorist**, historian of Sufism, and Ḥanafī religious scholar from present-day Afghanistan who died in Lahore (Pakistan), credited with writing the first Sufi work in **Persian**. His systematic **manual**, *The Revelation of Realities Veiled* (*Kashf al-Maḥjūb*), is an invaluable source of information on Sufism's formative years. Little is known about his personal life and Sufi associations, but his popular appeal remains broad and many regional pilgrims still make **visitation** to his **tomb** in Lahore.

ḤURŪFĪYA. An **esoteric** sectarian tradition founded in **Iran** during the late 14th century by a Sufi **ascetic** named **Faḍl Allāh Astarābādī**

(740/1340–796/1394). His early concern with the interpretation of **dreams** was eventually superseded by an interest in the esoteric meanings of letters of the **alphabet**, particularly as a vehicle for communicating a distinctive anthropology and prophetology. The underlying **theology** turns on such concepts as emanation and ongoing process in divine communication. Faḍl Allāh was executed for his views. The organization spread throughout the Middle East and was particularly influential among the **Bektashīya** and some Persian Sufi groups, but it never gained large numbers of adherents.

ḤUSĀM AD-DĪN ÇELEBĪ (c. 623/1226–683/1284). Anatolian Sufi from a family of ***akhīs***, disciple of **Rūmī** who became the third leader of the **Mawlawīya**. Rūmī himself appointed him as ***shaykh*** of two *khānqāhs*. He convinced Rūmī to begin writing his major **didactic** work, the *Spiritual Couplets*, and served as the **poet's** secretary. He also crafted what would become the disciplinary regime of the **order** and was largely responsible for turning the founder's **tomb** into a center for the whole order.

ḤUSAYN IBN 'ALĪ (4/626–61/680). Son of **'Alī** and the **Prophet's** daughter **Fāṭima**, acclaimed by **Shī'īs** as the "proto-**martyr**." When he led a small force against Yazīd, Umayyad family heir to the caliphate, he and his family band and supporters were slaughtered at Karbalā' in **Iraq** on the 10th of Muḥarram (the first Islamic lunar month). His story soon became the stuff of legend, attributing countless **wonders** to the holy man. In Sufi circles, his story was perhaps most influential among the **Bektāshīya**, but he does figure as a link in the **lineages** of many **orders** that trace their origins to the Prophet.

ḤUṢRĪ, ABŪ 'L-ḤUSAYN (d. 371/982). Ascetic from Baṣra and later associate of **Shiblī** in Baghdad. Sufi authors often cite his observations on self-denial.

– I –

IBERIAN PENINSULA. Western-most region of Europe, bordering on France to the northeast and otherwise bounded by the Mediterranean Sea on the south and southeast, and the Atlantic Ocean to the north and west. Prior to the arrival of Islam across the Straits of Gibraltar in 93/711, the peninsula had been largely under the sway of Arian Christian Visigothic kings. Muslim forces soon controlled approximately the southern two-thirds of the peninsula, a region known in Arabic as *al-andalus*, or **Andalusia**. Major cities included Toledo, Seville, Cordoba, and Granada. During the eighth and ninth centuries, Cordoba was the capital of the Umayyad Emirate; it remained the capital after Umayyad rulers proclaimed themselves caliphs. After the caliphate collapsed into feudal decentralization in 423/1031, two successive Moroccan regimes invaded and made Seville their capital. As the Christian kings gradually reconquered the peninsula from the north, Muslim regimes lost first Toledo, then Seville and Cordoba. By the late eighth/14th century, the sole surviving Muslim regime was the Nasrid dynasty in Granada, which held out until 898/1492. Some Iberian Sufi scholars have characterized Andalusian Sufism—Maghribī Sufism in general, for that matter—as retaining its flexibility and focus on the individual long after "Eastern" Sufism had become markedly establishment-bound. Among the more prominent Sufis of Iberian origin are Abū 'l-'Abbās al-**Mursī**, **Abū Madyan**, **Fāṭima of Cordoba**, **Ibn 'Abbād** of Ronda, **Ibn al-'Arabī**, **Ibn al-'Arīf**, and **Ibn Masarra**. The most influential of the **orders** in Andalusia was the **Shādhilīya**.

IBLĪS. *See* SATAN.

IBN 'ABBĀD AR-RUNDĪ (733/1333–792/1390). Iberian-born mystical author from the southern hill town of Ronda, prominent ***shaykh*** of the **Shādhilīya**. His family moved to Morocco when he was a boy, and he was educated at various Mālikī *madrasas* in **North Africa**. He became acquainted with a number of famous Sufi *shaykh*s, particularly in **Fez** and Salé, and studied classic **Arabic** Sufi texts of **Ghazālī** and **Abū Ṭālib al-Makkī**. Around the middle of the eighth/14th century, the Shādhilī **order** had made its way to Morocco and spread with the increasing popularity of the **aphorisms** of **Ibn 'Aṭā' Allāh**. Ibn 'Abbād's most important works include a commentary on those aphorisms and two collections of **letters** of spiritual **direction.** He counseled a simple life of devotion and self-scrutiny uncomplicated by the speculative approaches of fellow Iberians such as **Ibn al-'Arīf**, **Ibn al-'Arabī**, **Ibn Masarra**, and **Ibn Sab'īn**.

IBN 'AJĪBA, AḤMAD (1161/1746–1224/1809). Moroccan **exegete** and religious scholar, prolific author of Arabic commentaries on the mystical poetry and treatises of earlier Sufis, and affiliate of the **Darqāwīya**. An initial attraction to Sufism came via **Ibn 'Aṭā' Allāh of Alexandria's** *Book of* ***Aphoristic*** *Wisdom* (*Kitāb al-ḥikam*) and his joining an **order** marked a major **conversion** for him. His **autobiographical** account, *The Chronicle* (*Fahrasa*), is one of the more extensive of the **genre**; and his "glossary" of Sufi technical **terms**, *The Book of the Ascension in Perceiving the Realities of Sufism* (*Kitāb al-mi'rāj at-tashawwuf ilā ḥaqā'iq at-taṣawwuf*), suggests that he thought of the spiritual quest in terms of the **Prophet's Ascension**.

IBN AL-'ARABĪ, MUḤYĪ AD-DĪN (560/1165–638/1240). Iberian-born visionary mystical author whose extensive writings exerted profound influence on Sufi thought from the **Maghrib** to Malaysia. Born in Murcia, not far to the northeast of Granada, he moved to Seville as a boy and called that city home for over 20 years. During those years he also traveled in the Maghrib and Iberia, attaching himself to a number of Sufi ***shaykhs*** (including two **women**). When he was about 30, he embarked on more extensive travels that would take him more than once to Cairo, **Jerusalem**, **Mecca**, central **Anatolia**, and major cities in **Iraq** and **Syria**. His complex masterwork, the *Meccan Revelations* (*Al-Futūḥāt al-makkīya*), develops a sweeping conception of the spiritual life based on an intricate **theory** of **knowledge**. He also elaborated perhaps the most imaginative mystical **prophetology** in his *Bezels of Wisdom* (*Fuṣūṣ al-ḥikam*). Through the efforts of his principal Anatolian student, Ṣadr ad-Dīn al-**Qūnawī**, as well as later authors such as the **Persian poet Jāmī**, his often controversial thought enjoyed wide dissemination, and was a major ingredient in the ***wujūdī*** **controversy**. Emphasizing the importance of an immediate divine connection and spirit-**initiation**, he neither founded nor belonged to a formal **order**. He was buried in Damascus and his **tomb** remains a goal of pilgrim **visitation**.

IBN AL-'ARĪF (481/1088–536/1141). Iberian-born mystical author and religious scholar who taught in several important Spanish centers of traditional Islamic scholarship. He is closely associated with the city of Almeria, where **Ghazālī**-inspired Sufism thrived in opposition to the disapproval of government-sponsored religious authorities. His sole extant work is a brief theoretical **treatise** entitled *The Beauties of Mystical Sessions* (*Maḥāsin al-majālis*), which was influenced by the work of **Anṣārī** and in turn influenced the thought of **Ibn al-'Arabī**.

IBN AL-FĀRIḌ (576/1181–632/1235). Egyptian Sufi **poet** often acclaimed as the author of the finest mystical **lyric** poems in **Arabic**. He does not appear to have been formally affiliated with an **order**, preferring years of solitary life in the deserts of Egypt and the western **Arabian Peninsula**. His most celebrated poems are the ***Wine*** *Ode* (*al-Khamrīya*) and the *Greater T-Rhyming Ode* (*at-Tā'īyat al-kubrā*, formally titled the *Ode on Spiritual Sojourning* [*Naẓm as-sulūk*]). He crafted original, imaginative **metaphors** of the spiritual quest and of the divine-human relationship, beginning with the fundamental requirements of Muslim tradition and elaborating on their **inward** meanings.

IBN 'AṬĀ', ABŪ 'L-'ABBĀS (d. 309/921–2 or 311/923–4). 'Irāqī Sufi, prominent supporter of **Ḥallāj**, executed perhaps because of that support. He was involved in differences of opinion between the rather flamboyant Ḥallāj and the more theologically cautious **Junayd** and his circle.

IBN 'AṬĀ' ALLĀH OF ALEXANDRIA, TĀJ AD-DĪN AḤMAD (d. 709/1309). Egyptian mystical author and **hagiographer**, Shāfi'ī and/or Mālikī religious scholar, prominent member of the **Shādhilīya**. The most influential of the 20 extant works credited to him is the *Book of* ***Aphoristic*** *Wisdom* (*Kitāb al-ḥikam*), on which **Ibn 'Abbād**, Aḥmad **Zarrūq**, and **Ibn 'Ajība** wrote important **commentaries**. Sometimes referred to as the "Breviary" (**office**) of the Shādhilīya, the work's 262 thought-provoking sayings offer instruction on interpreting the seeker's inner life. The aphorisms are followed by four very brief "**treatises**," the last of which is actually a small collection of **supplicatory** prayers. In addition, he authored an account of the sayings of his **order's** founder, Abū 'l-Ḥasan ash-Shādhilī and of Abū 'l-'Abbās al-**Mursī**, his own ***shaykh*** (*The Subtle Graces of the Feats of Abū 'l-'Abbās al-Mursī and his Shaykh Abū* *'l-Ḥasan* [*Kitāb al-laṭā'if fī manāqib Abī 'l-'Abbās al-Mursī wa shaykhihi Abū 'l-Ḥasan*]) He was among the most vociferous critics of **Ibn Taymīya**.

IBN KHAFĪF, ABŪ 'ABD ALLĀH MUḤAMMAD (d. 371/982). Persian religious scholar (Ẓāhirī in **law** and Ash'arī in **theology**), **ascetic** and mystical author who founded a *ribāṭ* in Shiraz and whose thought influenced the later **organizations** of **Kāzarūnī** and **Suhrawardī**. He sympathized with Sufis who identified themselves with the views of **Ḥallāj** but also found the more "sober" approach of **Junayd** attractive.

IBN MASARRA (269/883–319/931). Iberian mystical author, philosopher, and **ascetic** of Cordoba. His travels in the central **Middle East** likely put him in touch with mystics in the tradition of **Junayd**. His critics accused him of "free thinking" because of the negative implications of his views on the soul for mainstream Islamic **theology**. Although he is not regarded as the founder of a formal Sufi **organization**, he did accept disciples and teach them his distinctive mystical philosophy. None of the works attributed to him have survived.

IBN MASHĪSH, 'ADB AS-SALĀM (d. 625/1228). Moroccan **ascetic** and mystic who was a disciple of **Abū Madyan** and teacher of Abū 'l-Ḥasan ash-**Shādhilī**. Later tradition accorded him the rank of "**pole** of the West," opposite number to the spiritual role of **'Abd al-Qādir al-Jīlānī** in the "east." His tomb is arguably the most important goal of Sufi **visitation** in Morocco.

IBN-I MUNAWWAR, MUḤAMMAD (d. late sixth/12th century). Persian hagiographer, author of a major life of **Abū Sa'īd** ibn Abī 'l-Khayr, *The Secrets of God's Mystical Oneness* (*Asrār at-tawḥīd*), one of the most extensive integrated accounts dedicated to any single **Friend of God**.

IBN SAB'ĪN (c. 613/1217–669/1270). Andalusian Sufi and Aristotelian philosopher from Murcia. Some religious scholars criticized him for monistic tendencies and he went into exile, first in Morocco and eventually Tunisia. Continued pressure from religious authorities prompted him to move farther east, to Cairo, where controversy continued to surround him. An order of followers under the name Sab'īnīya was never widely established.

IBN SĪNĀ, ABŪ 'ALĪ (a.k.a. Avicenna) (370/980–428/1037). Persian philosopher and mystic born in **Central Asia**. He was the author of a series of three Persian-language "visionary **recitals**" (each entitled a *risāla*, "**treatise**," in their titles, but belonging to the **genre** of *ḥikāyāt*, "narratives"), a genre later taken up by Shihāb ad-Dīn Yaḥyā as-**Suhrawardī** "Maqtūl," as well as an **allegorical** work called the *Book of the* ***Ascension*** (*Mi'rājnama*). The recitals, cast in the first-person, lay out a cosmic landscape across which the spiritual seeker must journey. In the fourth work, also in Persian, he prefaces a traditional version of the **Prophet's** Ascension with a psychological and epistemology framework and then intersperses an allegoresis into the text of the story. He explains from the outset that his purpose is to unveil the inner **meaning** of the narrative.

IBN TAYMĪYA (661/1263–728/1328). 'Irāqī-born **theologian**, Ḥanbalī religious scholar, and influential anti-Sufi polemicist. He spent much of his life in **Damascus**, where he was active in political affairs, and was imprisoned for a time in Cairo on charges of theological anthropomorphism. His critique of what he considered deviant beliefs and practices of some Sufis (particularly **visitation**) later became an important ingredient in the **reformist** ideology of the **Wahhābī** movement in the **Arabian Peninsula**.

IBN AL-WAQT. *See* MOMENT.

IBRĀHĪM IBN ADHAM (c. 122/730–161/777). Khurāsānī ascetic (born in Balkh, in present-day Afghanistan) who traveled widely in the **Middle East**. Subject of a popularly embellished legend, he is said to have traded his royal prerogatives for a life of **poverty** and to have had a special relationship to **Khiḍr**. A now-defunct Sufi **order** named after him apparently had a relatively short history.

IBRĀHĪM IBN AL-KHAWWĀṢ (d. c. 291/904). 'Irāqī itinerant **ascetic** who spent time in the **Iranian** city of Rayy and is buried there.

Hagiographical sources associate him especially with an emphasis on the centrality of the virtue of **trust**. He is said to have declined even to associate with the enigmatic **Khiḍr** lest his reliance on anyone diminish his **trust** in **God**. Often cited by Sufi authors, his most famous disciple was Ja'far al-**Khuldī**. A work on **poverty** attributed to him is no longer extant.

IḤSĀN. *See* SPIRITUALITY.

IḤYĀ' 'ULŪM AD-DĪN. Abū Ḥāmid al-**Ghazālī's** masterwork of pastoral and mystical theology, *The Revitalization of the Religious Disciplines*. Written after his withdrawal from teaching in 488/1095, the work is structured in four quarters and further divided into a total of **forty** "books" covering the full range of beliefs and practices he regarded as essential to a healthy spiritual development. He begins with matters of worship and social relationships, sections he regarded as pertaining to all good Muslims, concluding the first half of the work with a book on the **Prophet** as exemplar. Advising caution for anyone who would go further, he moves into major sections on evils against which the more spiritually advanced person must guard, and the loftiest virtues. The last quarter in particular calls for a more rarified level of spiritual **knowledge** as well as a much higher form of discipline.

IJĀZAT AT-TABARRUK. *See* AUTHORITY.

IKHLĀṢ. *See* SINCERITY.

ILHĀM. *See* INSPIRATION.

ILLUMINATION. A way of describing how **God** works in the **hearts** of the spiritually advanced, and the name given to a school of **Persian** Muslim philosophy associated with Shihāb ad-Dīn Yaḥyā as-**Suhrawardī** "Maqtūl." In the first sense, Sufis speak of God "casting a **light**" into the heart by which the individual receives a higher form of **knowledge**. The school of thought taught the esoteric "wisdom of illumination" (*ḥikmat al-ishrāq*), which is founded on a metaphysics of light as a cosmic reality.

'ILM. *See* KNOWLEDGE, DISCURSIVE.

IMĀMZĀDA. *See* TOMB.

IMPLEMENTS. Practical and **symbolic** accoutrements associated especially with membership in Sufi **organizations**. In addition to important items of **clothing** and **headgear**, and objects such as the **begging bowl**, **staff**, and **rosary**, Sufis often carried items such as a jug or ewer (called the *ibrīq*) associated with ritual purification, and a kerchief (*rūymāl*). An item of critical importance to daily ritual is the prayer mat (*muṣallā*), which is in turn symbolically connected to the *sajjāda*, the ***shaykh*'s** prayer **carpet** that is often a major emblem of **authority**.

INCLINATIONS. A variety of spiritual **experience** manifest in "thoughts" that one can discern and understand only with subtle skills and exquisite sensitivity resulting from **knowledge** of the **science of hearts**. As they elaborated refined methods of **psychological** analysis, Sufi theorists underscored the importance of attending to even the most ephemeral movements of spirit called *khawāṭir* (sg. *khāṭir*). These elusive thoughts combine both a discursive "content" and an affective "feeling," and can originate either from God (through an **angelic** intermediary), from the **ego**-soul, or from **Satanic** whispering. A related inner movement is known by the term *wārid/wāridāt*, sometimes translated as "oncoming" thought, but it is distinguished from the *khāṭir* in that the *wārid* includes no verbal or cognitive element.

INDIA. Formerly the whole of the **South Asian** land mass that now includes the nation states of **Pakistan** and Bangladesh, as well as India. Prior to 1367/1947 the three states constituted the Indian subcontinent and were part of the British Empire. India's Muslim minority amounts to around 12 percent of a total population of nearly one billion. Islam became a major factor in Indian history around the sixth/12th century, with Muslim rule extending over much of the subcontinent through the 10th/16th century under the **Mughal** dynasty. Indian cities of importance in the history of Sufism include **Ajmīr**, Bijapur, **Delhi**, **Golconda**, Gwaliyar, and Panipat. Sufi **orders** most important there have included the **Chishtīya**, **Kubrāwīya**, **Naqshbandīya**, **Qādirīya**, **Shaṭṭārīya**, and

Suhrawardīya. Many major individual Sufis of Indian origin are cross-referenced at those entries.

INDONESIA. The largest **Southeast Asian** nation, made up of some 3,000 islands, and the modern state with the largest population of Muslims. Sufi missionaries may have participated in the introduction and spread of Islam on its two principal islands, Sumatra and Java, beginning in the seventh/13th century. But Sufi **organizations** as such began to appear in the later 1500s. Among the more important Sufi **orders** in Indonesia are the **Qādirīya** and branches of the **Shādhilīya**. The three most influential Indonesian Sufis were the 11th/17th century figures **Ḥamza Fanṣūrī**, **Rānīrī**, and **Samaṭrānī**.

INITIATION. A state of belonging to a Sufi **order** or **lineage** or of being inducted into a noninstitutional form of the Sufi **path**, as well as the **rituals** and processes associated with induction. Initiation is described as involving a wide range of experiences. "Spirit initiation" can occur through **dreams** or **visions**, when an important Sufi from the past appears to an individual and confers on that person the **cloak** of initiation. In such accounts it is often **Khiḍr** who functions as the initiator. More commonly, aspirants to membership in an order are initiated by a living ***shaykh***. The critical sign of the relationship is the **oath** (*bay'a*, *mubāya'a*) or bond (*'ahd*) by which typically the new member, after completing an extended period of **formative** probation, swears unstinting allegiance and docility to the *shaykh's* every command. Sources speak of the "knot" (*'uqda*) that symbolizes the covenant between disciple and *shaykh*. The *shaykh* invests the aspirant with the cloak (sometimes with a laying on of hands and/or a handclasp [*muṣāfaḥa*]), and imparts an individually chosen secret formula of **invocation** or personal **litany**, thereby providing access to **companionship**. The practice of investment with a belt or girdle (*shadd*) is common to **chivalric** groups but found among some Sufis also, notably the **Bektāshīya** and the **Mawlawīya**. Its symbolism was analogous to binding as in a marriage contract. One's declaration of spiritual affiliation is known as *tasammā*. *See also* AUTHORITY; GOVERNANCE; HIERARCHY.

INSPIRATION. One possible avenue or source of **knowledge** that may be associated with mystical **experience**. Sufi theorists have discussed at length the role of *ilhām* in the overall process of spiritual development. The term originated in a scriptural text (Qur'ān 91:8) which uses a verb that means "to cause one to gulp down," referring to **God's** causing the **ego**-soul to swallow its sins and awe of God. Some **exegetes** explained that God thus "explained" sin to the soul, but Muslim authors generally speak of inspiration primarily as the prerogative of **Friends of God**. Sufi authors, however, typically hold inspiration in lower regard as a source of knowledge because of its highly individualized quality.

INSTITUTIONS. A complex of formal **organizational** structures, including methods of **governance** and the exercise of **authority**, as well as the larger aspects of Sufi material culture such as the development of specific **architectural** forms and functions, most notably **residential facilities** and **tombs**. Making many institutions possible has been the funding provided by the traditional mechanism of the religiously motivated **endowment**. *Dargāh*, an important **Persian** term often used to refer a variety of institutional settings, from residential to funerary, means "court" and offers a sense of the "royal" atmosphere that has prevailed in many Sufi venues. The Arabo-Persian term *jamā'at-khāna* (assembly hall) can likewise refer to facilities of more than one function, as can the Turkish *āsitāne*.

INSTRUCTION. Alongside the various elements of spiritual **formation**, the basic education of a Sufi aspirant in Muslim tradition and in the tradition of the **order**. This aspect of general training (*tadrīb*) is typically the task of a ***shaykh*** who specializes in *ta'līm* (as distinguished from *tarbīya*), imparting fundamental religious and more basic mystical **knowledge** as it relates directly to discipline and ethical character development. Sources use a variety of terms to refer to various aspects of instruction, from *tahdhīb* (especially *ethical* matters), to *taḥkīm* (often connoting discipline in **behavior**), to *talqīn* (from a verb than means "to prompt," and suggests the imparting of a more arcane form of instruction).

INTAMĀ. *See* ORGANIZATION.

INTASABA. *See* ORGANIZATION.

INTERCESSION. The ability or power to play an intermediary role between God and human beings, whether in this life or after the death of either the intercessor or the beneficiary, or both. Muslims have long debated the question of whether any human being could play such a role (*shafā'a*). A key Qur'ānic text for those who deny the possibility is 2:254, which refers to Judgment **Day**, when there will be no leniency as a result of "friendship or intercession." However, the following verse (2:255) seems to leave open the possibility that under some circumstances, God might countenance intercession: "For who is it that can intercede before Him, except with His permission?" Why, they reason, would the scripture even mention "His permission" were there not some situation in which intercession might be acceptable? Popular Islamic piety in many parts of the world has in fact included prayer of intercession addressed to many **Friends of God** as well as to the **Prophet**. Recitation of such prayers, or depositing petitions written on scraps of paper around the **tombs** of holy figures, is often an integral part of **visitation**. *See also* ESCHATOLOGY.

INTIMACY. An aspect of spiritual **experience** related to **ecstasy** and mystical **union**. An aspect of spiritual experience sometimes listed among the **states** (by **Kalābādhī**, **Sarrāj**, and **Ghazālī**, for example) and frequently in relation especially to **desire**, **proximity, recollection**, and **love**. Intimacy can refer, for example, to "the lover's daring in the Beloved's presence," even to the point of making very bold demands. Though it is not always included among lists of **stations** or states, intimacy (*uns*) figures prominently in many of the **manuals'** analyses of the spiritual path. **Qushayrī**, for instance, locates intimacy (paired with awe [*hayba*]) after the dyad of **constriction** and **expansion** and just ahead of a triad of features associated with ecstasy. As is the case with many such pairings, the juxtaposition of a kind of hesitancy or dread with intimacy is quite a striking reminder of the complexity of Sufi understandings of the mystical life.

INTOXICATION. A frequent **metaphor** to describe the condition of an advanced mystic's **experience** of **ecstasy** or **annihilation**. The ultimate stage of **love**, intoxication (*sukr*) with the **wine** of the Beloved's **beauty** is often characterized by the experiences of perplexity and bewilderment. In short, it suggests complete loss of control and surrender to the power of God.

INVESTITURE. *See* CLOTHING; INITIATION.

INVOCATION. A form and method of **prayer** often individually assigned by a ***shaykh***, which can be either silent or vocal. Usually referred to with the term *dhikr* ("invoking, recalling, remembering," also translated as **recollection** in reference to collective or group invocation **rituals** called *dhikr al-ḥaḍra*), invocation involves rhythmic repetition of a **name** of God, syllable, word (such as *Allāh*), phrase (such as *subḥān Allāh*, Glory to God) or **litany** tailored to the spiritual needs of the individual seeker. Practitioners often use a **rosary** to keep track of repetitions and changes of invocatory expressions, and the ritual can involve **breath control**, especially in the case of silent or "hidden" invocation (*dhikr al-khafī*). Invocation at set times during the day is called *dhikr al-awqāt* or "**office**." Specific uses of invocation are among the factors that distinguish one order from another, and those that consider it a central practice typically developed very detailed instructions.

INWARD. A dimension of reality accessible only to those with the acute insight to penetrate beneath **outward** appearances of **form** to the spiritual **meaning**. Sufi theorists, however, underscore the **hermeneutical** principle that inward (*bāṭin*) meaning invariably presupposes an outward reality whose requirements cannot be ignored.

IQBĀL, SIR MUḤAMMAD (c. 1293/1876–1357/1938). European-educated **Indian** religious scholar, philosopher, **poet** and mystical author in **Persian** and **Urdu**, and **reformer**. A major theme in his critique of Sufism involved an emphasis on healthy psychological development as an antidote to the notion of **annihilation** and related excesses. In a work dedicated to his son Jāwīd, he uses the Dantesque **literary** conceit of a cosmic journey under the guidance of **Rūmī**, whose **didactic** tradition he espouses. Adopting much of the idiom of Sufi poetry, he nevertheless warned against any signs of the abdication of rational, intelligent belief. He does not seem to have belonged to any particular Sufi **order**.

ĪRĀN. Modern nation-state occupying the largely high arid plateau between **Iraq** and the **Persian** Gulf on the west and southwest; the Caucasus, the Caspian Sea, and **Central Asia** to the north; Afghanistan and **Pakistan** to the east; and the **Arabian** Sea to the south. Also known more generically as Persia (a name deriving originally from a western province called Fars), the formerly Zoroastrian region was Islamized from the mid-seventh/first century when the last Sasanian king was deposed. Scores of major Sufis have hailed from Persia, including, for example, **'Abd al-Qādir al-Jīlānī**, **Ḥāfiẓ**, **Ibn Khafīf**, **Kirmānī**, **Najm ad-Dīn Dāyā Rāzī**, **Rūzbihān Baqlī**, **Sa'dī**, **Sahl at-Tustarī**, **Sanā'ī**, **Shabistarī**, **Simnānī**, the **Suhrawardīs**, and **Yaḥyā ibn Mu'ādh**. The Sufi **order** most prominent there over many centuries has been the **Ni'mat-allāhīya**.

'IRĀQ. Modern nation-state generally covering the land mass formerly known as Mesopotamia, just north of the **Arabian Peninsula**, south of **Turkey**, west of **Iran**, and east of Jordan and **Syria**. Many famous Sufis have hailed especially from **Baghdad** and **Basra**, including **Rābi'a**. With the exception of the **Qādirīya**, few of the more significant still-surviving Sufi **orders** originated in Iraq, but the region has the distinction of being one of the most fertile seedbeds for the germination of what became seminal movements and schools led by figures cross-referenced under the Baghdad and Basra entries.

'IRĀQĪ, FAKHR AD-DĪN. *See* FAKHR AD-DĪN.

'IRFĀN. *See* KNOWLEDGE, MYSTICAL.

'ĪSĀWĪYA. Moroccan Sufi **order** founded by Muḥammad ibn 'Īsā al-Mukhtārī (c. 842/1467–930/1523), who studied with disciples of **Jazūlī** and was noted for his **clairvoyance**. The order's teachings reflect considerable influence of the **Shādhilīya**, and its **lineage** includes major figures of that order. 'Īsāwā (a plural referring to the order's members) enjoyed some success in establishing their **institutions** in Algeria and Tunisia, as well as in **Egypt** and **Syria**. An important symbolic focus of the order remains the founder's **tomb** in Meknes.

***ISHĀRA*. *See* ALLUSION.**

***'ISHQ*. *See* LOVE.**

***ISHRĀQ*. *See* ILLUMINATION.**

***ISLĀM*. *See* SURRENDER.**

ISLĀM. Name of the third of the "Abrahamic" religious traditions, that grew out of the preaching of **Muḥammad**, from an **Arabic** term meaning "grateful **surrender**." Upon the death of the **Prophet**, in 10/632, a dispute arose concerning the transfer of leadership authority. A minority insisted that the Prophet had designated **'Alī** as his "caliph," and as they continued to affirm his legitimacy, they came to be known as the Supporters or Party—**Shī'a**—of 'Alī. The majority position asserted that the Prophet had designated no successor and wanted the leadership issue decided by a group of elders. They argued that this was indeed the "example" (*sunna*) of the Prophet, and their interpretation of **historical** events has come to be known as the foundation of **Sunnī** Islam.

Within less than a century after the death of the **Prophet**, the tradition had spread from the **Arabian Peninsula** eastward through **Iran**, into **Central Asia**, and as far as the Indus River; northward into **Iraq** and **Syria**; and westward across **North Africa** to the **Iberian Peninsula**, eradicating much of the Byzantine Empire. After the death of the last of the "Rightly Guided Caliphs" ('Alī according to Sunnī reckoning), the first of a series of dynasties arose. The **Umayyads** established their new capital in **Damascus** where they presided over a dramatic expansion until brought down in 133/750 by the **'Abbāsids**. From their newly founded capital of **Baghdad** the 'Abbāsid caliphs remained, at least symbolically, the universally acknowledged leader of all Muslims. But during its five-century tenure, the 'Abbāsid dynasty steadily lost control over its far-flung realm as governors in distant provinces broke away and proclaimed themselves *amīrs* (regional rulers) and even caliphs (claiming universal authority). In 656/1258, Baghdad was sacked by Mongol descendants of Genghis Khan, virtually putting an end to the caliphate as an effective institution.

During the subsequent 250 years or so, political fragmentation saw numerous Muslim-led political entities come and go, including the very important two and a half century rule of the **Mamlūk dynasty** headquartered in Cairo. Meanwhile, Islam continued to spread in **Southeast Asia** and sub-Saharan Africa. By the early 10th/16th century, three emerging "Gunpowder Empires" began to reconsolidate regional power. Occupying the territories of the Byzantine Empire, and then some, the Sunnī **Ottoman Turks** ruled most of the central **Middle East**, **North Africa**, and much of Eastern Europe. From its capital at Delhi, the Sunnī **Mughal** dynasty dominated **South Asia**. Geographically in the middle, the "Twelver" Shī'ī **Ṣafawid** dynasty reunited Iran. As these empires diminished through the 12th/18th and 13th/19th centuries, colonial powers carved up many predominantly Muslim areas into what would become modern nation-states.

ISMĀ'ĪL SHAHĀD, SHĀH (1193/1779–1246/1831). Indian religious scholar, **reformer** and preacher against Sufi "excesses," grandson of **Shāh Walī Allāh of Dehlī** and disciple of **Aḥmad Brelwī**. Ironically, the **tomb** of this man who railed against popular "funerary innovations" has become famous in more recent times.

ISOLATION. An aspect of mystical **experience** that suggests radical detachment from all that is not **God**, resulting in more perfect readiness for ultimate **union**. One example of how Sufi **theorists** developed the concept is **Anṣārī**'s placement of *tafrīd* in his two **typologies** of spiritual progress. In his earlier **Persian** work *The Hundred Fields*, *tafrīd* precedes **knowledge** (*'ilm*) and is numbered 70 of 100 **stages**. In the **Arabic** *Dwelling Places of the Wayfarers*, he locates isolation much later in the list, at number 98, just after "de-husking" (*tajrīd*, a process of becoming utterly vulnerable through the stripping away of all defenses) and prior to conjoining in union (*jam'*).

IṢṬILĀḤĀT. *See* LEXICONS; TERMINOLOGY.

ISTINBĀṬ. *See* HERMENEUTICS.

ITTIḤĀD. *See* UNION.

– J –

***JABARŪT*.** *See* REALMS.

***JADHB(A)*.** *See* MYSTIC.

JA'FAR AṢ-ṢĀDIQ (c. 80/699–148/765). Medinan-born **traditionist**, **exegete**, and religious scholar and leader of the early **Shī'ī** community who counseled against open revolt against the **Sunnī** majority. He was eventually acknowledged by most Shī'ī Muslims as the sixth in the line of ***imāms***, though the larger community split over whether to follow his first-designated son Ismā'īl, who predeceased his father, or the later-designated son 'Abd Allāh. Those who took the former option became known as Ismā'īlīs, while those who chose the latter (eventually giving their allegiance actually to Mūsā, another son of Ja'far by another mother, since 'Abd Allāh died without a male heir) are now known as "Twelvers." Beyond his powerful standing as a paragon of virtue, Ja'far's greatest significance for Sufism lies in his contribution to **symbolic** exegesis. His **Qur'ānic hermeneutic** profoundly influenced that of **Dhū 'n-Nūn**. In addition, he formulated three foundational **typologies** or analyses of spiritual progress: 12 sources of mystical knowledge; 12 heavenly constellations of the heart; and **forty** lights emanating from the divine **light**. He occupies a place of honor in the **lineages** of many Sufi organizations. *See also* NUMBERS.

JAHĀNĀRĀ (1023/1614–1092/1681). Indian mystic and **hagiographer**, older sister of **Dārā Shikūh**, initiated by Mullāh Shāh into the **Qādirīya**. This **celibate** daughter of the **Mughal** emperor Shāh Jahān (builder of the Tāj Maḥal) later became a member of the **Chishtīya** and wrote a biography of its founder. Buried in Delhi near the tomb of **Niẓām ad-Dīn Awliyā'**, she is among India's most famous Sufi **women**.

JALĀL AD-DĪN ḤUSAYN AL-BUKHĀRĪ "MAKHDŪM-I JAHĀNĪYĀN" (707/1308–785/1384). Indian mystic initiated into Sufism by Naṣīr ad-Dīn Maḥmūd **Chirāgh-i Dihlī**; ***shaykh*** of the **Chishtīya** in Ucch (present-day **Pakistan**). He traveled widely in the **Middle East** and **Central Asia** and eventually was put in charge of 40 *khānqāhs*.

Traditional accounts credit him with having met the **Prophet** during a trip to **Medina**.

JALĀL AD-DĪN RŪMĪ. *See* RŪMĪ, JALĀL AD-DĪN.

***JAM'*.** *See* UNION.

JAMĀ'AT ALĪ SHĀH (d. 1371/1951). Indian Naqshbandī reformer and ***shaykh*** of the school of **Rae Bareilly**. He was deeply involved in ongoing mid-14th/20th century debates among religious scholars over the validity of Sufism.

***JAMĀ'AT KHĀNA*.** *See* INSTITUTIONS.

***JAMĀL*.** *See* BEAUTY.

JAMĀL AD-DĪN (JAMĀLĪ KANBŌH), ḤĀMID IBN FAḌL ALLĀH (d. 942/1536). Indian hagiographer and **poet**, member of the **Suhrawardīya** in Delhi. His hagiographical account of major **Suhrawardī** and **Chishtī** ***shaykh***s, *Lifestories of the Knowers [of God]* (*Siyar al-'ārifīn*), is regarded as the first Indian multi-**lineage** biographical anthology in the memorial **genre** and among the highest quality of its kind.

JĀMĪ, MAWLĀNA 'ABD AR-RAḤMĀN (817/1414–898/1492). Persian mystical **poet** and **hagiographer** from Herat (present-day Afghanistan), member of the **Naqshbandīya**. He is most celebrated for his collection of **didactic** poems in the **couplet** structure, *The Seven Thrones* (*Haft awrāng*), and for his major hagiographical work, *Warm Breezes of Intimacy* (*Nafaḥat al-uns*). The final section of the latter work is dedicated to short sketches of the lives of nearly three dozen **women** Sufis. Of the seven didactic poems, the most important for the history of Sufism are *The Rosary of the Pious* (*Subḥat al-abrār*) and ***Joseph*** *and Zulaykhā*, but all of these works are suffused with **ethical** themes. Among his more important mystical **treatises** is the *Gleams of Light* (*Lawā'iḥ*), a summation of the thought of **Ibn al-'Arabī**.

***JAWĀWNMARDĪ*.** *See* ETHICS.

JAZŪLĪ, ABŪ ABD ALLĀH AL- (d. c. 869/1465). North African religious scholar of Berber descent, mystical author and member of the **Shādhilīya**, and eponym of the branch of that order called the Jazūlīya. Traditional accounts claim that when his followers exhumed his body for reburial, it was incorrupt (a mark of sanctity in many popular religious traditions). He thus became a patron **Friend of God** of the Moroccan city of Marrakesh. Two extant works, of the many attributed to him, are a collection of supplications on behalf of the Prophet and a "litany of success," *The Proofs of Excellence* (*Dalā'il al-khayrāt*).

JERUSALEM. Ancient capital of King **David** and site of the temple of **Solomon**, captured by Muslim armies under the caliph 'Umar in 15/638. The city, known in Arabic as *al-Quds* (The Sacred One), figures in Islamic tradition generally as the goal of the **Prophet's Night Journey** and point of origin of his **Ascension**. Under the **Umayyad** dynasty, the city rose to symbolic prominence as the third holiest place, after **Mecca** and **Medina**. Late first/seventh century caliphs made the former site of Solomon's temple an architectural showpiece and a visual/theological counterstatement to the Byzantine complex of the Holy Sepulcher. By aligning the **Dome of the Rock** axially with the slightly later Al-Aqṣā mosque, with an open courtyard with ablution fountain in between, they both imitated and considerably outshone the Sepulcher's alignment of a basilical hall (the actual church) and small domed structure (the aedicule of the Resurrection) with a small open space (now long since covered over) in between. **Hagiographical** sources occasionally tell of visits by **Friends of God** to the sacred sites in Jerusalem.

JESUS. Second-to-last in the line of **prophets**, son of Mary. Known in **Arabic** as 'Īsā, he was born miraculously before his mother had married and spoke miraculously as an infant to defend her against the calumnies of her townspeople and family members. For Sufis, Jesus represents an important model of **trust** in God. Some authors develop **metaphorically** the concept of Mary's pregnancy and parturition as a prototype of the seeker's bringing forth the "Jesus of the Spirit." Just as Jesus disciplined the beast of burden, so the seeker's spirit must tame and ride the "Donkey of the Body." Jesus had the miraculous gifts of healing and restoring life, and the Sufi must learn to cultivate the spiritual counterparts of those marvels. Many Sufis have regarded Jesus as the paragon of **asceticism**.

JIHĀD. *See* STRUGGLE.

JĪLĪ, 'ABD AL-KARĪM AL- (767/1365–811/1408 or 826/1423 or 832/1428). Irāqī mystic and author, descendant of **'Abd al-Qādir al-Jīlānī**, most famous for his theoretical work *The Perfect Person* (*Al-Insān al-kāmil*). The concept of the **Perfect Person** originated in alchemical speculation about the relationships between macrocosm and microcosm. It was significantly reinterpreted by **Ibn al-'Arabī** and **Shabistarī**, and Jīlī further developed the notion as a symbolic model of the goal of the spiritual quest; namely, the return to one's original divine form. Though the highest example of this condition was the Prophet **Muḥammad**, it has also been embodied in other individuals of high sanctity. He was one of the major interpreters of the thought of Ibn al-'Arabī, and, like the seventh/13th-century **Andalusian**, developed a highly imaginative **spirituality** and **cosmology**.

JOSEPH. The **prophet** Yūsuf, son of the Muslim prophet (and Biblical patriarch) Jacob (Ya'qūb). The **Qur'ānic** telling of the story of Joseph is unique in that the scripture dedicates an entire chapter (Sīra 12) to an integral account of only one prophet, parallel in many respects to Genesis 39–50. Stories of prophets typically appear piecemeal in the Qur'ān, but Joseph appears significantly only in this segment. For Sufis, Joseph became a prime **symbol** of the divine **beauty**, in whose presence the human seeker experiences bewilderment and loss of self. Sufi poets such as **Jāmī** crafted the tale of Joseph's relationship with the lover **Zulaykhā** into a masterpiece of **didactic** mystical romance. Many features of the Qur'ān's account take on special **metaphorical** significance for Sufis. The jealousy of Joseph's brothers at their father's predilection for the younger son becomes the "wolf" of **ego** that threatens to devour unwary seekers. God rescues Joseph from the well or "pit" into which the brothers had consigned him, transforming his suffering into a garden. Sufi poets see the well as a symbol of the world and Joseph's eventual rescue as a sign of the resurrection. Joseph's shirt becomes a powerful reminder of the healing properties of divine beauty; placed over the eyes of Jacob, who had gone blind from grief over losing Joseph, the shirt restores the old man's sight.

JOURNEY. A major **metaphor** for the spiritual quest, often described as leading the seeker through various regions or **realms** of the cosmos. For Sufis, journey imagery takes its fundamental significance from three paradigmatic divinely enjoined journeys of the **Prophet**: his departure or "emigration" (***hijra***) from Mecca to Medina in 1/622; the combined experience of the **Night Journey** and **Ascension**; and the **pilgrimage** to Mecca that **Muḥammad** undertook from Medina in 9/630. Sufi authors have often developed these themes at considerable length, drawing out their **inward** meanings as models of various aspects of spiritual transformation.

In addition, **Ibn al-'Arabī**, who discerned no fewer than 16 journeys in the **Qur'ān**, developed the concept of multiple journeys as a model of the spiritual life: away from **God**, as when a sinner departs in shame; toward God, as when the obedient move toward the divine even if only the elect among them actually enjoy God's presence; and in God, where especially the prophets and saints sojourn eternally. Many other Sufi authors have elaborated similarly on journeying as a metaphor. The 10th/16th century **Turkish** Sufi Vāhidī paired seven aspects of the journey (to, for the sake of, toward, with, in, through, and by God) with seven levels of **invocation** and seven dimensions of the **soul**. In the seventh/13th century, Majd ad-Dīn **Baghdādī** wrote of journeys at three levels of spiritual advancement, using a by-then standard triple **typology** of the masses, the elect, and the elect among the elect. The ultimate goal of any journey is, of course, the "arrival," often expressed in various terms, such as *waṣl* (pl. *wuṣūl*) and the cognate *ittiṣāl*, roughly synonymous with **ecstasy**—the goal of the mystical journey. Perhaps the most celebrated literary development of the theme is that of **'Aṭṭār**, for whom the key metaphor for the **stages** (*manāzil*) of the quest is the valley.

JUDGMENT, FINAL. *See* DAY OF JUDGMENT.

JUNAYD, ABŪ 'L-QĀSIM MUḤAMMAD AL- (d. 298/910). Central figure among the mystics of **Baghdad**, of **Persian** origin; author, and Shāfi'ī legal scholar; nephew of **Sarī** and critic of **Ḥallāj**.

Known especially as chief proponent of "sober" mysticism, he advocated a reserved approach to claims about, and expression of, spiritual **experience**. Like **Muḥāsibī**, he focused on the essential aspects of spiritual **struggle** and **self-scrutiny**. He emphasized the centrality of "second sobriety," insisting that the experience of **ecstasy** must be considered secondary to one's ability to sustain life at the level to which one invariably returns after any such mystical apogee. His influence on subsequent **generations** of Sufi theorists and practitioners is pervasive, and many Sufi **lineages** lead back through him to the **Prophet** and his family and immediate successors. Junayd's principal written works are several brief **treatises** on the divine transcendent **unity** (*tawḥīd*).

JURISPRUDENCE. *See* LAW.

JŪZJĀNĪ, ABŪ 'ALĪ AL- (c. 353/964). Early theorist on sainthood. He described **Friends of God** as **annihilated** with respect to the **ego** so that **God** alone might **abide** in the individual's awareness. His sayings are recorded by a number of the **manualists**.

– K –

KA'BA. Structure at the center of **Mecca's** main sanctuary, whose name derives from an **Arabic** root meaning "to shape into a cube." According to variant traditions, **Adam** first built the Ka'ba and **Abraham** and his son Ismā'īl rebuilt it many centuries later. When the structure was rebuilt again during the lifetime of the **Prophet**, **Muḥammad** was asked to replace the "black stone" in one of its corners. It was probably not the only "ka'ba" in the **Arabian Peninsula** then, but Islamic tradition soon rendered the others irrelevant. It has since been rebuilt several more times and now stands some 43 feet high with four sides ranging in width from 36 to 43 feet, considerably larger than it was during the early seventh century. Sufi **poets**, perhaps most notably **Ibn al-Fāriḍ**, have developed the image of the Ka'ba as a complex **metaphor** for the **Beloved**, the **journey's** end, the inner **pilgrimage**, and the macrocosmic counterpart to the human **heart**. **Poets** often refer to specific quality or individual or value as the *qibla* (orientation) of seekers, that is the "direction" of the Ka'ba to which Muslims align themselves for ritual **prayer**. *See also* JERUSALEM.

KĀKĪ, QUṬB AD-DĪN BAKHTĪYĀR (d. 633/1235). Of **Central Asian** origin, **Indian** mystic, member of the **Chishtīya** and successor to its founder. He was known particularly for his **ecstatic experience**, and traditional accounts assert that he died during an **audition** session. He founded a *khānqāh* in **Delhi** and his most famous follower and successor in leadership of the order was **Farīd ad-Dīn Ganj-i Shakar**.

KALĀBĀDHĪ, ABŪ BAKR MUḤAMMAD AL- (d. 380/990 or 384/994). Central Asian historian and **theorist** of Sufism. The more famous of his two extant works is the **Arabic manual** *Exploration of Sufi Teachings* (*Kitāb at-ta'arruf*), a major source of information on individual Sufis and their views. The 75 generally brief chapters arrange a broad spectrum of material largely on a historical model. Its five sections offer a general background for the subject, an analysis of Sufi beliefs juxtaposed with the elements of a widely accepted creedal statement, a discussion of mystical **knowledge** and the various **stations** and **states**, a **lexical** survey of idiosyncratic Sufi **terminology**, and an overview of major ritual and practical aspects of Sufi life. One of his overriding concerns is to demonstrate the compatibility of authentic Sufism with mainstream Islamic beliefs and practices as represented by the Ash'arī school of **theology**.

KALENDERHANE. *See* RESIDENTIAL FACILITY.

KARĀMA(-ĀT). *See* WONDERS.

KARRĀMĪYA. A sectarian movement with **ascetical** and other themes analogous to those of concern in Sufism, founded by 'Abd Allāh Muḥammad ibn Karrām (c. 190/806–255/869) in **Persia**. Traveling widely through **Iran** and the Arab **Middle East**, he developed a quasi-philosophical system that positioned itself between the rationalist Mu'tazila and hard-core **traditionists**, and emphasized rejection of the world. After the founder's death, his **tomb** in **Jerusalem** soon became an important goal for **visitation**. Though it never spread far to the west, it was strong during the early medieval period as far to the east as **Central Asia**, with a stronghold in **Nishapur**. It apparently did not survive the Mongol invasions of the early seventh/13th century.

KASB. *See* LIVELIHOOD.

KĀSHĀNĪ, ʻABD AR-RAZZĀQ AL- (d. 730/1330). Iranian author of important **lexicon** of Sufi **terminology**, disciple of the school of **Ibn al-ʻArabī**. In addition to his **commentary** on the latter's work, he also wrote an important document on the values of **chivalry** and related organizations, *The Gift of Brothers concerning the Special Features of Chivalry* (*Tuḥfat al-ikhwān fī khaṣā'iṣ al-fityān*). There he describes systematically the stages of progress, beginning with the fundamental virtues of proper **behavior** and moving toward higher levels of spiritual **initiation** (*walāya*) and purity.

KASHF. *See* UNVEILING.

KASHF AL-MAḤJŪB. *See* ḤUJWĪRĪ.

KASHKŪL. *See* BEGGING BOWL.

KATAPHATIC. From the Greek compound *kata-phasis*, "speaking out," hence, "expressing freely," the opposite of **apophatic**. Sufi mystics and theorists have often debated the wisdom—and even the very possibility—of giving full expression to higher levels of spiritual **experience**. Those who, like **Ḥallāj** and **Bāyazīd**, have argued that the individual experiencing **ecstasy** or mystical **union** under whatever guise cannot but give expression to that experience are sometimes called "intoxicated" Sufis. As an approach to **theology**, the term refers to the conviction that one can appropriately speak affirmatively of the divine attributes and of human capacity to know **God** through them.

KATTĀNĪ, ABŪ BAKR AL- (d. 322/934). An early member of the **Baghdad** school of Sufism, often quoted in the fourth/10th century **manuals** on a wide range of topics.

KAYGUSŪZ (QAYGHUSŪẒ) ABDĀL (d. c. early ninth/15th century). Turkish mystical author and **poet** traditionally associated with the **Bektāshīya**. He is said to have founded an important **residence** of the **order** in Egypt and he is said to be buried in Cairo in the vicinity of the **tomb** of **Ibn al-Fāriḍ**. As a poet his use of imagery was highly original, but he may also have been influenced by **Yūnus Emre**.

KĀZARŪNĪ, ABŪ ISḤĀQ IBRĀHĪM AL- (352/963–426/1033). Persian mystic and founder of an **order** that bears his name, perhaps **initiated** by **Ibn Khafīf**. He was born and lived virtually his entire life near Shiraz in southwestern **Iran**, and his followers founded 65 *khānqāhs* in the region. His order emphasized social concern and was actively involved in aid to the needy and travelers. Though the order expanded for a time to **Anatolia, Syria**, and even **China** and **India**, its influence outside of Iran was relatively short-lived.

KHĀDIM. *See* GOVERNANCE.

KHĀLIDĪYA/MUJADDIDĪYA. Alternative names of an important early-modern branch of the **Naqshbandīya** and the dominant development of that order through most of the central **Middle East**. A Kurdish religious scholar named Mawlānā Khālid Baghdādī (d. 1243/1827), who was initiated in Delhi by a Mujaddidī ***shaykh***, is widely credited with founding the branch.

KHALĪFA. *See* SUCCESSOR.

KHALWA. *See* RETREAT.

KHALWAT DAR ANJUMĀN. *See* RETREAT.

KHALWATĪYA. An **order** founded during the eighth/14th century and spread early on in northwestern **Persia**. A number of prominent initiates into the order went on to found separate branches, especially in **Turkey, Middle Eastern** and eastern European lands under **Ottoman** rule, and across **North Africa** as well. The name of the organization derives from a favored spiritual practice of "isolation" or "seclusion" (*khalwa*), a form of **retreat**. The Khalwatī-Jarrāḥīya (or

Helveti-Jerrāhi) order, now very important in Turkey, resulted from a 12th/18th century split.

KHAMRĪYA. *See* IBN AL-FĀRIḌ.

KHĀNQĀH. *See* RESIDENTIAL FACILITY.

KHARĀBĀT. *See* RUIN.

KHARAQĀNĪ, ABŪ ’L-ḤASAN ‘ALĪ AL- (c. 349/960–425/1033). Persian ascetic and mystic, ***shaykh*** of **Anṣārī**. Traditional accounts claim that **Bāyazīd initiated** him in a **dream**, so that he falls into the category of **Uwaysīs**. Many later Sufis claimed spirit-**initiation** through him, and he was eventually incorporated as a major link in the **Naqshbandī lineage**. Though he left no writings, his sayings are often cited in **manuals** and other Sufi writings, including a **hagiographic** work by one of his disciples.

KHARRĀZ, ABŪ SA‘ĪD AḤMAD AL- (d. 286/899). Iraq-born **ascetic**, prolific author and mystic who was an associate of **Bishr** and **Dhū ’n-Nūn**, a disciple of **Sarī**, and one of **Junayd’s *shaykh***s. He is most famous for his **Arabic** *Book of Authenticity* (*Kitāb aṣ-Ṣidq*), among the earliest handbooks of spirituality, and another work on mystical **psychology**, in which he adds the concept of “natural tendencies” (*ṭab‘*) to the lexicon of Sufi psychological terms. He was also arguably the first to develop the **genre** of the mystical **allusion** and penned one of the earliest works on the status of **Friends of God**.

KHATM AL-ANBIYĀ’. *See* SEAL.

KHATM AL-AWLIYĀ’. *See* SEAL.

KHATM AL-WILĀYA. *See* SEAL.

KHĀṬIR/KHAWĀṬIR. *See* INCLINATIONS.

KHAWF. *See* FEAR.

KHAYR AL-MAJĀLIS. *The Best of Assemblies*, a major collection of **discourses** of **Naṣīr ad-Dīn** by **Chishtī** poet Ḥamīd ad-Dīn Qalandar in the mid-eighth/14th century in Delhi.

KHIḌR/KHAḌIR. The "Green One," a mysterious character who figures prominently in Sufi lore as a **Friend of God** who **guided** a **prophet**, as the seeker whose arcane **knowledge** allowed him to discover the "Fountain of Life," and as "spirit-**initiator**." He is one of only three significant figures not specifically identified in the **Qur'ān** and to whom later tradition has attached names. Qur'an 18:61–83 tells how Mūsā (**Moses**) and his unnamed servant (usually identified as Joshua) head off in search of the "Confluence of the Two **Oceans**." The two have brought along a fish to eat, but when Moses looks away momentarily, the fish comes to life and swims away. This they take as a sign that they must retrace their steps, for they have apparently gone too far unawares. Turning back, they meet the figure whom **God** describes as "one to whom we gave mercy from ourselves and to whom we taught a knowledge from our presence" (Qur'ān 18:64). Recognizing this person as a guide, Moses asks to follow him. The guide hesitates, insisting that Moses will be too impatient with the guide's actions. Moses promises to hold his peace on pain of being left to journey on alone. As they proceed, Khiḍr performs three actions that Moses deems morally untenable: he scuttles a ship, murders a boy, and rebuilds a wall for people of questionable character. At each juncture, Moses criticizes Khiḍr's actions. Finally, Khiḍr has had enough; he agrees to explain himself, but then Moses is on his own. He sank the ship because he knew an evil king was planning to do great harm with it; he killed the youth to prevent his parents from having to grieve his inevitable rebelliousness; and he rebuilt the wall so that the owner's orphaned children would eventually be able to inherit the treasure their father had buried beneath it for them.

Sufi **exegetes** associate Moses with **outward** knowledge and Khiḍr with the **inward**, esoteric knowledge that comes uniquely from the divine presence. Sufi authors transform Khiḍr into the master of the mystery to which all seekers must surrender themselves in their quest for guidance on the **Path**. Spiritual aspirants must be willing to endure this ***shaykh*'s** apparently draconian authority in view of higher meanings. Khiḍr functions as the spirit-*shaykh* who appears in

dreams and **visions** to **initiate** Sufis and invest seekers with the patched **cloak** of spiritual **poverty**. As one who reads hearts and sees with the very eyes of God, Khiḍr is the epitome of the spiritual guide. Serious seekers must be willing to set out on the very ship (the body) that Khiḍr scuttled, as a token of authentic spiritual poverty.

KHIRQA. *See* CLOAK.

KHULDĪ, JA'FAR AL- (d. 348/959). A member of the circle of **Ruwaym** and **Junayd** in **Baghdad**, whose **aphorisms** appear often in the early **manuals**. His **lineage** is believed to be the earliest extant record of its kind.

KHURĀSĀN. Northeastern province of **Iran**, a region that the modern nation-state now shares with Afghanistan and **Central Asia**. Khurasan's borders were quite fluid throughout medieval and early modern times, determined by changing political regimes. It was home to one of the most important early formative Sufi movements, one broadly identified with "**Intoxicated**" Sufism. From its principal cities, especially **Nishapur**, Tus, and Marw, came dozens of major Sufis including **Abū Sa'īd ibn Abī 'l-Khayr**, **Aḥmad-i Jām**, **Anṣārī**, **'Aṭṭār**, the **Bākharzī's**, **Bishr**, Abū 'Alī ad-**Daqqāq**, the **Ghazālī** brothers, **Sarrāj**, and **Shaqīq**.

KIBRĪT AL-AḤMAR, AL-. *See* DISCERNMENT.

KĪMĪYĀ-YI SA'ĀDAT. *See* GHAZĀLĪ, ABŪ ḤĀMID.

KIRMĀNĪ, AWḤĀD AD-DĪN (c. 567/1171–635/1238). Persian poet most famous for his collection of **quatrains**, reputedly numbering some 1,700. He traveled widely throughout the **Middle East**, and became personally acquainted with **Ibn al-'Arabī** during a stay of several years in central **Turkey**. Other influences on his thought included Farīd ad-Dīn **'Aṭṭār** and Shihāb ad-Dīn Yaḥyā as-**Suhrawardī**. He spent his last few years in the **Baghdad** area, where he was appointed ***shaykh*** of a local *ribāṭ*. He is said to have taught many disciples and traditional accounts credit him with a variety of **wonders**.

KITĀB AL-LUMA'. *See* SARRĀJ.

KITĀB AR-RI 'ĀYA. *See* MUḤĀSIBĪ.

KITĀB AṢ-ṢIDQ. *See* KHARRĀZ.

KITĀB AT-TA 'ARRUF. *See* KALĀBĀDHĪ.

KITĀB ṬABAQĀT AṢ-ṢŪFĪYA. *See* SULAMĪ.

KITĀB AṬ-ṬAWĀSĪN. *See* ḤALLĀJ.

KNOWLEDGE, DISCURSIVE. Generally expressed by the **Arabic** term *'ilm*, which can also be translated as traditional or acquired knowledge. An important class of scholars in traditional Islamic societies are known as *'ulamā'*, those who possess *'ilm*, which in turn is sometimes associated with reason or intellect (*'aql*). Elaborating their distinctive epistemologies, Sufi authors have discussed at length the various types of knowledge. In general, they argue that one can attain discursive knowledge through one's own effort, by a disciplined study of the principal Islamic religious sources (scripture and **exegesis**, Prophetic **tradition**, and religious **law**) as well as through familiarity with important Sufi sources. Most authorities on the subject teach that by itself this type of knowledge is insufficient for genuine spiritual development because it can leave one with only an **outward** understanding that lacks penetration to the ultimate **meaning** of the sources represented by **mystical** knowledge. In Sufi training, seekers pursue this sort of knowledge with help from **instructing *shaykhs***, but must progress beyond that level through the aid of *shaykhs* who can help them move further into genuinely **experiential formation** and a higher level of mystical **knowledge**.

KNOWLEDGE, MYSTICAL. Generally expressed by the **Arabic** term *ma'rifa*, which can also be translated as infused or experiential knowledge. Although there are alternative opinions, most Sufi authors argue for the superiority of *ma'rifa* over *'ilm* (discursive **knowledge**). They emphasize the purely gratuitous, **graced** nature of this mode of knowing. Discursive knowledge does not of itself eventuate in mystical knowledge, regardless of the level of the seeker's effort or the competence of teachers. In Sufi training, seekers pursue this sort of knowledge with help from **formative *shaykhs***.

KONYA. Central **Anatolian** city that saw the emergence of one of **Turkey's** most important **orders**, the **Mawlawīya**. In early antiquity it was known as the city of Iconium in the Roman province of Lycaonia visited by St. Paul. During medieval times it became the capital of the **Saljūqid** sultanate of **Rūm** and an important center of Turkish Sufism. The town remains particularly important because of its association with the **poet Rūmī**, whose **tomb**, now enshrined in a 10th/16th century **Ottoman** complex, is a major site for **visitation**.

KUBRĀ, NAJM AD-DĪN (540/1145–617/1220). Central **Asian** mystic, religious scholar, author, and founder of the **Kubrāwīya**. Broad travels through the **Middle East** put him in touch with several Sufi ***shaykhs***, and he eventually became established as a *shaykh* himself. Sa'd ad-Dīn **Ḥammūya**, Majd ad-Dīn **Baghdādī**, and **Najm ad-Dīn Dāyā Rāzī** are three of his most prominent students. Kubrā's key writings explore in particular various refined aspects of the **science of hearts**, outlining 10 stages of spiritual development and contributing significantly to the development of mystical **psychology**. He laid the foundation for a system of **color symbolism** that later authors of his order would elaborate further.

KUBRĀWĪYA. Order of **Central Asian** origin founded by Najm ad-Dīn **Kubrā**. Important members of the order include **'Alī Hamadhānī**, **Bākharzī**, **Ḥammūyā**, Majd ad-Dīn **Baghdādī**, **Najm ad-Dīn Dāyā Rāzī**, and **Nasafī.** The order made some limited headway in Afghanistan, **India**, **China**, and **Turkey**, with the **Firdawsīya** and **Nūrbakhshīya** numbered among its major branches.

KULĀH. *See* HEADGEAR.

KŪRĀNĪ, IBRĀHĪM IBN ḤASAN AL- (1025/1616–1102/1690). Kurdish mystic who taught in **Medina** and influenced large numbers of students from all over the world who then returned home to disseminate his thought. His influential disciples include the **Indonesian** author 'Abd ar-Ra'ūf as-**Sinkilī** and Zayn al-Mizjājī (1053/1643–1138/1725), who went on to mentor a major **Chinese** Sufi leader, **Ma Mingxin**, who studied with Zayn in his native Yemen.

– L –

LĀHĪJĪ, SHAMS AD-DĪN MUḤAMMAD (d. 912/1506). Persian mystical **poet** and ***shaykh*** of the **Nūrbakhshīya**. He came from northern **Iran** but spent much of his life in Shīrāz and there accepted students in his *khānqāh*. His **commentary** on the mystical poetry of **Shabistarī** reveals considerable influence of **Ibn al-'Arabī**.

LAHORE (LĀHAWR). Major city in the **Panjāb**, second-largest city in present-day **Pakistan**, former capital of various Muslim political regimes. It had been home to a number of important Sufis and is the site of the much-visited **tomb** of **Hujwīrī**.

LĀHŪT. *See* REALMS.

LĀL SHĀHBĀZ QALANDAR (d. c. 661/1262). Indian wandering **dervish** from Iran, who lived mostly in **Sindh**, member (generally by way of exception) of the **Suhrawardīya**. Though he was **initiated** into the **order** by **Bahā' ad-Dīn Zakarīya**, he preferred the life of the ***qalandar*** and shared a love of **dance** with the **Malamatīya**. He claimed **Hallāj** as his mystical forebear. His real name was Mīr Sayyid 'Uthmān, and he received the nicknames Lāl ("red") because he liked to wear that **color**, and Shāhbāz ("king's **falcon**") because of his mystical devotion.

LAMA'ĀT. *See* FAKHR AD-DĪN 'IRĀQĪ.

LANGUAGES. Sufi authors, and **historians** whose works help document the history of Sufism, have written in a wide range of languages from several different major language families. Most important for the early centuries are **Arabic** (Semitic) and **Persian** (Indo-European). From the eighth/14th century on, as Sufism became established in **Central** and **South Asia**, and in **Anatolia**, regional languages such as **Sindhī**, **Panjābī**, and **Turkic** tongues such as Chaghatai and what came to be known as **Ottoman** emerged as important means of **literary** expression. As Sufism took root in **Southeast** and **East Asia** from around the 10th/16th century, mystical texts in **Malay,** Javanese, and **Chinese** extended the daunting task of translating Sufi concepts into new frameworks of thought and culture. Moving into Eastern Europe with Ottoman expansion in the 16th century and later, Sufism added works in Slavic tongues to its vast library. Sufis in **East Africa**, especially during early modern times, began to produce works in **Swahili**. Meanwhile, back in South Asia, the Indo-Persian hybrid tongue called **Urdu** emerged as an essential early modern language of Sufism.

LAṬĪFA. *See* ANECDOTE; for plural, *laṭā'if*, *see* PSYCHOLOGY.

LAW. Systems and methods of praxis-oriented interpretation of the primary sacred texts, **Qur'ān** and **Ḥadīth**, along with the codification of religious requirements deriving from those systems and methods. By the second/mid-eighth century, Muslim religious scholars responsible for adapting the sacred sources to changing social and cultural circumstances had begun to develop regional variations in methods of interpretation. Over the next century or so, those methods coalesced into more formal "schools of thought" called *madhhabs*, each with its distinctive approach to jurisprudence (*fiqh*). The growing corpus of the results of religious jurisprudence has long been known by the comprehensive term *sharī'a*, "revealed law," embracing the full range of what Muslims have considered religious requirements and ethical responsibilities. Critics of Sufism through the centuries have often argued that Sufis as a whole disregard the **outward** stipulations of religious law and replace fundamental practice with innovations of their own design, thereby removing themselves from the community of true Muslims.

Manuals by a number of Sufi theorists and historians have set out explicitly to refute that criticism by situating Sufism as a legitimate religious discipline. They argue that far from disregarding the core disciplines of **exegesis**, Ḥadīth scholarship, and law, Sufism actually presupposes and builds upon them by seeking their **inward meanings** (*istinbāṭ*). Most of the major Sufi authors had significant academic backgrounds in one or more of the four **Sunnī Law** schools. For example, **Anṣārī**, **'Abd al-Qādir al-Jīlānī**, and **Hujwīrī** were Ḥanbalī; **Kalābādhī** and **Tirmidhī** were Ḥanafī; **Ghazālī**, **Muḥāsibī**, **Qushayrī**, and the **Suhrawardīs** were Shāfi'ī; **Ibn 'Abbād** and most of the major **Shadhilīya** figures were associated with the Mālikī school; and **Abū Ṭālib al-Makkī** was conversant with Ḥanbalī, Shāfi'ī, and Mālikī approaches to jurisprudence. The principal **institution** associated with the teaching of religious law is the *madrasa*, "place of study."

LAWĀ'IḤ. *See* JĀMĪ.

LAYLAT AL-QADR. *See* REVELATION.

LETTERS. An important medium of spiritual (and administrative) communication for many major Sufi ***shaykh***s. Generally called *rasā'il* or *maktūbāt*, the epistolary output of some teachers has been considerable. Two of the most prolific and best known letter-writers are **Ibn 'Abbād** of Ronda and Sharaf ad-Dīn **Manīrī**, but authors more celebrated for their **poetry**, such as **Rūmī**, have also left valuable collections of letters. Along with **discourses**, this **genre** often provides the most significant personal data about the authors.

LEXICONS. Scholarly tools designed to help readers of mystical works by interpreting the often idiosyncratic technical terminology (*iṣṭilāḥāt*) that Sufis have devised in their attempts to express the ineffable. Some of these glossaries or dictionaries of key terms appear as segments of larger **manuals**, such as those of **Hujwīrī**, **Kalābādhī**, and **Sarrāj**. Others, such as **Kāshānī's**, are separate works. Some authors, such as Abū Ḥāmid al-**Ghazālī** and **Ibn al-'Arabī**, composed shorter lexicons as companions to their own major works, sometimes in response to specific requests from their students for help in deciphering technically demanding material—what some authors call "the elucidation of ambiguities/obscurities" (*bayān al-mushkilāt*). The mystical lexicon is naturally an invaluable **genre** for historians of Sufism as well.

LIGHT. Primary **metaphor** for the divine self-manifestation to the human **heart**. Sufi **poets** derive much of their love for light imagery from the Qur'ānic "Verse of Light" (24:35): "**God** is the Light of the Heavens and the Earth. His light (*nūr*) is like a niche in which there is a lamp that is within a glass, and the glass like a shining star; kindled from a sacred olive **tree** neither of east nor west, whose oil would nearly glow even if no **fire** touched it. Light upon light, and God guides to His light whom He will." The classic development of the theme is that of **Ghazālī's** *Niche of Lights* (*Mishkāt al-Maṣābīḥ*), a theme later picked up by the "***Shaykh*** of **Illumination**," Shihāb ad-Dīn Yaḥyā as-**Suhrawardī**, whose cosmology is suffused with light imagery. Countless Sufi poets and authors have elaborated further on the theme. In addition, an important mystical development of the theme is that of the light of **Muḥammad** (*nūr muḥammadī*), a pre-eternal element of the **Prophet's** cosmic presence.

LINEAGE. Continuity in **authority** and legitimacy as manifested in stable **institutions** and **organizational** structures and expressed as a "chain" (*silsila*) or "**tree**" (*shajara*, a type of genealogical chart). Virtually every Sufi **order** has paid considerable attention to maintaining a sense of organizational integrity, tracing its spiritual pedigree back through a succession of major ***shaykhs*** as far back as the **Prophet** himself. These tables of spiritual descent became the Sufi counterpart of the *isnād* (chains of transmitters) that assured the veracity of sayings of the Prophet. Some orders further developed **lineages** related to specific concerns such as the transmission of **blessing** from a founder to a current leader, the chain of authority to confer **initiation** into the order, and genealogies of *shaykhs* responsible for spiritual **formation**. The lineage or genealogy enshrines an order's spiritual legacy or inheritance (*wirātha*).

LITANIES. Vocal **prayers** structured as a list of formulaic phrases and sometimes with repeated refrains. **Names of God** and phrases from the **Qur'ān** frequently punctuate these prayers. Typically referred to with the **Arabic** terms *ḥizb* (lit. "section," pl. *aḥzāb*) and *wird* (lit. "access, coming" pl. *awrād*), they were often composed by famous mystics and handed down as part of the heritage of an **order**. A given prayer's unique power derived from the sanctity and distinctive spirituality of the one who composed it. Litanies could function as part of the content of communal **recollection rituals**. Some litanies are kept secret to the extent that they are specially selected and bestowed on a seeker only on full **initiation** into an order. Litanies performed at the individual's discretion, not necessarily under prescribed circumstances, are called *rawātib* ("things arranged," sg. *rātib*), and some litanies have been available to devout Muslims outside the context of the orders.

LITERATURE. A major medium of Sufi communication in over a dozen **languages** and a host of **genres**. Along with **architecture**, the visual **arts, dance**, and **music**, the many forms of literary expression and documentation provide an enormous range of data for the history of Sufism. Here, as with the many other sources for that history, one cannot discern a neat line between the **experiential** and the "factual" aspects of the record. Some of the world's premier religious **poetry** has flowed from the tongues and pens of Sufis, beginning as early as the second/eighth century with the **love lyrics** of **Rābi'a**. She was followed not long thereafter by **Ḥallāj**, whose **Arabic** lyrics are beautiful in their stark simplicity. **Persian** became an important Sufi literary language from about the late sixth/12th century on, with major authors such as **Sanā'ī, 'Aṭṭār**, **Ibn al-Fāriḍ**, and **Rūmī** perfecting the **didactic** genre of **couplets** in addition to producing large collections of lyric work. By the eighth/14th century, **Turkish** was becoming an important Sufi literary tongue, and by early modern times, poets were crafting mystical works in regional languages such as **Malay**, **Urdu**, **Sindhi**, and **Swahili**. A variety of poetry dedicated preeminently to the **praise** of the **Prophet** is well exemplified by the work of **Būṣīrī**. In recent years, considerable scholarship has pointed out that Sufi poetry is not merely mystical sentiment in verse, but literary art of the highest quality.

Important prose works written by and for Sufis came to the fore especially with the Arabic **manuals** of the fourth/10th century, by **Sarrāj**, **Makkī**, **Kalābādhī**, and others. **Hujwīrī** introduced Persian as a major prose Sufi language with his fifth/11th century manual. From that period on, the kind of **hagiographical** material Hujwīrī included in his manual came into its own as the subject of freestanding works by **Sulamī** in Arabic and **Anṣārī** in Persian, as well as other authors such as **Jāmī**. A host of other prose genres including **autobiographical** accounts, **commentary**, **discourses**, **letters**, **recitals**, and **treatises** have been produced by major Sufis through late medieval and early modern times in considerable profusion, providing much of our information about the history of Sufism. *See also* ALLEGORY; ANECDOTE; APHORISM; *DĪWĀN*; EXEGESIS; HISTORIOGRAPHY; LEXICONS; METAPHOR; SYMBOLISM; THRENODY; WISDOM.

LIU CHIH (c. 1081/1670–?). Chinese religious scholar from Nanking, **hagiographer** and translator of Sufi texts into Chinese. He was well schooled in Buddhist thought as well as in that of the indigenous Chinese religious traditions, Daoism and Confucianism, and sought to present Islam as altogether compatible with the ancient Chinese religious heritages, neo-Confucianism in particular. In his works dedicated to introducing Chinese readers to Islam and related cultural contexts, he frequently mentions important Sufi writings by **Jāmī**, **Najm ad-Dīn Dāyā Rāzī**, and **Nasafī**. Among his more important contributions were a biography of the **Prophet** and a full Chinese translation of Jāmī's *Gleams* (*Lawā'iḥ*). Along with **Wang Daiyu**, he remains one of the most important sources for the history of Sufism in China.

LIVELIHOOD. Acceptable means of sustaining the daily life and activities of Sufi **organizations** and **institutions** as well as the itinerant lifestyle of solitary **dervishes**, including both gainful labor and mendicancy. Sufi authorities and **orders** have supported a wide range of attitudes toward modes of livelihood, referred to in general by the **Arabic** term *kasb*, "acquiring, gain." Those that have espoused an active life and more lay-oriented daily life, such as the **Shādhilīya**, have emphasized the need for scrupulous honesty in all one's mercantile dealings. A few organizations adopted an official policy of never accepting donations from the very wealthy, lest they be subtly co-opted and beholden to the rich and powerful; others have been pleased to receive from any generous hand and have lived in relative comfort, or even frank affluence. Voluntary donations are typically known as *futūḥ*. A few orders, along with noninstitutional Sufis, have made a policy of living in genuine material, as well as spiritual, **poverty**, accepting only what they needed to sustain a fairly meager, austere lifestyle.

LOVE. An aspect of mystical **experience** often ranked high in Sufi psycho-spiritual or developmental **typologies**. Sufi talk about love (typically using the Arabic words *'ishq*) presupposes not only that **God** is positively disposed to the individual seeker in such as way as to allow the servant to experience intimacy, but also that the individual has been granted the capacity to respond by giving God praise. Thus, even though many **poets** employ the **metaphors** of romantic love, they do not imply anything like a simple mutuality of enjoyment or infatuation. Sufi authors sometimes pun on the most common Arabic terms for love, *ḥubb* and *maḥabba*, suggesting that one related root meaning, "to produce seed," gives an insight into the "seminal" significance of love which takes root in the heart. According to **Qushayrī**, and other authorities, the seeker's love is the **heart's** "bubbling" over with **desire** for the presence of the Beloved (*ḥubab*, bubbles on water). Love is the heart's perfect focusing on the goal of **union**, implying that the lover has no awareness of anything else.

LUBB. *See* HEART.

LYRIC POETRY. Forms of literary expression adapted by Sufi poets in many **languages**, including **genres** such as the ***ghazal*** (short lyric), *qaṣīda* (**ode**), *qiṭʻa* ("fragment"), and *rubāʻī* (**quatrain**). Lyric poems are generally distinguished from longer forms associated with narrative used for **didactic**, romantic, and epic purposes. Sufi lyricists, beginning in the eighth and ninth centuries, developed a variety of genres as daring vehicles for expressing ineffable dimensions of the complex **experience** of divine-human **love**. Among the great lyricists are **ʻAṭṭār**, **Bīdil**, Mīr **Dard**, **Ghālib**, **Ḥāfiẓ**, **Ḥamza Fanṣūrī**, **Ibn al-Fāriḍ**, **Fakhr ad-Dīn ʻIrāqī**, **Kirmānī**, **Niẓāmī**, **Rūmī**, **Sanāʾī**, **Sulṭān Bāhū**, and **Yūnus Emre**.

– M –

MA FUCHU (c. 1209/1794–1291/1874). Chinese religious scholar of Yunnan who composed over half of his three dozen works in **Arabic** as well as one in **Persian**. He was a major interpreter of Islamic concepts, particularly the notion of "the true pure religion," in relation to neo-Confucian thought. He also translated into Chinese other Sufi texts, including **Ibn al-ʻArabī's** prophetological masterpiece, *Bezels of Wisdom*.

MA HUALONG (d. 1288/1871). Descendant of **Ma Mingxin**, leader of the Hui rebellion in northwest **China** (1862–76), and a **martyr** of his Sufi *menhuan* (**lineage**).

MA LAICHI (c. 1091/1680–1180/1766). Chinese member of the Āfāqīya branch of the **Naqshbandīya**, noted for its involvement in political affairs, and perhaps also of the **Suhrawardīya** and **Qādirīya**. He traveled extensively and studied with ***shaykh***s in **Bukhara**, **Mecca**, and Yemen. Ma's Sufi community used the silent **recollection** typical of the Naqshbandīya, being therefore known as the Khafīya suborder ("Old Teaching"), and was the first *menhuan* in Gansu where his **tomb** remains a site of **visitation**. Twenty active *menhuan* of his group remain today.

MA MINGXIN 1132/1719–1196/1781. Chinese Sufi who established the Jahrīya (**recollection** aloud, hence "New Teaching") brand of practice to Gansu in 1761. Some Muslims, including **Ma Laichi's** group, accused the order of extroverted **ritual** practices too suspiciously similar to those of Daoists and Buddhists. He studied for nearly 16 years with a Yemenī ***shaykh*** named Zayn al-Mizjājī (1643–1725) and elsewhere in the **Arabian Peninsula**.

MA QIXI (1274/1857–1333/1914). Chinese religious scholar and popular **preacher** who had been a member of the Khafīya Sufi **order** but later instituted a **reform** movement. He was assassinated at the command of a leader of the Sufi order as a result of his opposition.

MA ZHENWU (d. c. 1378/1958). Chinese Jahrī Sufi, grandson of **Ma Hualong**. He led and, with members of his order, fomented Hui uprisings in 1952. In 1958, he was arrested and accused of being a counterrevolutionary, partly because of the wealth that was at his disposal as executor of the order's **endowments**.

MADHHAB. *See* LAW.

MADHŌ LĀL ḤUSAYN (d. c. 1056/1646). Panjābī lyric poet and member of the **Qādirīya**, still popular in **Pakistan**. He was most famous for his highly personal and expressive distichs, known as *kafis*, in which he vigorously defended the concept of ontological **unity** in the ***wujūdī* controversy**.

MADĪḤ. *See* PRAISE.

MADRASA*. See* LAW.

MAGHRIB. Arabic term meaning "place where the sun sets," generally understood as referring to **North Africa**. Comprised of the modern nation-states of Morocco, Algeria, Tunisia, and Libya, the region has been largely dominated by the Mālikī school of **law**. Among the more important Sufis from the region are **Ibn 'Ajība**, **'Alawī**, **Dabbāgh**, **Darqāwī**, **Fāsī**, **Ibn Mashīsh**, **Jazūlī**, **Sanūsī**, **Shādhilī**, and **Tījānī**; the major orders have been the **Darqāwīya**, **Khalwatīya**, **Shādhilīya**, **Sanūsīya**, and **Tījānīya**.

MAGHRIBĪ, MUḤAMMAD SHĪRĪN (d. 810/1408). Persian Sufi author and **poet** from Tabriz in northwestern **Iran**, ***shaykh*** of the **Kubrāwīya**, major figure in transmitting the thought of **Ibn al-'Arabī**. He was much influenced by both **Rūmī** and **Shabistarī**.

MAḤABBA*. See* LOVE.

MAḤBŪB*. See* BELOVED.

MAḤMŪD AL-BAGHDĀDĪ, SĪDĪ (d. 1088/1678). West African Sufi ***shaykh*** of what is now the southern Saharan nation-state of Niger. Legendary sources say he traveled to West Africa from **Baghdad**. **Hagiographical** accounts attribute numerous **wonders** to him, but he is still more renowned for his personal charisma and for his "luminosity" and the depth of his **knowledge** of the spiritual life. He is said to have died a **martyr** for the faith. An **order**, called the Maḥmūdīya after its "founder," made the spiritual **retreat** and circular **dance** prominent practices.

MAḤW*. See* EFFACEMENT.

MAJD AD-DĪN BAGHDĀDĪ. *See* BAGHDĀDĪ.

MAJDHŪB*. See* WAYFARER.

MAJLIS*. See* RECOLLECTION; RITUAL.

***MAJNŪN*. *See* PERPLEXITY.**

MAKKĪ, ABŪ ṬĀLIB AL-. *See* ABŪ ṬĀLIB AL-.

MAKKĪ, 'AMR IBN 'UTHMĀN AL-. *See* 'AMR IBN 'UTHMĀN AL-.

***MAKTŪBĀT*.** *See* LETTERS.

***MALAKŪT*.** *See* REALMS.

***MALĀMA*.** *See* BLAME.

MALĀMATĪYA. A doctrinally eclectic movement related to Sufism, with roots in northeastern Iran. **Ḥamdūn al-Qaṣṣār** is widely acknowledged as the founder of the movement, with significant influence of his teacher, Abū Ḥafṣ al-**Ḥaddād**, and Abū 'Uthmān al-**Ḥīrī**. As **Sulamī** explains in his important *Treatise* (*Risāla*) on the tradition, the name means "those who bring **blame** upon themselves," and reflects the underlying principle that understating one's spiritual status and concerns is preferable to garnering social and religious approval by any sort of outward display or symbolism. Individuals who lived lives of actual material **poverty** were not to appear impoverished. Even to credit oneself very privately with success in religious deeds, or to hope for a heavenly reward, was a spiritual failure. The tradition traces its origins to none other than the **Prophet**, whom the **Qur'ān** extols as impervious to blame (5:54). In its more extreme forms, the tradition promoted **behavior** and **ethics** calculated explicitly to evoke disapproval and rejection. A tendency to favor withdrawal from the public in all **ritual** practices may have influenced, for example, the **Naqshbandīya**. Some scholars point out that the tradition at least initially represented a reaction not so much to **institutional** Sufism as to the **Karrāmīya** of Nishapur, who gravitated toward public display of their piety. As an **organization**, the movement was particularly important in **Central Asia**, but enjoyed considerable success in **Turkey** and the **Balkans**, as well as portions of the Arab **Middle East**.

MALANG. Technical term, possibly of Hindi origin, used in **South Asia** to refer to ***qalandar***-like mendicants who attach themselves sporadically to various holy places. Popular usage seems on the whole to restrict the term *qalandar* to individuals with specifically Sufi connections, while *malang* refers more generically to religiously motivated beggars. Some, of course, are considered charlatans, but many are popularly regarded as spiritually potent, if socially marginal. Female *malangs* are rare but not unheard of. The word, which means "transverse, across" in **Malay**, took on the extended meaning of unfortunate or star-crossed, and has become associated with **poverty** in **Southeast Asia**, and hence with **asceticism**; but it does not appear to be a common term there for Sufis as such.

MALAY. A major **Southeast Asian language** that developed as an important regional medium of Islamic communication in part through the writings of Sufis. A member of the Malayo-Polynesian language family, it became the preferred medium of literary and political culture of much of the region, including large parts of **Indonesia**, particularly Sumatra and western Java. Major Sufi-oriented writers in the language include **'Abd aṣ-Ṣamad of Palembang**, **Ḥamza Fanṣūrī**, **Rānīrī**, and **Sinkilī**. Along with others, they were largely responsible for making Sufi and Islamic teachings more widely available to the cultural elite of the region. For example, a little-known 12th/18th century scholar of Sumatra, Kemas Fakhr ad-Dīn of Palembang, produced a Malay adaptation (generally known as *The Compendium* [*Kitāb mukhtaṣar*] but lacking its own formal title) of a sixth/12th century **Arabic** Sufi text by ***Shaykh*** Walī Raslān of Damascus (*Treatise on the Divine Transcendent* ***Unity*** [*Risāla fī 't-tawḥīd*]), thus facilitating the spread of elements of **Junayd's** teachings in the Southeast Asia.

MALAYSIA. Formerly known as Malaya, a modern nation-state of **Southeast Asia** with a majority Muslim population. It now occupies the southern portion of a peninsula, sharing a border with Thailand, and two of its 10 states are on the north coast of the island of Borneo. Sufism likely arrived there in the sixth/12th century. Malaysia played an important role in the Islamization of the region. Its **language**, **Malay**, was the *lingua franca* of the region and, thanks to the work of

Ḥamza Fanṣūrī especially, became arguably the most significant vehicle of Sufi literary expression in Southeast Asia. The most important of the **orders** in the region has been the **Qādirīya**, but the **Naqshbandīya** was also a presence there, as were several smaller orders.

MALFŪẒ(-ĀT). *See* DISCOURSE.

MĀLIK IBN DĪNĀR (d. c. 131/748). Basran preacher, **storyteller**, and **ascetic** familiar with **Ḥasan al-Baṣrī** and **Rābi'a al-'Adawīya**. His moral maxims, most notably his teaching about the centrality of **struggle** with one's own internal enemy, are often quoted by **manualists** and other Sufi authors.

MAMLŪK DYNASTY (648/1250–923/1517). Originally slave-soldiers of **Turkic/Central Asian** origin, the Mamlūks ruled the central Middle East, especially Egypt and Syria-Palestine, for two and a half centuries following the demise of the Ayyūbid dynasty. In addition to their significant patronage of **literature** and the **arts** in general, a number of the sultans fostered Sufism by building major architectural foundations and associating themselves with Sufi ***shaykhs*** and **orders**. Some of the richest records of Sufi **institutional** development are available in Mamlūk **endowment** documents. Famous Sufis who lived under their Cairo-centered rule include **Ibn 'Aṭā' Allāh of Alexandria** and **Ibn al-Fāriḍ**. The dynasty held off the Mongols in 659/1260 but later succumbed to the Ottoman conquest of most of the Middle East.

MA'NĀ. *See* MEANING.

MANĀM. *See* DREAMS.

MANĀZIL AS-SĀ'IRĪN. *See* ANṢĀRĪ.

MANĀQIB. *See* HAGIOGRAPHY.

MANĀQIB AL-'ĀRIFĪN. *See* AFLĀKĪ.

MANIFESTATION. A gift of **God** to the advanced mystic in which the seeker **experiences** an inkling of the divine majesty and grandeur by way of an **illumination**. Typically referred to with the **Arabic** term *tajallī*, talk about this aspect of divine disclosure emphasizes God's majesty and the transformation wrought in the seeker in its wake.

MANĪRĪ, SHARAF AD-DĪN (661/1261–782/1381). Indian regional leader of the **Firdawsīya** and author, who lived much of his life in what is now the state of Bihar. Enjoying royal patronage in his own *khānqāh*, he became a renowned spiritual **guide** of the order, a branch of the **Kubrāwīya** that arrived first in India. His fame rests largely on four collections of **letters** of spiritual direction and a commentary on a work of Abū Najīb as-**Suhrawardī**. Sprinkling generous citations of **Persian** poetry throughout his letters, the ***shaykh*** covers a wide range of topics, from the most mundane concerns of Muslims seeking to inculcate Islamic spiritual values into every daily act to the more refined intricacies of the most advanced mystical pedagogy. Whatever his subject, he treats it not in the interest of theory as such, but out of genuine pastoral care for his addressees. Sharaf ad-Dīn himself evidently considered a collection now called *The Hundred Letters* (*Maktūbāt-i ṣaḍ*) as an integral and essential document on the spirit of the Firdawsīya, and wanted a text of the collection available to members. As such, the letters seem to have functioned as miniature **treatises** on the spiritual life. In addition to his letters, Sharaf ad-Dīn—or to be more precise, his disciples—also left substantial collections of **discourses**, the substance of his teaching at "assemblies" in response to the expressed needs, often rooted in matters of religious practice, of those gathered.

MANṬIQ AṬ-ṬAYR. *See* 'AṬṬĀR.

MANUALS. An important **genre** developed by Sufis as early as the fourth/ninth (or perhaps even the second/eighth) century as a vehicle for defending Sufism against its critics as well as providing an overview of Sufi **history** and **spirituality**, and setting the boundaries of **Sunnī** Sufism. These compendia typically combine **hagiography**, **lexicography**, and mystical theory. In some cases they also supply the only extant bits of **poetry**, **letters**, and other writing attributed to a number of famous Sufi authors. One of the earliest examples of the form is that of **Kharrāz**, but the most famous manuals are those attributed to **Abū**

Ṭālib al-Makkī, Abū Ḥāmid al-**Ghazālī**, **Kalābādhī**, **Hujwīrī**, **Qushayrī**, **Sarrāj**, and Abū Ḥafṣ ʻUmar as-**Suhrawardī**. The term *ishārāt* ("**allusions**") is sometimes used to refer to catechism-like instructional manuals.

MANUSCRIPT ARTS. Calligraphy, illumination, and illustration with miniature **paintings**. Wealthy Muslim patrons of the **arts** over the centuries have considered a number of texts by major Sufi authors worthy of being copied by noted calligraphers. But in addition, many Sufi texts, especially in various genres of **poetry** and **hagiography**, have also been deemed worthy of illumination and illustration by accomplished designers and miniaturists. More often than not, the images chosen interpret their texts primarily at a fairly straightforward narrative level—what one might call a literal interpretation. Some of the most sophisticated artists, however, have added subtle **symbolic** and even **allegorical** associations through their visual exegesis of the texts.

MANZIL. *See* STAGES.

MAQĀM. *See* STATION.

MARABOUT(ISM). Based on the French pronunciation of the **Arabic** for "one who is bound" [i.e., to God] (*marbūṭ*; in a cognate usage one who takes residence in a *ribāṭ* [originally a frontier fortress] is called a *murābiṭ*) referring to revered holy persons and the socio-religious phenomenon of saint veneration in formerly French-colonial **North** and **West Africa**. *See also* BLESSING; FRIEND OF GOD.

MAʻRIFA. *See* KNOWLEDGE, MYSTICAL.

MARTABA (pl. MARĀTIB). *See* RECOLLECTION.

MARTHĪYA. *See* THRENODY.

MARTYR. One who dies for the sake of religious values. The Arabic *shahīd* is from the same root as the word for "witness" (*shāhid*), a term of importance in describing various aspects of mystical **experience**. Some Sufis who were executed because particular expressions of their faith were judged heretical have been considered martyrs in a literal sense. **Metaphorically** speaking, one can be martyred spiritually by dying for love through **annihilation** in mystical **union**. The Arabic root for both witness and martyr are tucked away significantly in the Arabic terms for **contemplation**, *mushāhada*, and the essential Muslim confession of faith, *shahāda*.

MA'RŪF AL-KARKHĪ (d. 200/815). Mystical **ascetic** whose name includes mention of the neighborhood of **Baghdad** in which he lived. He was a disciple of **Farqad** as-Sabakhī and a mentor of **Sarī "as-Saqaṭī." Manualists** and **hagiographers** have preserved many of his sayings on **love** and the meaning of Sufism and many **orders** trace their **lineages** back through him. Some sources credit him with offering the earliest explicit definition of Sufism: grasping spiritual realities and rejecting creaturely concerns.

MASHYAKHA. *See* AUTHORITY.

MASJID. *See* MOSQUE.

MATHNAWĪ. *See* COUPLETS.

MAWLĀNĀ. Arabic **honorific** meaning "Our Master/Patron," bestowed on a number of renowned teachers and Sufis over many centuries. Perhaps the most famous Sufi who is known to many Muslims even today by this title alone is the seventh/13th century Persian mystic **Rūmī**.

MAWLAWĪYA. Name eventually given to the **order** comprised of disciples of **Rūmī**, the Arabic term means "belonging to the Master," referring to the foundational figure's honorific title, ***mawlānā***. Many scholars suggest that Rūmī himself may not have specifically intended to found an order, a conclusion deduced in part from the fact that his own son **Sulṭān Walad** was appointed ***shaykh*** only after three predecessors in the post had died. Because of its use of axial-circular movement in its principal **ritual** for **audition**, the order became widely known by the popular designation "Whirling Dervishes." Each of the several distinct stages of the ritual represents a higher degree of mystical vision. When members join other orders in their paraliturgical ceremonies, they stand out because of their distinctive tall conical **headgear**. The order developed a fairly complex **organizational** structure, with an elaborate hierarchy of positions and roles and spaces dedicated to various specific **ritual** practices. Aspirants or trainees in the order originally underwent a "trial" of 1,001 days of menial work to serve the community.

Although the order is to be found now mostly in **Turkey**, it had spread widely during **Ottoman** times through the **Balkans** and various parts of the central **Middle East**. It has generally been most identified with the **Turkish** pronunciation of the name, Mevleviye. In 1344/1925, a decree of Atatürk officially outlawed all **dervish** orders in the newly proclaimed Republic of Turkey, but since the 1370s/1950s, the Mevlevīs have been allowed to celebrate the birthday of Rūmī in December. A significant branch of the order has become increasingly important in the United States.

MAWLID. *See* BIRTHDAY.

MAWSIM. *See* TIMES, SACRED.

MAYBUDĪ, RASHĪD AD-DĪN (d. 520/1126). Persian religious scholar, **exegete**, and mystic. A student of **Anṣārī**, he wrote an amplified esoteric scriptural commentary based on his teacher's work. His work begins with a Persian rendering of the **Qur'ānic** text in question, discusses its **outward** meanings, and proceeds to an interpretation of the **inward** significance.

MAZĀR. *See* VISITATION.

MEANING. An important feature of Sufi **hermeneutics** typically juxtaposed to **form**, as **inward** is juxtaposed to **outward**. Meaning (*ma'nā*) is thus the spiritual dimension of all things sensible.

MECCA. Ancient city in the west-central **Arabian Peninsula**, birthplace and home of **Muḥammad**, goal of Muslim **pilgrimage**. Among Mecca's major links with Sufism is the centrality of the **Ka'ba**, whose metaphorical dimensions Sufi **poets** (especially **Ibn al-Fāriḍ**) have often developed as a symbol of the **veiled** beauty of

Fig. 1. Tomb of Shaykh Salīm Chishtī (Akbar's spiritual guide), in courtyard of Akbar's mosque, Fatehpur Sikri. Note graves to the right.

Fig. 2. Sufi Musicians at tomb of Salīm Chishtī at Fatehpur Sikri: instrumentalists play two-headed drum and keyboard with hand-pumped bellows, called harmonium, while two singers clap. Note burial behind them.

Fig. 3. Courtyard of Mawlawīya tekke, *showing chimneyed dervish cells around the perimeter, with the mosque housing Rūmī's tomb to the right. Konya, Turkey.*

Fig. 4. Khānaqāh *of Faraj ibn Barquq in Cairo's Northern Cemetery, early 9th/15th century, showing prayer hall with small dome over* miḥrāb*, one of two flanking domed tomb chambers, with shaykh's residence along the right and portion of Sufi residence wing on the left.*

Fig. 5. Egyptian Sufis of the Bayyūmīya-Aḥmadīya and Burhānīya-Shahāwīya orders (as indicated on the two wall banners) gather with their families in the 8th/14th century mosque-tomb complex of the Mamlūk Amīr Sirghitmish, Cairo.

Fig. 6. Sufis with Shaykh of Halveti-Jerrahi order (seated at right rear, looking toward camera), gathering for group spiritual direction session after samā' ceremony. Note images of major figures from the order's history on back wall. Istanbul, 1988.

Fig. 7. Dome of the Rock, Jerusalem, 73/692, with churches on Mount of Olives in background. The octagonal structure stands over the site traditionally identified as the place from which Muhammad Ascended to the Throne of God, a paradigmatic experience for Sufis.

Fig. 8. Tomb of Shaykh Muhammad Rahim Bawa Muhaiyaddeen, in his mazār *in Coatesville, Pa. Note the shaykh's turban mounted on pillar.*

Fig. 9. Indian calendar poster showing five goals of pilgrimage and visitation: upper right, Ka'ba in Mecca; upper left, Prophet's Tomb, Medina; lower right, tomb of 'Abd al-Qādir al-Jīlānī in Baghdad; lower center, tomb of Mu'īn ad-Dīn Chishtī, Ajmer, India; lower left, Dome of the Rock and Al-Aqsā Mosque, Jerusalem.

Fig. 10. *Sufis by a Mountain Spring, c. 1590.*

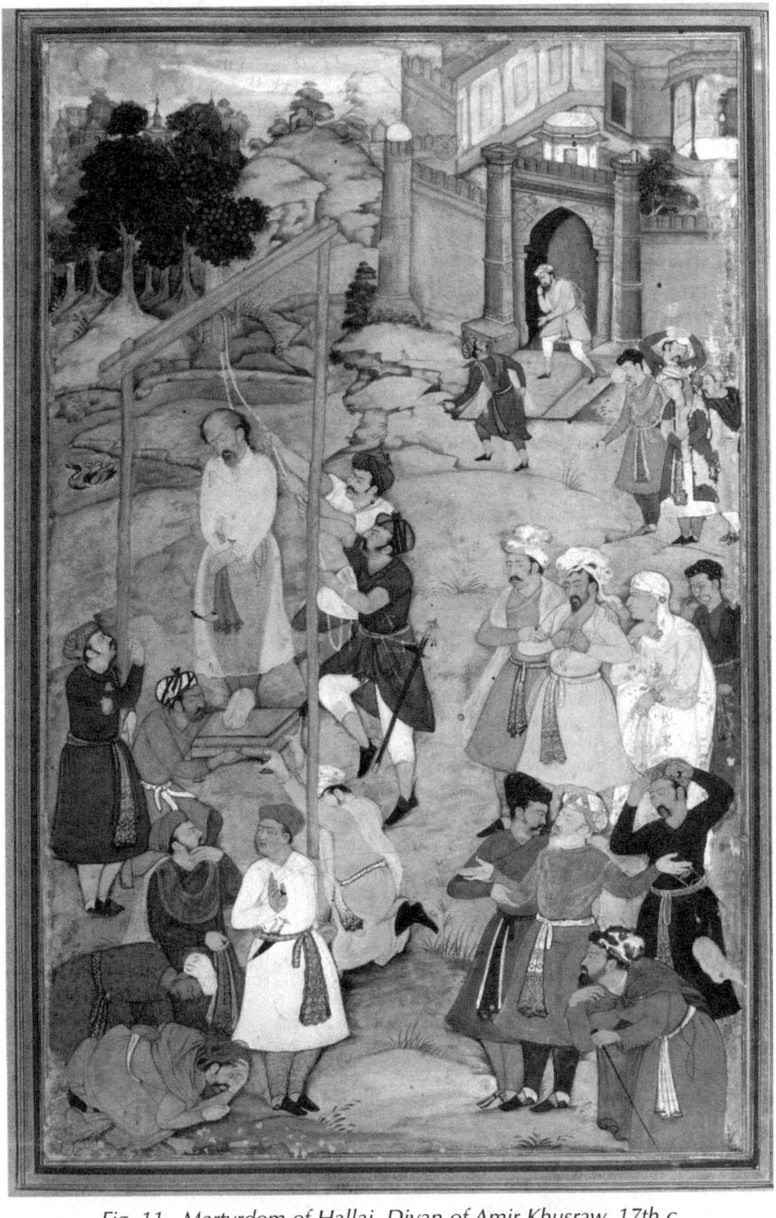

Fig. 11. Martyrdom of Hallaj, Divan of Amir Khusraw, 17th c.

Fig. 12. *Allegorical image of mystical journey (Safawid Persia, c. 1650)*

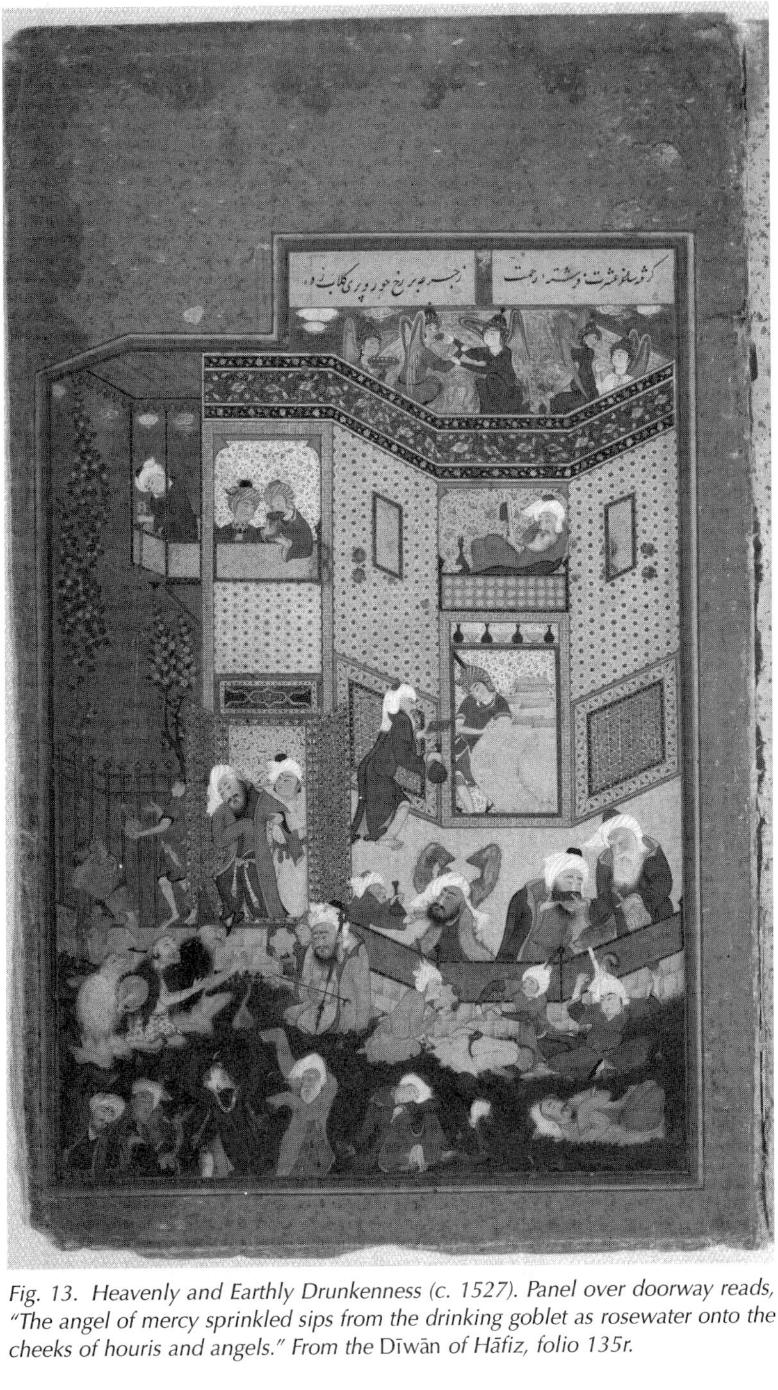

Fig. 13. Heavenly and Earthly Drunkenness (c. 1527). Panel over doorway reads, "The angel of mercy sprinkled sips from the drinking goblet as rosewater onto the cheeks of houris and angels." From the Dīwān of Hāfiz, folio 135r.

Fig. 14. Sa'dī's Dream of Angels while writing poetry, showing three moments in one frame: a student (lower right) dreams that his shaykh, Sa'dī, (reclining at center with a book) is composing poetry praising God as angels descend with gifts of light. The student rushes to the shaykh's door to visit him, appearing again at the door (lower left). Jāmī's Subhat al-abrār, *46.12.147a.*

Fig. 15. Dārā Shikūh with Miān Mīr and his disciple Mullā Shāh. Album painting, c. 1635, Mughal, India. S86.432.

Fig.16. Sufis Dancing; note frame drums, sleeves flowing over hands, and one dancer being assisted in ecstasy (without turban). S86.0035 2r.

Fig. 17. Brass candlestick, with texts from Sa'dī's Bustān: *the moth, symbol of the mystical lover willing to die in the candle's flame, complains that when the honey of the beloved burns down and the sweetness departs from the lover, the lover's own head bursts into flames like that of the unrequited lover Farhād (who committed suicide when he could not have the king's wife, Shīrīn, the "Sweet One").*

Fig. 18. Prince and Holy Man. A royal seeker, with his traveling retinue, receives spiritual direction from a Sufi shaykh. (India, Mughal

Fig. 19. Sufi in Ecstasy in a Landscape, c. 1650–60, Iran, Isfahan.

Fig. 20. Mosque complex of Ottoman Sultan Bayezit I, Bayezit II, showing one wing of a residential facility for Sufis just this side of the domed prayer hall—a matching unit stands on the far side of the prayer hall; and to the left of the minaret is a wing of the medical facility. Edirne, Turkey, near the Bulgarian border.

the divine beloved. Prior to the 13th/19th century **Wahhābī** reforms, the holy city was an important center of the **Naqshbandīya**, and major members of the **Qādirīya** and **Tījānīya** studied there. It was common, in fact, for members of many different **orders** to pursue careers in religious studies in both Mecca and **Medina**, eventually returning to their homelands as teachers. Among the more famous Sufis who resided there for significant periods is the **manualist Abū Ṭālib al-Makkī**. Mecca is the *qibla*, the ritual orientation toward which Muslims turn in daily ritual **prayer**. *See also* JERUSALEM.

MEDINA. Formerly known as Yathrib, the city came to be known as the "City of the Prophet" (*madinat an-nabī*), "The City" for short, after the ***hijra***. Some of the earliest paragons of the kind of devotional life later Sufis would hark back to as exemplary lived in Medina. Their spiritual status derived largely from their having enjoyed personal relationships with the Prophet. This was particularly true of devotees known as the "People of the **Bench**," who were noted for their austerity and attachment to the Prophet because they were content with spending their days on a bench (or perhaps in a portico) near the leader's humble abode.

MENHUAN. *See* CHINA.

METAPHOR. An implied verbal comparison of the sort that Sufi authors often fashioned to describe subtle aspects of the divine-human relationship. Their imaginative figures of speech sometimes involved puns on the various meanings of **Arabic** terms, such as those for **love**, for example. But Sufi metaphors (*majāz* in Arabic) have often had the effect of appearing to tread on forbidden territory in attempts to say what, by definition, no human language can. Sufi authors developed the semantic fields of **wine** and **intoxication**, of the divine **beloved's** devastating **beauty**—the polo player who mercilessly swats the head of the lover downfield with the mallet of her eyebrow, of treasure hidden in **ruins**, of **pilgrimage** to the **Ka'ba** of the heart, of the beloved as sugar-crunching parrot, or/and of the desirability of death-by-drowning in the **ocean** of divine unity, among many others. *See also* ALLEGORY; POETRY; SYMBOLISM.

MIDDLE EAST. The modern nation states that comprise West and Southwest Asia. These include principally **Egypt**, Israel, the **Arabian Peninsula**, Jordan, **Syria**, Lebanon, **Turkey**, and **Iran. Arabic**, **Persian**, **Kurdish**, and **Turkish** are the principal **languages** of the region.

MIRACLES. *See* WONDERS.

MI'RĀJ. *See* ASCENSION.

MĪR DARD. *See* DARD, KHWĀJA MĪR.

MĪR KHURD, MUḤAMMAD BIN MUBĀRAK (eighth/14th century). Indian hagiographer and member of the **Chishtīya**, author of the first extant Indian Sufi biographical anthology. From a family of Sufis, he was a student of **Farīd ad-Dīn Ganj-i Shakar** and later of **Niẓām ad-Dīn Awliyā'** in Delhi. His chief work, *Life Stories of the* ***Friends of God*** (*Siyar al-awliyā'*), recounts the personal histories of major seventh/13th and eighth/14th century Chishtī figures and remains a critical source of information about Sufi life under the Tughluq dynasty of north-central India.

MIRROR. An important multivalent **symbol** in Sufi **poetry** and **theoretical** works. Most commonly, the mirror is a **metaphor** for the **heart** that functions properly only when burnished to a high sheen, but it can also stand for the whole person in relationship to others. The **Prophet** is reported to have said, "The believer is mirror to the believer." Some mystics, such as Aḥmad al-**Ghazālī**, **Ibn al-'Arabī**, and **Yūnus Emre**, like to talk about the need for the **lover** and **Beloved** to reflect one another. Mīr **Dard** considered all of created reality a mirror that reflects **manifestation** of the divine **beauty**. **Rūmī** describes the Prophet himself as a mirror, and says that death is a mirror that reflects everyone's true face. **Friends of God**, too, are mirrors that faithfully reflect the divine reality.

MIRṢAD AL-'IBĀD. *See* NAJM AD-DĪN DĀYĀ RĀZĪ.

MĪTHĀQ. *See* COVENANT, DAY OF.

MIYĀN MĪR (957/1550–1045/1635). Nickname of **Indian** mystic ***Shaykh*** Muḥammad Mīr of Sind, an **ascetic**, **Uwaysī** and member of the **Qādirīya**. From a family of Sufis, he is perhaps most noted as a spiritual counselor to **Mughal** rulers Jahāngīr, Shāh Jahān, and the latter's son, **Dārā Shikūh**. Mīr spent many years in Lahore, pursuing traditional religious studies and studying with various Sufi teachers, before being acknowledged as a spiritual authority in his own right. In spite of his own austere personal discipline, he preferred not to wear the traditional Sufi **cloak**, regarding it as ostentatious. **Theologically** he was a proponent of *waḥdat al-wujūd*. His most famous disciple was **Mullāh Shāh Badakhshī**, who became the *shaykh* of prince Dārā Shikūh and his sister **Jahānārā**.

MOMENT. A dimension of mystical **experience** expressed as a timeless instant (*waqt*) in which one is aware most acutely of one's spiritual **state**. A Sufi is known as the "son of the moment" (*ibn al-waqt*), that is, one who is perfectly attuned to the condition that **God** has chosen for him or her. The moment, or instant, is thus a kind of intense focused spiritual imperative that requires the individual's complete and undivided attentiveness.

MOSES. Major **prophet** of whom the **Qur'ān** speaks frequently and to whom the scripture often likens **Muḥammad**. As a paradigm of mystical **experience**, Moses plays his most prominent role as the *Kalīm Allāh*, the "One who conversed with **God**." Sufi poets are fond of several **metaphorical** features of Moses' story as symbols of crucial features of the spiritual life. For example, "the white hand," a reference to God's turning the prophet's hand white with leprosy, is a sign of God's transforming power; the "rod" or "staff" a reminder of how the prophet's absolute trust in God led to the unleashing of spiritual power that devoured the forces of deceit and evil represented by Pharaoh's magicians; and his confrontation with the Egyptian ruler symbolizes the seeker's need for continual struggle against the **ego**. Leading the Israelites on the Exodus, Moses models the ideal spiritual **guide**. But even Moses needs guidance, and perhaps his most important scriptural episode, from the Sufi perspective, is his search for the Confluence of the Two Seas in the company of the mysterious **Khiḍr**.

MOSQUE. From the Arabic *masjid*, "site of prostration," the term refers primarily to the place where Muslims perform their daily **ritual** prayer at the five prescribed times. Though the term did not originate as a technical term for a specific kind of building, it has largely come to be associated with **architectural** function. The earliest "mosque" structure was apparently a section of the **Prophet's** own house in **Medina**. Eventually, as the Muslim community grew and spread, more and more purpose-built mosques came into being under the influence of regional designs and decorative styles. Originally the *muezzin* made the call to prayer from the Prophet's roof, but in time a separate architectural feature, a tower called the minaret, gave the call greater audibility. Inside the mosque, two early features were a niche called the *miḥrāb*, which pointed the direction of prayer toward **Mecca**; and a pulpit, or *minbar*, from which a sermon was delivered. *See also* INSTITUTIONS.

MOTH. One of the most popular poetic **metaphors** of the pinnacle of mystical **experience**. Many **poets** allude to the moth's fatal attraction to the candle's flame as a symbol of **annihilation**. A moth may see the flame from afar and return to describe its lovely glow to companions; or approach still more boldly into the room and live to tell of the flame's warmth. But, like the mystic who has gone the distance to **ecstasy**, the moth who makes the ultimate commitment will not survive to wax eloquent about the experience.

MU'ĀDH, YAḤYĀ IBN, AR-RĀZĪ. *See* YAḤYĀ IBN MU'ĀDH.

MU'ĀSHARA. *See* COMPANIONSHIP.

MUBĀHA. *See* COMPETITIVENESS.

MUBĀYA'A. *See* INITIATION.

MUGHAL DYNASTY. Major **South Asian** ruling family that traced its political lineage and legitimacy back to Mongol roots (Mughal is a variant of Mongol). Rising to power in Afghanistan, the dynasty's founding ancestor, Bābur, eventually moved to establish a base of power in northern **India**. Under his son Humāyūn and grandson Akbar, the dynasty expanded its dominion over north and central India from its capital in **Delhi**. Akbar and his son Jahāngīr were particularly open, and even fervently attached, to Sufis and patronized their **institutions**. The most influential **orders** during the reigns of these two sovereigns were the **Chishtīya** and **Qādirīya**, and many members of the Mughal house were known to seek the counsel of renowned Sufi ***shaykh***s. Jahāngīr's son Shāh Jahān (who built the Tāj Maḥal) had two children who became famous Sufis: **Dārā Shikūh** and his sister **Jahānārā**.

MUḤĀḌARA. *See* PRESENCE.

MUHAIYADDEEN, BAWA (d. 1407/1986). Sri Lankan ***shaykh*** who established an **order** eventually known as the Bawa Muhaiyaddeen Fellowship in the United States during the 1970s. Centered in the Philadelphia area, the teacher emphasized the centrality of **recollection** and the wisdom of universal understanding among adherents of all religious traditions. His writing on the cause of world peace is perhaps his most widely known. When the *shaykh* died, his mostly born **American**-born followers constructed his **tomb** in Coatesville, Pennsylvania, and it has since attracted **visitation** from Sufi **pilgrims** from various orders.

MUḤAMMAD, PROPHET (c. 570–12/632). Last of a series of divine emissaries to the human race (hence known as the "**Seal** of the Prophets" [*Khatm al-anbiyā'*]), who delivered the consummate revelation known as the **Qur'ān** and whose relationship with God made him the model of the ideal spiritual life for Sufis. Born in **Mecca** toward the latter part of the sixth century, Muḥammad is said to have had his first experiences of **revelation** at about the age of 40. During the subsequent 23 years or so, he uttered the words of the sacred scripture, largely in the form of preaching. After the young Muslim community undertook the ***Hijra***, the Prophet's role added legislation and political leadership to ethical and spiritual example. Virtually every aspect of Muḥammad's way offers an important clue as to the **inward** values toward which all Muslims should strive. The Prophet's simplicity of life and repudiation of all ostentation and luxury made him the paragon of self-denial for the early **ascetics** as well as for later generations. His "unscriptured" (or "illiterate," *ummī*) condition came to symbolize the need for the individual to be present before **God** without precondition, in full realization of the priority of divine initiative in all things. Sufis have always gravitated to (and perhaps sometimes fabricated) **Ḥadīths** that suggest spiritual concerns and qualities, such as the Prophet's attitudes toward prayer and other practices. The Prophet's relationships with his wives, children, and **Companions** also exemplified important values, characterized as they were by kindness and justice. But above all, it was Muḥammad's **Ascension** that most captured the imagination of later Sufis as an image of the ultimate spiritual **experience**. Sufi **poets** in all the major Islamicate literary languages have developed virtually every feature of the Prophet's life and relationships as paradigms of specific aspects of the spiritual path, and have sung in **praise** of his lofty **virtues**.

MUḤAMMAD GHAWTH GWĀLIYĀRĪ. *See* GWĀLIYĀRĪ.

MUḤĀSIBĪ, AL-ḤĀRITH IBN ASAD AL- (d. 243/857). ʿIrāqī mystical teacher and theorist, author of some of the earliest detailed analyses of mystical **psychology**. A major work is his *Book of the Observance of the Rights of God* (*Kitāb ar-riʿāya li-ḥuqūq Allāh*). Its chief target is **ego**-centricity in all its forms, and his strength is his unrelenting focus on the need for intense **self-scrutiny**—a focus that won him the nickname al-Muḥāsibī, "the one who takes account of himself." Some of his critics accused him of being too friendly with the rationalist methods of the speculative **theologians**, but virtually all later Sufis acknowledge the importance of his contribution to the **science of hearts**.

MUḤĀSABA. *See* SELF-SCRUTINY.

MUḤIBB. *See* ORGANIZATION.

MUʿĪN AD-DĪN CHISHTĪ (d. 633/1236). Indian *shaykh* and major figure in the early history of the **Chishtīya** in the subcontinent. Prior to making his base in the city of Ajmīr, where he would spend the last 20 years of his life, Muʿīn ad-Dīn traveled extensively, teaching and gathering followers. Though he had remained **celibate** during his travels, he took two wives after settling in Ajmīr, the better to emulate the **Prophet**. He set a tone of simplicity and austerity, insisting that members of the **order** rely entirely on the kindness of others for their **livelihood** and avoid hoarding in any form, even so much as a day's sustenance. His **tomb** in Ajmīr became a center of Chishtī life and remains a regional goal of pilgrim **visitation** for members of many faiths.

MUJĀHADAT AN-NAFS. *See* SELF-DISCIPLINE.

MUKĀSHAFA. *See* UNVEILING.

MULK. *See* REALMS.

MULLĀ SHĀH BADAKHSHĪ (992/1584–1072/1661). Indian mystic, **poet**, disciple of **Miyān Mīr**, member of the **Qādirīya**, and ***pīr*** of **Dārā Shikūh** and his sister **Jahānārā**. He came from Badakhshan (northeast of Afghanistan) and after moving to Kashmir, he became engaged in Sufism and eventually headed for Lahore to become Miyān Mīr's disciple. He remained celibate and maintained a severe ascetical regimen, emphasizing allegedly extraordinary feats of **breath control**. He is credited with a large output of **Persian lyric** and **didactic**, as well as a partial scriptural **commentary**.

MULTĀNĪ, BAHĀ' AD-DĪN ZAKARĪYA. *See* BAHĀ' AD-DĪN ZAKARĪYA.

MUNĀJĀT. *See* ANṢĀRĪ.

MUNĀJĀT. *See* PRAYER, PERSONAL.

MUNĀQARA. *See* CONTEST.

MUNĀWĪ, 'ABD AR-RA'ŪF AL- (952/1545–1031/1621). Important **Egyptian** religious scholar and Sufi **hagiographer**, initiated as a Sufi by **Sha'rānī**. He maintained connections with various orders, including the **Shādhilīya**, **Khalwatīya**, and **Naqshbandīya**. His most important Sufi work was an anthology of Sufi lives, including sketches of some three dozen Sufi **women**, called *Shining Stars of the Biographies* *of the Masters of Sufism* (*Al-Kawākib ad-durrī ya tarājim aṣ-ṣādāt aṣ-ṣūfīya*). He also composed a **lexicon** of mystical **terminology**.

MUNQIDH MIN AḌ-ḌALLĀL, AL-. *See* GHAZĀLĪ, ABŪ ḤĀMID AL-

MUNSHID. *See* SINGING.

MUNTASIB. *See* ORGANIZATION.

MUQADDAM(A). *See* AUTHORITY.

MUQĀTIL IBN SULAYMĀN (d. 150/767). Early **exegete** who was born in Balkh (Afghanistan) but lived much of his life in **Baghdad** and died in **Baṣra**. He wrote perhaps the first complete scriptural **commentary**, more concerned with situating the sacred text within a narrative framework than with analyzing its grammatical details. His approach opened the way to further developments in Sufi **exegesis** concerning the **Prophet** with his interpretation of the **Qur'ān's** "Verse of Light" (24:35). In his view, the Prophet participates in the divine **light** and illumines the world through the other prophets as well. Later Sufi exegetes would develop at great length the theme of light mysticism in relation to **Muḥammad**.

MURĀBIṬ. *See* MARABOUT(ISM).

MURĀQABA. *See* CONTEMPLATION.

MURAQQA'A. *See* CLOAK.

MURĪD. *See* DISCIPLE.

MURSĪ, ABŪ 'L-'ABBĀS AL- (616/1220– 686/1287). Iberian-born successor to Abū 'l-Ḥasan ash-**Shādhilī** and a pivotal figure in the origins of the **Shādhilīya**. After the founder transferred the **order** from Tunis to **Alexandria**, Mursī adopted a different attitude toward relations with **political** authorities, declining to accept the patronage of the new **Mamlūk** rulers of the region. He studied the work of the Ash'arī theologian Juwaynī (who had taught the elder **Ghazālī**), who was of the Shāfi'ī **Law** school, but it was the Mālikī school with which the order was always chiefly associated. His meager literary output included mainly some **litanies** after the manner of his own ***shaykh***. Among his disciples were **Būṣīrī** and **Ibn 'Aṭā' Allāh of Alexandria**.

MURSHID. *See SHAYKH.*

MUṢĀFAHA. *See* INITIATION.

MUṢALLĀ. *See* PLACES.

MUSHĀHADA. *See* CONTEMPLATION.

MUSHKILĀT. *See* LEXICONS; TERMINOLOGY.

MUSIC. An important ingredient in the **rituals** and **prayer** practices of many Sufi **organizations**. Some **orders** prefer unaccompanied forms of **singing**, in keeping with the long-standing practice of "*a capella*" recitation of the **Qur'ān**. Reticence to use musical instruments may in some instances be related to the belief that musical accompaniment can have the effect of stimulating the emotions in undesirable ways. However, many Sufi groups, such as the **Chishtīya** and **Mawlawīya**, have developed elaborate traditions of ensemble music accompanied by a wide variety of string, wind (especially flutes and other woodwinds), and percussion instruments. Some traditions, such as **Qawwālī**, add keyboard instruments capable of the considerable volume needed to support large groups of singers.

MUṢṬAFĀ. *See* PROPHET, NAMES OF.

MUSTAṢWIF. *See* SUFISM.

MUTAJARRID. *See* ORGANIZATION.

MUTAṢAWWIF. *See* SUFISM.

MUTASHABBIH. *See* ORGANIZATION.

MUZAMZIM. *See* SINGING.

MYSTERY. A quality or dimension of spiritual **experience**. Sufi authors speak of mystery as both a macrocosmic **realm** by means of the term *ghayb*, the "unseen or hidden," and a microcosmic human faculty (*sirr*, "inmost nature"), sometimes identified as a level within the **heart**. Some further speak of the heart's "mystery within mystery," a still deeper level of experience.

MYSTIC. A generic name referring to individuals possessed of the highest levels of spiritual **experience**. Arabic terms that function as synonyms for "mystic" include *'āshiq* (lover), *'ārif* (one endowed with intimate **knowledge**), *sālik* (**wayfarer**), *majdhūb* (one drawn to **God** through *jadhba*, effortless attraction), and *fatā* (young man, hero).

– N –

NAFAḤĀT AL-UNS. *See* JĀMĪ.

NAFS. *See* EGO.

NĀGAWRĪ, ḤAMĪD AD-DĪN. *See* ḤAMĪD AD-DĪN.

NĀ'IB. *See* GOVERNANCE.

NAJĪB. *See* CHIEF.

NAJM AD-DĪN DĀYA RĀZĪ (573/1177–654/1256). Persian mystical author and **exegete**, member of the **Kubrāwīya** and disciple of Najm ad-Dīn **Kubrā** and Majd ad-Dīn **Baghdādī**. He traveled extensively in the central **Middle East**, with a longer sojourn in **Anatolia**, encountering a number of major seventh/13th century Sufis, including Abū Ḥafṣ 'Umar as-**Suhrawardī**. His chief work is *Path of the God-servants to the Starting Point and the Return (Mirṣad al-'ibād)*, an influential **manual** of mystical spirituality whose 40 chapters recall **Moses' forty** nights of communion with **God**. One of his principal contributions is his clear, careful analysis of the essential ingredients of the **science of hearts**, including a critique of the qualifications of an effective ***shaykh***.

NAKHSHABĪ, ABŪ TURĀB AN- (d. 245/860). Central Asian ascetic, follower of Ḥātim al-Aṣamm ("The Blind," d. 237/851). He was renowned for the quality of his complete **trust** in God (*tawakkul*), and is known to us largely from anecdotes and sayings preserved in the classical **manuals**.

NAKHSHABĪ, ḌIYĀ' AD-DĪN AN- (d. 751/1350). Persian author and **poet** who became affiliated with the **Chishtīya** after moving from his native Uzbekistan to **India**. Though he is most famous for his charming *Book of the Parrot (Ṭūṭī-nāma)*, his importance for the history of Sufism lies in an anthology of utterances and stories of famous ***shaykhs***—a blend of **hagiography** and **lexicography**, and a treatise-like work that includes samples of Sufi "exhortations and preaching."

NAMES OF GOD. *See* GOD.

NAQĪB. *See* CHIEF; RITUAL.

NAQSHBAND, KHWĀJA BAHĀ' AD-DĪN (718/1318–791/1389). Central Asian Sufi leader from near **Bukhara** in present-day Uzbekistan, traditionally named as the founder of the **Naqshbandīya**. Traditional accounts consider him the seventh *khwāja* ("master") in a line that originated with **Yūsuf Hamadhānī**, and some regarded him as a spiritual descendant of **Ja'far aṣ-Ṣādiq**. He is said to have been mystically initiated by **Ghijduwānī**, some of whose teaching he adopted in his own spiritual principles. Eight key practices that apparently originated with his initiator included **breath control**, observing one's footsteps, spiritual introspection as a kind of journey, isolation even in public (*khalwat dar anjuman*), recollection, control and observation of one's thoughts, and remembering **God**. Naqshband later added awareness of time dedicated to various activities, keeping track of deeds of remembrance, and wakefulness of the **heart**. The name Naqshband, associated with embroidery, may derive from the notion that the name of God is stitched onto the heart of the seeker. As part of his own spiritual training, he apprenticed to at least two major ***shaykhs*** of the **Yasawīya**. Naqshband focused on the importance of silent **recollection** and preferred a way of life that called as little attention to itself as possible. No major written work of his is extant and his followers apparently did not publish his discourses.

NAQSHBANDĪYA. Order of **Central Asian** origin that eventually came to be active across a broader expanse of territory than any but the **Qādirīya**. It was particularly important also in the **Balkans**, **Turkey**, **Persia**, Afghanistan, and **India**, and there is evidence of its spread as far eastward as parts of present-day **Indonesia**. The organization has played a major role in the history of Sufism in **China** as well. During the 14th/19th century, the order's resistance to foreign domination of Central Asia and the **Caucasus** resulted in disastrous losses at the hands of Russian forces. Among the order's most famous members are Khwāja 'Ubayd Allāh **Aḥrār**, **Bāqī Bi-'llāh**, **Aḥmad Brelwī**, the poet **Jāmī**, **Mīr Dard**, Khwāja Muḥammad **Parsā**, and Aḥmad **Sirhindī**. One of its main branches, the *Mujaddidī*, or "renewer," suborder was a particularly influential **reform** movement in India. The order was far more **politically** active than the Qādirīya and members typically were married and had active family lives. Leaders of the order have traditionally been very concerned with maintaining a strictly observant compliance with all strictures of Islamic **Law** while still allowing some latitude of spiritual practice within the organization. One of the order's more distinctive ritual exercises involves **visualizing** one's ***shaykh*** while meditating.

NASAFĪ, 'AZĪZ AD-DĪN (d. c. 680/1282). Central Asian Sufi theorist and ***shaykh*** of the **Kubrāwīya**, disciple of Sa'd ad-Dīn **Ḥammūyā**. Among his most important works for the history of Sufism is his *Disclosure of Spiritual Truths* (*Kashf al-ḥaqā'iq*), a **treatise** in which elaborates on **cosmological** themes. He was also interested in the symbolism of the ***Imām***, especially in relation to the concept of **Friends of God**. He wrote a treatise on the **Perfect Person** (*Insān-i kāmil* in Persian), and his theories evidently had an impact on Ḥajjī **Bektāsh Walī**.

NASHĪD. *See* SINGING.

NASĪMĪ, 'IMĀD AD-DĪN (d. 820/1417). Ḥurūfī lyric poet whose **Turkish** writing was much influenced by the work of **Ḥallāj**. He left poetry in **Persian** and is said to have written in **Arabic** as well. Before associating himself with the founder of the Ḥurūfīya, he had been a disciple of **Shiblī** in **Baghdad**. His poetry gained popularity thanks to dissemination by ***qalandars***. He was executed in Aleppo, **Syria**, flayed alive in a gruesome manner of death that recalled that of the earlier mystical martyr.

NAṢĪR AD-DĪN CHIRĀGH-I DIHLĪ (c. 675/1276–757/1356). South Asian student and **successor** of **Niẓām ad-Dīn Awliyā'**, and major ***shaykh*** of the **Chishtīya**. From the **order's** *khānqāh* in **Delhi** he led the organization for over thirty years, generally maintaining close relations with the Tughluq sovereigns. Although he left no writing of his own, his disciples compiled a substantial record of his thought, as represented especially by his **discourses**, even during the *shaykh*'s lifetime. One of his most renowned disciples was **Gīsū Darāz**.

NĀṢIR MUḤAMMAD 'ANDALĪB (1105/1693–1172/1759). Indian mystical author, father of Mīr **Dard**, and member of the Mujaddidī **Naqshbandīya**. As a **Persian** poet, he took the pen name 'Andalīb, "**Nightingale**," and wrote a lengthy allegorical work identifying himself indirectly with the **Prophet** by explaining that the Nightingale who seeks the **Rose** is actually the Prophet.

NAṢRĀBĀDHĪ, ABŪ 'L-QĀSIM IBRĀHĪM AN- (d. 367/977). Disciple of **Shiblī** and teacher of **Qushayrī's** mentor, Abū 'Alī ad-**Daqqāq**. He was noted for the fire of his religious devotion.

NĀSŪT. *See* REALMS.

NA'T. *See* PRAISE.

NEO-PLATONISM. A late classical philosophical system whose broad influence throughout the eastern Mediterranean world is evident also in some aspects of Sufi **cosmology** and theories of **knowledge**. Its influence filtered into Islamic circles during late antiquity and early medieval times. Greek philosophical texts became increasingly available in Arabic translations commissioned especially during the second–third/ninth century by **'Abbāsid** caliphs in **Baghdad**. Some early-modern European scholars have discerned extensive parallels between Sufism and neo-Platonic thought because they interpreted some Islamic mystical traditions as monistic and/or pantheistic. Some have made the connection more specifically with the so-called **Illuminationist** school (*ḥikmat al-ishrāq*), with its hierarchical cosmos of **light** and **angelic** orders as well as emanationist elements. Another important example of an arguable neo-Platonic link with Sufism is the work of the **Iberian** mystic **Ibn Sab'īn**; and the thought of **Ibn al-'Arabī** is suffused with neo-Platonic language. There is also evidence of possible neo-Platonic influence on Sufi thought in **orders** with historic connections to **Shī'ī** thinkers and political institutions and in the concept of the **Perfect Person**. Finally, scholars have identified neo-Platonic elements in the thought of major **Southeast Asian** Sufis **Ḥamza Fanṣūrī** and **Samaṭrānī**.

NEO-SUFISM. A contested designation for some early modern **reform**-oriented movements characterized by a heightened awareness of the **Prophet's** defining role in Islamic spirituality and a desire to purge excesses and "innovations" from the tradition. Among the major figures associated with neo-Sufism are **Aḥmad ibn Idrīs** of Algeria and his follower al-Ḥajj 'Umar, and Aḥmad ibn Muḥammad at-**Tījānī** of Morocco and his followers Muḥammad ibn 'Ali as-**Sanūsī**, 'Uthmān al-Mīrghanī (12081793–1269/1852), and Ibrāhīm ar-Rashīd (1228/1813–1291/1874). Some scholars associate 13th/19th century "muridism" in the **Caucasus**, for example, with the larger movement of neo-Sufism, while others argue that the Caucasian resistance activities of Sufi groups in Daghestan and Chechnya and elsewhere do not constitute a clearly distinguishable movement worthy of the name neo-Sufism.

NIFFARĪ, 'ABD AL-JABBĀR AN- (d. 354/965 or 366/976). 'Irāqī mystical author of the paradox-laced *Book of Mystical Stayings* (or *Standings, Kitāb al-mawāqif*) and *Mystical Addresses* (*Mukhāṭabāt*). More than perhaps any other early Sufi theologian, he breaks the molds of traditional mystical psychology with his strikingly original analysis of spiritual **experience**. Writing in more or less thematic clusters of **aphorism**-like statements, he obliterates whatever sense of separateness or individuality his reader might otherwise consider operative in the divine-human relationship. His apothegms defy categorization and virtually dare the reader to identify a logical sequence. In the mystical moment of "**standing**," which Niffarī ranks higher than infused **knowledge**, the seeker seems to experience a kind of **annihilation** as the divine presence overcomes human individuality.

NIGHT JOURNEY. An **experience**, called the *isrā'*, in which the **Prophet** is said to have been "carried" or "made to travel at night" by **God**, "from the **mosque** of the sanctuary to the Farther Mosque." Traditional interpretations came to identify the former location with the **Ka'ba** and the latter with the present site of the early eighth century Al-Aqṣā ("farther") mosque in **Jerusalem**, just south of the late seventh century **Dome of the Rock**. Traditionally situated in time just prior to the Prophet's **Ascension**, the journey has been interpreted by some authors as involving physical locomotion, while most Sufi authors have considered it as primarily a spiritual experience. *See also* MECCA.

NIGHTINGALE. A major poetic **metaphor** used by Sufi **poets** to refer to the **lover** who is so enamored of the **rose** as to be completely oblivious to the danger of its thorns. Utterly enthralled by the **beauty** of the beloved, the **bird** sings its heart out across great distances until the opportunity arrives to risk the pain of union. In the latter respect the bird is a metaphor for the **soul**, but as a singer, it naturally came to be associated with revealing angel **Gabriel** and with the **Prophet**. Along with the **falcon**, the nightingale is one of the more important of the many birds that figure prominently in poetic imagery.

NI'MAT ALLĀH WALĪ, SHĀH (c. 731/1331–834/1431). Syrian-born **Persian** mystical author who was introduced in **Mecca** to a Sufi **lineage** deriving from **Abū Madyan**. He traveled widely through the **Middle East** and **Central Asia**, where he established himself as a founding ***shaykh*** of a new **order**, before finally settling in central Iran. He spent the greater part of his life there in the city of Kirman and was buried in Mahan, where his **tomb** remains an important site. His extensive body of writing includes a number of **theoretical** and **exegetical** works as well as lyric **poetry**. Deeply influenced by the thought of **Ibn al-'Arabī**, he became a major interpreter of the theology of *waḥdat al-wujūd* (ontological **unity**).

NI'MAT-ALLĀHĪYA. Persian order founded by **Ni'mat Allāh Walī**, historically influential in **Central Asia** and **India**, but today largely limited to Iran and with important groups in western Europe. It traces its **lineage** back to **'Alī** and is generally identified as a **Shī'ī** order. The founder's son, Khalīl Allāh (c. 773/1371–860/1465), left Persia for southern **India** and there established a branch of the order. Over the subsequent century or so, the Iranian branch declined as a result of conflicts with **Ṣafawīd** political authorities. The Indian branch flourished until the early 13th/late 18th century. The last of the Indian ***shaykh***s, Ma'ṣūm 'Alī Shāh, was sent to revive the order in Persia. The organization ran afoul of both the Ṣafawid rulers and the now well-established Shī'ī religious establishment because of politically threatening claims on the part of the order's leadership to divinely sanctioned authority. Ma'ṣūm 'Alī Shāh was forced to leave the capital, Isfahan, and while traveling toward northeastern Persia was arrested and eventually executed (1211/1796); his death was interpreted as **martyrdom**. The order flourished in (post-Ṣafawid) Iran during the 13th/19th and 14th/early 20th centuries before being officially disallowed by the Islamic Republic of Iran beginning in 1400/1979.

NĪSHĀPŪR. Central Asian city in **Khurasan**, a place of great historical importance in the early history and development of "*adab* Sufism"; that is, organizational developments presupposing specific regimens of **behavior** and **ethics**. Among the more influential Sufis who figured prominently in that early history **Yaḥyā ibn Mu'ādh** and Abū 'Uthmān al-**Ḥīrī**, as well as the founder of the ascetical movement known as the Karrāmīya. Noted Sufis who contributed significantly to the religious culture of the city include Abū Ḥāmid al-**Ghazālī**, **Qushayrī**, and **Tirmidhī**. The poet Farīd ad-Dīn **'Aṭṭār** was one of the city's more famous later Sufis.

NIYĀZĪ MIṢRĪ EFENDI (1027/1617–1105/1694). **Turkish** mystical **poet** during the **Ottoman dynasty** who wrote in both **Arabic** and Turkish. Although his family had links to the **Naqshbandīya**, he was initiated into the **Qādirīya** and studied with a ***shaykh*** of the **Khalwatīya** as well. He became a popular **preacher** and developed a reputation for effecting saintly **wonders**. An **order** named after him survived for a time in western Turkey and Greece but never developed significantly.

NIẒĀM AD-DĪN AWLIYĀ' (a.k.a. Muḥammad Badā'ūnī) (c. 640/1243–725/1325). **Indian** religious scholar and Sufi leader largely responsible for the wide dispersion of the **Chishtīya** in the subcontinent. A disciple and major successor of **Farīd ad-Dīn Ganj-i Shakar**, he insisted on limited **political** involvement and emphasized the spiritual benefits of active service of the poor and needy. A collection of his Persian **discourses**, *Morals for the Heart* (*Fawā'id al-fu'ād*), enshrines important aspects of his spiritual legacy. Among his most influential successors were **Burhān ad-Dīn Gharīb** and **Naṣīr ad-Dīn Chirāgh-i Dihlī**.

NIẒĀMĪ GANJAWĪ, ILYĀS IBN YŪSUF (c. 535/1141–606/1209). Āzarbayjānī **poet** from the city of Ganja in the **Caucasus**, most famous for his 30,000 verse romantic/**didactic**/epic anthology *The Quintet (Khamsa)*. Written in the literary **genre** of rhyming **couplets** known as *mathnawī*, two of the five poems have been especially important in the history of Sufism. *The Treasury of Mysteries (Makhzan al-asrār)*, much influenced by the work of **Sanā'ī**, delves deeply into the intricacies of human motivation. *Majnūn and Laylā* recounts the romantic tale of a young man desperately smitten (*majnūn* means "possessed by a *jinn*") with Laylā, a story often interpreted as the quintessential relationship between **lover** and **Beloved**. His intricate character development of major **women** in his stories is particularly noteworthy.

NORTH AFRICA. The largest portion of a region known in Arabic as the *maghrib*, the area is generally said to include (east to west) Libya, Tunisia, Algeria, and Morocco. (The *maghrib* technically also includes the **Iberian Peninsula**.) Major **orders** of the region include the

Darqāwīya, Idrīsīya, **Qādirīya**, **Sanūsīya**, **Shādhilīya**, and **Tījānīya**, along with various suborders of the largest of these. Major Sufis important in the region include **Abū Madyan**, **Ibn 'Abbād**, **Ibn 'Ajība**, **'Alawī**, **Darqāwī**, **Ibn Mashīsh**, **Jazūlī**, **Tījānī**, and **Zarrūq**.

NUMBER SYMBOLISM. Deriving mystical meaning from numbers either in themselves, or with reference to their alphabetical counterparts. Every letter in the **Arabic alphabet** (*abjad*) has been associated with a numerical value. Some numbers are particularly important in Islamic traditional generally, as for example, five: the daily **ritual prayers**, the so-called pillars (profession of faith, **pilgrimage**, alms, **fasting**, ritual prayer), the five members of the "family of the **Prophet**" (the Prophet, Fāṭima, **'Alī**, Ḥasan, and Ḥusayn). Seven is similarly symbolic in relation to the repetition of certain ritual actions, or clusters of **Friends of God** in the Sufi cosmic **hierarchy**, or the number of valleys traversed on the mystical **journey**. The number **forty** is associated with **retreat** as well as with another cluster of Friends of God. Among the more theologically important numbers is 99, associated with the total of the Beautiful Names of **God**.

NŪR. *See* LIGHT.

NŪR MUḤAMMADĪ. *See* LIGHT.

NŪRBAKHSH, JAWĀD, DR. (1346/1927–). Contemporary ***shaykh*** of the Khāniqāhī **Ni'mat-Allāhīya**, **poet** and religious scholar. He was an active founder of *khānqāhs* throughout **Iran** during the later 14th/20th century, before moving to the United States and later to England, to continue his work at spreading the order and spearheading a large publishing enterprise focused on the **order's** history and thought. The London-based retired psychiatrist has published numerous English writings designed to interpret the order's traditional teachings for a contemporary readership, perhaps most notably in the multivolume encyclopedic *Sufi **Symbolism***.

NŪRBAKHSH, MUḤAMMAD SAYYID (d. 869/1465). Shī'ī founder of the **Nūrbakshshīya**, disciple of Khuttalānī (d. 826/1423), a major student of **Kubrā**.

NŪRBAKHSHĪYA. Branch of the **Kubrāwīya** founded by Muḥammad **Nūrbakhsh** in Persia. The order did not survive in strength for long under the **Ṣafawid** dynasty, but has enjoyed a rebirth in **Iran**, **India**, and Kashmir since the 12th/18th century. Like other orders of that time and place, its leadership had to make a choice between allegiance to a **Shī'ī** regime or leave, and even though they sought an accommodation with the regime, the arrangement was not entirely satisfactory.

NŪRĪ, ABŪ 'L-ḤUSAYN AN- (c. 226/840–295/907). Disciple of **Sarī "as-Saqaṭī,"** associate of **Junayd**, and important, if sometimes wayward, member of the **Baghdādī** circle of Sufis. His family was of **Khurāsānī** origin. His effusive views on **love** of God rendered him theologically suspect among some religious scholars, and many of his **ecstatic** utterances have been preserved in the writings of others. His one major extant work, *The Stations of Hearts (Maqāmāt al-qulūb)*, centers around an **allegorical** description of the **heart** as a fortress of seven battlements under the safekeeping of **fear** and **hope**.

NUSSĀK. *See* ASCETICISM.

– O –

OATH. A pact (*'ahd*) or swearing of allegiance (*bay'a*) between the seeker and the spiritual director that forms an important part of the rites of Sufi **initiation**. The aspirant symbolically hands his or her will over to the ***shaykh*** in a gesture of trust, acknowledging the full **authority** of the one entrusted with guidance along the **path**.

OBEDIENCE. An attitude of complete openness to being guided, by God ultimately and one's spiritual guide (***shaykh***) more immediately. Taking the **oath** of **initiation**, the seeker agrees to surrender entirely to whatever the *shaykh* requires, even if a given directive seems to contradict good sense. A classic illustration refers to the willingness even to "water a dry stick," purely because it is the guide's directive for the seeker at this moment, or to be like the cadaver in the hands of those who prepare it for burial.

OCEAN. Metaphor employed by numerous Sufi **poets** and **theorists** to allude to the multiple dimensions of the essence, attributes, presence, and transcendent reality of **God**. Authors typically use the term in compounds, such as ocean of existence, of **fire**, of **intimacy**, or engulfing ocean (referring to the ancient **cosmological** notion that the earth is encircled by a vast sea). This expansive metaphor, signaled by the Arabic *baḥr* and Persian *daryā*, functions particularly in relation to the metaphors of **journey** into the immeasurable unknown and **annihilation** by **drowning** in the divine mercy and goodness.

ODE. Literary **genre** most often referred to by the Arabic term *qaṣīda*, generally one of the lengthier forms of **lyric poetry** sometimes employed as panegyric. It typically uses a monorhyme scheme in which both hemistichs in the first verse end in the same sounds, and subsequent verses end in those same sounds. The prime literary model of the form is the pre-Islamic **Arabic** ode, which begins with a lover's lament over the traces of a lost beloved. The second large section describes the lover's quest to find the beloved, though the seeker may boast of having "gotten over" the pain of separation. A third large section treats a main theme, often in **praise** of a ruler or personification of sanctity. Many great Sufi poets—including **'Aṭṭār**, **Ghālib**, **Ibn al-Fāriḍ**, and **Rūmī**—developed the form into a vehicle of mystical expression in Arabic, **Persian**, **Turkish**, **Urdu**, and a host of other languages. The ode has been adapted as a vehicle for religious expression perhaps more widely than any other single Islamicate literary form. *See also* LITERATURE.

OFFICE. Special set of communal or individual **prayer** texts chosen by some Sufi **orders** as a distinctive way of **ritually** sanctifying the hours of the day. Texts for this breviarylike liturgy of the hours are sometimes unique to a particular order, because a founder or other holy figure associated with the group composed it. Four terms commonly used are *waẓīfa* (duty), *wird* (access), *ḥizb* (portion, litany), and *rātib* (repetitive, prearranged text), and their respective plurals. As a "duty" the **litany** was also referred to as *waẓīfa*. These texts were often assigned for recitation at regular daily times, much like a monastic "liturgy of the hours" or office, or for particular occasions, since they gave one "access" (*wird, awrād*) to a particular "segment" (*ḥizb, aḥzāb*) of **time**. They may refer either to larger set texts or collections of shorter prayers assembled specifically for one aspirant by the ***shaykh***. These texts can function rather like *mantras* assigned by a **Hindu** *guru*, kept secret from all but the aspirant in question and specially chosen. Some prayers composed by famous *shaykhs* have taken on virtually magical significance, so that their use has expanded well beyond membership in an order. One of the most famous examples is **Ibn ʿAṭāʾ Allāh's aphoristic** *Book of Wisdom*, a standard text of the **Shādhilīya**.

ONENESS. The **union** or melding of the **lover** with the **Beloved**, often expressed by the term *ittiḥād*. This mode of **experience**, related to **intimacy**, differs from **annihilation** in that the latter assumes total loss of self whereas oneness does not. Mystical oneness is expressed through a number of **metaphors** as well as concepts such as **ecstasy** and "arrival" (*waṣl*). Some Sufi authors have discussed the state of oneness in such a way as to suggest a monistic or pantheistic worldview, but most have been at pains to explain that mystical oneness does not necessarily imply a **theologically** unacceptable loss of distinction between Creator and creature. The debate has been focused in the ***wujūdī*** **controversy.**

ORDER. Principal mode of formal Sufi **organization** most commonly referred to with the term *ṭarīqa* (pl. *ṭuruq*), "path" or "way." The earliest focal points for the gathering of spiritual seekers and devotees were local mosques and the **residences,** or *zāwiyas*, of men and women whose reputations for virtue and learning attracted followers. As these circles of disciples grew, so, gradually, did the need for **institutional** structures designed for accommodating larger and more diverse groups in more focused communities of purpose. **Abū Saʿīd ibn Abī 'l-Khayr** is generally credited with crafting the first basic formal **rule** or charter for the regulation of community life, but the organization was limited to a single foundation. It was during the first half of the sixth/12th century that the earliest major orders developed under the leadership of **ʿAbd al-Qādir al-Jīlānī**, Aḥmad ar-**Rifāʿī**, and Abū Najīb as-**Suhrawardī** and his nephew Abū Ḥafṣ ʿUmar as-**Suhrawardī**. Some of the orders had particularly close ties to *futūwa*, or **chivalry**-oriented, organizations. Many orders grew so expansively that they spawned branch foundations or "suborders" (often called *ṭawā'if*, sg. *ṭā'ifa*, "party, faction").

Among the principal orders are the **Badawīya**, **Bektāshīya**, **Chishtīya**, **Darqāwīya**, **Dasūqīya**, **Firdawsīya**, **Khalwatīya**, **Kubrāwīya**, **Malāmatīya**, **Mawlawīya**, **Naqshbandīya**, **Ni'matallāhīya**, **Nūrbakhshīya**, **Qādirīya**, **Rifā'īya**, **Sālimīya**, **Sammānīya**, **Sanūsīya**, **Shādhilīya**, **Shaṭṭārīya**, **Suhrawardīya**, **Tījānīya**, and **Yasawīya**. Practices and internal structures of all kinds varied from one order to another. Among the more common distinguishing attributes were modes of **livelihood**, degrees of **political** activism, social integration or preference for isolation, relative emphasis on daily communal life, and styles of **prayer** and **ritual**. Certain organizations, such as the **Karrāmīya**, **Qalandarīya**, **Qizil-bāsh**, and **Ṣafawids**, manifest features that have prompted some to include them in this category.

ORGANIZATION. Structures and principles governing the establishment, functioning, and spread of Sufi **orders** and **institutions**. The earliest historical records of formal organization are *silsilas*, genealogies tracing the spiritual **lineages** or pedigrees of prominent individual Sufis who identified themselves with (*intasaba*, *intimā*) a particular organization. Evidence of the earliest attempts to organize institutional structures took the form of **rules** authored by leading Sufis who typically came to be identified as founders of orders. Within the various orders, organizational concerns grew more complex as the groups grew locally and, in many instances, expanded regionally and transregionally by founding new branches. In general, the larger the institution, the more elaborate its methods of regulating communal life and delegating **authority** became.

Overall organizational structures vary from one order to another. Some original foundations have insisted on maintaining centralized control over their branches, while others have allowed considerable autonomy in derivative foundations. Within a given local foundation, daily life saw different duties assigned to members of various ranks. Mid-level members were called by a variety of names, such as *'azīzān* (dear ones) or *mutajarrid* (devotee). In some organizations a special category was reserved for members who did not belong to the dominant ethnic group of the order, as with the term *tilmīdh* (pupil), referring to lower level members of the **West African** Mukhtārīya order not of the Kunta lineage.

Another important aspect of organization has to do with varying attitudes toward acceptance of members outside the core of an order, affiliates (sometimes known as *awlād aṭ-ṭarīqa*, "children of the Path"; *muḥibb*, "lover[s]"; *mutashabbih*, "one who emulates"; or *muntasib*, "one who seeks a connection" [Bektāshīya]), who participated only in a limited number of the organization's activities and often played a supporting role. Early gatherings centered on ***shaykhs*** whose authority derived from their spiritual attainment and piety. As the organizations grew into more formal institutional structures with multiple foundations, systems for maintaining the organizations naturally grew more complex. Structures of **governance** thus merit a separate consideration. *See Also* RANKS.

OTTOMAN DYNASTY. Beginning with a confederation of **Turkic** tribes in **Anatolia** under the leadership of a certain 'Uthmān (Osman in Turkish, hence Ottoman), a succession of rulers advanced on the ancient Byzantine Empire from both the European and Asian sides, gradually reducing it to the environs of Constantinople. In 857/1453, Mehmet the Conqueror took the city, which eventually came to be known as Istanbul. Through much of the 10th/16th and 11th/17th centuries, Ottoman sultans ruled much of the Mediterranean basin and central **Middle East**. Ottoman lands gradually diminished, until they included what is now the nation-state of Turkey, and in the 1920s the dynasty was supplanted by the secular regime of Muṣṭafā Kemāl Atatürk

Under Ottoman rule, a number of Sufi **orders** flourished, most notably the **Bektāshīya**, **Mawlawīya**, and **Naqshbandīya**. Sultans such as Bayezit II (r. 886/1481–918/1512) and Sulaymān the Magnificent (r. 927/1520–974/1566) were major patrons of various Sufi orders and famous ***shaykhs***, **endowing** and building considerable **institutional** complexes for them. Some Sufi **residential facilities** were incorporated into mosque-centered imperial complexes along with *madrasas*, medical schools and hospitals, and caravanserais. As under other major dynasties, an ongoing matter of concern and discussion for Sufis was the degree to which **political** involvement was appropriate to any given order.

OUSPENSKY, P. D. (1296/1878–1367/1947). A Russian teacher of music and mystical theories, follower of Georgy **Gurdjieff**, credited by some with passing along Sufi ideas and practices. This less than accurate association appears to derive from Ouspensky's being influenced by the "theosophical movement" of Madame Blavatsky. This "theosophy," however, is not directly connected with **theosophical** notions developed in classical Sufi sources.

OUTWARD. Form, exteriority, praxis; all things visible or whose significance is readily apparent, or whose significance one evaluates purely on the basis of a literal or superficial **hermeneutic**. The outward, or exoteric *(ẓāhir/ī)*, is therefore an aspect of reality accessible to the vast majority of individuals who, at the very least, are willing to seek the informed view of specialists in the practice-oriented dimensions of the sacred sources and religious **law**. All **meaning** presupposes both outward and **inward** dimensions, but Sufism presumes that every seeker must move beyond mere appearances to the spiritual resonance of all things.

– P –

PAINTING. Illumination or illustration, particularly in manuscripts of mystical **poetry** or **hagiography**. In addition to numbering important **calligraphers** within their ranks, some Sufis have also been accomplished painters and illuminators. Favorite Sufi subjects have been scenes described especially in **didactic** poems and narratives of the **Friends of God**. In addition, some painters have used visual images to give a distinctively Sufi twist to the interpretation of texts not overtly mystical in tone, playing on the frequently ambiguous imagery stories of romance and intoxication, for example. Except in some cases of narrative images used to illustrate stories of holy persons, one is frequently hard-pressed to tell whether a particular image depicts a scene of earthly dalliance and love or suggests a more **metaphorical** or even **allegorical** allusion to celestial or spiritual encounter.

PĀKISTĀN. Modern nation-state founded in 1367/1947 with the "partition" of **India** for the express purpose of segregating Muslim and

Hindu populations. Originally comprised of "western" and "eastern" sections, Pakistan was split again when "eastern Pakistan" seceded in 1391/1971 to become the nation-state of Bangladesh. The city of Lahore was home to a number of important Sufis during medieval and early modern times, and the provinces of **Sind** and **Panjab** (two of the nation's four) boast their own long traditions of mystical **poetry** in several vernaculars. In addition, a number of Pakistan's major **Persian** and **Urdu** language literary figures were Sufis. Among the most prominent in modern times is Sir Muḥammad **Iqbāl**, and the **Qādirīya** is perhaps the most influential order still active in Pakistan.

PANJĀBĪ. An Indo-Aryan **language** written in **Persian** script and spoken especially in central and eastern portions of the Indo-Pakistani province of Panjāb, which was divided with the partition of India in 1367/1947. A number of important Sufi **poets** wrote in Panjābī, including **Bulhe Shāh**, **Madhō Lāl Ḥusayn**, and **Sulṭān Bāhū**, and it is the principal language of the popular Sufi-inspired **song** tradition called *qawwālī*. This performance art is based on a **lyric** form consisting of rhymed **couplets** and a recurring refrain. One distinctively Panjābī poetic **genre** is the lengthy narrative romance, sometimes clearly allegorical, which has often reworked themes from the **Persian didactic** repertoire.

PARADISE. The heavenly "garden" (*janna*), ultimate goal of faithful Muslims and the symbol of union with **God** for spiritual seekers. Sufi **poets** play with the **metaphorical** possibilities and ambiguities of paradise imagery, weaving it together with themes of **annihilation**, **intoxication**, and mystical **union**. On the other hand, some of the most influential Sufis, beginning with **Rābiʿa**, have insisted that the true mystical lover will never seek primarily either to gain paradise or avoid infernal punishment, for **heaven** and **hell** are both mere distractions from the ultimate goal of the authentic seeker, the **Face** of God.

PARSĀ, KHWĀJA MUḤAMMAD (d. 822/1419). Central Asian *shaykh* of Bukhara, intellectual leader of the **Naqshbandīya**, and one of the most important disciples of the founder, Bahā' ad-Dīn **Naqshband**. A sub-**order** was eventually named after him, and members of the now largely inactive group considered their leader's **tomb** in **Medina** an important goal for **visitation**.

PASHTO. An Iranian-based Indo-Aryan **language** spoken in portions of (especially southern) Afghanistan and (northwestern) Pakistan. Sufi **poets** who have produced significant works in Pashto include Mīrzā Khān Anṣārī and the **Chishtī** Raḥmān Bābā (both early 12th/18th century).

PATH. *Ṭarīqa* (pl. *ṭuruq*), the way of spiritual seekers, and by extension, the particular approach or method developed by, or distinctive of, particular Sufi **orders**. Some ***shaykhs*** have taught that individual seekers make their way along the path at their own pace, focusing on purification, illumination, or spiritual union, depending on their levels of proficiency and maturity. Some sources also use the technical term for "path" as a synonym for Sufi order. A classic Sufi triad lists *ṭarīqa* as the second level of spiritual development, after *sharī'a* (revealed **law**) and before *ḥaqīqa* (ultimate **reality**).

PATIENCE. An attitude of perfect willingness to endure whatever **God** sends, so important that many theorists list it as a **station** along the **path**. The **prophet** Jacob, father of the prophet **Joseph**, is often cited as epitomizing the virtue of *ṣabr*, which the **Qur'ān** calls "beautiful." It has merited a place among the stations of spiritual progress embodied in the **typologies** of nearly all the major Sufi **theorists**, and is typically situated toward the beginning of the lists (of **Ghazālī**, **Makkī**, **Kalābādhī**, and **Sarrāj**, for example), in the vicinity of renunciation, **poverty**, **trust**, and **fear**.

PERFECT PERSON. Metaphor, developed by **Ibn al-'Arabī** and further interpreted by 'Abd al-Karīm al-**Jīlī** and others, for the embodiment of spiritual perfection, the individual who most of all reflects divine self-**manifestation** in the world. Some authors have identified the **Prophet** as the Perfect Person (*al-insān al-kāmil*), while others have seen the role as fulfilled in the person of the ideal ***shaykh***. Ultimately the role of the Perfect Person is to straddle the line between the seen and unseen worlds for the benefit of all spiritual seekers. Because of its tendency to aggrandize the Prophet above the merely human, the concept has generated considerable disapproval from Sufism's critics through the centuries. The concept may represent an element of **neo-Platonic** influence in Sufi thought.

PERPLEXITY. A critical aspect of mystical **experience** characterized by bewilderment (*ḥayra*), confusion, and a loss of ability to process one's condition rationally. Poets talk of the experience of becoming a "fool for God," one possessed (*Majnūn*) by the madness of a **lover's** apparently unrequited passion for ultimate **union** with the **Beloved**.

PERSIAN. An Indo-European **language**, the "modern" development of which is spoken largely in **Iran**, parts of Afghanistan (where it is known as Dārī, and **Central Asia** (especially the republic of Tajikistan). Beginning in the early fifth/11th century, modern Persian developed into an important literary language, and Sufi authors soon thereafter began producing major works of mystical literature in Persian, throughout **South Asia** as well as lands further west. **Anṣārī**, Rūzbihān **Baqlī**, **'Ayn al-Quḍāt al-Hamadhānī**, **Hujwīrī**, and **Sa'dī** were major prose authors; and among the most celebrated **poets** are Awḥād ad-Dīn **Kirmānī**, Farīd ad-Dīn **'Aṭṭār**, **Ḥāfiẓ**, **Jāmī**, **Niẓāmī**, Jalāl ad-Dīn **Rūmī**, and **Sanā'ī**.

PILGRIMAGE. One of the five **pillars of Islam**, involving a visit of several days to the **Ka'ba** in **Mecca** and its environs during the official *ḥajj* season from the eighth to the 13th days of the 12th lunar month of the Muslim calendar. A "lesser" pilgrimage, called the *'umra*, is a laudable devotional practice, involving a briefer visit, with reduced ritual activity, to Mecca at any time during the year. In addition, the widespread practice of **visitation** represents a phenomenon similar in many ways to "official" pilgrimage practices, but not formally recognized as a religious duty. Most pilgrims to Mecca try to make a form of visitation to the **tomb** of the **Prophet** in **Medina** before or after the *ḥajj* or *'umra*, but this practice is considered an optional devotional, recommended but not integral to the **ritual** associated with pilgrimage. *See also* PLACES; TIMES, SACRED.

PILLARS OF ISLAM. Five essential practices widely known as "pillars" (*arkān*), including profession of faith (*shahāda*), ritual **prayer** five times daily (*ṣalāt*), major **pilgrimage** once in a lifetime (*ḥajj*), almsgiving (*zakāt*), and **fasting** (*ṣawm*) during the month of Ramaḍān. So fundamental are they that a theorist such as **Abū Ṭālib**

al-Makkī describes the pinnacle of **knowledge** as full comprehension of the meaning of the pillars.

PĪR. *See SHAYKH.*

PLACES. Locations rendered especially sacred or venerable by reason of some remarkable event said to have occurred there or by association with a particular holy figure. The most important of such places are, naturally, those associated with the life of the **Prophet**, his family, and his **Companions**, mostly in **Mecca** (goal of formal **pilgrimage**), **Medina**, and **Jerusalem**. In local and regional lore, such holy sites are often identified with the **tombs** of **Friends of God** and associated **shrines**, and are frequently transformed into goals for pilgrim **visitation** and are marked with distinctive **architectural** monuments. Many important places figure prominently in a calendar of especially sacred **times**. Some Sufi **orders** associate special sanctity with the sites of their organizations' original foundations. In addition, Sufis have developed various **institutional** structures designed to provide venues for a wide range of activities. Such venues include **residential facilities** as well as **mosques** dedicated especially to the use of certain Sufi groups, and smaller oratorylike facilities known by the generic Arabic term *muṣallā*, a "place for ritual prayer."

POETRY. A major medium of **symbolic**, **metaphorical**, and **allegorical** expression of Sufi concepts and values, beginning at least as early as the **Arabic** works of **Rābi'a al-'Adawīya**. Sufi poets have developed and adapted numerous **genres** of **literature** in over a dozen major Islamicate **languages**, and **manuscript arts** have adorned countless mystical poetic works with **calligraphy** and **painting**. It seems clear that many Sufi poets drew considerable inspiration from the tradition of pre-Islamic Arabic **odes**, which classically begin with lamentation at the traces of the lost beloved's campsite. The lover goes on to describe at length the beauties of the beloved, often moving entirely into the realm of nature metaphors, before talking about the experience of embarking on the by no means promising journey to recover her. Sufi poets have drawn on many other linguistic and cultural traditions as well, in the centuries-long evolution of Islamic mystical verse. Their best works demonstrate an intimate link between mystical **experience** and the creative imagination. Major poets include **'Aṭṭār**, **Bīdil**, **Bulhe Shāh**, Mīr **Dard**, **Ghālib**, **Ḥāfiẓ**, **Ḥamza Fanṣūrī**, **Ibn al-Fāriḍ**, **Fakhr ad-Dīn 'Irāqī**, **Jamāl ad-Dīn (Jamālī Kanbōh)**, **Jāmī**, **Kirmānī**, **Niẓāmī**, **Rūmī**, **Sanā'ī**, **Sulṭān Bāhū**, and **Yūnus Emre**. *See also* CALLIGRAPHY; COUPLETS; DIDACTIC POETRY; DĪWĀN; LYRIC POETRY; PRAISE; THRENODY.

POLE. Pinnacle of the Sufi **cosmological hierarchy**. Individual Sufi leaders have sometimes been identified as the cosmic axis, pivot, or pole (*quṭb*) "of the age," suggesting that the cosmic hierarchy is subject to **metaphorical** renewal in that it is composed of living individuals. In that sense the term refers to the highest level of sanctity among **Friends of God**. Some consider the pole of each age to be the manifestation of the spirit of the **Prophet** for that time, and in certain **orders** the ***shaykh*** is regarded as the pole. The word "pole" is preferable to "axis" in this context, because the former preserves the tent metaphor carried on in the term *awtād* ("tent pegs") discussed in the entry **supports**. The term *ghawth*, Arabic for "assistance," is often used as virtually synonymous with *quṭb*, but some theorists rank *ghawth* second to the pole.

POLITICS. Engagement by Sufis and their leadership with rulers and political institutions. **Orders** varied considerably with respect to both stated policies and actual practice, running the gamut from a preference for remaining totally aloof to hobnobbing with the powerful and prestigious. An excellent example of the former preference is evident in the lives of some of the great early **Chishtīya** leaders of the seventh/13th and eighth/14th centuries, while many **Naqshbandīya** leaders, as well as later Chishtīya leaders, argued for greater political activism. Somewhere in the middle of that spectrum, a number of orders and ***shaykhs*** were willing to serve as spiritual guides, teachers, and advisors to rulers and their families while seeking to maintain a measure of autonomy and freedom from reliance on the royal dole for survival. Royal patronage of Sufi **institutions** in the form of **endowments** has been a major factor in the survival and development of many major **organizations**.

POSTNIŞIN. *See* AUTHORITY.

POVERTY. The choice to forego acquisition of possessions and wealth for the sake of more perfect dedication to **God**, and a fundamental attitude based on the realization of one's radical neediness and utter dependence on God. Sufi **orders** have taken a wide variety of positions concerning material poverty (*faqr*) and means of **livelihood**, ranging from legislated virtual destitution to willingness to live amid great wealth while cultivating detachment from it. The underlying concern for all Sufis, however, has been the virtue of spiritual poverty characterized by the refusal to arrogate unto oneself any claim to power or self-sufficiency. As such, poverty ranks among the **stations** most often listed by Sufi **theorists** and **manualists**, usually toward the beginning of their lists along with conversion or **repentance** and **asceticism**. One of the notable exceptions in this respect is that **Qushayrī** locates poverty well down the list among the more advanced **states**.

PRAISE. An attitude ultimately due only to **God** but reflected in **poems** dedicated to the **Prophet** and **Friends of God** as well. Paeans in honor of **Muḥammad** are generally known either as *na'ts* (characteristic, virtue) or *mawlids* (**birth**-[story]). The former typically dwell on the lofty estate of the Prophet especially as manifest in the ways his **Ascension** suggests a perfect relationship with **God**, while the latter detail the marvels attendant upon the holy person's birth. The term *mawlid* often applies to stories of saints' very early lives as well. Poems of praise understood more generally as applying to the Prophet as well as to Friends of God are often called *madīḥ* (panegyric). Among the most famous prophetic encomia is that of **Būṣīrī**, while mystical poets such as **Jāmī**, **Niẓāmī**, and **Sanā'ī** made the *na't* a standard feature as a prologue to their **didactic** works.

PRAYER, PERSONAL. Important forms of devotional expression that include impromptu, "free" prayer in the form of **supplication** (*du'ā*) as well as established forms of **recollection** (*adhkār*) handed down across many **generations**. Personal prayers called *munājāt* (intimate conversations, also occasionally characterized as "epigrams"), and a large category called **litanies**, composed by famous Sufis, have also come to comprise a considerable body of **literature**, a treasury of spiritual sentiment that offers seekers rich sources of inspiration.

PRAYER, RITUAL. One of the five **pillars of Islam**, to be performed at each of five prescribed **times** (dawn, later morning, shortly after midday, later afternoon or evening around sundown, and at night) during the day as determined by astronomical calculations. The principal positions involve standing, bending at the waist, sitting on one's heels, and prostration while touching one's forehead to the ground, all while oriented toward the *qibla* of **Mecca**. Each occurrence is preceded by a ritual ablution. Sufi **poets** have often reflected on the **symbolic** and **metaphorical** dimensions of both the times and movements of the **ritual**.

PREACHING. Addressing religious gatherings, whether in a formal sermon on Friday after the midday ritual **prayer** at a **mosque** (then called the *khuṭba*) or for special occasions (such as a *mawlid*, a holy person's **birthday**, or death-anniversary). Some Sufi ***shaykhs*** were celebrated for their ability to move hearers with their preaching. Preaching is also sometimes associated with the role of the **storyteller**, the individual who regales audiences with edifying tales (*qiṣṣa*) of **Friends of God**.

PRESENCE. An aspect of spiritual **experience** implying perfect attentiveness to God, often juxtaposed with **absence**. Presence (typically called *ḥuḍūr*, sometimes with cognates *ḥaḍāra* and *muḥāḍara*) paradoxically may involve a certain "absence" from created beings the better to focus on God. A variation of the concept is expressed in the term *ḥaḍra*, usually referring to the presence of the **Prophet** experienced in certain **dance rituals**.

PROPHET, NAMES OF. Muḥammad has been known by a host of **honorific** titles and terms of respect and endearment. Sufis have been particularly fond of the terms *Muṣṭafā*, the pure or chosen one, and *Aḥmad*, a variation on Muḥammad. Royal titles such as *sulṭān* and *shāh* are quite common, as are terms that emphasize the Prophet's beauty and elegance, such as the Lamp or Candle, Light, Jewel, and Rose.

PROPHETIC EXAMPLE. The full range of behavior, attitudes, and teachings modeled by the **Prophet Muḥammad** and held up for emulation by all Muslims. Called the *sunna* and enshrined chiefly in the

Ḥadīth literature, this reservoir of idealized values and conduct represents for Sufis the epitome of spiritual maturity and a kind of map for one's travel along the mystical **path**.

PROPHETS. Spokespersons and messengers in an unbroken chain beginning with **Adam** and culminating in **Muḥammad**, commissioned to articulate divine guidance for humanity. Some prophets, referred to by the **Arabic** term *nabī* (one who gives tidings), are sent to particular peoples. Others, to whom the term *rasūl* (messenger, apostle) applies, are sent to all people and are given a scripture of universal authority to communicate to them. In Sufi **literature**, the prophets and their respective stories frequently function **metaphorically**, each representing a specific spiritual virtue, value, or symbolic function of particular significance in Sufi life and thought. Some Sufi authors have associated various prophets with specific **colors** and levels of **heaven**. Major prophets include **Abraham**, **David**, **Jesus**, **Joseph**, **Khiḍr**, **Moses**, and **Solomon**.

PROXIMITY. An aspect of spiritual **experience** often juxtaposed with **distance**. Proximity, or nearness, (*qurb*) is a variation on the theme of **intimacy** or familiarity (*uns*), but is slanted rather toward the **ethical** dimension of **obedience** and fulfilling one's duties toward **God**. A story tells how a friend of **Dhū 'n-Nūn** once wrote to him, praying that he would experience God's proximity. Dhū 'n-Nūn replied, "May God cause you to experience his distance," for the experience of the divine proximity brings the possibility of complacency.

PSYCHOLOGY. Sufi analysis of the inner faculties (sometimes called "subtle centers," *laṭīfa*) and functions of the individual human person. Beginning in about the second/eighth century, major Sufis began sorting out key aspects of human personality, focusing especially on characteristic modes of relating to, or attempting to avoid, God. In the classical Sufi **manuals** that developed as a major mystical genre from the fourth/10th to early seventh/13th centuries, **theorists** organized these modes into **typologies** designed to assist seekers in identifying signs within their inner selves, the better to negotiate the spiritual **path**. Focusing on the centrality of the **heart**, these systematic observations on spiritual **experience** came to be known generically as the **science of hearts**.

– Q –

QABḌ. *See* CONSTRICTION.

QĀDIRĪYA. One of the oldest and most widespread **orders**, named after **'Abd al-Qādir al-Jīlānī**, who is traditionally credited with founding the first formally constituted order. In fact, the order did not assume any definitive **organizational** character until some years later. Early **disciples** of the ***shaykh*** in **Baghdad** received the **cloak** from him and were in turn given the **authority** to **initiate** others. Some sources allude to the importance of being initiated via a **dream** or **vision** of the founder. It appears that there was some latitude in the assignment of forms of **recollection** and **litanies** to individual initiates. In general the order's many regional developments exhibit somewhat less uniformity than those of other orders. Its many foundations have typically operated independently and have followed the principle of hereditary succession to leadership. The history of its diffusion is less well documented than that of many other organizations. Among the order's key **ritual** practices are the **retreat**, **breath control**, **contemplation**, and **fasting**.

In some regions communal or individual devotion to 'Abd al-Qādir has developed in less formally institutional ways and includes elements of pre-Islamic popular piety. Though its nominal central authority has historically resided in Baghdad, the order has been important across **North Africa** (especially after the sixth/12th century) and the **Middle East** as well as large sections of **South** and **Central Asia** (mostly after the 10th/16th century). It has spawned numerous sub-branches, such as an Egyptian group named after the poet **Ibn al-Fāriḍ**. **Political** involvement has varied regionally, running the gamut from armed resistance to, or support of, colonial powers, to a preference for nonintervention. Among the order's more prominent members are **'Abd al-Ḥaqq Dihlawī**, **Bībī Jamāl Khatūn**, **Dārā Shikūh**, **Eshrefoğlu Rūmī**, **Jahānārā**, **Miyīn Mīr**, **Mullā Shāh**, **Niyāzī Miṣrī**, and **Qi Jingyi**.

QALANDAR. Originally referred to itinerant, "antinomian," mendicant **dervishes**, unattached to any particular **institutional** framework. As individuals, *qalandars* (also known in Turkish as *torlaks*) distinguished themselves by flaunting social and religious conventions in

clothing as well as **behavior**. Some apparently went out of their way to marginalize themselves for reasons of spiritual commitment, convinced that one ought not to seek human approval through conformity to "official" religious or social norms. Their **asceticism** included a decided antipathy to any kind of formal learning. In this respect their approach was meant to attract less attention than that of the **Malāmatī** dervishes. Ironically, the *qalandars* soon developed their own brand of conformity by affecting similar features such as shaving the head completely (including eyebrows), wearing coarse garments and **headgear**, and carrying **standard** and drum.

Non-Muslim antecedents of the *qalandars* are said to have been part of Muslim societies as early as the third/ninth century. These curious folk have naturally had their detractors, but their defenders also include such major figures as **Jāmī**. He insisted that although *qalandars* represent perhaps a less disciplined approach to the mystical life, they are nonetheless to be considered genuinely religious in intent. As a movement, the phenomenon reached a peak around the seventh/13th century and was widely recognized as a loosely **organized** equivalent of an **order** known as the **Qalandarīya**.

QALANDARĪYA. An **order** sometimes characterized as antinomian, arguably of **Central Asian** origin, with uncertain connections to the **Malāmatīya** and **Bektāshīya** and whose members are known as ***qalandars***. One of the earliest sources on the tradition was written by **Anṣārī**. Jamāl ad-Dīn as-Sāwī (d. c. 630/1222) is generally credited with spreading the movement to the central **Middle East**, and its **institutions** developed in a number of areas, notably **Egypt** and **Turkey** (where members are known as *torlaks* and where they were also once called *abdāl*). The order was represented as far to the east as **India**. Some scholars suggest the movement evidences Buddhist **ascetical** influence, although the movement played down the role of self-denial and the practice of **retreat**. Most rejected the comforts of a settled life, but some communities did maintain **residential facilities** in the Middle East and India. They were typically **celibate** mendicants, and cultivated absolute sincerity and nonattachment to possessions as the most fundamental **virtues**. A similar movement of contemporaneous origin is known as the **Ḥaydarīya**.

QALANSUWA. *See* HEADGEAR.

QALB. *See* HEART.

QANĀʿĀT. *See* RESIGNATION.

QARANĪ, UWAYS AL-. *See* UWAYS AL-.

QAṢĪDA. *See* ODE.

QAṢṢĀR, ḤAMDŪN AL-. *See* ḤAMDŪN.

QĀWUK. *See* HEADGEAR.

QAWWĀL(Ī). A type of Sufi **singing** especially popular in **Pakistan** and **India**, based on **musical** settings of mystical **poetry**, often in **Urdu** and **Persian** as well as **Panjābī** and Hindī. The lead accompaniment is provided by an accordionlike instrument called the harmonium, with a bellows pumped with one hand and a keyboard played by the other. Hand drums, and sometimes bowed strings, supply the other principal instrumental accompaniment. A lead singer sets the often intense emotional tone by presenting the text, while backup vocalists support him especially on refrainlike passages. The overall effect of this form of entertainment is that of alternately lifting and lowering the listeners through both the mystical content of the lyrics and the shifting intensity of melody and rhythm.

Praising the **Prophet** and extolling **love** of **God**, each performance models the mystical movement toward **ecstatic intoxication** and the eventual descent to **sobriety**. The musical tradition is especially, but no longer exclusively, associated with the **Chishtīya**. **Hagiographical** sources tell of how important figures, such as **Kākī**, are said to have died during performances, which occur regularly at the **tomb** shrines of **Friends of God**, especially on death anniversaries. Like various other forms of **audition** rituals, *qawwālī* has often drawn fire from critics who argue that, like all forms of music, it represents a spiritual danger and must therefore be condemned as “un-Islamic.”

QAYYŪM. *See* GOVERNANCE.

QI JINGYI, HILĀL AD-DĪN (1067/1656–1132/1719). Popular **preacher**, generally considered founder of the **Chinese** branch (*menhuan*) of the **Qādirīya**, still revered as Grand Master Qi by China's Sufis. According to traditional accounts, he apprenticed with **Naqshbandī** ***shaykhs*** Khwāja Āfāq and Khwāja ʻAbd Allāh. He taught the necessity of **ascetical** solitude, individual **prayer**, and material **poverty**. His **tomb** in Linxia remains a focal point of Qādirī life in China.

QIBLA. *See* PRAYER, RITUAL.

QIṢṢA. *See* STORYTELLING.

QIZIL-BĀSH. A Turkish term meaning "red head," referring to the **headgear** worn by members of certain **Shīʻī** sectarian groups that manifested some superficial similarities to Sufi **orders**. Developing especially after the late seventh/13th century, these organizations took root in **Turkey**, the central **Middle East**, and **Persia**. There is evidence that during **Ottoman** times, some allied themselves with the **Bektāshīya** for legal protection against government intervention in their affairs. During the regime of the order at the heart of the **Ṣafawid dynasty**, the name applied to people who attached themselves to the ruler the way **disciples** apprentice to a Sufi ***shaykh***. In Persian **painting** especially, the *qizil-bāsh* are recognizable by the *tāj* composed of a tall crimson spike at the center of a turbanlike wrap of 12 folds of white cloth (symbolizing the 12 *Imāms*).

QUATRAIN. Short **lyric poem** consisting of four hemistichs, hence called the *rubāʻī* (pl. *rubāʻīyāt*, "in fours"). Many Sufi **poets** have chosen the **genre** with an *a-a-(x)-a* rhyme scheme as a compact vehicle for expressing surprisingly complex concepts as well as for more ephemeral, occasional sentiments. Surely the most famous author of the genre is ʻUmar Khayyām, but many other important Sufis wrote in the form, including **Kirmānī** and **Rūmī**.

QUBBA. *See* TOMB.

QŪNAWĪ, ṢADR AD-DĪN AL- (606/1210–673/1274). Anatolian religious scholar of **Persian** descent, stepson and major disciple of **Ibn**

al-'Arabī. Particularly through his commentary on Ibn al-'Arabī's prophetological work *Bezels of Wisdom*, he was largely responsible for setting in motion the long tradition of interpreting his teacher's work with special attention to the concept of **being** (*wujūd*). His more than two dozen works make him an indispensable guide to penetrating the dense thought of his mentor. He was a major influence in establishing links between Sufi thought and the metaphysical themes that would fuel debate for centuries to come concerning the relationships between ontological and experiential **unity**. In the city of **Konya**, Ṣadr ad-Dīn was a well-known teacher of traditional religious disciplines and a friend of **Rūmī**. He was known as an authority on the **poetry** of such major Sufis as **Ibn al-Fāriḍ**. Although he seems not to have been initiated into one of the more widespread orders, Qunawī was a key link in a spiritual and intellectual **lineage** that descended from Ibn al-'Arabī well into early modern times. Perhaps his most famous student was **Fakhr ad-Dīn 'Irāqī**, but other important members of the lineage include **Jīlī**, **Kāshānī**, **Maghribī**, **Shabistarī**, **Sha'rānī**, 'Alā' ad-Dawla **Simnānī**, and **Zarrūq**.

QUR'ĀN. Islam's most sacred text, believed to have been revealed by **God** to the **Prophet Muḥammad** through the intermediary **Gabriel**, and delivered by the Prophet orally between 610 and 12/632. In its printed form, it is organized in 114 *sūras* (roughly equivalent to chapters) arranged in more or less descending order of length. Scholars have long found it useful to divide the texts into **Meccan** and **Medinan** periods, with the former further divided into early, middle, and late Meccan. The earliest material is, in general, found in many of the shorter chapters, though some chapters actually contain material from several time periods.

Since very early times, Sufis **exegetes** have authored some highly influential commentaries on the scripture. In their reading of the sacred word, Sufis have typically gravitated toward those texts that provide greatest insight into the divine-human relationship. Texts such as the Throne and Light verses, particularly weighty for all Muslims, have evoked some elaborately symbolic exegesis. But, in addition, Sufi **poets** and **theorists** have delved deeply into texts that suggest God's love, mercy, and closeness to human beings. In particular, texts that describe the paradigmatic **experience** of the Prophet have attracted a great deal of attention.

In this regard, Sufi poets and commentators focus on allusions to the Prophet's unique relationship with God as suggested in texts that speak of God's caring for him since his orphaned youth and of the moments and processes of divine **revelation**, such as that **visionary** event suggested in Sūra 53. They key in on the dynamics of texts in which God speaks to Muḥammad in a more "personal" way (rather than in the context of commanding him what to instruct the community). In addition, if not quite as importantly, Sufi authors suffuse their discourse with citations of the sacred word, thus giving rise to the phrase "Qur'ānization of the memory." These and similar thematic interests are important ingredients in the development of Sufi **hermeneutics**.

QUR'ĀN, MEMORIZING. Learning the entire sacred scripture by **heart** (*ḥifẓ al-qur'ān*), particularly as a devotional deed. Recitation of the sacred scripture by a *qārī* (one who recites [professionally]) is generally done from memory rather than relying on a written text, even when the reciter has a book ceremonially in view. Sufi poets love to talk about the resonances between memorizing the sacred word and remembering the **Beloved** always.

QURB. *See* PROXIMITY.

QUSHAYRĪ, ABŪ 'L-QĀSIM 'ABD AL-KARĪM AL- (375/986–465/1072). Major **Central Asian** religious scholar, Sufi **manualist** and **hagiographer**, disciple of Abū 'Alī ad-**Daqqāq** and **Sulamī**. He spent many years studying Shāfi'ī **Law** and Ash'arī **theology** before traveling to **Baghdad**, where he took a post as religious scholar for the sultan. He eventually returned to **Nishapur**, where he died. In 437/1045, he wrote his most famous work, the ***Treatise*** *(on Sufism),* a.k.a. *The Letter to the Sufis* (*Ar-Risāla fi 't-taṣawwuf*, or *Ar-Risālat al-qushayrīya*) with the intention of supporting the religious authenticity and legitimacy of Sufism. After laying out basic tenets of Sufism in relation to mainstream Islamic tradition, a **hagiographical** section offers sketches of 83 famous mystics. He then provides extended definitions of three dozen technical terms, followed by more detailed analyses of some four dozen **stations** and **states**. The manual concludes with discussions of various aspects of Sufi **ritual** and practice, such as **audition**.

QUṬB. *See* POLE.

QŪT AL-QULŪB. *See* ABŪ ṬĀLIB AL-MAKKĪ.

– R –

RĀBI'A AL-'ADAWĪYA (c. 95/714–185/801). Early **woman poet**, **ascetic**, and mystic of **Basra** around whom numerous elements of legend and lore have gathered. Among her important acquaintances were **Ḥasan al-Baṣrī**, **Mālik ibn Dīnār**, and **Shaqīq al-Balkhī**. She is widely credited as the first to speak boldly about divine-human **love**, a major theme of anecdotes about her as well as of the fragmentary poems and **prayers** that survive in the works of later authors. Some scholars have argued that she was the first genuine Muslim mystic, for it was she who first presumed to move beyond simple asceticism. She is one of the few women who consistently merited a place in **hagiographic** anthologies over the centuries.

RĀBIṬA. *See* VISUALIZATION.

RAE BAREILLY (a.k.a. Rāy Barēlī). Indian town in the **Panjab** founded by Makrand Rāy in 1068/1657, birthplace of Sayyid **Aḥmad Brelwī**. The town has been prominently associated with a 13th/19th century movement initiated by Sayyid Aḥmad that was critical of some aspects of Sufism at large. Though the founder and his followers were themselves Sufis, they sought to distinguish themselves from the generality of Sufis by purging their own practice of elements they regarded as un-Islamic. Because of their critical stance especially in relation to veneration of **Friends of God** at their **tombs** and the inappropriate exaltation of living ***shaykhs***, other Sufis labeled the reformers "**Wahhābīs**."

RĀJA 'ABD ALLĀH, ENGKU MUDA (d. 1274/1858). Malay ruler who was also a ***shaykh*** of the **Naqshbandīya**, and whose son carried on the family link with Sufism.

RAMAḌĀN. Ninth lunar month of the Islamic ritual calendar, during which Muslims are enjoined to fast from before sunrise to after sundown. **Fasting** during the 30-day period is not required of younger children or the very elderly, pregnant or nursing women, the ill, or individuals on arduous journeys. No other lunar month is named in the **Qur'ān**. The most momentous night of the month, *laylat al-qadr* (Night of Power), generally identified as the night on which the **Prophet** received the initial **revelation**, is also mentioned in the scripture. Although many Muslims locate that night on the 27th of the month, many also believe that because the precise date is not known, one is advised to be especially attentive to devotion and charitable conduct during all of the odd-numbered nights during the last third of the month. Sufi **poets** often allude to the scriptural text (Qur'ān 53:9) in which the Prophet experienced an apparition traditionally identified as **Gabriel**, and is said to have come as close as "two bow-lengths or nearer" (*qāba qawsayn aw adnā*) to **God**. Poets often interpret the verse as alluding to the inauguration of the Prophet's mystical **experience**. *See also* RITUAL; TIMES, SACRED.

RĀNĪRĪ, NŪR AD-DĪN (d. c. 1068/1658). Of **Indian** origin, member of the **Rifā'īya** and Aydarūsīya, major religious scholar who studied in **Mecca**. He authored **Malay** and **Arabic** works in which he argued against the ***wujūdī*** theological orientation of **Ḥamza Fanṣūrī** and Shams ad-Dīn as-**Samaṭrānī**. His seven-year sojourn in the Sumatran city of Acheh made him an adopted son of **Indonesia**.

RANKS. Degrees (*darajāt*) in the **hierarchical** ordering of **cosmological realms**, levels of spiritual progress on the **journey** as described in a variety of **typologies**, and individual persons or groups in Sufi **organization** and **authority** structures. Sufi **theorists** and **hagiographers** in particular provide information on a host of specific designations that underscore the elaboration of often complex models of both **institutional** developments and individual spiritual search. The diverse models documented by a variety of authors reveal important aspects of the evolution of highly structured Sufi thought on a wide range of topics.

RAQṢ. *See* DANCE.

RĀTIB. *See* OFFICE.

REALITY, ULTIMATE. Standard designation of the third and highest level of mystical learning and **experience**. Beyond the revealed **law** (*sharīʻa*) and the Sufi **path** (*ṭarīqa*) lies the "really real" or ultimate reality (*ḥaqīqa*). A saying attributed to the **Prophet** associates the first level with his words, the second with his deeds, and the third with his spiritual **states**. "Ultimate reality" is therefore accessible only to spiritual **journeyers** most advanced in the **science of hearts**.

REALMS. Levels or spheres of **cosmology** or **experience** indicated by various compounds with the term *'ālam* ("world"). Sufi **theorists** speak of a number of realms as a way of distinguishing aspects of the complex spiritual quest and the several "landscapes" through which mystical seekers must navigate and with which humans have varying degrees of affinity. As such, these realms are at the heart of some of the most important Sufi theories of **knowledge**, though their names and functions vary somewhat from one author to another. What follows is an overview of a fairly widely diffused understanding of the subject.

At the bottom of a **hierarchy** is the realm of earthly sovereignty or humanity (*'ālam al-mulk/nāsūt*), dominated by sense perception. Above that is the realm of lordly dominion or hidden mystery (*'ālam al-malakūt/ghayb*) in which the seeker gains access to more profound spiritual realities, for there resides the celestial archetypes of the Preserved Tablet, the Pen with which **God** writes, and the **Qur'ān** itself. Still "higher" is the realm of divine power (*'ālam al-jabarūt*) where authorities variously locate the human imagination and names of God. Spiritual seekers gain access to the upper realms through the intellectual and imaginative capacities of the **heart**, and some authors further identify the realm of lordly dominion and/or that of divine power as the realm of imaginative similitudes (*'ālam al-mithāl*). Above them all is the realm of pure divinity (*'ālam al-lāhūt*), to which human beings have no ordinary access. A more generic cosmological feature is the realm of principles or "pillars" (*arkān*), sometimes associated with complex models of the heart or **soul**.

REASON. A source of **knowledge** that many Sufi authors disparage as secondary at best, because reliance on rational processes can lead one to imagine that discursive knowledge (*'ilm*) is sufficient. Some Sufi authorities insist that reason and intellect (both translating the term *'aql*) make available knowledge that is, at best, partial, and, at worst, downright false and deceptive. **Rūmī**, for example, regards reason as "a highway robber," lying in wait for unsuspecting travelers. One who relies on reason, he cautions, is like a person who stands on the roof and still insists on the necessity of a ladder. Others, such as Abū Ḥāmid al-**Ghazālī**, allow reason a more significant role, for example, in the process of **exegesis**.

RECITALS, VISIONARY. A **genre** called the *ḥikāya* (literally, "narrative") developed as a vehicle for mystical expression, especially by **Ibn Sīnā** and Shihāb ad-Dīn Yaḥyā as-**Suhrawardī**. The highly imaginative genre typically offers a first-person perspective on an inward spiritual **journey** in search of one's long-forgotten origins, the traveler riding the steed of nostalgia and recalling assorted encounters with intriguing symbolic personifications of spiritual realities.

RECOLLECTION. Both an essential Sufi **ritual** and a state of spiritual attentiveness, *dhikr* can involve both remembering and mentioning one's relationship to **God**. In general the practice involves a rhythmic repetition of some word (often *Allāh* or one of the 99 names of God) or phrase (such as "God is supreme"), and often entails controlled **breathing**. The answer to the question of whether one ought to practice silent or hidden (*khafī*) or vocal (*jalī* or *jahrī*) recollection became one of the distinguishing features of individual **orders**, and the issue occasionally gave rise to considerable controversy. One order famous for its insistence on silent recollection is the **Naqshbandīya**. Communal recollection (*dhikr al-ḥadra*, *majlis adh-dhikr*) is, of course, vocal and is sometimes referred to as **audition**. Organization of the practice involves breaking the material down into segments (*marātib*, sg. *martaba*) or formulae (*ḍarb*). This can include recitation of **poetry** as well as solo or ensemble devotional **singing** and group **dancing**. Individual recollection, whether silent or audible, often involves use of a **rosary** to count repetitions. Many orders practice a form of **office** called "recollection at set **times**" (*dhikr al-awqāt*).

REFORM. According to an Islamic tradition, God will raise up a "renewer" (*mujaddid*) at the dawning of each (Islamic) century. A number of major Sufis have been identified as the "renewers" of their respective ages, and several Sufi and **neo-Sufi** organizations have explicitly identified themselves as reform-oriented (such as the Mujaddidī **Naqshbandīya**, the followers of Sayyid **Aḥmad Brelwī**, and the **Deobandīs** Reformist movements within Sufism have generally focused on eradicating ritual or popular practices deemed excessive (such as seeking **wonders** or veneration at the **tombs** of **Friends of God**) or concepts regarded as theologically "innovative" or even downright heretical (such as those associated with the ***wujūdī* controversy**).

REMEMBRANCES. A **hagiographic genre** (*tadhkira*, often translated "memorial"), generally an anthology of short biographical sketches of famous **Friends of God**. Sometimes also called *siyar* (life stories) or *akhbār* (records, accounts), the type is particularly well-represented in **Persian** and **Turkish**, and is of enormous importance as a source of the history of various **orders** and their leading ***shaykhs***. This is especially true in the case of the richly documented history of the **Chishtīya**. Among the more famous examples of the genre are major works by **'Aṭṭār** and **Jāmī** (though the latter does not use the technical term in its title). Like earlier works in the genre called **generations**, this form is generally arranged chronologically; unlike the earlier genre, its function is that of commemorating in a devotional, almost **contemplative** way, the values represented by spiritual giants of the past.

RENUNCIATION. *See* ASCETICISM.

REPENTANCE. Turning back (*tawba*), hence a kind of conversion, to **God** from one's sinfulness to seek divine forgiveness. Many Sufi **theorists** locate repentance as the first among a progression of **stations**, as a precondition for dedication to one's relationship to God. Some Sufi authors describe repentance as a turning "away" from all that is not God. Others, such as **Ruwaym**, emphasize that genuine repentance requires that one repent even of repenting itself, as if warning of the danger of complacency and of self-congratulatory willingness to rest in this humble beginning. God Himself is known by the name *at-tawwāb*, the ever-turning, reminding the seeker that repentance is always an option.

RESIDENTIAL FACILITY. Accommodations for members of formal and generally stable Sufi **orders**, including their administrative personnel, as well as for itinerant **dervishes**. Known most commonly by the terms *ribāṭ* (used across a wide geographical area) and *zāwiya* (mostly western), *khānqāh* (mostly eastern), and *tekke* (**Arabic**, **Persian**, and **Turkish**, respectively), often extensive **institutions** have developed around original Sufi foundations and their branches as well as around **tombs** of famous ***shaykhs***. Larger complexes were typically sustained through **endowments**. The *ribāṭ* was originally a frontier fortress in which warriors took shelter while expanding Islamic rule, and eventually came to be thought of, metaphorically, as a residence for **ascetics** and others engaged in the inner *jihād*. During medieval times, most such facilities were located in cities rather than in frontier regions.

Sufi residential facilities have frequently been part of extensive complexes, attached to a variety of other **architectural** functions, such as **mosques**, schools, and the equivalent of social service agencies. Some orders have also maintained residences for families attached to members of the organization, and some facilities have been dedicated to **women** only. Many orders made the founding of such facilities an integral part of their programs of expansion into new territories. Institutions known by the Persian terms *jamā'at khāna* and *dargāh* sometimes combined residential and more public functions. The term *duwayra* ("small enclosure") is also often used to refer to a local lodging, while *ṭibaq* (pl. of *ṭabaqa*) often refers to the individual rooms or cells of dervishes. The Turkish usage *kalenderhāne* refers to residences of ***qalandars***.

RESIGNATION. One of the **stations** on the **path**, *qanā'a* can also be translated "**contentment**." One experiences resignation or contentment when one is truly satisfied with what **God** has apportioned. It is not a question of having what one wants, but of wanting what one has in full confidence that God grants precisely what the individual needs at any given **moment**.

RESURRECTION. Fundamental element of Islamic belief, that human bodies will rise from the grave to rejoin their souls prior to final, comprehensive judgment. The concept is unconnected with **Jesus** (as it is in Christian belief), for Muslims believe Jesus did not die in the first place. No such notion existed among the pre-Islamic Arabs, who believed that at death one entered a kind of oblivion. Some Sufi **poets** elevate mystical **love** above "a hundred resurrections," and speak of the spiritual resurrection that occurs when one returns to life after dying to one's **ego**-centric tendencies. The term "Day of Resurrection" (*yawm an-nashr*) is often synonymous with "**Day of Judgment**" (*yawm al-qiyāma*).

RETICENCE, SPIRITUAL. A **station** on the spiritual **path** characterized by heightened circumspection and watchfulness over one's inward movements and feelings. Some translators render the term *wara'* as "scrupulous attentiveness" or "abstention." The preference for "reticence" here suggests that in this critical spiritual station the individual seeker remains guarded and careful not to be presumptuous in any way in God's presence.

RETREAT. Withdrawal (*'uzla*) from ordinary social interaction for the purpose of dedicating oneself wholly to spiritual **exercises** and **ascetical** disciplines. **Orders** place varying degrees of emphasis on retreat-related practices, but most recommend at least some recourse to isolation and solitude (*khalwa*). The most common regimen involves a period of **forty** days (Arabic *arba'īnīya*; Persian *chilla*) of intensified **prayer**, **fasting**, and consultation with one's ***shaykh***. Some use the term *khalwa* in a more generic fashion to refer to specific actions, rather than a longer interval, to be performed occasionally. These include the practice of going off on one's own for shorter periods. More extreme forms of retreat include suspending oneself upside down in a well.

REVELATION. Divine self-disclosure specifically as mediated through **angelic** and **prophetic** messengers. Technically called *waḥy*, this dimension of **God's** communication of the divine will and word ended, strictly speaking, with the last **Prophet**, whose reception of divine messages began on a night toward the end of the month of **Ramaḍān**

called the Night of Power (*laylat al-qadr*). Some Sufi authors, insisting that God would surely not so limit his self-disclosure to humankind, speak of a post-prophetic "extension" according to which the communication is ongoing, but is referred to by other terms, such as **light**, **manifestation**, and **unveiling**.

RIBĀṬ. *See* RESIDENTIAL FACILITY.

RIḌĀ'. *See* CONTENTMENT.

RIFĀ'Ī, AḤMAD AR- (c. 512/1118 [or 499/1106]- 578/1182). 'Irāqī Shāfi'ī religious **Law** scholar and founder of the **Rifā'īya**. Some sources credit him with having written miscellaneous **poems**, **prayers**, **litanies**, and **discourses**. He is said to have gathered remarkably large numbers of followers to hear him speak on special occasions, and to have emphasized the importance of **poverty** and **asceticism**.

RIFĀ'ĪYA. One of the earliest **orders**, founded in southern **Iraq** by Aḥmad ar-**Rifā'ī** and eventually established prominently throughout the central **Middle East**, **Turkey**, and **North Africa**. It also spread as far to the east as **Indonesia** and **Malaysia**, possibly as a result of the **preaching** of **Rānīrī**. Some scholars suggest that it was the most extensive of the orders prior to the dramatic spread of the **Qādirīya**. The order soon developed a reputation for emphasizing **wonders** and extreme behavior not unlike that associated with ***qalandars***. One such **ritual**, still popular even in **Southeast Asia**, is called the *dabbūs* ("awl"), in which various parts of the body are pierced with no permanent sign of damage. Some are reported to have even removed their eyeballs from their sockets. Members of the organization have commonly been dubbed the "Howling Dervishes" as a result of certain ritual practices. It remains a major order in **Egypt** today, thanks in part to the influence long ago of one of the order's most famous sons, Aḥmad al-**Badawī**.

RISĀLA. *See* TREATISE.

RISĀLAT AL-QUSHAYRĪYA. *See* QUSHAYRĪ.

RITUAL. The whole complex of patterned **behavior** oriented to Sufi communal, social, and devotional life, including not only the five **pillars of Islam**, but a host of activities sometimes distinctive of individual **orders**. These include practices of **asceticism**, **audition**, **breath control**, **companionship**, **dance**, **initiation**, **invocation**, **litanies**, **office**, personal **prayer**, **recollection**, **retreat**, **singing**, and **visualization**. In addition, ritual **spatial** contexts are known by various terms, including *dā'ira* or *ḥalqa* (circle), and *majlis* (session), and are frequently governed by calendrical acknowledgment of sacred **times**. Some orders designate an individual called a *naqīb* as the director of liturgical life in the community.

RITUAL OBJECTS. Implements used to facilitate religious exercises and devotions. Many Sufi **orders** have developed a characteristic cluster of objects that, in addition to distinctive items of **clothing** and **headgear**, **banners**, and **standards**, may allow one to get some sense of the users' identify. Some dervishes carry **staff** and/or **begging bowl**, and the **rosary** is very common. A few organizations use **weapons** as emblematic implements of their order. An important ritual item, for Sufis as for all Muslims, is the prayer **carpet** (*sajjāda*), whose central design has traditionally been a niche that recalls the **light** imagery of **Qur'ān** 24:35.

ROSARY. Primarily a **ritual object** (most commonly called a *tasbīḥa* or *subḥa*, "a device for offering praise") consisting of varying numbers of beads, used for keeping count of **prayers** and **invocations**, but also a **symbol** of **authority** passed down from the ***shaykh*** of an **order** to a **successor**. The various orders employed rosaries of different sizes, with clusters of beads arranged variously. The **Qādirīya** use 99 beads in groups of 33; the **Tījānīya** group 100 beads in clusters of 12, 18, 20, 20, 18, and 12; and the **Khalwātīya** have a rosary of 301 beads. Most are of relatively small beads for easy manipulation, but some are of larger scale and meant to be worn around the neck.

ROSE. Symbol of the **beloved**, with which the **nightingale** is hopelessly enamored; and of the **Prophet**. **Poets** have developed virtually every aspect of the rose's many qualities—thorny and dangerous yet exquisitely designed, irresistibly beautiful, and intoxicatingly fragrant—as **metaphors** of the perils and attractions of mystical **experience**.

RUBĀ'Ī. *See* QUATRAIN.

RŪDHBĀRĪ, ABŪ 'ALĪ AḤMAD AR- (d. 322/934). Early **'Irāqī** Sufi and religious scholar of **Baghdad** who figures in the **lineages** of both the **Kubrāwīya** and the **Ni'mat-allāhīya** and was acquainted with **Junayd** and **Nūrī**. He famously repudiated the **ritual** of **audition** because it is so readily misinterpreted by outsiders. He emphasized the need to abide by all injunctions and prohibitions of the **law** and recommended **asceticism**. Noted for his **patience** under pressure, he is credited with composing lyric **poetry** in **Arabic** and his sayings and **letters** are cited often by the **manualists**, especially by **Sarrāj**.

RŪḤ. *See* SPIRIT.

RUIN. Poets love to use the **metaphor** of ruined structures (*kharābāt*) to express the paradox that great riches are often hidden in the most unexpected of places. Only the individual who has experienced the **annihilation** of the **ego** will truly be able to discover the wealth that lies behind the unimpressive façade.

RUKH. *See* FACE.

RUKHṢA. *See* DISPENSATION.

RULE. Institutional charters designed to formalize **organizational** and **governance** structures and codes of **behavior** in Sufi **orders**. Early rules are attributed to **Abū Sa'īd ibn Abī 'l-Khayr** and **'Abd al-Qādir al-Jīlānī**. These documents lay out a wide range of disciplinary and **ritual** parameters, including circumstances under which a **dispensation** may be allowed; detail the various **ranks** within an order's **hierarchy** and their respective roles and duties; and may also spell out the order's characteristic approaches to the role of saintly **wonders**, means of **livelihood**, and **political** involvement. Some authors, such as Abū Ḥafṣ 'Umar as-**Suhrawardī**, associated with the founding of orders have composed major **manuals** that have incorporated the characteristics of extended rule.

RŪM. Standard Islamic designation for the central lands of the former Byzantine Empire (i.e., **Anatolia** and immediate environs), based on the view that it was the "Rome" of the East. It came to be the center from which the **Ottoman Turkish** dynasty extended its rule over much of the old Byzantine realm, and beyond.

RŪMĪ, MAWLĀNĀ JALĀL AD-DĪN BALKHĪ (604/1207–672/1273). Major **Persian** mystical **poet** widely popular through translation into many languages, perhaps best known as the original "Whirling **Dervish**." He was born in Balkh (in northern Afghanistan) where his father, **Bahā' ad-Dīn Walad**, was a major religious scholar. After leaving Balkh, the family lived in various Middle Eastern cities for about a decade. Rūmī was about 20 years old when they settled in the central **Anatolian** city of Konya, then under **Saljūqid Turkish** rule. Rūmī inherited the position of religious scholar his father held at the Saljūqid court, but he found that the academic formality of the work it entailed was uncongenial to his personal spiritual needs. His relationship with an itinerant dervish named **Shams ad-Dīn** of Tabrīz (in northwestern **Iran**) proved to be a dramatic influence, leading Rūmī to pursue a mystical course. He dedicated a ***dīwān*** of some 35,000 verses of **lyric poetry** to Shams. He also authored an important book of **discourses** and a collection of **letters**, but perhaps his most famous work is the 25,000-verse didactic *Spiritual* ***Couplets*** (*Mathnawī-yi ma'nawī*). He is credited with founding the **Mawlawīya**, and with originating a kind of paraliturgical **dance** that gave his **order** the nickname Whirling Dervishes.

RUWAYM IBN AḤMAD, ABŪ MUḤAMMAD (d. 303/915). Early mystic of **Baghdad** and an associate—perhaps a friendly rival—of **Junayd**. He distinguished himself partly in his relative de-emphasis on **trust** in favor of realistic stewardship and responsibility. He left no written work and his thoughts are known chiefly from the compendia of **manualists** like **Sarrāj**.

RŪZBIHĀN BAQLĪ (522/1128–606/1209). Persian mystical author from Shiraz, in southwestern Iran. He is celebrated especially for an **Arabic exegetical** work, *The Brides of Elucidation* (*'Arā'is al-bayān*), a Persian **commentary** on **ecstatic** utterance (especially of

Ḥallāj), and for his elaboration of the concept of mystical **love**. His seminal contribution lay in the development of a systematic yet non-scholastic language with which to describe the indescribable, particularly in his Persian **treatise**, *The Jasmine of the Lovers* (*'Abhar al-'Āshiqīn*). He also authored a remarkable **diary**, *The Revelation of Secrets* (*Kashf al-Asrār*), an **autobiographical** work in which he recounts powerfully and allusively the evolution of his personal spiritual **experience**. Although he founded a *ribāṭ* in Shiraz, his institutional following remained largely local and was relatively short-lived. He may have had some connection with the **Kāzarūnīya** at some point in his life.

– S –

ṢABR. *See* PATIENCE.

SACHAL SARMAST, 'ABD AL-WAHHĀB (1152/1739–1242/1826). A major **Sindhī poet** who wrote also in **Persian** and **Urdu**, and was much influence by Shāh **'Abd al-Laṭīf**. Lovers of his poetry have dubbed him the "[Farīd ad-Dīn] **'Aṭṭār** of Sind."

SA'DĪ, MUṢLIḤ AD-DĪN (c. 580/1184 [or c. 610/1213]–692/1292). Persian author of **wisdom** literature and **poet**, among the most famous citizens of Shiraz, **Iran**. Widely traveled, he may have been at some point a member of the **Suhrawardīya** and, in any case, apparently spent the latter part of his life affiliated with some sort of formal Sufi **organization**. He penned a fine ***dīwān*** of **lyric** and panegyric poems but is perhaps best known as the author of two **didactic** works in Persian, *The Orchard* (*Bustān*) and *The Rose Garden* (*Gulistān*). The first is entirely poetry while the latter blends prose and poetry seamlessly, interweaving anecdotes with **aphoristic** wisdom; in both he offers wry observations on a wide range of human foibles and dilemmas, generally with a Sufi twist. Among Persian-speakers, however, his lyric poems remain a favorite choice.

ṢADR. *See* HEART.

ṢAFAWID DYNASTY (907/1501–1135/1722). Persian rulers whose family line originated in Kurdistan, moved to Azerbaijan (west of the Caspian Sea) and reigned successively from capitals in Tabriz, Qazvin, and Esfahan. During the late seventh/13th-early eighth/14th century, the line became identified as an **order** under the leadership of ***shaykh*** **Ṣāfī ad-Dīn** of Ardabīl, a **Sunnī** Muslim. But by the late 10th/15th century, the members of the now-revolutionary political movement distinguished themselves by **headgear** featuring a red spike (whence the nickname ***qizil-bāsh***, red head) wrapped with 12 turns of white cloth (for the 12 *Imāms*), and under the first sovereign of the dynasty, **Shī'ī** Islam became the creed of the realm in 907/1501. During the reigns of the Shāhs Ṭahmāsp (r. 930/1524–984/1576) and 'Abbās I (r. 996/1588–1038/1629), to name two of the greatest, much Sufi-related **literature** and **art** flourished under royal patronage. However, popular or "folk" Sufi orders outside the dynastic structure occasionally presented a threat to the royal establishment's brand of Sufism. Despite the dynasty's official aversion to Sufi movements that posed a potential political threat, a number of orders spread throughout Iran and the thought of **Ibn al-'Arabī**, in particular, garnered considerable, if often critical, attention. Even when it was not a question of **institutional** Sufism, the history of the dynasty is suffused with elements of mystical thinking.

ṢĀFĪ, FAKHR AD-DĪN 'ALĪ (867/1463–939/1532). Persian author, member of the **Naqshbandīya**, and student of Khwāja 'Ubayd Allāh **Aḥrār**.

ṢĀFĪ AD-DĪN ARDABĪLĪ (650/1252–735/1334). Persian Sufi leader regarded as the spiritual ancestor of the **Ṣafawid order**. In his mid-20s he began a relationship with *Shaykh* Zāhid Gīlānī, and eventually assumed leadership of the ***shaykh's*** followers who came to be known by the name of their new head.

SAHL AT-TUSTARĪ, IBN 'ABD ALLĀH (203/818–283/896). Prominent early Sufi **exegete** and mystical **theorist**, teacher of such major figures as Aḥmad ibn Sālim of Baṣra and **Ḥallāj**. A prominent faction among his disciples in Baṣra eventually developed into a school of thought called the **Sālimīya**, an organization made known especially by one of Sahl's most famous followers of a later generation, **Abū Ṭālib al-Makkī**. Two of the most influential works produced in Sahl's name are a volume of mystical exegesis and an anthology of his teachings. Many of his sayings are also preserved by the major **manualists** in particular. One of his most significant contributions to **hermeneutics** is his elaboration of the fourfold meanings of each **Qur'ānic** verse: the literal, symbolic, ethical, and eschatological or mystical (roughly analogous to the four senses of scripture developed by several Fathers of the Church). Other important concepts that Sahl developed include aspects of his theology of **light** and views on the role of **Friends of God**.

SAḤW. *See* SOBRIETY.

SAINT. *See* FRIEND OF GOD.

SAINTHOOD. The office, status, condition, or authority of a **Friend of God**. Generally referred to by the Arabic terms *walāya* and *wilāya* (used somewhat interchangeably and ambiguously), sainthood refers to a high level relationship in a human being who enjoys the protection and patronage of **God** in ways other people can scarcely imagine. The status brings with it unique capabilities and **wonders**, and the ability to share divine **blessing** with others.

SAJJĀDA. *See* CARPET.

SALAF. Collective noun referring to the "ancestors," that is, forerunners in the faith, generally identified as the **Companions** of the **Prophet** and the second generation of Muslims, the Followers, and their "followers" in the third generation. They thus comprise what is considered the "era" of the Prophet, representing for some Muslims a kind of spiritual Golden Age. Sufi theorists such as **Abū Ṭālib al-Makkī** refer often to the age of the Salaf as epitomizing the values of simplicity and ascetical discipline, as modeled especially by the Prophet himself. The 14th/20th century movement known as the *salafīya* sees itself as a reformist force and is on the whole thoroughly inimical to the unacceptable innovation (*bid'a*) they believe Sufism represents. The *salafīs* share that critical stance with the **Wahhābī** movement.

ṢALĀḤ AD-DĪN ZARKŪB (d. 656/1258). Anatolian dervish, close friend and source of inspiration for **Rūmī**, whom the poet was said to have encountered while walking through the area of the bazaar where the goldsmith (*zar-kūb*) had his shop. According to lore, the goldsmith's rhythmic hammer work moved the poet to begin dancing. Ṣalāḥ ad-Dīn had been a student of Rūmī's ***shaykh***, Burhān ad-Din Muḥaqqiq, and the poet later betrothed his own son **Sulṭān Walad** to the goldsmith's daughter.

SĀLIK. *See* WAYFARER.

SĀLIMĪYA. A school of thought connected with proponents of Mālikī **Law** in **Baṣra** and associated especially with **Sahl at-Tustarī** and **Abū Ṭālib al-Makkī**. This school, which takes its name from one of Sahl's disciples called Ibn Sālim, was thus intimately related to a particular theological-legal interpretation of Sufism but was not an **order** as such.

SALJŪQID DYNASTY. A **Turkic** regime that swept westward across the **Middle East**, from central **Asia** through **Persia** and into **Iraq**, conquering **Baghdad** in 447/1055. Interrupting the tenure of the **'Abbāsid** dynasty, they weakened the authority of the Caliph by limiting its authority to the religious realm and establishing the parallel **political** institution of the Sultanate. Important members of the dynasty's administration became influential patrons of major Sufis, including Abū Ḥāmid al-**Ghazālī**. Sufism underwent significant expansion under the dynasty in Iraq and Persia, under the leadership of such luminaries as **Abū Sa'īd ibn Abī 'l-Khayr**, **Anṣārī**, and **Qushayrī**. A branch of the dynasty continued north-westward through Syria and established itself in central the central **Anatolian** city of **Konya** (c. 483/1081–707/1307), where the family of **Rūmī** would later settle and enjoy the patronage of the royal authorities.

SALMĀN AL-FĀRISĪ (d. c. 36/656). A convert from Christianity and a devotee noted for his intimate relationship with the **Prophet**, known as both "The **Persian**" and "The Pure One." Tradition has it that he identified the Prophet through certain bodily marks. A barber by trade, he became a patron of skilled tradespeople. His ethnic nickname stuck and he eventually became something of a symbol of the importance of Persians in the larger Muslim community. He was also adopted as an important religious presence by several **Shī'ī** fringe groups.

SAMĀ'. *See* AUDITION.

SAM'ĀNĪ, ABŪ QĀSIM AḤMAD AS- (487/1094–534/1140). Persian mystical author most famous for his work on the inner significance of the names of **God**. His *Refreshment of Spirits* (*Rawḥ al-arwāḥ*) was likely the first such commentary composed in Persian and blends prose and poetry. From a family of Shāfi'ī religious scholars, his erudition in the traditional Islamic disciplines shines through in his work, which is permeated with themes of **love**, mercy, and forgiveness.

SAMARQAND. Major **Central Asian** city in present-day Uzbekistan. It was an important location in the history of the **Naqshbandīya**, especially under the leadership of Khwāja **Aḥrār**. It was a center of art and culture under the Timūrid dynasty.

SAMAṬRĀNĪ, SHAMS AD-DĪN AS- (a.k.a. Shams ad-Dīn of Pasai) (d. 1039/1630). Indonesian religious scholar and Sufi **theorist** active at the court of Sulṭān Iskandar Muda of Acheh, capital of northern Samatra. He wrote several works in **Arabic** and **Malay** and was the sulṭān's ***shaykh***. Influenced by the thought of **Ibn al-'Arabī**, he was a major participant in the ***wujūdī*** **controversy** against the views of **Rānīrī**.

SAMMĀNĪYA. A branch of the **Khalwatīya** founded by 'Abd al-Karīm as-Sammān (1132/1718–1189/1775) in the **Arabian Peninsula** as part of a **reformist** movement in Sufism. A pupil of his son brought the **order** to the Sudan. There the man who later became the Sudanese Mahdī studied with a ***shaykh*** of the order and eventually fashioned his own Mahdist movement along the lines of the Sufi organization. The order spread soon to **Egypt**, Ethiopia, and the Horn of Africa, and a student of the founder traveled back home to Sumatra to establish an **Indonesian** branch, but the order never succeeded in becoming a major global presence. Some suggest that the order was brought to Sumatra, **Indonesia**, by **'Abd aṣ-Ṣamad of Palembang**.

SANĀ'Ī, ABŪ 'L-MAJD MAJDŪD (d. 525/1131). Major **Persian** Sufi **poet**, author of both **didactic** and **lyric** works. Born in Ghazni (in present-day Afghanistan), the center of the Ghaznawid dynasty, he enjoyed the patronage of various political and religious officials, but during travels in **Central Asia** he also came into contact with the **Saljūqid dynasty**. His only credible link with Sufi **organizations** came as a result of travels to Herat (in western Afghanistan), where he seems to have associated with **Anṣārī's** family. Sanā'ī seems to have been influential in the growing popularity of religious poetry in court circles. His most famous poem is the didactic work in rhyming **couplets** called *The Hidden Garden of Ultimate Reality and the Revealed **Law** of the Path* (*Ḥadīqat al-ḥaqīqa*). Widely regarded as the first mystical work of the genre in Persian, the over-5,000-verse poem was a significant influence on Farīd ad-Dīn **'Aṭṭār** and **Rūmī** and bears thematic affinities with the work of **Sa'dī**.

SANŪSĪ, ABŪ 'ABD ALLĀH MUḤAMMAD AS- (c. 838/1435–895/1490). Maghribī mystical author, religious scholar, and **ascetic**. He studied Sufism in what is now the state of Algeria and sometimes engaged in the so-called **fast** of **David** (fasting one day, eating the next) that became widespread among some **North African** Sufis. Sanūsī's influence as a religious scholar was significant through the 13th/19th century, extending across the **Middle East** and as far east as **Indonesia**. As a Sufi he showed an affinity with the spiritual tenor of **Abū Madyan**.

SANŪSĪ, MUḤAMMAD IBN 'ALĪ AS- (1202/1787–1276/1859). North African religious scholar and founder of the **Sanūsīya**. He went from Algeria to **Fez** (Morocco) to study Sufism and became associated with several branches of the **Shādhilīya** (and possibly also with the **Darqāwīya** and **Qādirīya**). Sanūsī later met and was briefly and at different times a disciple of both Aḥmad at-**Tījānī** and **Aḥmad ibn Idrīs**. After he succeeded the latter in **Mecca**, he gradually transformed the followers of ibn Idrīs into the beginnings of the Sanūsīya. Some regard him as an important Sufi **reformer**.

SANŪSĪ, SAYYID AḤMAD (1290/1873–1351/1933). North African mystic and third ***shaykh*** of the **Sanūsīya**. By his time the **order** had spread southward to Chad and it was there that he spent many years. He is perhaps best known for an ill-fated military resistance to French colonization around Chad and the Sudan, for his political activism within the **Ottoman** administration of the region, and for eventually supporting Atatürk's fight against the allies. He ended his life in **Medina**, no longer welcome in lands under European colonial rule.

SANŪSĪYA. Sufi **order** that originated in the environs of **Mecca** but took root seriously only after its founder, Muḥammad ibn 'Ali as-**Sanūsī**, moved back to **North Africa**, finding at length a congenial setting in Libya. It spiritual heritage, handed down via the founder's teacher **Aḥmad ibn Idrīs**, is rooted in that of the **Shādhilīya**. *Zāwiyas* of the **organization** (the first founded in 1259/1843) became the signature **institution** across Libya and mid-Saharan Africa, and the manner in which these **residential facilities** (typically with attached schools) were founded became a hallmark of the order. Special devotion to the **Prophet** is also a crucial feature of the tradition. It spread through both its links with nomadic tribespeople and its choice of sites along trade and **pilgrimage** routes. It eventually expanded further southward into sub-Saharan regions, and during the early 14th/20th century became increasingly **political** in its stance of resistance to European powers, particularly the French and Italians. Today the order is most important in Libya.

SĀQĪ. *See* CUPBEARER.

SARAKHSĪ, ABŪ 'L-FAḌL MUḤAMMAD IBN ḤASAN (d. 387/997 or 414/1023). **Central Asian** ***shaykh***, influential **Khurāsānī** teacher of the much more famous **Abū Sa'īd ibn Abī 'l-Khayr**. This teacher-disciple relationship is often cited as an example of a particularly potent bond that resulted in the student's far outstripping the master in historical impact.

SARI ṢALṬŪḲ (seventh/13th century). A quasi-legendary **Turkish** warrior **dervish** who, according to the ninth/15th century epic-like work that bears his name in its title, marched with Muslim forces confronting the Byzantine armies. Like a very bold chaplain, he strode ahead of the troops while reciting **litanies** and functioning as a mediator between the seen and unseen worlds. He came to be identified in popular lore as a disciple of Ḥajjī **Bektāsh**, friend of a number of famous Sufi leaders, as well as spiritual patron and missionary preacher of the **Bektāshīya**.

SARĪ "AS-SAQAṬĪ," ABŪ 'L-ḤASAN (155/772–253/867). Oft-quoted **Baghdad ascetic**, known as "the street vendor," whose meeting with **Ma'rūf al-Karkhī** introduced him to Sufism. He traveled widely in the central **Middle East** and, after settling in Baghdad, became the teacher of many important Sufis, including **Junayd**, **Kharrāz**, and **Sumnūn**. Some sources credit him with producing a **rule**, but he left no extant writings and his thought is known only from citations in **manuals** and **hagiographical** sources. He eventually downplayed the importance of outward asceticism as a mode of living, emphasizing the centrality of acting upon one's **love** of **God** and neighbor.

SARRĀJ, ABŪ NAṢR AS- (d. 378/988). Major **theorist** of **Khurasan** and author of an influential **manual**. Few details of his personal life are available, apart from sketchy information about his studying with Ja'far al-**Khuldī** and Ibn Sālim (of the **Sālimīya**), and an indication that Abū 'l-Faḍl as-**Sarakhsī** was among his own students. His sole surviving work is the *Book of Light Flashes* (*Kitāb al-Luma'*), an extensive compendium of Sufi **hagiography**, **lexicography**, and theory. Its 152 brief chapters are organized in 12 "books," beginning with a kind of sociology of religious knowledge that situates Sufi modes of knowing above (but complementary to) the disciplines of **tradition**, **exegesis**, and **law**. He then moves through the various aspects of distinctively Sufi interpretations to those disciplines. Over a fourth of the work is dedicated to Sufi practice, detailing specifics of **behavior**, **dress**, and related matters of **ritual** and communal life. In the final five books, Sarrāj discusses **audition**, **ecstasy**, **miracles** and **wonders**, **terminology**, and the peculiarities of ecstatic utterance. Along with the work of **Abū Ṭālib al-Makkī**, it is among the earliest such works in **Arabic** and a source of much of what we know about countless early Sufis who left no writings of their own.

SATAN. Originally either a *jinn* (created of smokeless fire) or an **angel**—a much-debated issue, Iblīs forfeited his status when he refused **God's**

command that all the angels do homage to the newly created **Adam**. He argued that it made no sense for creatures of fire to bow before a creature of clay. Satan and his minions are at liberty to attempt to lure human beings away from attentiveness to God, but his power is of course limited. Sufi authors, and especially **poets** such as **Ḥallāj**, have often discussed sympathetically the dilemma in which God's command left Iblīs: he was to worship none beside God and yet bow to Adam. It was as though God had commanded him to jump into the water without getting wet. Satan thus becomes paradoxically a model of the mystic: the **lover** of God whose dedication to acknowledging God's absolute unity tragically separated him from the object of his devotion.

SAWĀNIḤ. *See* GHAZĀLĪ, AḤMAD AL-.

SCIENCE OF HEARTS. The general term (Arabic, *'ilm al-qulūb*) Sufi **theorists** and **manualists** use to refer to the whole complex of spiritual disciplines designed to aid the seeker along the **journey**. The disciplines are integral to Sufi **formation** and **instruction** in the quest for mystical **knowledge**, and spiritual guidance of a ***shaykh*** is another specific aspect of the science. Any number of disciplines contribute to this science, including prominently **exegesis** and **hermeneutics** and the use of various **typologies** and **psychological** models, and the understanding of technical **terminology** used in the **discernment** of spirits. It involves tutelage in various forms of **self-discipline, self-scrutiny**, and **asceticism** needed to engage in the ongoing **struggle**, including **contemplation** and various forms of **prayer** and **recollection**. Authentic science of hearts is the opposite of "self-direction" (*tadbīr*), against which **Ibn 'Aṭā' Allāh** and others caution.

SEAL. The concept that a given individual represents finality, hence a kind of closure (*khatm*, seal), in a line of succession. The term is used to refer to **Muḥammad** as the last **prophet** (*khatm al-anbiyā'*), and to a number of prominent Sufis considered by their followers (or themselves) to be the greatest of the **Friends of God** (*khatm al-awliyā'*).

SELF-DISCIPLINE. A large concept including principally a range of methods of **struggle** (*mujāhada,* from the same root as *jihād*) against one's **ego**-soul (*nafs*) as well as various forms of **asceticism**. These include, for example, **self-scrutiny**, the **contemplative** disciplines, and all applied aspects of the **science of hearts**.

SELF-SCRUTINY. Taking account (*muḥāsaba*) of one's inner spiritual movements, a major ingredient in the process of **discernment** that is an integral component of the **science of hearts**. All of the Sufis with prominent reputations as spiritual guides (***shaykhs***) developed their distinctive approaches to self-scrutiny, and some, such as **Muḥāsibī** (whose nickname derives from his legendary competence in this area) developed seminal works of spiritual **psychology** around this central issue.

SEMĀHĀNE. *See* INSTITUTIONS.

SEPARATION. An aspect of spiritual **experience** associated with painful distance from the **Beloved** and often juxtaposed with **union**. Separation (*farq*) results from the seeker's shortcomings, yet, paradoxically, there can be no union without separation. Only when one becomes aware of the distance resulting from one's disobedience can one know the true status of one's creatureliness and need of **God**.

SERVANT. The most common term used to describe a human being from a religious perspective. **God** alone is master, and each individual is ideally *'abd Allāh* (the plural here is *'ibād*) a servant of God. Sufi authors on the whole presuppose this as the baseline, so to speak, of the spiritual life. Common Arabic parlance often uses cognate terms, such as *'abīd* and its plural, *'ubbād*, to refer to pious persons or devotees.

SEXUALITY. Awareness of, and practice in relation to, the sexual nature of human beings. An important but too-seldom acknowledged or studied theme in much mystical **poetry**, issues of sexuality and **gender** relationships are frequently a backdrop or subtle undercurrent in Sufi descriptions of interaction between **lover** and **Beloved**. Poetic intimations of especially male-to-male sexual connection frequently take the form of admiring descriptions of the beardless, downy-cheeked youth. Some famous Sufis insist that the seductive beauty of young boys is a function of the power of multiple diabolical forces attending the youths (whereas only one demon is at work in feminine charms). These often suggest homosexual relationships, of course, but one cannot always attribute them simply and definitively to homosexuality. **Rūmī** is among the most famous poets to speak often of his close male friendships, describing **Shams** and others as inspirational alter-egos; and critics in his own day and later have sought to discredit the poet for leaving his family to pursue a relationship with the wandering **dervish**. Heterosexual imagery also underlies countless metaphors of the divine-human relationship, as in the stories of **Joseph** and **Zulaykhā**, and Laylā and Majnūn.

SHABISTARĪ, MAḤMŪD ASH- (d. c. 737/1337). Persian author and **poet** from Azerbaijan, with spiritual ties to the **Kubrāwīya**. His most famous work is the **didactic** poem in rhyming **couplets** called the *Rose Garden of Mystery* (*Gulshan-i rāz*). In the same **genre** is his *Treatise on (Mystical) Felicity* (*Sa'ādat-nama*) and he is credited with two prose works of mystical theology as well as a small number of **lyric** poems. Much of his work explores the theme of spiritual development through **experiential knowledge** and bears the stamp of **Ibn al-'Arabī**. Later followers such as Shams ad-Dīn Muḥammad **Lāhijī** produced significant commentaries, particularly on the *Rose Garden*.

SHADD. *See* INITIATION.

SHĀDHILĪ, ABŪ 'L-ḤASAN ASH- (c. 593/1196–656/1258). Moroccan mystic and **Friend of God**, founder of the **Shādhilīya**. Rather sketchy details of his life suggest that he traveled in the central **Middle East** for a few years in search of the **pole** of his era, eventually identifying him in **Ibn Mashīsh**, whom he met back in Morocco. When his teacher was murdered, he traveled east to what is now Tunisia and established himself in the town of Shadhila for around 20 years before moving again to **Alexandria**, Egypt. There he further developed down-to-earth spirituality characteristic of his order, a simple approach with broad appeal as well as lofty aspirations to guide the more spiritually advanced among his disciples. He downplayed external practices that tended to bring attention to themselves, such as **audition**, and emphasized unassuming personal devotion (particularly in the form of **supplication** and **litanies**, some composed by him) and **self-scrutiny**. Much of what is known of the ***shaykh*'s** thought is contained by writings of his disciples, such as **Ibn ʻAṭā' Allāh**, whose *Subtleties of Grace* (*Laṭā'if al-minan*) remains an essential source. Perhaps his only theological extravagance was his belief that he was the spiritual pole of his era. And one of the ironies of his otherwise unpretentious life is that his followers attributed countless **wonders** to him and developed his **tomb** as a focus of extensive devotion and **visitation**, despite the founder's repudiation of saint-veneration. He was succeeded by Abū 'l-ʻAbbās al-**Mursī**.

SHĀDHILĪYA. The **order** founded by Abū 'l-Ḥasan ash-**Shādhilī**, a major **organization** across **North Africa** and into the central **Middle East**. As successor to the founder, Abū 'l-ʻAbbās al-**Mursī** actively expanded the order through the founding of *khānqāhs*, and the order's third master, **Ibn ʻAṭā' Allāh**, further developed its devotional legacy as well as its mystical theology through his very popular writings. His teachings were in turn further developed and disseminated by **Ibn ʻAbbād ar-Rundī**. Eventually the order spread globally, with branches in Turkey and as far eastward as China and Indonesia. The order's overall **organization** remained quite fluid, with subordinate **institutions** maintaining considerable independence. Above all the spirit of the order appealed to devout lay persons, for it did not require specific **clothing** or community living, though it strongly recommended regular contact with a spiritual **director**. Among the Sufi founders profoundly influenced by the Shādhilī spirituality are **Darqāwī**, **Jazūlī**, **Wafā'**, and **Zarrūq**. With an affinity not unlike that demonstrated by Catholic religious orders that adopted the spirit of earlier orders, such as the Benedictines or Jesuits, other orders that branched off of the Shādhilīya include the **ʻĪsāwīya** and Jazūlīya.

SHĀH WALĪ ALLĀH OF DELHĪ (1114/1703–1176/1762). Major **Indian** religious scholar, reformer, translator of the **Qur'ān** into **Persian**, member of the **Naqshbandīya** and **Qādirīya**, and author who sought to reconcile mystical trends and mainstream theology. This thrust is particularly evident in several Persian works that explore psychological aspects of mystical **experience** and enter prominently into the ***wujūdī* controversy**. According to tradition, he had numerous **visionary** experiences featuring the **Prophet** and his family. He identified Sufism with the third of the essential elements of religious experience, *iḥsān* (making beautiful, synonymous with **spirituality**, after *islām* and *īmān*, **surrender** and faith). Acknowledging major differences in individual seekers, he maintained an important distinction between one who is "drawn" to **ecstasy** (*majdhūb*) and the **wayfarer** who makes slower progress (*sālik*), although the latter could eventually become one of the former. Two of the spiritual **typologies** he developed to assist in the evaluation of one's progress were three stages of acknowledgment of the divine unity, and four dimensions of divine **manifestation**. The history of Sufism, he believed, unfolded in four cycles: the first began with the Prophet, the second with **Junayd**, the third with **Abū Sa'īd ibn Abī 'l-Khayr**, and the fourth with **Ibn al-'Arabī**.

SHAHĀDA. *See* CREED.

SHAHĪD. *See* MARTYR.

SHĀHID. *See* WITNESS.

SHAJARA. *See* LINEAGE.

SHAME. An aspect of spiritual **experience** expressed by the Arabic term *ḥayā'*. It is particularly prominent in the more **ascetical** traditions within Sufism, implying a heavy emphasis on compunction for sin and a desire for true **repentance**.

SHAMS AD-DĪN TABRĪZĪ (d. 645/1247). Wandering **dervish** (perhaps associated with a ***qalandar***, **chivalric**, or ***akhī*** movement) who became an alter-ego of **Rūmī**. He may also have had links to the **Kubrāwīya**. He came to **Konya** in 642/1244 and soon became acquainted with Rūmī and his family. The two began to spend a great deal of time together and the poet acknowledges the dervish as a prime inspiration for much of his **poetry**. Shams left a single work in prose, the quasi-**autobiographical** ***Discourses*** (*Maqālāt*) in which he speaks of the centrality of love for the **Prophet**. Rūmī's family and friends grew increasingly jealous of the relationship and some have argued that one of the poet's sons, 'Alā' ad-Dīn, may have been involved in the murder of Shams.

SHAQĪQ AL-BALKHĪ (d. 194/810). Persian mystic and author, from present-day Afghanistan, credited with writing the first systematic program for a series of **forty**-day **retreats**, and with being the first in his region to discuss mystical **states**. The **Khurāsānī's** short **Arabic** work outlines the requirements of four resting places along a **journey**, beginning with **ascetical** self-denial and progressing through **fear** and **longing** for heaven, to **love**. His plan may well have been an important influence on further development of such psycho-spiritual schemas with their extensive elaboration of various **stations** and states.

SHA'RĀNĪ, 'ABD AL-WAHHĀB ASH- (897/1492–973/1565). Egyptian religious scholar and Sufi **hagiographer**. He traces his ancestry back to an early member of the **Shādhilīya**, and his family had been involved with Sufism for generations. He became the leader of the family's own version of a Sufi **order**, showing influences of the **Badawīya** as well as the Shādhilīya, but inclining to a populist approach that emphasized conscientious adherence to fundamental legal prescriptions. The order has not been active since the early 13th/19th century. Theologically, he was a defender of **Ibn al-'Arabī**, and one of his own more famous students was **Munāwī**.

SHARḤ. *See* EXEGESIS.

SHARĪ'A. *See* LAW.

SHAṬḤ. *See* ECSTASY.

SHAṬṬĀRĪYA. Indian order founded in the ninth/15th century by a member of the **Suhrawardīya** family, Shāh 'Abd Allāh (d. 890/1485), and later spread to **Indonesia**. The theory behind the **organization's** practice was intimately bound up with **cosmology** and the influence of celestial bodies on human life. Major members of the order include Muḥammad Ghawth **Gwāliyārī** and **Sinkilī**. Not unlike the **Chishtīya**, the order gravitated toward **political** activism.

SHAWQ. *See* DESIRE.

SHAYKH. From the Arabic for "elder," referring in its most general sense to a tribal, religious, or organizational leader. In the context of Sufism, the term refers especially to individuals entrusted with the critical aspect of spiritual guidance and **formation** called the **science of hearts**, or with leadership of an **order**. The term *shaykh* and the feminine form, *shaykha*, as well as its Persian equivalent, *pīr*, can, by extension, mean "venerable." Both terms can refer to senior Sufis who exercise various specific kinds of institutional **authority** in Sufi orders.

Sufi authors speak of the importance of the *shaykh at-ta'līm*, whose role is that of **instruction** in a wider range of often less arcane concerns and matters of personal and communal discipline. Some scholars argue that this broadly educative role was dominant until about the fourth/10th century, at which time the *shaykh* began to assume a more spiritually oriented function, that of the soul-mentor. The term *shaykh at-tarbīya*, "formative guide," refers to the function of forming seekers in the inner disciplines essential to progress on the path. The moral authority of such a guide has been nearly absolute in many orders, and seekers are counseled to think of themselves as akin to the cadaver in the hands of one who prepares it for burial. This change arguably occurred as Sufi **theorists** elaborated in their **manuals** the science of hearts as a map for the spiritual **journey**. In the case of the **Naqshbandīya** in modern times, the *shaykh's* role has also included a mediating function in relation to the person of the **Prophet**, assisting the seeker to connect with that paragon of **intimacy** with **God**. That same order has emphasized the importance of the practice of **visualization** of one's *shaykh*. Slightly more technical and precise in relation to the role of spiritual direction is the Arabic *murshid*, "one who confers right guidance." Sometimes the term *bābā*, "papa" is used as a synonym.

Apart from the Sufi connections, the term *shaykh* often used to refer to the leader of, for example, a tribe, or conferred **honorifically** on someone with special credentials for religious leadership and knowledge.

SHIBLĪ, ABŪ BAKR IBN JAḤDAR ASH- (247/861–334/945). Religious scholar and early **'Irāqī** Sufi, disciple of **Junayd** and erstwhile associate of **Ḥallāj**. His eccentric behavior marginalized him and some of his claims to spiritual authority drew criticism of religious authorities. He **initiated** a number of influential disciples, including al-**Ḥuṣrī**, **Ibn Khafīf**, and **Naṣrābādhī**, but his views survive only in extensive citations of his mystical **allusions** gathered especially in the major **manuals**.

SHĪʿĪ SUFISM. Official or formal adoption by particular **orders** of Shīʿī teachings, **ritual** and **symbolism**. This involves particularly the explicit acknowledgment of a major role for the Shīʿī *Imāms* in an order's genealogy. Many organizations trace their **lineages** through figures of central importance in Shīʿī tradition, such as **ʿAlī**, **Jaʿfar aṣ-Ṣādiq** and some of the earlier *Imāms*, but only a few **Persian** orders have embraced Twelver Shīʿī tradition quite integrally. These include chiefly the present-day Dhahabīya, Khāksār, **Niʿmat-allāhīya**, and **Nūrbakhshīya**. One could also include for historical completeness the case of the long-defunct **Ṣafawīs**. Affinities between Sufism and Shīʿī tradition in general include such features as similarities in the roles of ***shaykhs*** and the *Imāms* (e.g., **authority** in interpretation); characteristics (e.g., power and **wonders**) and functions (e.g., **intercession** and position in the cosmic **hierarchy**, including that of **pole**) shared by **Friends of God** and the *Imāms*; and the types of ritual observances practiced in relation to those paragons of sanctity and sources of **blessing** (e.g., **visitation**).

SHĪRĀZ. Major southwestern **Persian** city, not far from the ancient pre-Islamic Acahemenid Dynasty city of Persepolis (sixth century BCE). It was home to many famous Sufis, including **Ḥāfiẓ**, **Ibn Khafīf**, **Rūzbihān Baqlī**, and **Saʿdī**. Townspeople in general had a reputation of old for devotion and **asceticism**.

SHRINE. Structure or **architectural** complex associated with a **prophet** or **Friend of God**, typically a goal for pilgrim **visitation** (*mazār*, place to which one goes on *ziyāra*). Most such **institutions** (sometimes funded by **endowments**) are associated with **tombs** of holy persons, but some, such as Jerusalem's **Dome of the Rock**, enjoy elevated status by association with episodes in the life of the holy person.

***ṢIDQ*.** *See* AUTHENTICITY.

SILSILA. *See* LINEAGE.

SIMILITUDE. An extended simile, analogous to a parable except that it relies less on developed narrative details, meant to teach a spiritual or ethical point or principle. The **Qur'ān** contains many similitudes (*amthāl*, s.g. *mathal*) "coined" by the divine pedagogue, and Sufi authors pick up and extend those scriptural leads in addition to fashioning their own in prose and poetic works alike.

SIMNĀNĪ, 'ALĀ' AD-DAWLA (659/1261–736/1336). Persian mystic and author, son of a powerful and influential family during the period of Mongol Il-khānid rule of **Iran**. According to tradition, he experienced a conversion precipitated by a **vision** and a protracted illness, developing into a redoubtable apologist for Islam in debate with the Buddhist monks who visited the Mongol courts. His familiarity with Sufism remained informal and self-taught for a time, but he eventually cultivated a series of more formal relationships with influential ***shaykhs*** in **Baghdad** and Persia. His clearest **institutional** link was with the **Kubrāwīya** via **Iraq**. He wrote a number of important works of theory in which he contests the thought of **Ibn al-'Arabī**. Perhaps the most distinctive aspect of his thought is his development of **'Ayn al-Quḍāt Hamadhānī's psychological** concept of the seven "spiritual subtleties" associated with the inner faculties. Each is further paired with a specific symbolic **color** and **prophet**. A major theme underlying his work is a balancing of Sunnī and **Shī'ī theological** elements with Sufism.

SIMNĀNĪ, SAYYID ASHRAF JIHĀNGĪR (d. c. 829/1425). Sufi saint, teacher, and **theorist** of **Persian** origin (Khurasan), who spent much of his adult life in **India**. Claiming affiliation to 14 different **orders**, he was most intimately claimed by the **Chishtīya**. He speaks at length of the importance of rituals of **audition**, and a significant portion of one of his extant works, in the **genre** of mystical **discourse**, functions also as a **hagiographical** source for his order.

SĪMURGH. A mythical **bird** from pre-Islamic lore, a hybrid of features of the eagle and griffon with elaborate flowing plumage, that functions as a **symbol** of **God**. In the **Persian** national epic, *The Book of Kings* (*Shāhnāma*), the wondrous creature was known to visit great royal heroes when they were in dire straits, to avail them of its magical powers. Dwelling in the remote Elburz Mountains, the bird becomes the symbol of divine kingship in **'Aṭṭār's** *Conference of the Birds* (*Manṭiq aṭ-ṭayr*) where the poet fashions an elaborate pun. When a bedraggled group of a mere 30 birds (*sī murgh* in Persian) appear at the mountain palace asking for the Sīmurgh, they find themselves standing before a large **mirror** and discovering the object of their quest within themselves.

SIN. *See* VICE.

SINCERITY. A quality of spirit characterized by a perfect lack of self-consciousness, the diametric opposite of hypocrisy. Many theorists and **manualists** locate *ikhlāṣ* at various junctures among the **stations** or **states**, but virtually all major Sufi authors discuss the quality at some point even if they do not analyze it so systematically as that. A genuinely sincere seeker does not act out of a hope for reward or fear of punishment and is unaffected by, indeed unaware of, other people's opinions of him or her. Sincerity is a feature that most of all describes the individual's relationship with **God**, and **Muḥāsibī**, for example, further analyzes sincerity into degrees of docility and promptness in responding in sincerity.

SIND. A region straddling the lower Indus River and occupying parts of present-day **Pakistan** and **India**. The region was important in the history of Sufism especially through the **Mughal dynasty**, and several Sufi authors crafted **Sindhī** into an important mystical literary **language**. The two most prominent Sufi orders there have been the **Naqshbandīya** and **Suhrawardīya**. Most of the all, the region is famed for its countless **tombs** of **Friends of God**, and as a land of pilgrims intent on **visitation**. Many Muslims still long to be buried in the Maklī Hills, where many famous holy persons are interred.

SINDHĪ. An Indo-Aryan **language** spoken by about 20 million Pākistānīs (about 80 percent of the total) and Indians, whose 52 letters are written in a variation of the **Arabic** script. It became an important vehicle for Sufi **poets** in late medieval and early modern times in **South Asia**. Sufi authors who wrote notably in the language include **'Abd al-Laṭīf** and **Sachal Sarmast**.

SINGING. One of the forms of **music** used by many Sufi groups for communal **ritual** in particular. **Recollection** rituals of many orders include devotional songs (*anāshīd*) as well as instrumental music. Some orders incorporate into their ceremonies a formal role for the office of chanter (*muzamzim*) or groups of singers (*munshidūn*). Two of the major orders that have developed important song repertoires are the **Mawlawīya** and the **Chishtīya**, the latter most closely associated with ***qawwālī***. Song styles can be both accompanied instrumentally and a cappella.

SINKILĪ, 'ABD AR-RA'ŪF AS- (c. 1620/1030–1104/1693). Malay religious scholar, from western Sumatra (Indonesia), and **Friend of God** who brought the **Shaṭṭārīya** to **Southeast Asia** and was a major ***shaykh*** of that order as well as of the **Qādirīya**. Traditional accounts credit him with introducing Islam to Acheh. He apparently did not find the theological positions of fellow Malay scholars **Ḥamza Fanṣūrī** and **Samaṭānī** on the ***wujūdī*** **controversy** congenial, but refrained from the head-on attacks for which **Rānīrī** was well known. He is believed to have translated the **Qur'ān** into Malay for the first time.

SIRHINDĪ, AḤMAD (971/1563–1034/1624). Major **Indian** religious scholar and mystical author from the **Panjab**, *pīr* of the **Naqshbandīya** under the **Mughal** dynasty. As a Sufi leader he was **politically** active, offering advice to rulers concerning needed religious reforms. And, as his hundreds of **letters** in **Persian** suggest, he sustained personal relationships with a large number of individuals. A major theme in his writing is the central role of the "renewer" or **reformer** whom God promised to raise up each (Islamic) century and whose function was, in effect, to extend the influence of the **prophets** beyond the age of prophetic **revelation**. His followers named him the "renewer (*mujaddid*) of the age" and his branch of the **order** came to be known as the *Mujaddidīya*. The concept of **intoxication** plays a signal role in his theory of how **Friends of God** model mystical **experience**.

SIRR. *See* HEART.

SOBRIETY. One's "natural" spiritual condition, prior to **ecstatic experience**, and, according to some, the optimal condition after such experience as well. According to the latter view, "**intoxication**" is at best a temporary spiritual experience, for the human person is not created to survive long at, let alone sustain, such a pitch of intensity. Some Sufi authors, such as **Junayd**, speak of a "second" sobriety (*saḥw*) according to which one returns from a state of ecstatic intoxication to a sustainable level of spiritual engagement.

SOLOMON. A **prophet**, son of **David**, known for his wisdom and for his unusual relationship to Bilqīs, Queen of Sheba. An important aspect of his special **knowledge** was his facility in communicating with all living beings, especially the **birds** and the *jinn* (creatures of smokeless fire whom the king enlisted to build his temple). The crested hoopoe (*hudhud* in Persian) assisted him in his military conquests as a kind of airborne divining rod, reconnoitering for sources of water. A story in which a mere ant confronts the king with his arrogant dismissal of the powerless of this world describes a moment of spiritual conversion about which Sufi **poets** comment often.

SOUL. A human faculty (generally referred to by the **Arabic** term *nafs*) whose status and function varies according to context. According to the **Qur'ān**, the *nafs* can function as an obstreperous **ego** (*an-nafs al-ammāra*, the overweening soul) with its selfish and even downright evil designs that contend with **spirit** for the attentions of the **heart**. In that role, the soul stands as the prime enemy against which the seeker must **struggle**. It can also act as a moral compass, calling the individual to act justly; *an-nafs al-lawwāma*, the blaming soul, is akin to conscience. There is also the tranquil soul, *an-nafs al-muṭma'inna*, representing a condition occurring in the presence of **God**. The various aspects of soul each suggest different features of the Sufi **psychological** analysis of spiritual **experience**.

SOUTH ASIA. Region consisting principally of three nation-states that once comprised **India** alone, from which **Pakistan** was partitioned in 1367/1947, with the former East Pakistan separating to form

Bangladesh in 1391/1971. (Sri Lanka is also included, and some would also include the Himalayan nations of Nepal, Tibet, Sikkim, and Bhutan, but none of the latter has ever had significant Muslim populations.) Major **orders** include the **Chishtīya**, **Firdawsīya**, Kāzarūnīya, **Kubrāwīya**, **Naqshbandīya**, **Qalandarīya**, **Shaṭṭārīya**, and **Suhrawardīya**.

SOUTHEAST ASIA. Generally taken to include the nation-states of Vietnam, Laos, Cambodia, Thailand, Burma, **Malaysia**, **Indonesia**, Singapore, Brunei, and the Philippines. The most important language prior to modern times in the communication of Sufism is **Malay**. Major Sufis include **'Abd aṣ-Ṣamad of Palembang**, **Ḥamza Fanṣūrī**, **Rānīrī**, **Samaṭrānī**, and **Sinkilī**. Numbered among the more influential orders are the Aḥmadīya, **Chishtīya**, **Naqshbandīya**, **Qādirīya**, **Rifā'īya**, **Shādhilīya**, and **Shaṭṭārīya**.

SPAIN. *See* ANDALUSIA.

SPIRIT. A human faculty (generally referred to by the **Arabic** term *rūḥ*) that typically represents positive inner impulses and drives. It engages in a tug-of-war with the **ego-soul** to win over the ever-changeable **heart**. Some Sufi **psychological** theories add the element of "natural disposition" to the mix, interposing it between spirit and heart. In addition, many Sufi authors describe the spirit as highly mobile, able to depart from the body during sleep and returning during the waking state; though it leaves the body at death, it will be united with the body in **resurrection**.

SPIRITUALITY. One English equivalent for the Arabic term *iḥsān*, "making/doing the beautiful," the third key ingredient mentioned in the "**Ḥadīth** of **Gabriel**," along with *islām* (**surrender**) and *īmān* (faith). It is an especially important concept in Sufi thought, representing as it does a high level of spiritual progress.

STAFF. An **implement** used by many Sufi **orders** as both a practical device and a **symbol** of the seeker's **pilgrim** status. On a more symbolic level, the staff functions in the lore of many **orders** as an article of spiritual heredity, handed down from as far back as **Adam**.

Like the **begging bowl** and **cloak**, the staff thus becomes a link to exemplary pilgrims past.

STAGES. Milestones or resting places along the spiritual **journey**. Often expressed by the term *manāzil* (sg. *manzil*, place at which one settles down), stages of various kinds are laid out and analyzed in the diverse **typologies** Sufi **theorists** have devised. Tempting as it may be to read descriptions of, for example, **stations** and **states** and other types of "stages," in a linear or progressive fashion, the **metaphor** of traveling toward the goal of **union** is rarely understood as a simple passage from one stage to another, never to revisit "earlier" stages. Instead, the **wayfarer**'s advance in some ways encompasses all stages traversed as a condition for progress.

STANDARD. A flag (*'alam*), among the **ritual implements** and identifying marks of specific Sufi groups or famous individuals. When members of more than one **order** gather for a joint **ritual** occasion, one might see different **colored** standards flying (often triangular in shape) or hanging as **banners** (typically rectangular cloth panels) on nearby walls. Some **Friends of God** have had their own standards, sometimes inscribed with the individual's name along with a pious wish expressed in such formulae as "May God sanctify/ennoble his/her spirit/countenance." Standards are often hung in the holy person's **tomb** as well. Devotees celebrating **birthdays** of famous Sufis often carry standards in ritual processions.

STANDING. A **metaphor** used to express a feature of mystical **experience** in which **God** positions or "stays" an individual in a particular **moment** or spiritual **stage**. It was **Niffarī** who most significantly injected the term (*waqfa*, with the active participle *wāqif*) into the Sufi **lexicon**.

STATE. A dimension of spiritual **experience** generally characterized as fleeting and irretrievable, in the sense that it is a pure gift of **God** unrelated to human effort. Sufi authors offer various opinions as to what aspects of experience qualify as states, as well as about the precise relationships between states and **stations**. **Sarrāj**, for example, lists 10 states (*ḥāl/aḥwāl*), including meditation, **proximity**, **love**, **fear**, **hope**,

desire, **intimacy**, tranquility, **contemplation**, and **certitude**. **Qushayrī**'s list of 43 aspects of experience begins with 21 stations, with the 22nd marking a transition to the states, which include [satisfaction], servanthood, **desire**, steadfastness, sincerity, **authenticity**, **shame**, freedom, **recollection**, **chivalry**, **discernment**, moral character, largesse, jealousy, sainthood, supplication, **poverty**, **Sufism**, proper demeanor, experiential **knowledge**, **love**, and desire. **Hujwīrī**'s presentation combines aspects of both stations and states without distinguishing them as such, discussing various aspects of experience under the rubric of "pulling back veils."

STATION. A dimension of spiritual **experience** generally characterized as of some duration and resulting, at least to some degree, from individual striving. **Sarrāj** precedes his list of 10 **states** with seven stations (*maqam/maqāmāt*): **repentance**, **reticence**, **asceticism**, **poverty**, **patience**, **trust**, and **contentment**. **Abū Ṭālib al-Makkī** talks of "stations of certitude and states of those endowed with certitude" as an overall heading for his detailed descriptions of **repentance**, **patience**, **hope**, **fear**, **asceticism**, **trust**, **contentment**, and **love**. Among the authors who developed a lengthier list but did not always distinguish so systematically between stations and states, Abū Ḥāmid al-**Ghazālī** stands out. He lists 10 items, some of which are actually clusters: repentance, patience and gratitude, poverty and asceticism, acknowledging the divine unity and trust, love and desire, intention and sincerity and **authenticity**, **contemplation** and **self-scrutiny**, meditation, and recollection of death. **Qushayrī** provides a list of some 43 aspects of spiritual experience, the first 22 of which he apparently considers stations. These include: **repentance**, **struggle**, **retreat**, reverential awe, **reticence**, silence, **fear**, **hope**, sorrow, hunger, humility, resistance to **ego**, envy, backbiting, contentment, trust, gratitude, **certitude**, patience, self-awareness, and satisfaction. Concerning satisfaction, he acknowledges various opinions as to whether it is a station or a state. His own view compromises: it begins as a station and develops into a state. **Abū Sa'īd ibn Abī 'l-Khayr** spoke of 40 stations, beginning with intention and culminating in **Sufism** itself. **Anṣārī** developed the longest list of stations, which he names "resting places." It includes 100 aspects of experience (to be precise, two different lists of 100 stations) in groups of 10 for easier memorization.

STORYTELLING. An important medium for communicating edifying tales (*qiṣṣa*, pl. *qiṣaṣ*) and lore about major holy persons such as **prophets**, as well as about **Friends of God**. Some Sufi authors, such as **Abū Ṭālib al-Makkī**, have expressed grave reservations about the dangers of listening to such professional raconteurs (*qāṣṣ*, pl. *quṣṣāṣ*). They argue that one can be led astray by their beguiling tales, which are, ultimately, meant only to entertain and distract rather than truly edify.

STRUGGLE. An ongoing aspect of ordinary spiritual **experience**, a form of daily **asceticism** and self-discipline. Typically expressed with the **Arabic** term *jihād*, this striving is generally interpreted by Sufi authors as predominantly an inward combat (*mujāhada*) aimed at vanquishing one's **ego/soul** and its baser tendencies.

SUBSTITUTES. A group of living persons called *abdāl* (sg. *badal*), variously numbered at four, seven, 40, or 70, who form an essential part of the Sufi **cosmological hierarchy**. These **Friends of God** are divinely chosen to communicate **blessing** and mediate **wonders** in post-prophetic ages. Members of the larger group of substitutes are further distinguished as **authentic** ones (*ṣiddīqūn*), **supports**, and **poles**. Some authors argue that the number of substitutes—whose identity at any one time is known only to very few people—remains constant, since when one of them dies, another "substitutes" for him.

SUCCESSOR. The technical name (Arabic, *khalīfa*) for the assistant to the founder, superior or "senior" ***shaykh*** of an **order** who is designated to assume the leadership in the **governance** of the **organization** at the death of the current leader. Successorship has been hereditary in some orders, elective in others, while in still others the *shaykh* chose the heir to his **authority**.

ṢŪF(Ī). *See* SUFISM.

SUFISM. Generic term (*taṣawwuf* in Arabic) commonly used to describe various aspects of the Islamic **mystical** tradition and its **institutions**. Some scholars have argued that it derives from the **Arabic** term *ṣūf* (wool), suggesting that the earliest Sufis were **ascetical** types known for wearing rough woolen garments. Some Sufi **theorists** list the term toward the top of their rosters of **stations** or **states**, suggesting that one attains the inner reality of Sufism only long after espousing it as a way of life. Significant cognate technical terms include *mustaṣwif* (Sufi pretender) and *mutaṣawwif* (one to aspires to be a Sufi).

SUHRAWARDĪ, ABŪ ḤAFṢ ʻUMAR AS- (539/1145–632/1234). Major **Persian**-born religious scholar, Sufi theorist and **preacher**, student of his uncle Abū ʼn-Najīb as-**Suhrawardī** and of **ʻAbd al-Qādir al-Jīlānī**. His most important contribution is his beautiful **manual**, *The Benefits of Intimate Knowledge* (*ʻAwārif al-maʻārif*), arguably the last of the truly seminal works in its **genre**. It became essential reading for a number of **orders** in addition to the **Suhrawardīya**, particularly the **Chishtīya**. He also had significant connections with **chivalric** groups and, working with several rulers interested in the movement, injected a distinctively Sufi element into that **institutional** tradition. His most influential associates included **Bahāʼ ad-Dīn Zakarīya** and **Najm ad-Dīn Dāyā Rāzī**. He spent much of his life in **Baghdad** and was buried there.

SUHRAWARDĪ, ABŪ ʼN-NAJĪB ʻABD AL-QĀHIR AS- (c. 490/1097–563/1168). Major Sufi ***shaykh***, author, and religious scholar from western **Iran**, widely regarded as founder of the **Suhrawardīya**. He traveled to **Baghdad** and was initiated into an **order** by an uncle of his, but returned to Isfahan (in west-central Persia) to apprentice to Aḥmad al-**Ghazālī**. Again he headed for Baghdad, resuming for a time a teaching position on a faculty of Islamic **law** and **tradition**. He remained an influential independent teacher for the rest of his life, numbering Najm ad-Dīn **Kubrā** and his own nephew, Abū Ḥafṣ ʻUmar as-**Suhrawardī**, among his most famous followers. His sole influential work is the *Rules of **Behavior** for Sufi Seekers* (*Kitāb ādāb al-murīdīn*), one of the earliest texts of its kind, covering a full range of issues in the daily life of aspirants to **institutional** Sufi life.

SUHRAWARDĪ "MAQTŪL," SHIHĀB AD-DĪN YAḤYĀ AS- (549/1154–587/1191). Father of the "**Illuminationist**" school (*Ishrāq*) influential in the evolution of religious epistemology, he became known as "the murdered one" after his politically motivated execution in Aleppo (Syria) at the order of the Ayyubid ruler. His **Arabic** and **Persian** writings have been characterized as predominantly philosophical, but he exerted considerable influence in the formation of aspects of **theosophical** or speculative Sufism. Perhaps of greatest interest for the history of Sufism are his "visionary **recitals**" (*The Red Intellect [ʿAql-i surkh]*, *The Tale of the Occidental Exile* [*Qiṣṣat al-ghurba al-gharbīya*], and *The Treatise on the Birds* [*Risālat aṭ-ṭayr*]), and a short treatise on **love**. He was very much attracted to the thought of **Ḥallāj**, whom he considered a final link in a chain of Sufis (including also **Bāyazīd**, **Dhū 'n-Nūn**, and **Sahl**) through whom ancient **Iranian** wisdom was preserved. His metaphysics of **light** continued to make its mark on the writings of later Sufis as well.

SUHRAWARDĪYA. An order traditionally said to have been founded in **Baghdad** by Abū Ḥafṣ ʿUmar as-**Suhrawardī**, nephew of Abū 'n-Najīb as-**Suhrawardī**. The **organization** quickly spread throughout the **Middle East**, moving as far east as **Indonesia** and establishing an important presence in north and northwest **India** especially, where it took shape in the 10th/15th century. Major figures in the order include **Bahā' ad-Dīn Zakarīya**, **Fakhr ad-Dīn ʿIrāqī**, and **Ḥamīd ad-Dīn Nagawrī**.

SUKR. *See* INTOXICATION.

SULAMĪ, ʿABD AR-RAḤMĀN AS- (325/937–412/1021). Exegete and **hagiographer** and theorist from **Nīshāpūr**, of a family of religious scholars and **ascetics**. He was a disciple of **Naṣrābādhī** and is credited with writing one of the most important sources on the **Malāmatīya**. Of his scores of writings, he is perhaps best known for biographical anthologies of famous Sufis (he compiled about 1,000 lifestories in all, but only a shorter version of some 100 remains—a work called the *Generations of the Sufis* [*Ṭabaqāt aṣ-Ṣūfīya*]), and two very valuable **Qur'anic** commentaries that have preserved the exegetical **allusions** of many of the earliest Sufis.

SULAYMĀN ÇELEBĪ (d. 822/1419). Turkish poet, author of one of the most famous poetic accounts of the **birth** of the **Prophet**. The text is still widely recited on anniversaries of death and other such occasions, in addition to the Prophet's birthday.

SULṬĀN BĀHŪ (1039/1629–1102/1691). Major **Panjābī poet** during the reign of the **Mughal** Shāh Jahān, and author of nearly two dozen **Persian** Sufi texts. He was a member of the **Qādirīya** and a proponent of the concept of ontological **unity**, *waḥdat al-wujūd*. His short, earthy lyrics remain popular because they are memorable and folksy, even down to the way he ends nearly every verse with "*Hū*"—Arabic for He, that is, **God**. This pronominal name of the deity remains one of the most common syllables that Sufis repeat during rituals of **recollection** or **audition**. It was this literary habit that won him the name Bā-hū ("with Him").

SULṬĀN WALAD (623/1226–712/1312). Turkish poet and author, son of **Rūmī**, among the founding members of the **Mawlawīya**. Many scholars credit him with actually organizing the **order** formally, and with initiating the first movements to expand the **organization** beyond Konya. His **Persian** writings include **lyric** poems as well as longer **didactic** works in rhyming **couplets**, and he appears to have penned some of the earliest extant Turkish religious poems from the land of **Rūm**.

SUMNŪN IBN ḤAMZA "AL-MUḤIBB" (d. c. 298/910). Important early Sufi of **Baghdad**, follower of **Sarī as-Saqaṭī**, known as "The Lover." His sayings and views, including bits of **poetry**, are extant only in the **manuals** and **hagiographical** works. He is best known for his observations on **patience** and mindfulness of **God** at all times.

SUNNA. *See* PROPHETIC EXAMPLE.

SUNNĪ. "Having to do with the *sunna*," generally used in juxtaposition to the term ***Shī'ī***. *Sunnī* is in effect an abbreviated form of "People of the *sunna* and the Assembly/Community" (*ahl as-sunna wa' l-jamā'a*), a term that originally designated the majority of Muslims after differences of opinion as to how the community should choose a **successor** to the **Prophet**. According to the Sunnī interpretation of history, the Prophet had not designated his cousin and son-in-law 'Alī as his successor (as the Shī'a claimed). The caliph was to be chosen from a group of elder-peers, and not necessarily from the family of the Prophet. Most Sufi **orders** have identified themselves as Sunnī. Acceptance of the legitimacy of all four "Rightly Guided Caliphs" (**Abū Bakr**, 'Umar, 'Uthmān, and **'Alī**) is a hallmark of Sunnī thought—hardcore Shī'ī tradition regards the first three as illegitimate usurpers. Some Sunnī orders trace their **lineages** back to the earlier caliphs (the **Naqshbandīya** and **Yasawīya** to Abū Bakr, and the **Rifā'īya** to 'Umar, for example). **Hujwīrī** identifies the first four caliphs as symbols, respectively, of **contemplation**, **self-discipline**, friendship with **God**, and guidance to the ultimate **reality**.

SUPPLICATION. A form of personal **prayer** generally referred to with the Arabic term *du'ā*, "calling upon" God. The term *adhkār* ("invocations," plural of *dhikr*) is sometimes used as a synonym. Many Sufis are credited with composing prayers of petition, and some have been collected, thus constituting in effect a **genre**. These originally spontaneous, free expressions of the questing **heart** are often intense and volatile, sometimes overflowing with passion and thus easily misinterpreted as inappropriate or even **theologically** suspect.

SUPPORTS. A group of four individuals among the **substitutes** who form an important part of traditional Sufi **cosmological hierarchy**. The governing metaphor is that these "tent pegs" (*awtād*, also called *'umūd*, columns, or *arkān*, pillars) are needed to hold down the spiritual cosmos by overseeing the four quadrants of the universe from their abode in the center.

ṢŪRA. *See* FORM.

SURRENDER. A fundamental attitude and prerequisite for all spiritual **experience** expressed by the Arabic term *islām*. Often translated "submission," *islām* actually connotes an important element of more active response of gratitude to **God's blessings**.

SWAHILI. A Bantu **language** spoken by some 40 million people in **East Africa**, named after its early identification with the coastal regions (*sawāḥil*). As a result of extensive Muslim influence, the language gradually incorporated a great deal of **Arabic** vocabulary. A number of mystically tinged works have survived in Swahili, particularly in the form of texts on the themes of the **Prophet's birth** and **Ascension**.

SYMBOLISM. A wide range of **literary** and visual means of expressing truths that Sufis have generally regarded as inexpressible in a literal way. These include literary **metaphor**, **similitude**, and **allegory**; use of **number**, **alphabet**, and **color** in symbolic fashion; and the use of a wide range of objects, such as **banners**, **carpet**, **standards**, items of **clothing** and **headgear**, and **ritual implements**. The latter types of symbolism might also appear in visual presentations through the media of **calligraphy** and **painting** and the **manuscript arts**.

SYRIA. Ancient region of the **Middle East**, and a modern nation-state, bounded on the north by **Turkey**, on the east by **Iraq**, on the south by Jordan, and on the west by the Mediterranean, Lebanon, and Israel/Palestine. Its capital, **Damascus**, became the capital of the **Umayyad** dynasty in 41/661 and was home to a number of famous Sufis over the centuries. Among the Sufis most famously associated with Syria are **Dārānī**, **Dhū 'n-Nūn**, **Ibn al-'Arabī**, and Yaḥyā as-**Suhrawardī**.

– T –

ṬABAQA. *See* RESIDENTIAL FACILITY.

ṬABAQĀT. *See* GENERATIONS.

TADHKIRA. *See* REMEMBRANCES.

TADHKIRAT AL-AWLIYĀ'. *See* 'AṬṬĀR.

TADRĪB. *See* FORMATION.

TAFRĪD. *See* ISOLATION.

TAFṢĪL. *See* DISCERNMENT.

TAFSĪR. *See* EXEGESIS.

TAHDHĪB. *See* INSTRUCTION.

TAḤKĪM. *See* INSTRUCTION.

ṬĀ'IFA. *See* ORDER.

TĀJ. *See* HEADGEAR.

TAJALLĪ. *See* MANIFESTATION.

TA'LĪM. *See* INSTRUCTION.

TALQĪN. *See* INSTRUCTION.

TAMHĪDĀT. *See* 'AYN AL-QUḌĀT.

TAMKĪN. *See* FIXITY.

TAMZĪQ. *See* BEHAVIOR.

TANZĪH. *See* THEORY.

ṬĀQIYA. *See* HEADGEAR.

TARBĪYA. *See* FORMATION.

ṬARĪQA. *See* ORDER.

ṬARṬŪR. *See* HEADGEAR.

TASAMMA. *See* INITIATION.

TAṢAWWUF. *See* SUFISM.

TAṢAWWUR. *See* VISUALIZATION.

TASBĪḤA. *See* ROSARY.

TASTE. An element of spiritual **experience** describing an essential dimension of the seeker's relationship to **God**. Tasting (*dhawq*) is related **metaphorically** to imbibing the **intoxicating** beverage of the divine presence. Some authors, such as Abū Ḥāmid al-**Ghazālī**, use the term to distinguish firsthand experience from mere intellectual or notional assent to a truth.

TAWAHHUM. *See* CONTEMPLATION.

TAWAJJUH. *See* CONTEMPLATION.

TAWĀJUD. *See* ECSTASY.

TAWAKKUL. *See* TRUST.

TAWBA. *See* REPENTANCE.

TAWḤĪD. *See* GOD.

TA'WĪL. *See* EXEGESIS, ESOTERIC.

TEKKE/TAKĪYA. *See* RESIDENTIAL FACILITY.

TERMINOLOGY. Distinctive technical vocabulary developed by Sufi **poets** and authors and catalogued and analyzed by theorists in **lexicons** and **manuals**. As a part of the organic process of profound imaginative reflection on various aspects of personal **experience**, original Sufi minds began early on to generate a rather idiosyncratic vocabulary, some based on **Qur'ānic** usage and some not. By the ninth/15th century, scholars of the history and practice of Sufism began to assemble lists of distinctive Sufi language under the heading of *iṣṭilāḥāt*, conventional or agreed usage or, simply, "technical terms." They further distinguished expressions that were especially problematical, and therefore in particular need of elucidation, called *mushkilāt*. Finally, they referred to expressions of an especially high level of spiritual acumen, some of which they referred to as "**allusions**" (*ishārāt*), because they hinted with deceptive simplicity at very complex realities; and some—the most difficult and demanding of all—they called *shaṭaḥāt* (sg., *shaṭḥ*), **ecstatic** utterances characterized by a quality of being "shaken to overflowing," much the way flour escapes over the rim of a sieve when it is overloaded.

TESTAMENT. Term referring to instructions for **successorship** handed on by a ***shaykh***. The term *waṣīya* can also mean an official government document appointing an individual to leadership of local Sufi groups.

THANVĪ, MUḤAMMAD ASHRAF 'ALĪ (1280/1863–1362/1943). Major **Indian** Sufi leader, religious scholar, and **exegete**. Among his reported output of approximately 600 volumes are an important commentary on **Rūmī's** *Spiritual* ***Couplets*** and a seminal **treatise** on Sufism.

THEOLOGY, MYSTICAL. Theories developed through **symbolic exegesis** of the foundational Islamic sources, above all the **Qur'ān** and **Ḥadīth**, and elaborated in **manuals** and **treatises**. The critical questions have generally focused on the divine-human relationship and on the terms in which one can appropriately describe it. More **ascetically** inclined Sufis have typically drawn the line at simple, abject **servanthood**, on the grounds that the basic reality is human nothingness in the face of **God's** sublimity. **Theologically** moderate Sufis have often assumed greater scope in the relationship, arguing that **love** is its essential feature, presumptuous as it might seem to claim that a creature can relate lovingly to its creator. At the other end of the spectrum, some have insisted that the fully realized human relationship with God cannot but involve the loss of self in complete **union**. Another set of theological issues associated with Sufi tradition has to do with **sainthood** and the possibility of **intercession**. Mystical theologians whose views have accorded a major role to sainthood have in general also supported the notion that the individual believer has hope of intercession in connection with final judgment, and, short of that ultimate accounting, the option of seeking saintly aid for more immediate needs. But since those to whom the term "mystic" typically refers are generally engaged more directly with God, these issues are strictly speaking peripheral to genuinely mystical theologies. Perhaps the single most important ongoing theological discussion has been that of the ***wujūdī*** **controversy.**

THEORY, MYSTICAL. A range of often highly technical discussion ranging from matters of **ritual** and practice, to methods of spiritual direction and the various psycho-spiritual aspects of the **science of hearts**, to analyses of the most rarified reaches of mystical **union** and **ecstatic experience**. An early popular distinction between the so-called "**sober**" and "**intoxicated**" mystics arose on the basis of a divergence of views concerning the results of mystical experience and the personal status of the individual. Among the most widely contested theoretical issues are those at the center of the ***wujūdī* controversy**. Sufi theorists have often opted for a more **apophatic** approach, emphasizing *tanzīh*, eschewing images of **God**, rather than its theological opposite number, *tashbīh*, settling for apparent commonalities between the human and the divine.

THEOSOPHICAL SUFISM. Strictly speaking, a hybrid of **theology** and philosophy; in this context, a reference to Sufi thought of a more speculative bent. Theosophical Sufism has generally been associated with the work of Shihāb ad-Dīn Yaḥyā as-**Suhrawardī** and **Ibn al-'Arabī** and his school.

THRENODY. Lamentation or elegy (*marthīya*), a **genre** dedicated to **poetic** expression of grief over the loss or painful absence of the beloved, whether human or divine. The genre has been important in varying degrees, and in different contexts, in **Arabic**, **Persian**, **Swahili**, **Turkish, Urdu**, and other **languages** as well. However, since various **poetic** forms have been used post-classically to express elegiac sentiments, this is more a thematic category than a genre strictly speaking. Although the predominant Islamic adaptation of threnody has been associated with mourning for the martyred **Shī'ī** *imāms*, Sufi poets have developed the ancient tradition and applied it to mystical yearning for the separated **Beloved**.

TĪJĀNĪ, AḤMAD IBN MUḤAMMAD AT- (1150/1737–1230/1815). Algerian-born ***shaykh*** and religious scholar, founder of the **Tījānīya** who claimed that none other than the **Prophet** had disclosed his new spiritual path to him in a **vision**. Though he had been initiated into the **Khalwatīya** and **Shādhilīya**, he considered his way a significant departure from the earlier **orders**. He considered his own authority definitive and laid claim to being the "**seal** of **sainthood**." Just prior to his death in **Fez**, he apparently left detailed instructions to his **successors**, along with a document later adopted as the order's **office**.

TĪJĀNĪYA. Founded in Tlemcen in Algeria in 1195/1781 by Aḥmad ibn Muḥammad at-**Tījānī**, the **order** was a dominant influence in large portions of **North** and **West Africa**, including Algeria, Morocco, Senegal, Guinea, Western Sahara, Nigeria, Ghana, and Togo, as well as, but much later and to a lesser extent, in **Egypt**, Sudan, and Ethiopia. Though the founder had been initiated into both the **Shādhilīya** and the **Khalwatīya**, members were not allowed to give their allegiance to any other orders at the same time lest their loyalties be divided. Like the Shādhilīya, this order downplayed the need for demanding ascetical practice and generally took a dim view of **visitation** to **tombs** of holy persons—a bit ironic, perhaps, given the enormous popularity of the founder's tomb as a goal of visitation. In some parts of Africa, the order functioned as a counterbalance to the perceived elitism of the **Qādirīya**, for the order's members were largely uneducated. **'Umar ibn Sa'īd Tall** was among the most important figures in the dissemination of the order. During the 13th/19th century, the order mounted some of the fiercest resistance to French colonialism.

TILMĪDH. *See* ORGANIZATION.

TIMES, SACRED. Sufis, like all Muslims, have oriented their worship and **ritual** life around a calendar generously sprinkled with religiously important observances. The universally acknowledged times include those associated with the five **pillars** (especially ritual **prayer**, the season of the formal **pilgrimage**, and the **fast** of **Ramaḍān**). Many others govern regional and local observances associated with **birthdays,** mystical "**weddings**," and related **visitation** rituals. Common relevant terms are "season" (*mawsim*) and "anniversary" (*ḥawlīya*), and specified **places** generally play a prominent role as well.

TIRMIDHĪ, MUḤAMMAD IBN 'ALĪ AL-ḤAKĪM AT- (d. c. 285/898). Central Asian theorist, **exegete**, major figure in the development of Sufi understandings of **sainthood**. His most important work,

Seal** of the **Friends of God (*Khatm al-awliyā'*) analyzed various ranks or levels in the **hierarchy** of sanctity. From a **theological** perspective, his work is significant in that it proposes a structure of post-prophetic holiness parallel to that of **prophethood**, which is "sealed" with **Muḥammad**. He bases his hierarchy on the relative degrees of experiential **knowledge** manifest in the lives of the individual saints. He also distinguished between those whose Friendship with **God** depends primarily on adherence to the prescriptions of the **Law** and those granted sainthood purely by divine grace.

TOMB. Burial place, grave, or mausoleum, specifically of **prophets**, **Shī'ī** *imāms*, major ***shaykhs*** and **Friends of God**. Called variously *imāmzāda* (P, *imām's* son), *turba/türbe* (A/T, dust, earth), *qubba* (A, dome), and the **Chinese** term derived from the latter (*gongbei*), tomb settings range from very simple markers, either alone or in the midst of cemeteries, to elaborate **shrine** complexes. Two other specific terms refer to the overall enclosure of the site (*ḍarīḥ*) and the grave itself or the burial vessel (*tābūt*). Some tombs, generally the larger and more elaborate ones, bury the deceased in a chamber below the one into which pilgrims are allowed entry, displaying a cenotaph to public view. Virtually any tomb of an individual popularly acknowledged as a paragon of sanctity and source of **blessing** can become a magnet for local or regional pilgrim **visitation**. Sufi tombs have sometimes been a prime target of **reformers**, most notably of the **Wahhābī** movement, which set about eliminating most such sites from the **Arabian Peninsula**.

Rituals commonly performed at tombs include a specific etiquette for entering and leaving the sacred space, standard **prayers** to be said (along with some latitude within which the pilgrim can express individual sentiments), particular modes of physical communication of the saint's blessing and power (such as touching the cenotaph or receiving an object that has touched it), and circumambulation of the grave. In some cultural contexts, it has been traditional to surround the gravesite with the saint's personal effects or symbols, or to mount the deceased individual's **headgear** on the grave marker.

***TORLAK.** See QALANDAR.*

TRADITION. *See* ḤADĪTH.

TRANSOXIANA. Region of **Central Asia** whose name means "Land beyond the Oxus River," also called the Jayḥūn and Amu Daryā, which flows through present-day Uzbekistan. To the northeast of **Khurasan**, the area was historically considered a kind of outer realm. The **Naqshbandīya** have been the dominant **order** in the region.

TREATISE. One of several **genres** of **literature** designed to reflect on the **historical**, **ritual, theoretical**, and **theological** dimensions of Sufism. Such works have been produced both in prose and **poetic** forms, but the majority are prose. Some, most notably the **manuals**, are comprehensive, including sections on **hagiography**, **lexicography**, and aspects of practice. Some are more specialized, analyzing a single theme in some detail. Many Sufi ***shaykhs*** have produced large collections of **letters** that function rather like miniature treatises. Disciples of many teachers have published **discourses** in which they assemble utterances thematically as well. Whatever their scope, treatiselike works typically begin by citing relevant **Qur'ānic** texts and **Ḥadīth**, then assemble apposite comments by famous Sufis, often supplementing their reflections with generous samplings of poetry originally written in the language of the treatise. The **Arabic** term *risāla* ("missive") is occasionally part of the titles of treatises, but the term is used for other genres as well. Shorter catechismlike **instructional** treatises, often in question/answer format, are called *ishārāt* (**allusions**); these have been produced in various regions across the globe, but have been particularly numerous in **South Asia**.

TREE, GENEALOGICAL. One form of device used to indicate an individual's **initiatic chain** or an **order's** spiritual pedigree and **lineage**. Like the *silsila* (chain), the *shajara* typically illustrates one's genealogy by listing major ***shaykhs*** all the way back to an "ultimate" spiritual authority, such as the **Prophet** or **'Alī**. Various orders have their distinctive preferences for including certain signature figures in their genealogies as emblematic of their unique charisms. Trees are often depicted in elaborate visual presentations, with names of major figures in the lineage framed in leaflike medallions hung from the "branches."

TRIAL. In the **formation** and **experience** of every Sufi, an element of testing (*balā'*) and hardship is inevitable and essential. This can run the gamut from the most pedestrian and mundane requirements of humiliating daily chores all the way to the pangs of suffering one experiences at the **separation** from one's **Beloved**. The true **lover** must rise above trial to the extent of not noticing—perhaps even enjoying—that one is being put to the test.

TRUST. A central value in all forms of Islamic **spirituality**, *tawakkul* means putting one's total reliance on God. Several major Sufi authors describe trust as one of the mystical **stations**, which, according to **Sarrāj**, for example, arises out of **patience** and in turn demands the next station, that of **acceptance**, just at the point where he makes a transition to a discussion of **states**. **Qushayrī** situates trust toward the upper end of his list of stations, between **contentment** and **gratitude**, a location similar to that of **Kalābādhī** except that the latter inverts the positions of gratitude and contentment.

TRUTH. Both a name for **God** and a reference to the ultimate standard of veracity and verification in spiritual **experience**. The basic Arabic term for truth, *ḥaqq*, is from the same root as the Sufi term for "ultimate spiritual **reality**," *ḥaqīqa*, the third level in the traditional tripartite Sufi model of religious questing in general, beginning with the revealed **law** (*sharī'a*) applicable to all Muslims, and narrowing to the **path** (*ṭarīqa*) on which Sufis in particular continue the journey toward ultimate truth.

TURBA/TÜRBE. *See* TOMB.

TURKEY. The modern nation-state that occupies the **Anatolian** Peninsula along with a portion of land on the European side of the Bosporus strait; a region known under Roman rule as Asia Minor and later constituting the heartland of the Byzantine Empire. Turkic tribes first entered the region in the late fifth/11th century following a **Saljūqid** military victory over a Byzantine expeditionary force at Manzikert in 464/1071. By the mid-seventh/13th century, the Saljūqid dynasty of **Rūm** had established a capital at **Konya**. From about 700/1300, a tribal group under the leadership of Osman began to rise to the head of a confederation of Turkic tribes and began to exert pressure on the Byzantine Empire. The confederation, known as the Osmanli Turks or **Ottomans**, established a series of capitals both in Anatolia and across the Bosporus. In 857/1453, Sultan Mehmet the Conqueror successfully laid siege to Constantinople and the Ottomans thereafter ruled until the early 14th/20th century from what came to be called Istanbul. A number of important **orders** flourished in Turkey and central Ottoman holdings, including the **Bektāshīya**, **Khalwatīya**, **Mawlawīya**, **Naqshbandīya**, **Shādhilīya**, and **Rifā'īya**. Sufis of major importance in the history of Turkey include Ḥajjī **Bektash, Eshrefoğlū Rūmī**, **Ghālib Dede**, **Kaygusūz Abdāl**, **Niyāzī Miṣrī, Qūnawī**, **Rūmī**, **Shams**, and **Yūnus Emre**.

TURKISH. A family of agglutinative **languages** currently spoken by various Turkic groups in **Central Asia** and **China** as well as virtually the entire population of the modern nation-state of **Turkey**. Ottoman Turkish, as well as some other dialects, classically used the **Arabic** alphabet/script and absorbed numerous words from Arabic and **Persian**. An important Central Asian literary language in the history of Sufism has been Chagatay Turkish, as well-exemplified by Mīr 'Alī Shīr Nawā'ī. **Yūnus Emre**, **Ghālib Dede**, and **Kaygusūz Abdāl** stand out among the greatest Sufi poets in the Ottoman literary tradition.

TYPOLOGIES. Conceptual models or pedagogical structures developed by **theorists** and **manualists** as summaries, "maps," or mnemonic devices for use in Sufi spiritual **formation** and **education**. These tools range from relatively simple and basic categorizations to very extensive and complex analyses of the human condition. They begin with a widely adopted tripartite classification of the human race, with respect to spiritual capacity and attainment, into the generality of persons (*al-'āmma*), the elect (*al-khāṣṣ/khuṣūṣ*), and the elect among the elect (*khāṣṣ al-khāṣṣ/khuṣūṣ al-khuṣūṣ*). The **science of hearts** elaborates on the characteristics of **soul** or **ego** in relation to the various types of deleterious influence and the diverse forms of inner movements, including **inclinations**, that are the stuff of spiritual **discernment**. Other typologies include, for example, programs analyzing the **stations** and **states**; relationships among the levels or contexts of the manifold spiritual **journey**; **cosmological** concepts dealing with the various **realms** and **hierarchies**; and diverse levels and kinds of **recollection** or **invocation**.

– U –

***'UDHRĪ* LOVE.** Designation of a conception of unconsummated **love** and a related form of **contemplation** of remote, unattainable **beauty** associated with a **poet** named Jamāl, from a tribe called the *Banū 'Udhrā*. Some early writers argued that it represented the height of longing and aspiration, and that no human being dared speak of an intimate relationship of **union** with God. Under the pens of poets like **Ibn al-Fāriḍ**, this tradition evolved into the theme of **martyrdom** in the cause of love.

'ULAMĀ'. *See* KNOWLEDGE, DISCURSIVE.

'UMAR IBN SA'ĪD TALL, AL-ḤĀJJ (1211/1796–1281/1864). Major **West African** religious scholar and leader in the spread of the **Tījānīya**, especially in Senegal. He was **initiated** into the order while making **pilgrimage** and designated **successor** for West Africa. He was involved in several waves of *jihād* with the support of his Sufi disciples, elevating the ***shaykh*** to leadership of state.

UMAYYAD DYNASTY. The first example of dynastic succession, strictly speaking, in Islamic history, ruling from **Damascus** from 41/661–133/750. It was under this dynasty that the **Dome of the Rock** was built in **Jerusalem**, and during whose tenure the beginnings of **ascetical** piety took root. From the Sufi perspective, and that of Islamic popular piety in general, the Caliph 'Umar ibn 'Abd al-'Azīz (d. 102/720, also known as 'Umar II, after the second "Rightly Guided Caliph" 'Umar ibn al-Khaṭṭāb, (d. 24/644) stands out among the Umayyads as a model of faith and **virtue**. Partly as a result of support from pious critics of the dynasty's "worldliness," the Umayyads were brought down and succeeded by the **'Abbāsids**.

UNION. A condition of **oneness** with the object of **love**, implying a mystical relationship of **ecstasy** and **annihilation** in **God**, the ultimate **Beloved**. This attainment of *jam'* is mentioned as a **state** occasionally by **theorists** such as **Anṣārī** and **Qushayrī**, both of whom discuss it in juxtaposition to separation and as a development occurring after **ecstasy**. Sufi authors sometimes use the term *ittiḥād* (achieving an identity of characteristics) more or less synonymously with *waḥda*, **unity**.

UNITED STATES OF AMERICA. *See* AMERICA.

UNITY, EXPERIENTIAL. Referred to by the Arabic expression *waḥdat ash-shuhūd*, which also connotes union through or in **contemplation,** witnessing, testimony, or vision. It implies that the ultimate goal of the mystical life is **experience** of **union** but not necessarily actual, metaphysical loss of self (or **annihilation**) resulting in monism. Some Sufi authors have used the term as virtually synonymous with *waḥdat al-wujūd* in the sense that *wujūd* can mean **ecstasy** in addition to "being" or "existence." However, the extended ***wujūdī*** **controversy** was based on a rather dramatic distinction between experiential unity and ontological **unity**.

UNITY, ONTOLOGICAL. Referred to by the Arabic expression *waḥdat al-wujūd*, understood in the sense that the individuality of the mystic is ultimately **annihilated** in the being of **God**. Developing the concept elaborated most prominently by **Ibn al-'Arabī**, some Sufis adopted the **metaphor** of drop losing itself completely in the **ocean** of divine unity. The resulting monism presented a problem for **reformist** Sufis like Aḥmad **Sirhindī**, who emphasized the importance of thinking of the mystic self as akin to the drop that becomes a pearl in that ocean, thus both maintaining a distinct identity and being wholly engulfed in divinity.

UNS. *See* INTIMACY.

UNVEILING. A common **metaphor** in Sufi literature for various aspects of the seeker's access to spiritual realities. Often expressed by the Arabic term *kashf*, or its cognate *mukāshafa*, the concept is analogous in a general way to that of **revelation** (which applies only to **prophets**). Some mystical authors elaborated fairly detailed **typologies** of unveiling. Khwāja Mīr **Dard**, for example, describes the overall process of unveiling with a four-part model: the seeker attains 1) intellectual unveiling through ethical uprightness; 2) creaturely unveiling in **dreams** through devotion and **self-discipline**; 3) divine unveiling in the ability to discern hidden signs and thoughts as a result of burnishing the **heart**; and 4) the unveiling of faith that presupposes a likeness to the prophets, who enjoy access to disclosure through **angelic** mediation and the

realm of imaginative similitudes. **Hujwīrī** has elaborated perhaps the most intricate theoretical presentation around the metaphor of unveiling.

'UQDA. *See* INITIATION.

URDŪ. A major Indo-Aryan **language** of **South Asia** that has been designated the "official" national language of **Pakistan**, but which is spoken also by many citizens of northwest **India** especially. Urdu is written in a Perso-**Arabic** script and includes many **Persian** terms, but is linguistically related more closely to Hindi. A number of major authors have written Sufi prose and verse in Urdu (especially an earlier form called Dakhni), including **Bīdil**, **Gīsū Darāz**, Mīr **Dard**, and **Shāh Walī Allāh**.

'URFĪ, MUḤAMMAD ASH-SHĪRĀZĪ (d. 1000/1591). Persian mystical poet known especially for his encomia of the **Prophet**, a genre of **praise** poetry called *na't*. He enjoyed the patronage of the **Mughal** ruler Akbar and decried the spiritual entropy of Sufism.

'URS. *See* WEDDING.

UWAYS AL-QARANĪ (d. c. 37/657). Early model of piety for Sufis, who without ever actually meeting the **Prophet** nevertheless exemplified perfect devotion. He was from Yemen, and perhaps the best-known reference to him is the Prophet's allusion to sensing the "breath of the Merciful from Yemen." Sufi tradition identifies Uways as the prototype of the Sufi **initiated** into the Path directly by **Muḥammad**. According to a saying of the Prophet reported by **Sarrāj**, Uways was capable of powerful **intercession** with **God**.

UWAYSĪ. A name given to Sufis considered to have been **initiated** into the mystical life without benefit or need of the presence of a ***shaykh***. Living outside the formal structures of an **order**, their "patron" is **Uways al-Qaranī** who "knew" the **Prophet** through divine grace across a great distance. An analogy may be seen in the "spirit initiation" often associated with **Khiḍr**.

– V –

VEIL. A **metaphor** commonly used in much mystical literature to refer to a covering that functions in spiritual **experience** in two principal, interrelated ways. First, it serves as a protection against almost certain destruction resulting from an experience of power or beauty beyond one's capacity to endure. In mystical **poetry**, it is often the Beloved's countenance that is veiled with the *ḥijāb* (the term **Hujwīrī** uses in his **manual**, *The Revelation of Realities Veiled*) much as the **Ka'ba** wears its *kiswa*. It can also function as a barrier between a mere human being, or an unworthy seeker, and a higher level of reality or truth than the individual in question is worthy of accessing. The seeker must proceed down a path of arduous discipline, gradually earning the removal of successive veils. Sufi **theorists** speak of mystical **knowledge** as a process of penetrating or lifting each veil and entering into progressively more demanding truths. *See also* UNVEILING.

VICE. **Ethical** failure that has fearsome destructive power, often described as sin (*dhamm*). Many Sufi authors, particularly those of a more **ascetical** bent, have developed catalogues of spiritual vices, including disobedience, hypocrisy, pride, slander, jealousy, and covetousness. **Muḥāsibī** is especially concerned with applying spiritual **discernment** to discovering one's vices, dividing them (along with many other traditional sources) into smaller (especially misuse of things) and greater (involving relationships between the individual and **God** or other persons). He focuses on seven particularly deadly vices which he calls "sins of the heart," with self-deception at the root of them all. Abū Ḥāmid al-**Ghazālī** situates sinful vices in the larger context of his fully developed pastoral theology, devoting the entire third quarter of his *Revitalization of the Religious Disciplines* to a detailed analysis of gluttony and sensuality; vices of the tongue; anger, malice, and jealousy; acquisitiveness and greed; love of status and hypocrisy; arrogance and conceit; and pride, the deadliest of them all. Other major Sufi authors have elaborated on the various vices as part of their discussion of **psychological** issues and the **science of the heart**.

VIGILANCE. A critical feature of **self-discipline**, **self-scrutiny**, and the **science of hearts** involving careful observation and custody (*ri'āya*) of all of one's spiritual faculties.

VIRTUE. An aspect of the **ethical** component of Sufism, situated within the larger context of Islamic moral reflection known as *'ilm al-akhlāq*. Essential Sufi virtues—the diametric opposite of **vice**—are represented prominently in the fundamental canons of **behavior** laid down by the various **orders**, as well as in the various **typologies** of **stations** and **states** (under which headings they are treated here).

VISION. Access to the sight (*ru'ya*) of the **Face** of **God**, ultimately. Traditional Islamic **theology** has long insisted that the believer who attains heavenly reward will enjoy the vision of God. This side of death, however, mystical **poets** in particular talk of their desire for a glimpse of the face of the (mystical) **Beloved**, however fleetingly, as a metaphor for **revelation** or **ecstasy**. This second type of vision may seem to represent a more immediately attainable experience because some mystics talk as though it can be granted in this life; but it remains a rare privilege indeed, and some authors caution against undue reliance on such experience. Finally, Sufi sources speak of visionary experiences with relative frequency, often in such a way that there is little clear distinction between vision and **dreaming**. Among the principal subjects of such visions are **Muḥammad**—and rather rarely, earlier **prophets** as well—and major Sufi figures and **Friends of God**, including notably the mysterious **Khiḍr**, who also fits in the category of prophet. Visionary experiences of this kind often function as the vehicle for "spirit **initiation.**" It is theologically significant that even **Moses** was not granted vision of God when he boldly asked God for that gift.

VISITATION. The practice of journeying to holy sites, particularly the **tombs** of important religious figures such as ***shaykhs***, founders of **orders**, and **Friends of God**. As a kind of local or regional **pilgrimage**, *ziyāra* (to a location called a *mazār*) involves often complex **ritual** requirements. Many books of etiquette and protocol have been produced to assist participants toward fuller engagement in the behavior expected of devotees at sacred **places**. In addition, larger works of geographical literature for pilgrims sometimes include material intended to guide pilgrims to major sites, occasionally illustrating their descriptions with elaborately detailed images and diagrams of the sites. **Guidebooks**, a subcategory of the large **genre** of geographical literature sometimes called *ziyāratnāma*, are helpful sources of information about popular piety as well as about the history of Sufism.

VISUALIZATION. An aspect of **behavior** required by certain orders (especially the **Naqshbandīya**) in which the individual Sufi "sees" and is present to the ***shaykh***. As the term *taṣawwur* (forming an image) implies, the practice involves summoning up in the imagination a mental picture of the *shaykh*. Another term, *rābiṭa* (mutual binding), suggests the practice's ultimate purpose, a conjoining of spirits in **companionship**. The practitioner can focus on an image of the *shaykh* as though standing before him, or imagine himself actually assuming the form and attributes of the *shaykh*, or imagine the *shaykh* entering into his **heart**. In its most complete form, the practice leads to a form of loss of self, or **annihilation**.

– W –

WAFĀ'ĪYA. Egyptian order named after Shams ad-Dīn Muḥammad ibn Aḥmad Wafā' (d. 760/1359) and his son 'Alī (d. 807/1404), distinctive for its development of **Ibn al-'Arabī's** thought on **sainthood**. The founding figures, originally from **North Africa**, wrote mystical **treatises** as well as **poetry, exegetical** works, and collections of **supplicatory prayer**. They had important connections with the **Shādhilīya**, and their **organization** is generally identified as a branch of that order. Eventually, however, the order adopted a structure and practices more elaborate than those of the Shādhilīya, a pattern observable in many other branches of that order. The founders of the Wafā'īya drew on the **theories** of **Tirmidhī** as well as on **Shī'ī** traditions concerning **Friends of God**.

WAHHĀB, MUḤAMMAD IBN 'ABD AL- (1115/1703–1207/1792). Arabian-born religious scholar and **reformer** best known for his sweeping attack on all forms of what he considered religious innovation (*bid'a*). Though he evidently studied Sufism in **Iran** as a young man, and even spoke publicly about Sufism's benefits, he later took up the study of Ḥanbalī **Law** in the Iranian city of Qum. A hallmark of his reformist thinking is his condemnation of all forms of popular piety associated with the veneration of **Friends of God**: acknowledging their burial places as especially holy sites, constructing often elaborate **tombs**, and promoting the practice of **visitation** and attendant **ritual**. He was the eponymous ancestor of the **Wahhābī** movement.

WAHHĀBĪ(YA) MOVEMENT. Major early modern-contemporary **reformist** development of Arabian origin and currently influential within many far-flung segments of the global Muslim community. Adherents of the school of thought generally follow eighth/14th century Ḥanbalī **Law** scholar **Ibn Taymīya**'s interpretations of certain issues of religious and devotional practice. In fact, the movement's legal interpretations have often been considerably more restrictive than those of Ibn Ḥanbal and his medieval interpreters. After the death of founder, Muḥammad ibn 'Abd al-**Wahhāb**, followers continued to advance militarily against regional rulers. They strengthened an ongoing alliance (initiated by their founder) with the emerging House of Sa'ūd and were a powerful support as the dynasty became the dominant power in the heart of the **Arabian Peninsula**. Contemporary Wahhābīs, with considerable financial support from the Saudi government and prominent members of the royal family, have served as patrons of **architectural** reform in many Muslim communities, funding drastic remodeling of mosques with a view to purging them of nearly all forms of decoration and visual embellishment. Sufism and forms of popular piety regarded as related to Sufism have been one of the principal objects of the movement's reformist zeal. For their part, later Sufi authors have styled their Wahhābī nemesis as representatives of **Satan** himself. Some features of the movement are similar to principles espoused by the **Salaf**.

WAḤDAT ASH-SHUHŪD. *See* UNITY, EXPERIENTIAL.

WAḤDAT AL-WUJŪD. *See* UNITY, ONTOLOGICAL.

WAḤY. *See* REVELATION.

WAJD. *See* ECSTASY.

WAJH. *See* FACE.

WALĀYA. *See* FRIEND OF GOD.

WALĪ. *See* FRIEND OF GOD.

WALĪ SONGO. The "Nine **Friends of God**," a designation for a cluster of holy persons traditionally said to have brought Islam to the **Indonesian** island of Java. The original nine are all known individually by the honorific title *Sunan* (Eminent One) sometimes followed by a name that indicates the area of Java in which they worked prominently. The original nine include Sunan Malik Ibrahim (d. 822/1419); Sunan Raden Rahmat [who worked in] Ampel (d. c. 875/1470); Sunan Raden Paku [who worked in] Giri in East Java (d. ninth/15th century); Sunan Kalijaga (d. ninth/15th century), credited with introducing shadow puppetry (*wayang kulit*) as a teaching device; Sunan Darajat (d. ninth/15th century); Sunan Bonang (d. 932/1525) in East Java; Sunan Gunung Jati (d. c. 978/1570) in West Java; Sunan Kudus (d. 10th/16th century), central and northern Java; and Sunan Muria (d. 10th/16th century), credited with introducing *gamelan* **music** to the island. The nine are not explicitly associated with Sufi organizations, but as culture heroes, they represent an important link via **sainthood** and popular piety. There is, however, an explicit link to Sufism in the later addition to the list of ***Shaykh*** Sitti Jenar, a late eighth/14th century Sufi missionary executed for his acceptance of the concept of ontological **unity**.

WANG DAIYU (b. c. 1001/1592). Major **Chinese** religious scholar said to be the first to translate Sufi thought into Chinese. He probably knew **Arabic**, **Persian**, and a **Turkic language**. He was schooled in the major Islamic religious disciplines in addition to the special disciplines of Sufism, and probably lived in Nanjing before moving to Beijing around 1055/1645. In the process of "translating concepts" from one religious tradition (Islam) into terms consonant with ancient

Chinese schools of thought, Wang favored the Confucian tradition as inherently more compatible than either Daoism or Buddhism with Islamic teachings. Wang may well have been familiar with the **Naqshbandīya**, an **order** that already had put down deep roots in China by his time, but Wang does not speak explicitly about personal connections to any specific Sufi individuals or **organizations**. In his major work, *The Real Commentary on the True Teaching*, however, he does mention some historically important Sufis, and was especially interested in **Abū Yazīd al-Bisṭāmī**.

WAQF. *See* ENDOWMENT.

WAQFA. *See* STANDING.

WĀQIF. *See* STANDING.

WAQT. *See* MOMENT.

WARA'. *See* RETICENCE, SPIRITUAL.

WĀRID. *See* INCLINATIONS.

WĀSIṬĪ, ABŪ BAKR AL- (d. c. 320/932). An **'Irāqī** mystic noted for characterizing the Mu'tazilī doctrine of free will as tantamount to the hybris of Pharaoh himself. He also famously condemned the teachings of **Malāmatīya** leader Abū 'Uthmān al-**Ḥīrī**. He left no extant written work, but Sufi **manualists** and other authors often quote his sayings; and an **exegetical** work by him was evidently incorporated in **Sulamī's** scriptural **commentary**. He was one of a number of Sufis from **Baghdad** who departed for points east in the wake of the martyrdom of **Ḥallāj**, bringing a new style of Sufism with them to **Khurasan**. One account says that Abū Bakr unsuccessfully sought refuge in no fewer than 70 towns before the city of Marv took him in.

WAṢĪYA. *See* TESTAMENT.

WAYFARER. Designating one of the two principal types of mystics, the *sālik* is distinguished from the *majdhūb*. The former makes slower progress on the **path**, beginning with gradual understanding of the signs of **God** in creation and within the **soul** and **heart**, and moving steadily upward by recognizing the divine in its lower manifestations. Pursuing the way of purgation and **self-scrutiny**, the wayfarer undergoes the lengthy disciplines of **asceticism** and **contemplation**, gradually being led to contemplate God's attributes. By contrast, the *majdhūb* is "drawn" by God along a less arduous illuminative path. This individual begins from above, as it were, with an awareness of the divine being and descends to an understanding of how all creatures share in the life of God. The one sees God in creation, the other creation in God.

WAẒĪFA. *See* OFFICE.

WEAPONS. Some Sufi **orders** (notably several of the **Shī'ī** groups) have employed various types of weapons as ritual **implements** or **symbols** of organizational identity. Representations of them appear on doorways of **residential facilities** and on the walls of **ritual places**, often in combination with other **ritual objects** or **implements** such as the **rosary** or **begging bowl**. Weapons sometimes gain spiritual significance with reference to major foundational religious figures in the tradition, especially the **Prophet** and **'Alī**. Ancient legend says that the Prophet bequeathed a formidable twin-tipped blade called "The Cleaver" (*Dhū 'l-Faqār*) to his son-in-law, who in turn handed it down to his own son, so that it became an heirloom down to the 12th Shī'ī *Imām*. **Bektāshī** dervishes use an axe as an important emblem of the order. **Metaphorically** speaking, the Sufi must wield *Dhū 'l-Faqār* in severing all attachments. And the dagger with which **Abraham** prepares to sacrifice his son Ismā'īl represents the death of the **ego** and the **annihilation** of the mystic.

WEDDING. A **metaphorical** reference to the death anniversary of a **Friend of God**. On the occasion of the *'urs*, devotees make special **visitations** to the **tombs** of their favorite holy persons to engage in often elaborate ceremony. The term *ḥawlīya*, "anniversary" is also used to refer to this annual **time**. A significant Sufi **genre** is the **guidebook** that details the ritual etiquette and **behavior** to be enacted at the celebration, as also at the observance of **birthdays** of holy persons.

WEEPERS. A group of early (second/eighth century) **ascetics** of **Basra** called *al-bakkā'ūn* (those who weep incessantly). They took their cue from a **Ḥadīth** in which the **Prophet** cautioned that anyone who had **knowledge** about what he knew would laugh little and weep copiously. Sufi authors sometimes associated them especially with a tearful John the Baptist (Yaḥyā), leaving open the possibility that laughing was not entirely to be condemned, for no less a figure than **Jesus** was so inclined.

WEST AFRICA. Largely sub-Saharan regions including the modern nation-states of Niger, Nigeria, Benin, Togo, Ghana, Burkina Faso, Ivory Coast, Mali, Senegal, and Mauritania. **Orders** of greatest importance in West Africa include the Hamawīya, **Qādirīya** and its Fāḍilīya and Murīdīya offshoots in Senega, the **Sanūsīya**, and the **Tījānīya**. Senegal is noteworthy in that a disproportionately large percentage of the population have traditionally belonged to Sufi orders. Timbuktu, capital of Mali, was among the region's leading centers of intellectual life during medieval and early modern times, and its library today contains thousands of manuscripts still waiting to be studied carefully. It was largely through so-called scholarly lineages that Sufism came to West Africa from **North Africa**, especially beginning in the 11th/17th century. Evidence of formal structure in the form of identification with the major orders began after 1215/1800, most notably when a leader of the Kunta lineage, Sīdī Mukhtār al-Kuntī (1142/1729–1226/1811) associated himself explicitly with the Qādirīya by being **initiated** into the order.

WHIRLING DERVISHES. *See* MAWLAWĪYA.

WILĀYA. *See* FRIEND OF GOD.

WINE. An important **metaphorical** ingredient in the mystical language of **intoxication**. Poets talk both of the alcoholic drink specifically, *khamr*, and of a more generic but spiritually potent beverage, *sharba(t)* (an Arabic/Persian word from which the English word *sherbet* derives). The Arabic root can connote a special level of understanding or comprehension, and is thus easily transferred to the repertoire of terms for mystical **experience**. The seeker's relationship to the **Beloved**, along with all the features of the Beloved and his/her responses to the **lover**, can be encompassed by these metaphorical references. Perhaps the most famous poem built around wine is **Ibn al-Fāriḍ's** *Khamrīya*, the "Wine Ode."

WIRĀTHA. *See* LINEAGE.

WIRD. *See* LITANIES.

WISDOM. A category of literature best exemplified in the history of Sufism by the **genre** known as the **aphorism** as well as some **didactic** works attributed to **Sa'dī**.

WITNESS. An aspect of spiritual **experience** rooted in the fundamental Muslim creed, known as the *shahāda*: attestation, confession, or witnessing to the ultimate truths of the faith. By extension, the witness (*shāhid*) is involved in both **visionary** experience properly so-called, and in **contemplation** (*mushāhada*). In the latter case, paradoxically, Muslim **theorists** point out that true witnessing can occur only after the conventional understanding based on a dichotomy between **knower** and known has been obliterated by loss of the "witnessing self."

WOMEN. Since very early in Islamic **history**, Sufis have acknowledged certain remarkable women as distinctive embodiments of holiness and virtue, and of spiritual **authority** as well. Recent scholarship has turned up more and more examples of women whose religious status won them the title of ***shaykha***, spiritual **director**. In many Muslim societies, women have exercised leadership roles in religious ritual settings, including even preaching, though typically ministering only to other women. In the history of Sufism, we find many examples of women, such as **Jahānārā** and **Rābi'a**, who enjoyed prominence as mystical leaders in their own right, and others who functioned as spiritual guides even for prominent Sufi men, such as **Ibn al-'Arabī,** who wrote short biographies of two of his own female spiritual guides. A few **orders**, including the **Bektāshīya**, allowed membership for women, sometimes establishing separate quarters for celibate female members. In some areas, such as Senegal and Sudan, women and children belong to orders but do not join fully in all **rituals**. Important **hagiographers**, such as **Jāmī**, 'Abd ar-Ra'ūf al-**Munāwī**, and **Sulamī** have broken the **gender** barrier by including life stories of numbers of significant Sufi women.

Anecdotes about several important Sufi men include prominent female characters (such as the sisters of **Bishr** and **Dhū 'n-Nūn**). Until relatively recent times, few Sufi women have left a written legacy, both because, in general, fewer women than men wrote and because women's works unfortunately merited less attention and were thus more often lost. Among the other more famous Sufi women are **Bībī Jamāl Khatūn**, **Fāṭima of Nishapur**, and **Fāṭima of Cordoba**. In addition, female literary characters have played very important roles in mystical **poetry**, particularly in **didactic** works, as symbols of the Divine **Beloved**. In a reversal of that role, there is perhaps no greater model of the hopelessly smitten **lover** of God than **Zulaykhā** in the story of the **prophet Joseph**.

WONDERS. Extraordinary deeds performed by **Friends of God** with the intervention of divine power. These marvels, known as *karāmāt*, run a wide gamut from fairly simple, homey acts, such as finding small lost treasures of value only to the owner, to altering the course of natural events. Islamic tradition early on developed a distinction between the "evidentiary miracles" vouchsafed only to **prophets** (*mu'jiza/-āt*) and deeds apparently wondrous of which an array of other persons seemed to be capable. For hard-core **theological** purposes, such deeds performed by the enemies of prophets were categorized as sleight of hand, magic (*siḥr*), while the term "marvel" or "wonder" was reserved for amazing acts attributed to saintly persons.

Wonder-stories are an integral part of Sufi **hagiographical** traditions. Accounts are often stock "types," and include a wide repertoire of spectacular deeds, from the ability to travel great distances instantly, to communicating with animals, clairvoyance, and causing miraculous supplies of food to materialize for the needy. Some Friends of God are famous for effecting wonders from beyond the grave. Sufi authors and **theorists** have expressed a variety of views as to the importance of saintly marvels. Many influential spiritual guides caution their followers against being unduly impressed at an individual's ability to perform amazing feats, for even **Satan** is capable of impressive pyrotechnic effects. The real marvel, some suggest, is that God brings about faith in the heart of one who had never before believed.

WORSHIP. A wide range of religious duties and devotional practices that come under the technical term *'ibādāt*, "worshipful deeds," a legal category juxtaposed to *mu'āmalāt*, which encompasses interpersonal and social relationships. For Sufis, worship as a general category thus includes the five **pillars** as well as various other forms of **prayer**, **ritual** and **ascetical** practices, or **exercises**. All of these constitute the essence of the life of a true **servant** (*'abd*, from which the Arabic term for worship derives).

***WUJŪDĪ* CONTROVERSY**. A long-running **theological** debate waged among important Sufi authors as to the central nature of spiritual **experience**, including ultimate **ecstatic union**. Especially during late medieval and early modern times, Sufi theorists often aligned themselves as favoring either *waḥdat ash-shuhūd*, experiential **unity** or *waḥdat al-wujūd*, ontological **unity**. In general, it was devoted followers of the thought of **Ibn al-'Arabī** who opted for the latter. **Reformists** and the more theologically cautious came down on the other side, arguing that ontological unity smacked of monism and obliterated any distinction between Creator and creature.

WUṢŪL. *See* JOURNEY.

– Y –

YAḤYĀ IBN MU'ĀDH AR-RĀZĪ (d. 258/872). A Sufi **preacher** from **Khurasan** whose thoughts survive only in sayings cited often by the **manualists** and **hagiographical** authors. Some scholars suggest that he was a follower of a certain Ibn Karrām (d. 255/869), who founded an **ascetical** movement (the **Karrāmīya**) and whom Sufi authors generally dismiss as a heretic. Yaḥyā's teaching, however, is generally upbeat, emphasizing hope and life-affirming acceptance of whatever good things **God** provides.

YAQĪN. *See* CERTITUDE.

YASAWĪ, AḤMAD (d. c. early seventh/13th century). Central Asian eponym of the **Yasawīya** and author of a collection of **aphoristic** poetry in a **Turkic** dialect. He hailed from a region in present-day Uzbekistan and was a significant figure in the history of Turkish mystical literature. His **tomb** in the southern Kazakhstan town of Turkistan remains an important regional shrine. After restoration it continued to attract Central Asian pilgrims through the latter days of the Soviet Union.

YASAWĪYA. An **order** of **Central Asian** origin arising from the teachings of Aḥmad **Yasawī**. The **organization's** structures of **governance** were not as tightly centralized as those of some other orders, and this may have been a factor in its eventual loss of dominance to the **Naqshbandīya** across Central Asia. Research on the organization's history is currently reassessing the order's role and its relationships with other Sufi groups in the region.

YĀSĪN, ABŪ 'L-QĀSIM BISHR (d. 380/990). Khurāsānī mystic said to have been the first spiritual teacher of **Abū Sa'īd ibn Abī 'l-Khayr**, and whose own **poetry** was probably the inspiration for that of his star pupil. The ***shaykh***'s **quatrains** are often quoted in the pupil's work, and the teacher evidently recommended the recitation of appropriate verses as prayers of **recollection**.

YŪNUS EMRE (d. c. 720/1321). Major **Turkish** mystical **poet** whose works influenced members of the **Mawlawīya**. He acknowledged a certain Ṭaptuḳ Emre as his spiritual guide, and some conclude that the "Emres" constituted a loosely organized Sufi presence across **Anatolia**. Yūnus left an important collection of **lyric** poems, akin to folk songs in structure and mood, that cover a wide range of traditional Sufi themes. One characteristic theme is that of the spiritual quest likened catching up with a caravan lest one be left alone in the mountains.

YŪSUF. *See* JOSEPH.

YŪSUF HAMADHĀNĪ (441/1049–534/1140). Persian *shaykh* acknowledged as a major influence on founders of both the **Naqsh-**

bandīya and the **Yasawīya** orders. He is traditionally acknowledged as the ancestor of a long line of *khwājagān*, spiritual masters. His own spiritual **lineage** connects him back to **Bāyazīd al-Bisṭāmī** and Abū 'l-Ḥasan **al-Kharaqānī**. Some scholars suggest that he was a student of **Anṣārī**.

– Z –

***ZĀHID*.** *See* ASCETICISM.

***ẒĀHIR(Ī)*.** *See* OUTWARD.

ZAKARĪYA, BAHĀ' AD-DĪN. *See* BAHĀ' AD-DĪN.

ZARRŪQ, AḤMAD (d. 899/1494). Mystical author of Moroccan origin whose writings exerted significant influence on various **orders** across **North Africa**. He became associated with the **Shādhilīya** while studying in **Egypt**, where he was particularly taken with the **Aphorisms** of **Ibn 'Aṭā' Allāh**. Zarrūq's **commentary** on that work, among the latest of many by major Shādhilī's, likened it to the "eyes of Sufism," for it combined fundamentals of **instruction** and **asceticism** with the higher disciplines of experiential **knowledge** and the **unveiling** of mysteries.

***ZĀWIYA*.** *See* RESIDENTIAL FACILITY.

ZAWQĪ SHĀH (1294/1877–1371/1951). Indian *shaykh* of the Ṣābirīya branch of the **Chishtīya**, among 14th/20th century leaders who wrote in defense of the Islamic foundations of Sufism. Writing in both **Urdu** and English, he responded to claims as to its non-Islamic origins as well as to criticisms about the unacceptability of certain beliefs and practices wrongly attributed to the core of Sufism. He was thus, in some ways, a modern counterpart to several of the classical and medieval **manualists**. **Politically** active, he spoke in favor of establishing an Islamic state in **Pakistan** and eagerly sought Christian converts to Islam.

***ZIYĀRA*.** *See* VISITATION.

ZIYĀRATNĀMA. *See* VISITATION.

ZUHD. *See* ASCETICISM.

ZULAYKHĀ. Name given to the **woman** in the story of **Joseph** to whom the Bible (Genesis 39ff.) refers only as the wife of Pharaoh's minister, Potiphar, and whom the **Qur'ān** (Sūra 12) identifies as the wife of "al-'Azīz," an official in the royal **Egyptian** court. In the scriptural accounts, this woman is so smitten with the **prophet** Joseph's **beauty** that she succumbs to temptation and schemes to seduce him. Sufi **poets** developed the character's personality well beyond the scriptural stories, understanding her as a type of the **lover** of **God** who loses her wits in the presence of the divine Beauty. Major poets, including **Jāmī** and **Rūmī**, for example, depict her most sympathetically as a "model" of the mystical seeker. They emphasize especially that Zulaykhā was not culpable for her attempted seduction of Joseph, for she was hopelessly under the spell of bewilderment. Poets love the expression "to cut one's hands" as a **metaphorical** allusion to the utter amazement to which one is driven in the presence of God. The expression picks up on the Qur'ānic episode in which, after being accused of less than honorable intentions regarding the prophet, Zulaykhā invites the noble women of Egypt to a feast. As they pick up knives to slice into their dessert oranges, she ushers Joseph into the room. Aghast at his comeliness, all the guests slice into their own hands in astonished distraction. In one mystical retelling of her story, Zulaykhā and Joseph live happily ever after, her youth restored when the two are at long last reunited in mystical bliss. In another ending, she prefers the love of God even to Joseph.

Glossary

Unless otherwise indicated, terms are Arabic: B = Berber; C = Chinese; P = Persian; T = Turkish. Unless otherwise noted, whole words in ( ) are Arabic "broken" plurals, suffixes in parentheses are (e.g., *-āt*) simple plurals, and *(a)* indicates the feminine form of the term.

Term	Definition
ābād	abode, spiritual dwelling place
'abd	servant (of God), godservant, believer, and spiritual seeker
'abīd (*'ubbād*)	devotee, worshipper
abdāl (sg. *badal*)	substitutes (40), personalities inhabiting upper realm of the cosmos
abrār (sg. *barr*)	devout ones (seven), a rank among *awliyā'*
adab (*ādāb*)	conduct, behavior, etiquette in discipline or devtional ritual
'adat	etiquette toward a holy person
'ahd	binding agreement or pact between disciple and *shaykh*
akh	brother, member of Sufi organization
akhyār	chosen ones (300), among Friends of God, rank within Sufi orders
'alam	flag or standard identifying a Sufi organization
'ālam	world, realm within Sufi cosmology
alast, rūz-i (P)	Day of Covenant, when creation reaffirmed God's Lordship
amghār (B)	elder, leader, roughly synonymous with *shaykh*
anāshīd (sg. *inshād*)	recitation of mystical poetry in Sufi ritual settings
'aql	intellect, reason, mind

arba'īnīya	"Forty"-(day) Sufi retreat
'ārif, 'arīf	mystic, one endowed with infused or experiential knowledge
arkān (sg. *rukn*)	pillars or supports, structural element in Sufi cosmology
'āshiq	lover (of God), spiritual advanced individual
āsitāne (T)	central residential facility of a Turkish order
āward-burd (P)	ritual discipline of breath control
awlād aṭ-ṭarīqa	offspring (i.e., associates) of (the/a) Sufi order
awliyā' (sg. *walī*)	Friends (of God), saints
awrād (sg. *wird*)	litanies, prescribed or individually assigned repetitive prayer
awtād (sg. *watad*)	tent-pegs or anchors (4), figures in the Sufi cosmic hierarchy
āya(-āt)	(divine) sign in creation and the self; verse of the Qur'ān
'ayn	eye, spiritual essence
'azīzān (P)	dear ones, members of certain Sufi orders
bābā (T)	father, Sufi *shaykh* particularly in the Baktashīya, missionary preacher
baḥr	ocean, metaphor for all-encompassing divine reality and presence
balā'	trial, purifying adversity
baqā'	abiding, permanence, spiritual survival in the wake of mystical experience
baraka	blessing, spiritual power, charisma communicated by Friends of God
barzakh	narrow passage between this world and the spiritual realms
baṣīra	spiritual insight, inward vision
basṭ	expansion, an aspect of mystical experience opposite of *qabḍ*
bāṭin	inward, concealed, opposite of *ẓāhir*
bay'a	oath of allegiance between Sufi seeker and the *shaykh*
bayt	house, of Sufi order; verse of poetry
bid'a	novelty, innovation; deviation from acceptable teaching and practice

bī shar‘ (P/A)	Lawless, antinomian, Sufis said to disregard Sharī‘a stipulations
bu‘d	distance, the experience of God's absence
buzurg (P)	great person, sometimes used of Friends of God
çelebī (T)	major superior of some Turkish orders
changdao (C)	*sharī‘a*; initial stage of Chinese Sufi initiation and spiritual progress
chilla (P)	"40"-(day) period of Sufi retreat
chilla khana (P)	place in which 40-day retreat is conducted
dā'ira	circle, ritual arrangement in a recollection ceremony
dam (P)	breath, holy person's breathing scriptural words over sick person
daocheng (C)	*ṭarīqa*; second level of Chinese Sufi training
darajāt	levels or ranks of attainment on the spiritual Path
ḍarb	liturgical division or portion of a recollection (*dhikr*) ritual
dargāh (P)	door-place, Sufi institution such as residence or tomb-shrine
darwīsh (P)	door-seeker, originally a mendicant, generic term for Sufi
dede (T)	elder, honorific given to spiritual guide, synonym for *shaykh*
destegül (T)	outer waist-length jacket with long sleeves
dhāt	essence, being
dhawq	taste, immediate awareness, aspect or level of mystical experience
dhikr	recollection, invocation, both individual and communal prayer ceremony
dil (P)	heart, seat of spiritual experience
du‘ā'	supplication, invocation, personal prayer
durūd	prayer recited during some *dhikr* ceremonies
dūst (P)	friend, synonymous with lover of God, or God Himself as Beloved
duwayra	enclosure, cloister, for small Sufi residential facility

eren (T)	Man of God, individual totally given to spiritual quest
fayḍ	overflowing, superabundance; grace bestowed by a holy person
fanā'	annihilation, loss of self, passing away (in God, *shaykh*, Prophet)
faqīr (*fuqarā'*)	poor person, mendicant, generic term for seeker of God
faqr	poverty, whether actual or spiritual
fard (*afrād*)	member of the lowest rank of Friends of God
farq	separation, experience of being apart from God or the Beloved
fatā	youth, courtly gentleman, synonym for seeker of altruistic values
fikra	meditation, spiritual consideration
fiqh	deeper understanding, common term for subject matter of jurisprudence
firāsa	power of spiritual perspicacity, a type of clairvoyance
fu'ād	heart at one of its deepest inner levels
futūḥ	voluntary charitable contributions to Sufi institutions
futūwa	chivalry institutionalized into organizations for ethical purposes
ghafla	heedlessness, spiritual torpor
ghawth	help, assistance, at top of cosmic hierarchy (syn. *quṭb*)
ghazal	short lyric love poem often adapted by mystical poets.
ghayb	unseen realm, home of cosmic hierarchy
ghusl	ritual for cleansing tombs of Friends of God during *'urs* ceremonies
ginān	poetic/song form popular among Ismā'ilīs
gongbei (C)	tombs of Sufi founders and leaders in northwest China especially
görüşme (T)	ritual salutation in Mawlawīya practice

ḥabs-i dam (P)	breath control, ritual discipline
ḥaḍāra	(divine) presence, five of which are metaphor for all reality (Ibn al-'Arabī)
ḥaḍra	gathering with invocation and ritual dance; presence of the Prophet
ḥajj	major pilgrimage to Mecca during specific ritual season
ḥakīm	wise one, sage, teacher of spiritual or metaphysical wisdom
ḥal (*aḥwāl*)	state, fleeting mystical experience that results from divine grace alone
ḥalqa	circle, gathering either for ritual or to listen to spiritual guide
ḥaqīqa	ultimate spirituality reality
ḥaqīqat al-muḥammadīya, al-	primordial spiritual reality of the Prophet Muḥammad
ḥaqq	truth, a common synonym for God; duty or right
ḥawlīya	turn of the year, Friend of God's death anniversary
ḥayā'	shame, embarrassment
haydarī	mendicant dervish, esp. in Turkey and Central Asia ("lionlike")
ḥayra	bewilderment, perplexity, condition of mystical experience
hayba	reverence, awe before God
ḥifẓ al-Qur'ān	having Qur'ān by heart
ḥikam	wisdom saying, aphorism, popular Sufi prayer form
himma	aspiration, attentiveness
ḥizb (*aḥzāb*)	1/16th part of Qur'ān, litany-like prayer or "divine office"
ḥubb	mystical love
ḥuḍūr	presence to God, entailing absence from creatures
ḥusnaẓ-ẓann	thinking well (of God), ability to accept God's design
ibn al-waqt	son of the moment, seeker who lives only in present experience
iḥsān	making beautiful, spiritual life well-lived

ijāzat at-tabarruk	license conferring authority of the *shaykh* of an order
ikhlāṣ	sincerity, spiritual uprightness
ikhwān	brothers in a Sufi order, brotherhood
ilhām	inspiration, sometimes also intuitive knowledge
'ilm	traditional, discursive, acquired knowledge
imāmzāda (P)	descendent of *imām*; common name for saint's tomb
insān al-kāmil, al-	complete person; image of spiritual perfection
intamā	asserting one's membership in an order
intasaba	documenting one's Sufi genealogy
'irfān	knowledge that is of infused, experiential, mystical origin
īshān (P)	"they," reference to major Sufi *shaykhs* in Central Asia especially
ishāra	allusion; a Sufi mode of communicating complex, paradoxical truths
'ishq	passionate, perhaps even romantic, love
islām	grateful surrender to God
isnād	supports; chain of transmission of sayings and anecdotes
ishrāq	illumination; identifying feature of an esoteric school of Sufism
isrā'	Night Journey of Muhammad, prior to Ascension
istighrāq	immersion; "drowning" in the ocean of divine oneness
iṣṭilāḥāt	distinctively Sufi terminology often documented in mystical lexicons
istinbāṭ	deeper interpretation; delving into inward meanings
ittiḥād	unification; bringing the human and divine into one
jabarūt	cosmological realm of absolute divine power
jadhb(a)	attraction; God's drawing the mystic to God-self
jam'	union; joining with God, spiritual focus
jamā'at khāna (P)	Sufi residential facility or meeting place
jamāl	the divine Beauty
jawānmardī (P)	youthful virility; code of spiritual ethics for members of confraternity

jihād	struggle; understood especially as self-discipline against egocentricity
kalenderhane (T)	residence of Sufis identified as *qalandars*
karāma(āt)	gratuitous marvels, wonders; saintly miracles as distinctive from prophetic
kasb	acquisition; Sufi means of livelihood and use of material goods
kashf	unveiling; a mode of divine disclosure to the spiritual seeker
kashkūl	Sufi begging bowl
kavuk (T)	quilted turban worn by some Turkish Sufis
khādim	attendant, steward, assistant-*shaykh* with special duties within an order
khalīfa	successor; chosen as heir to a *shakyh's* authority over an order
khalwa	seclusion, solitude; common term for spiritual retreat
khalwat dar anjumān	solitude in the midst of a throng, Naqshbandi retreat in everyday life
khamr	wine, beverage of mystical intoxication
khānqāh (P)	major type of Sufi residential facility, often linked with other functions
kharābāt	ruins; metaphor for God's favorite place to hide treasure
khatm al-anbiyā'	seal of the prophets; Muḥammad
khatm al-awliyā'	seal of the Friend of God; term given to certain leading saints
khāṭir (khawāṭir)	passing inclinations, movements of soul
khawf	salutary fear of God
khirqa	rag; Sufi cloak emblematic of initiated membership and poverty
khulla	intimacy; friendship with God, exp. of Abraham
khwāja	sir, master; honorific title of great teacher
kibrīt al-aḥmar, al-	red sulphur; alchemical power; metaphor for spiritual transformation
kufr-i ṭarīqat	infidelity on the Sufi Path; level of spiritual inebriation
kulāh (P)	tall, conical felt hat worn by some orders

lāhūt	cosmological realm of divinity itself
langar khāna (P)	free kitchen attached to Sufi institution
laṭīfa (*laṭā'if*)	anecdote (as literary genre); subtle centers in psychology
laylat al-qadr	Night of Power; time of inaugural revelation to the Prophet
lubb	a level of the human heart
madhhab	school of legal methodology in Islamic religious law
madīḥ	praise; genre of poetry especially in honor of saints and the Prophet
madrasa	place of study; traditional institution for study of Islamic law
maḥabba	love between humans and God
maḥbūb	beloved; common Sufi term for God
mahfil	gathering, assembly of participants in *dhikr*, musicians
maḥw	effacement; loss of self before God
majdhūb	one who is drawn by God; mystic who advances without personal effort
majlis	session, assembly; spiritual gathering; also collection of saint's sayings
majnūn	possessed by a *jinn*; metaphor for a mystic, one who is hopelessly smitten
makhdūm	"one who is served," honorific of major *shaykh*, teacher
makr	(divine) ruse, stratagem, machination; metaphor for God's transcendence
maktūb(-āt)	letter(s); collected epistolary writings of famous Sufis
malang (?)	Southeast Asian term for *qalandar*; dervish at Sehwan shrine in Sind
malakūt	cosmological realm of lordly dominion, of angels and pure spirits
malāma	blame; being thought ill of for God's sake
malfūẓ(-āt)	utterance(s); collected (originally) oral discourses of Sufi *shaykhs*

ma'nā	meaning; as distinct from mere outward form
manām	dreaming; important vehicle of divine disclosure requiring interpretation
manāqib (sg. *manqaba*)	virtue(s), meritorious deeds; genre of hagiographical account
manzil (*manāzil*)	resting place; respite or temporary stop on the spiritual path
maqām(āt)	station(s); lasting mystical experience resulting partly from one's effort
ma'rifa	knowledge; of experiential, infused, mystical origin
marbūṭ	one who is bound, attached, confined to a *ribāṭ*
marthīya	lament, threnody; usually poetry honoring a martyred saint
martaba (*marātib*)	segments; divisions of a formal recollection ceremony
mashāyikh	the collectivity of shaykhs as an institution
mashyakha	authority or office of the *shaykh*
masjid	place of prostration; hence, by extension, mosque
masnad	seating platform or cushion for *sajjāda nishīn*
mast (P)	intoxicated, mystically inebriated
mathnawī	rhyming couplet; poetic genre often used for longer, didactic works
mawlāna	our master; honorific title given to some outstanding religious figures
mawlid	birthday; celebration for a prophet or Friend of God
mawsim	season, annual observance of death of holy person
mazār	place of visitation; shrine, goal of pilgrimage, especially saint's tomb
menhuan (C)	sacred descent group; Chinese Sufi organization or order
miḥrāb	niche in back wall of mosque, indicating direction of Mecca
mi'rāj	ascension; Muḥammad guided tour of the heavens to the Throne of God
misbāḥa	praise-device; the rosary, made of up 33 or 99 beads for names of God

mīthāq	affirmation, confirmation (of God's Lordship), hence "Covenant"
mu'āshara	living with one another; life in Sufi communities
mubāḥa	competitiveness; a type of narcissistic behavior to be corrected
mubāya'a	exchanging loyalties; in the seeker's swearing allegiance to the *shaykh*
muḥāḍara	presence; the condition of unceasing remembrance of the Beloved
muḥāsaba	self-scrutiny; accounting for all inner developments in the self
muḥibb	lover; lay affiliate of a Sufi order
mujaddid	renewer, reformer expected at beginning of each new lunar century
mujāhadat an-nafs	struggle against the ego-soul; engaging in battle with the inner enemy
mujāwir	custodian of a Sufi shrine or tomb
mukabele (T/A)	evening portion of Mawlawīya *samā'* ritual
mukāshafa	unveiling; condition in which the seeker is intensely aware of the divine
mulk	cosmological realm of earthly sovereignty
munājāt	intimate prayers; brief, at times paradox-laced, form of discourse with God
munāqara	contest; hagiographic topos with saints competing in miracle power
munshid	singer of poetic verses; provides sung prayers at formal rituals
muntasib	lay associate of the Baktashī order
muqaddam(a)	deputy; group leader, representative of *shaykh*, with authority to initiate
murābiṭ	one who takes up residence in a *ribāṭ*
murād	"desired one," the spiritual guide as focus of aspirant's attention
murāqaba	self-awareness; major aspect of Sufi contemplative discipline
muraqqa'a	patched garment; cloak symbolizing Sufi initiation
murīd(-ūn)	seeker, disciple, aspirant, novice in an order

murshid	one who directs; a spiritual guide, synonym for *shaykh*
muṣāfaḥa	handshake; concluding symbol in Sufi initiation ceremony
muṣallā	place of ritual prayer; equivalent of a mosque-chapel
mushāhada	contemplation; a variety of experiential witnessing
mushkilāt	ambiguous, controversial expressions; technical Sufi terms
muṣṭafā	chosen one; one of the names of the Prophet
mustaṣwif	Sufi-pretender; one who affects Sufi ways
mutajarrid	one who strips oneself of distractions; committed devotee, recluse
mutaṣawwif	Sufi-aspirant; one who works at becoming a Sufi
mutashabbih	lookalike; one who acts like Sufis; affiliate of an order
mutawallī	administrator of a *waqf*, or pious endowment of an institution
muwallih	driven to distraction, ecstatic, enraptured
muzamzim	chanter; performer of musical texts in Sufi ritual
nafs	ego-soul; the often negatively inclined aspects of the self
nā'ib	deputy-*shaykh*, in some orders, to whom *muqaddams* reported
najīb (*nujabā'*)	noble one; name of seven Friends of God in cosmic hierarchy
naqīb	chief; custodian of liturgy or overseer of aspirants in some orders
nashīd (*anāshīd*)	musical poetic form
nāsūt	cosmological realm of humanity
na't	description, attribute; poetic genre extolling the Prophet's virtues
nawāfil (sg. *nafl*)	supererogatory, optional devotional prayer and rituals
niyaz penceresi (T)	mausoleum window allowing passersby to salute the deceased

nuqabā' (sg. *naqīb*)	preeminent ones; three Friends of God near top of cosmic hierarchy
nūr	light; primary metaphor for God
nūr muḥammadī	light of Muḥammad; aspect of the Prophet's pre-existence
nussāk (sg. *nāsik*)	those who practice asceticism
parsā (P)	an individual noted for devotion and piety
pīr (P)	elder; spiritual director, synonym for *shaykh*
pīrī-murīdī	system of traditional relationships between seekers and guides
pīrzāda (P)	descendant of spiritual guide, member of his order or organization
postnişin (T)	one who "sits on the sheepskin," *shaykh* of a *tekke*
qabḍ	constriction; an experience like desolation, opposite of *basṭ*
qalandar (P)	antinomian dervish; member of a class of itinerant mendicants
qalansuwa (P)	type of tall dervish headgear
qalb	heart; basic term for seat of knowledge and spiritual experience
qanā'āt	resignation; ability to surrender one's whole self to God
qaṣīda	ode; medium-length monorhyming poem often panegyric in tone
qāṣṣ	professional storyteller, entertaining with edifying tales
qawm	folk, generic name for Sufis
qawwāl/ī	chanter/popular devotional music, especially in South Asia
qawwūm	subsistent one, title given to highest figure in some saintly hierarchies
qibla	direction of ritual prayer, toward Mecca, as indicated by *miḥrāb*
qiṣṣa	tale, story; literary and oral hagiography
qizil-bāsh (T)	red head; reference to Sufis who wore red headgear

qubba	cupola, dome; type of structure for tombs of holy persons
qurb	proximity; the experience of nearness to God
quṭb	pole, axis; (one of) top figure(s) in Sufi cosmic hierarchy
rāhraw (P)	wayfarer; one who travels the mystic path and actual roads
rajā'	hope in God's mercy and forgiveness
raqṣ	dancing; ritual paraliturgical movement of various kinds
rātib	assigned prayer often associated with set times in the day
ribāṭ	frontier stronghold; Sufi residential facility
riḍā'	contentment; experience of God's satisfaction
risāla	treatise; important genre of Sufi instruction
riyā'	hypocrisy, vainglory
riyāḍāt	spiritual exercises, disciplines
rubā'ī	quatrain; important Sufi poetic genre
rubūbīya	Lordliness, as opposed to servanthood of human beings
rūḥ (*arwāḥ*)	spirit; human faculty in contest with ego-soul
rukh	cheek; important metaphor in Sufi love lyric
rukhṣ (*rukhṣa*)	indulgence, permission, dispensation from required practice
ṣabr	patience; the "beautiful" virtue modeled by Jacob, other prophets
ṣadr	center of one's being; an aspect of the human heart
ṣāḥibdil (P)	possessor/master of heart, i.e., a knower/mystical lover of God
saḥw	sobriety; experience of returning from ecstasy to "normal" awareness
sajjāda	prayer rug (where one prostrates self); symbol of Sufi authority
sajjāda nishīn (A/P)	Sufi leader who "sits on the prayer carpet"; heir-apparent of order

ṣāliḥ	upright person, noted for holiness and serenity
sālik	wayfarer; seeker who progresses through hard work, opposite of *majdhūb*
samā‘	audition; ritual "concert" often including music, singing, dance
sāqī	cupbearer; poetic metaphor for one who supplies mystical intoxication
ṣawm	fasting, both during Ramaḍān and in regimes specific to various orders
semāhāne (T)	place where Turkish orders hold rituals of audition
shadd	wrapping tightly; term used for part or all of some Sufi initiation rituals
shahāda	witnessing, profession; name of essential Muslim creed
shahīd	martyr; one who sacrifices self to the "death" of mystical love
shāhid	witness; term for one endowed with mystical experience
shajara	tree; chart of one's Sufi spiritual lineage or genealogy
sharḥ	expansion; either of one's spiritual center, or in textual exegesis
sharī‘a	revealed law; first level in spiritual journey
sharīf	noble, descendent of Prophet; title given to shaykhs in some orders
shaṭḥ (*shaṭḥīyāt*)	superfluity; ecstatic utterances, often paradoxical
shawq	desire for God
shaykh	elder; spiritual guide or director
shirk	association, setting up "partners" with God; idolatry
ṣidq	authenticity, righteousness, veracity
ṣiddīq	authentic, person of unassailable veracity and sincerity
silsila	chain of spiritual succession, Sufi genealogy
sirr	mystery; inner region of the human heart
ṣūf/ī	wool/wearer of wool; generic name for Muslim mystic

sukr	intoxication; metaphor for mystical ecstasy
sunna	example, especially of the Prophet; model for all Muslims
sūra	"chapter" of the Qur'ān
ṣūra	form; outward aspect, complement of inward meaning
ṭabaqa (*ṭibaq*)	dervish cell; part of Sufi residential facilities
ṭabaqāt	generations; successive groups of Sufis; major hagiographic genre
tadbīr	self-direction, as opposed to seeking out an authentic *shaykh*
tadhkira	remembrance, memorial; major hagiographic genre
tadrīb	training; aspect of Sufi education
tafrīd	isolating, setting apart for total dedication to God
tafṣīl	distinguishing, categorizing, hence spiritual discernment
tafsīr	amplification; exegesis, generic term for commentary
tahdhīb	instruction; especially with respect to ethical conduct
taḥkīm	discipline, imparting wisdom, an aspect of spiritual formation
ṭā'ifa	group, faction; common term for suborder
tāj	crown; name for an item of Sufi headgear
tajallī	manifestation of divine attributes, presence
tajrīd	isolation, seclusion for devotional purposes
ṭālib (P. ṭālibān)	student, seeker; name given to Sufi adepts, disciples
ta'līm	instruction; imparting knowledge of order's Islamic traditions
talqīn	prompting; imparting arcane knowledge through Sufi initiation
talwīn	coloration, variability of spiritual conditions and perceptions
tamkīn	fixity, stability in one's spiritual condition

tamzīq	rending one's garments in ecstasy
tanazzul	descent of the *majdhūb* from divine reality to created nature
tanzīh	eradicating images of God from one's mind; mystical *via negativa*
taqashshuf	asceticism, mortification, self-denial, simplicity of life
ṭāqiya	skull cap; Sufi headgear
taraqqin	ascent of the *sālik* from created nature to the divine presence
tarbīya	formation; shaping seekers in the inner, experiential aspects of the Path
ṭarīqa	path; generic name for a Sufi order
ṭarṭūr (*ṭarāṭir*)	high conical cap worn especially by Ḥaydarīs and related groups
tasamma	declaring one's spiritual connection; see Initiation, Organization
taṣawwuf	Sufism
taṣawwur	visualization (of *shaykh*'s image); meditative or contemplative technique
tasbīḥa	rosary or 33 or 99 beads for numbering the divine names
tawahhum	imagination; surmising, entertaining delusions
tawajjuh	"facing," contemplation, spiritual focus of saint on disciple
tawājud	seeking to "find and be found"; that is, to reach ecstasy
tawakkul	trust in God absolutely
tawba	turning around; repentance, early phase of spiritual path
tawḥīd	awareness and acknowledgment of God's transcendent oneness
ta'wīl	returning to origins; esoteric or symbolic exegesis
ta'wīdh	refuge taking; by extension, amulet from saint in which one takes refuge
tekke/takīya (T/A)	(Turkish) Sufi residential facility, often combining other functions
türbe/turba (T/A)	tomb, mausoleum; literally "earth, soil, dust"

'udhrī	notion of platonic love; contemplation of beauty (after 'Udhrī tribe)
'ulamā'	religious scholars; those endowed with *'ilm*
ūlū 'l-albāb	possessors of hearts, a synonym for spiritually advanced seekers
uns	familiarity, intimacy, quality of divine-human relationship
'uqda	knot, covenant with *shaykh*, part of initiation
'urs	wedding; holy person's death, hence meeting with Beloved/God
ustādh	master, teacher, Maghribi term for *shaykh*
'uzla	seclusion, withdrawal, lesser retreat
waḥdat ash-shuhūd	unity of experience/witnessing; experiential unity with God
waḥdat al-wujūd	unity of being; ontological oneness of all things
wahm	suspicion, conjecture, mistaken notion, opinion
waḥy	divine revelation given to prophets only
wajd	finding/being found; common term for mystical ecstasy
wajh	face; metaphor for presence of God, Beloved's countenance
walāya	status of a Friend of God, of one who enjoys divine patronage
walī	Friend of God, connotation of patron when referring to God
waqf	pious endowment; support in perpetuity for religious institutions
waqfa	standing, staying; an aspect of ecstatic experience
wāqif	one who experiences "standing" before God
waqt	moment; mystical time symbolizing the eternal now
wara'	abstinence; spiritual reticence
wārid(-āt)	spiritual oncoming; form of mystical enlightenment
waṣīya (waṣāya)	testament; *shaykh*'s final instructions to students or successor
waṣl (wuṣūl)	arrival, attainment of mystical union with God

waẓīfa (*waẓā'if*)	daily office prescribed for *murīd* by *shaykh*
wilāya	spiritual office or authority to rule
wirātha	spiritual heritage or legacy
wird (*awrād*)	litanies, often unique to an order, bestowed at initiation
wujūd	being, term related to those used for ecstasy
yaqīn	certitude, divine gift of conviction; central to Sufi epistemology
yār (P)	friend, whether human or divine; Abū Bakr called "Friend of the Cave"
yichan (C)	Chinese equivalent of Persian *īshān*, "they" (Sufi leading figures)
yuanjing (C)	Chinese Sufi practice of reciting whole Qur'ān at one session
zāhid (*zuhhād*)	one who practices asceticism, renunciation
ẓāhir(ī)	outward, apparent; as opposed to the hidden and inward meaning
zandaqa	free-thinking, doctrinal deviation, a charge often leveled at Sufis
zāwiya (*zawāyā*)	corner; small residence of *shaykh*, superseded by larger institutions
zhanxian (C)	writing saintly lineages on dead person's burial clothes
zhencheng (C)	*ḥaqīqa*; third and highest level of Chinese Sufi progress
zindīq	person judged guilty of *zandaqa*, charge leveled at some Sufis
ziyāra(-āt)	visitation, regional or local pilgrimage to holy person's tomb
zuhd	asceticism; self-discipline after the model of the Prophet

Bibliography

Over the past thirty years especially, a wide range of scholarly and popular literature on Sufism has become increasingly available in English as well as a host of Western and Eastern European languages. The present bibliography is biased toward relatively recent works in English but includes representative older works as well as more recent studies written in Western European languages. For reasons of space and because fewer readers will have access to them, works in Eastern European and Asian languages have not been included here. On the other hand, for the benefit of specialists in Sufism, the collection includes a section of texts and editions of primary-source material in Arabic and Persian. Space limitations required many hard choices in the final editing. Dozens of fine entries by Islamic Studies scholars, in such reference works as *Encyclopedia Iranica*, *The Encyclopedia of Islam* (both first and second editions), *The Encyclopedia of Religion*, *The Encyclopedia of Religion and Ethics*, and Cyril Glassé's *Concise Encyclopedia of Islam* (Harper & Row, 1988), thus had to be left out. The important work of those scholars, many of whose other studies are included here, are gratefully acknowledged. Also for reasons of space, articles and chapters published in volumes clearly dedicated entirely to Sufism, such as *The Journal of the History of Sufism* have not been listed separately. In a few instances, where full citation information was not available, or where individual works were "forthcoming" as of this writing, citations were nevertheless included in the list for the sake of near-completeness.

This bibliography begins with a variety of general and comparative works, then offers a selection of texts in Arabic and Persian, some of which include translations. Large sections of (mostly English) translations follow, including works of single authors as well as anthologized or excerpted material. Readers looking for useful overviews might turn to Carl Ernst's *Shambhala Guide to Sufism*, Annemarie Schimmel's

Mystical Dimensions of Islam, and Alexander Knysh's *Islamic Mysticism: A Short History*. Among translations of individual Sufis, William Chittick's *Sufi Path of Love* (listed under Rūmī here) and Barbara von Schlegell's *Principles of Sufism* (under Qushayrī) are fine places to start. Particularly useful collections of major Sufi texts in English translation include Michael Sells's *Early Islamic Mysticism* and John Renard's *Knowledge of God in Classical Sufism*.

In the category of "Focused Studies" are works that either investigate individual Sufis and their works in depth or analyze major themes and concepts across a broader spectrum of Sufi sources and historical data. Gerhard Böwering's *The Mystical Vision of Existence in Classical Islam* is an excellent choice for an advanced look at the hermeneutics of a major early Sufi exegete. The largest single category includes "Historical Studies" divided further by region. Here the possibilities are immense, and the reader has to begin by choosing an area of interest. Sachiko Murata's *Chinese Gleams of Sufi Light* (which might also have been listed under "Primary Sources: Translations") is a fine example of recent work on an important but still little-studied region in the history of Sufism. A goal of the bibliography in these sections has been to offer a geographical and chronological balance, moving well beyond those areas and periods that typically receive the most attention in studies of Sufism. Finally, a large segment on "Society, Politics, the Arts, and Gender" includes sections on institutions and ritual (the largest), as well as the literature, visual arts and architecture, and women in Sufism. Excellent examples are Raymond Lifchez's *The Dervish Lodge* (a work that might also have been listed under "Historical Studies by Geographical Region: Turkey and the Balkans") and Laleh Bakhtiar's *Sufi Women of America*.

An Internet search on "Sufism" turns up hundreds of sites, including many that provide lengthy lists of links (such as the "List of Sufi-related Sources" at www.world.std.com/~habib/sufi). There are far too many to offer even a substantial sample of them here, but most could be said to fall into one of five occasionally overlapping categories. In general, the Web site format does not allow for in-depth information, and on the whole sites tend to advocate views espoused by specific groups rather than offering broad coverage. A notable exception is the relatively small number of academically oriented sites intent on providing solid scholarly background on a full range of topics, works, and historical figures.

One of the best and most reliable of these is that of Professor Alan Godlas (www.arches.uga.edu/~godlas/sufism). Authors of many of the sites in this category are themselves Sufis, generally members of specific orders, but the most useful sites are those that strive for balance. In a second category are sites sponsored by particular Sufi orders, especially those with significant presences in America (e.g., that of the Bawa Muhaiyaddeen Fellowship, bmf.org). Some announce themselves as authoritative voices of Sufism as a whole, and Web surfers should in general be aware that such claims have very limited credibility.

Order-sponsored sites are related to a third group of sites, namely, those whose primary purpose is to advocate the works of particular Sufi authors. Many of these are sponsored by Sufi publishing houses and function much like online bookstores for books by authors such as Idries Shah (see Sufis.org). Fourth, a large number of sites espouse interpretations of Sufism, not as a distinctively Islamic phenomenon but as a global spirituality that transcends specific affiliation with any one confessional community (e.g., zensufi.com and the International Association of Sufism's ias.org). Finally, some sites are organized around anti-Sufism polemics of various kinds, most based on the belief that Sufism has from the outset represented a distortion and aberration of the core beliefs and values of the Islamic tradition (see, e.g., islam.org.au/articles/22/Sufism).

ABBREVIATIONS USED

AA	*Artibus Asiae*
AI	*Annales Islamologiques*
AIr	*Acta Iranica*
AO	*Ars Orientalis*
BJMES	*British Journal of Middle Eastern Studies*
BSOAS	*Bulletin of the School of Oriental and African Studies*
DI	*Der Islam*
HI	*Hamdard Islamicus*
HR	*History of Religions*
IA	*Islamic Art*
IC	*Islamic Culture*
IJMES	*International Journal of Middle East Studies*

IL	*Islamic Literature*
IQ	*Islamic Quarterly*
IrS	*Iranian Studies*
IS	*Islamic Studies*
JAAR	*Journal of the American Academy of Religion*
JAL	*Journal of Arabic Literature*
JAOS	*Journal of the American Oriental Society*
JAS	*Journal of Asian Studies*
JCR	*Journal of Comparative Religion*
JIS	*Journal of Islamic Studies*
JMBRAS	*Journal of the Malayan Branch of the Royal Asiatic Society*
JNES	*Journal of Near Eastern Studies*
JPHS	*Journal of the Pakistan Historical Society*
JRAS	*Journal of the Royal Asiatic Society*
JTS	*Journal of Turkish Studies*
KO	*Kunst des Orients*
MEJ	*Middle East Journal*
MES	*Middle Eastern Studies*
MIDEO(C)	*Mélanges d'Institut Dominicain des Études Orientales (au Caire)*
MW	*The Muslim World*
NS	*New Series*
REI	*Revue des Études Islamiques*
RS	*Religious Studies*
SI	*Studia Islamica*
SUNY	State University of New York Press
UP	University Press (same if separated as U . . . P)
WI	*Die Welt des Islams*
WO	*Die Welt des Orients*
ZDMG	*Zeitschrift der Deutschen Morgenländischen Gesellschaft*

OUTLINE OF CATEGORIES

I. General and Comparative Studies
   A. Sufism and Mystical Spirituality
   B. Comparative Studies

I. GENERAL AND COMPARATIVE STUDIES

A. Sufism and Mystical Spirituality

Aïssel, Selim. *De l'islam au soufisme: réflexions d'un ami gnostique*. Béning-lès-Saint-Avold: Éditions de la Lumière, 1998.

Anawati, G. C., and L. Gardet. *Mystique Musulmane*. Paris: J. Vrin, 1961/1986.

Andræ, Tor. *Islamische Mystik*. Stuttgart: W. Kohlhammer, 1980.

Andrae, Tor. *In the Garden of the Myrtles: Studies in Early Islamic Mysticism*. Albany: SUNY, 1987.

Arberry, A. J. *Introduction to the History of Sufism*. London: Longmans, Greene, 1943.

Arberry, A. J. *Sufism: Account of the Mystics of Islam*. London: Allen and Unwin, 1972.

Arena, Leonardo V. *Il sufismo*. Milan: A. Mondadori, 1996.

Bakhtiyar, Laleh. *Sufi: Expressions of the Mystic Quest*. New York: Avon, 1976.

Baldick, Julian. *Mystical Islam: An Introduction to Sufism*. London: I. B. Tauris, 1989.

Banani, A., et al., eds. *Poetry and Mysticism in Islam*. Cambridge: Cambridge UP, 1994.

Ben Stapa, Zakaria. "A Brief Survey and Analytical Discussion on the Origins and Nature of Sufism." *HI* 12 (1989): 75–91.

Bentounès, K., et al. *Le soufisme, cœur de l'Islam*. Paris: Table Ronde, 1999.

Bentounès, Hadj Adda, Cheikh. *La fraternité des coeurs*. Gordes: Relié, 2003.

Blochet, Ernest. *Études sur l'ésotérisme musulman*. Paris: Sindbad, 1979.

Bonaud, Christian. *Le soufisme: al-tasawwuf et la spiritualité islamique*. Paris: Maisonneuve et Larose/Institut du monde arabe, 1991.

Burckhardt, Titus. *An Introduction to Sufi Doctrine*. Trans. D. M. Matheson. Lahore: Sh. Muhammad Ashraf, 1959.

Caspar, Robert. *Cours de mystique musulmane*. Rome: Pontificio Istituto de Studi Arabi e d'Islamistica, 1993.

Chevalier, Jean. *Le soufisme: ou, L'ivresse de Dieu dans la tradition de l'islam*. Paris: CELT, 1974.

——. *Le soufisme*. Paris: Presses universitaires de France, 1991.

Chittick, William C. *Sufism: A Short Introduction*. Oxford: Oneworld Publications, 2000.

Corbin, Henry. *Face de Dieu, face de l'homme: herméneutique et soufisme*. Paris: Flammarion, 1983.

Danner, V. "Islamic Mysticism." *Studies in Comparative Religion* 10:1 (1976): 25–37.

De Jong, Frederick, and Bernd Radtke, eds. *Islamic Mysticism Contested: Thirteen Centuries of Controversies and Polemics*. Leiden: Brill, 1999.

Elwell-Sutton, L. P. "Sufism and Pseudo-Sufism." *Islam and the Modern World*. New York: St. Martin's, 1983.

Ernst, Carl W. *The Shambhala Guide to Sufism*. Boston: Shambhala, 1997.

Fadiman, J., and R. Frager, eds. *Essential Sufism*. San Francisco: HarperCollins, 1997.

Frembgen, Jürgen. *Reise zu Gott: Sufis und Derwische im Islam*. Munich: Beck, 2000.

Geoffroy, Eric. *Initiation au soufisme*. Paris: Fayard, 2003.

Gramlich, Richard. *Alte Vorbilder des Sufitums: Sheiche des Westens*. Wiesbaden: Harrassowitz, 1995.

——. *Alte Vorbilder des Sufitums: Sheiche des Ostens*. Wiesbaden: Harrassowitz, 1996.

Keddie, Nikki R., ed. *Scholars, Saints, and Sufis*. Berkeley: U of California P, 1972.

Kermānī, Karīm. *Soufisme au présent*. Paris: Harmattan, 2002.

Knysh, Alexander. *Islamic Mysticism: A Short History*. Leiden: Brill, 2000.

Lassalle, Philippe, and Jean-Bernard Sugier. *Rituels et développement, ou, Le jardin du soufi*. Paris: L'Harmattan, 1992.

Lings, Martin. *What Is Sufism?* Berkeley: U of California P, 1975.

Mandel, Gabriele. *Storia del Sufismo*. Milan: Rusconi, 1995.

Masihi, Multaqá al-Islami al-. *La spiritualité: une exigence de notre temps*. Tunis: U de Tunis, Centre d'études et de recherches économiques et sociales, 1988.

Meier, Fritz. *Essays on Islamic Piety and Mysticism*. Trans. and ed. John O'Kane and Bernd Radkte. Leiden: Brill, 1999.

Mohaghegh, M., and H. Landolt, eds. *Collected Papers on Islamic Philosophy and Mysticism*. Tehran: Imperial Iranian Academy of Philosophy, 1971.

Molé, Marijan. *Les mystiques musulmans*. Paris: Les Deux Océans, 1982.

Muhaiyaddeen, M. R. Bawa. *A Contemporary Sufi Speaks: The True Meaning of Sufism*. Philadelphia: Fellowship, 1995.

Nasr, Seyyed Hossein. *Sufi Essays*. Albany: SUNY, 1973.

———. "Sufism." *Cambridge History of Iran*. Cambridge: Cambridge UP, 1975. 4:442–63.

———, ed. *Islamic Spirituality*. 2 vols. New York: Crossroad, 1987–90.

Néaumet, J. *Le soufisme, la voie de l'unité: doctrine et méthode*. Paris: L'Originel, 1980.

Nicholson, R. A. *Studies in Islamic Mysticism*. Cambridge: Cambridge UP, 1921.

———. *The Mystics of Islam*. London: Routledge & Kegan Paul, 1963.

Nurbakhsh, Javad. *The Nurbabkhsh Encyclopedia of Sufi Symbolism*. 16 vols. London: Khanahiqahi Nimatullahi Publications, 1984–2004.

Ogén, G. "Did the Term 'sufi' Exist Before the Sufis?" *Acta Orientalia* 43 (1982): 38–48.

Padwick, Constance. *Muslim Devotions*. London: SPCK, 1960.

Pallavicini, Abd-al-Wâhid. *L'islam intérieur: la spiritualité universelle dans la religion islamique*. Paris: Bartillat, 1995.

Peirone, Federico, and Giuseppe Rizzardi. *La spiritualità islamica*. Rome: Studium, 1986.

Popovic, A., and G. Veinstein, eds. *Les Voies d'Allah: Les Ordres Mystiques dans le Monde Musulmane des origines à aujourd'hui*. Paris: Fayard, 1996.

Radtke, Bernd. "Between Projection and Suppression: Some Considerations concerning the Study of Sufism." In *Shi'a Islam, Sects and Sufism*. Ed. Frederick de Jong. Utrecht: Houtsma Stichting, 1992.

———. "Sufism in 18th C.: Attempt at Provisional Appraisal." *WI* 36:3 (1996): 326–64.

Renard, John. *Seven Doors to Islam: Spirituality and the Religious Life of Muslims*. Berkeley: U of California P, 1996.

Robinson, F. "Islamic History as the History of Learned and Holy Men." In *La Transmission du savoir dans le monde musulman pérphérique*. CNRS, Jeune Equipe, no. 42.004, Lettre d'information, no. 5, Paris, 1986. 1–10.

Schimmel, A. *Mystical Dimensions of Islam*. Chapel Hill: U of North Carolina P, 1975.

———. *Sufismus: eine Einführung in die islamische Mystik*. Munich: C. H. Beck, 2000.

Scholtz-Wiesner, R. F. von. *Lichtpfad der Menschheit: die Botschaft und Aufgabe unserer Zeit: Vorträge und Meditationen*. Heilbronn: Verlag Heilbronn, 1988.

Sirriyyeh, Elizabeth. *Sufis and Anti-Sufis: the defense, rethinking and rejection of Sufism in the modern world*. Surrey: Curzon, 1999.

Skali, Faouzi. *La voie soufie*. Paris: A. Michel, 1985.

Soares de Azevedo, Mateus. *Iniciación al Islam y al Sufismo*. Santafé de Bogotá, Colombia: Panamericana Editorial, 1995.

Stepaniants, Marietta T. *Sufi Wisdom*. Albany: SUNY, 1994.

Stoddart, W. *Sufism: The Mystical Doctrines and Methods of Islam*. Wellingborough, England: Thorsons, 1976.

B. Comparative Studies

Altmann, Alexander. "The Ladder of Ascension." In *Studies in Mysticism and Religion Presented to Gershom Scholem*. Jerusalem: Magnus, 1967.

Arnaldez, R. *Réflexions chrétiennes sur les mystiques musulmans*. Paris: O.E.I.L., 1989.

Asin Palacios, Miguel. *St. John of the Cross and Islam*. Trans. E. Douglas and E. Yoder. New York: Vantage, 1981.

Ben-Ami, I. "Folk Veneration of Saints Among the Moroccan Jews." In *Studies in Judaism and Islam.* Ed. S. Morag et al. Jerusalem: Magnes, 1981.

Cooper, David A. *Entering the Sacred Mountain: Exploring the Mystical Practices of Judaism, Buddhism, and Sufism*. Nevada City, Calif.: Harmony Books, 1995.

———. *Three Gates to Meditation Practice: A Personal Journey into Sufism, Buddhism, and Judaism*. Arlington Heights, Ill.: Skylight Paths, 2nd ed., 2000.

Desjardins, Arnaud. *Les chemins de la sagesse*. Paris: La Table Ronde, 1999.

Duez, Joël. *Mystique soufie et kabbalistique: Rituels secrets, Traité de la rose des sables (quête soufie des trésors)*. Paris: Guy Trédaniel, 1995.

Faruqi, I. *Sufism and Bhakti: Rumi and Sri Ramakrishna*. New Delhi: Abhinav, 1984.

Fenton, P. "Mystical Treatise on Perfection, Providence and Prophecy from Jewish Sufi Circle." In *The Jews of Medieval Islam*. Ed. D. Frank. Leiden: Brill, 1995.

———. "Some Judaeo–Arabic Fragments by Rabbi Abraham he-Hasid, the Jewish Sufi." *JSS* 26 (1981): 47–72.

Geels, Antoon. *Subud and the Javanese Mystical Tradition*. Surrey, Eng.: Curzon, 1997.

Gstrein, H. *Islamische Sufi-Meditation für Christen*. Vienna: Herder, 1977.

Guénon, René. *Aperçus sur l'ésotérisme islamique et le taoïsme*. Paris: Gallimard, 1992.

Guráieb, J. E. *El sufismo en el cristianismo y el islam*. Buenos Aires: Edit. Kier, 1976.

Hames, Harvey J. "Conversion Via Ecstatic Experience in Ramon Llull's *Llibre del Gentil e dels Tres Savis*." *Viator* 30 (1999): 181–200.

Hawley, John S., ed. *Saints and Virtues*. Berkeley: U of California P, 1987.

Henry, Gray, ed. *Merton and Sufism*. Louisville, Ky.: Fons Vitae, 2000.

Izutsu, Toshihiko. *Sufism and Taoism*. Los Angeles: U of California P, 1983.

Kieckhefer, R., and George D. Bond, eds. *Sainthood: Its Manifestations in World Religions*. Berkeley: U of California P, 1988.

Lee, Raymond L. M. "The Two Faces of Charisma: Structure, System, Praxis in Islam and Hinduism." *Journal for the Theory of Social Behavior* 22 (1992): 41–62.

Lobel, Diana. *Between Mysticism and Philosophy: Sufi Language of Religious Experience in Judah Ha-Levi's* Kuzari. Albany: SUNY, 2000.

Malter, H. "Personifications of Soul and Body: A Study in Judaeo–Arabic Literature." *Jewish Quarterly Review* n.s. 2 (1912): 453–79.

Massoudi, Mehrdad. "On the Qualities of a Teacher and a Student: An Eastern Perspective Based on Buddhism, Vedanta, and Sufism." *Intercultural Education* 13:2 (2002): 137–55.

Moulinet, Philippe. *Le soufisme regarde l'occident*. Paris: L'Harmattan, 2002.

Neumann, Wolfgang. *Der Mensch und sein Doppelgänger: Alter Ego-Vorstellungen in Mesoamerika und im Sufismus des Ibn 'Arabi*. Wiesbaden: F. Steiner, 1981.

Pastner, Stephen, and Rhonda Berger-Sofer. "Rebbe and Pir: Ideology, Action, and Personhood in Hassidism and Sufism." In *Studies in Islamic and Judaic Traditions II*. Ed. W. Brinner and S. Ricks. Atlanta: Scholars, 1989.

Rebetez, René. *La odisea de la luz: ciencia y sufismo*. Bogotá, Colombia: Ediciones Martinez Roca, 1997.

Renard, John. "The Dominican and the Dervish: A Christian Muslim Dialogue that Might Have Been—Between Thomas Aquinas (d. 1274) and

Jalal ad-Din Rumi (d. 1273)." *Journal of Ecumenical Studies* 29:2 (1992): 189–201.

Roest-Crollius, Ary A. *Spiritual Experience in the Meeting of Islam and Hinduism: The Case of Dārā Shikūh*. Tokyo: Sophia U, 1988.

Satz, Mario. *Umbría lumbre: San Juan de la Cruz y la sabiduría secreta en la Kábala y el sufismo*. Madrid: Hiperión, 1991.

Seale, Morris S. "The Ethics of Malāmatīya Sufism and the Sermon on the Mount." *MW* 58 (1968): 12–23.

Sells, Michael. *Mystical Languages of Unsaying*. Chicago: U of Chicago P, 1994.

Shayegan, Darius. *Les relations de l'hindouisme et du soufisme: d'après le Majma' al-Bahrayn de Dârâ Shokûh*. Paris: Éditions de la différence, 1979.

Vanderjagt, A. J. "Knowledge of God in Ghazālī and Anselm." *Sprache und Erkenntnis im Mittelalter* 2 (1981): 853–61.

Weber, Max. "Religious Rejections of the World and Their Directions." In *From Max Weber: Essays in Sociology*. Trans. and ed. H. H. Gerth and C. Wright Mills. New York: Oxford UP, 1946, 1977. 323–59.

Willar, Lise. *Soufisme et hassidisme*. Paris: Harmattan, 2003.

Woodward, Ken. *The Book of Miracles: The Meaning of Miracle Stories in Christianity, Judaism, Buddhism, Hinduism, and Islam*. New York: Simon and Schuster, 2001.

Yahyá, 'Uthman. *Mission en Turquie: recherches sur les manuscrits du soufisme*. Paris: P. Guenthner, 1958.

Zaehner, R. C. *Hindu and Muslim Mysticism*. New York: Schocken, 1960.

II. PRIMARY SOURCES

A. Original Languages (Limited Selection, some with translations)

'Abd al-Haqq Muhaddith Dihlawī. *Akhbār al-akhyār fī asrār al-abrār*. Delhi: Muhammad Mirzā Khān, 1280/1863.

Anṣārī, Khwāja 'Abd Allāh. *Kitāb-i Ṣad Maydān*. Ed. S. de Beaurecueil. *Mélanges Islamologiques* 2 (1954): 1–90.

———. *Manāzil as-Sā'irīn*. Ed. and trans. S. de Beaurecueil. Cairo: Institut Francais d'Archéologie Orientale, 1962.

———. *Kitāb Ṣad Maydān*. In S. de Beaurecueil, author, ed., and trans. *Khwaja 'Abdullah Ansari: Mystique Hanbalite*. Beirut: Imprimerie Catholique, 1965.

———. *Abdullah Ansārī of Herat (1006–1089): An Early Sufi Master*.Trans. A. G. Ravan Farhadi. Surrey: Curzon, 1994.

Asad ibn Mūsā. *Kitāb az-zuhd*. Ed. R. G. Khoury. Wiesbaden: Harrassowitz, 1976.

ʿAṭṭār, Farīd ad-Dīn. *Tadhkirat al-Awliyā'*. Ed. R. A. Nicholson. London: Luzac, 1959.

Baghdādī, Majd ad-Dīn. *Risāla dar safar*. Ed. Karāmāt Raʿnā Husaynī. In *Wisdom of Persia*. Ed. H. Landolt and M. Mohaqqeq. Tehran: McGill U Institute of Islamic Studies, Tehran Branch, 1971. 179–90.

Bobozhonov, B., Ulrike Berndt, et al. *Katalog sufischer Handschriften aus der Bibliothek . . . Usbekistan*. Stuttgart: Steiner, 2002.

Fansuri, Hamzah. *The Poems of Hamzah Fansuri*. Ed. and trans. G. W. J. Drewes and L. F. Brakel. Dordrecht, Netherlands: Foris, 1986.

Ghazali, Abu Hamid al-. *Ihya' ʿulum ad-din*. 4 vols. Beirut: Dār al-Kutub al-ʿilmīya, n.d.

Gril, Denis. "Sources manuscrites de l'histoire du soufisme à Dār al-Kutub." *AI* 28 (1994): 97–185.

Ḥallāj. *Kitāb aṭ-Ṭawāsīn*. Ed. Paul Nwyia. *Mélanges de l'Université Saint-Joseph* 47 (1972) 183–237. Also: Ed. Louis Massignon. Paris: Paul Geuthner, 1913.

Hujwīrī, ʿAlī ibn ʿUthmān al-. *Kashf al-mahjūb*. Ed. V. A. Zhukovskij. Leningrad: Dar al-ʿulum, 1926.

Ibn ʿAbbād ar-Rundī. *Ar-rasā'il aṣ-ṣughrā': Lettres de direction spirituelle*. Ed. Paul Nwyia. Beirut: Imprimerie Catholique, 1957, rev. 1972.

Ibn ʿArabī. *Fuṣūṣ al-hikam*. Ed. A. Affifi. Cairo: n.p., 1946.

Ibn al-ʿArīf. *Maḥāsin al-majālis*, Critical edition of Arabic text with trans. by M. Asin Palacios (French trans. of his Spanish). Paris: Paul Geuthner, 1933.

Ibn ʿAṭā' Allāh. *La sagesse des maîtres soufis = Latā'if al-minan*. Ed. Éric Geoffroy. Paris: B. Grasset, 1998.

Ibn al-Jawzī. *Kitāb al-quṣṣāṣ wa'l-mudhakkirīn*. Critical ed. and trans. Merlin L. Swartz. Beirut: Dar el-Machreq, 1986.

Ibn Sabʿīn. *Correspondance philosophique [de] Ibn Sab'in avec l'empereur Frédéric II de Hohenstaufen*. Ed. Şerefettin Yaltkaya. Paris: E. de Boccard, 1943/1999.

Jāmī, ʿAbd ar-Raḥmān. *Nafaḥāt al-uns*. Ed. Mahdī Tawḥīdpūr. Tehran: Kitābforūshī-yi Maḥmūdī, 1337.

Kalābādhī, Abū Bakr al-. *At-taʿarruf li-madhhab ahl at-taṣawwuf*. Ed. Mahmud Amin an-Nawawi. Cairo: Maktabat al-Kulliyat al-Azhariya, 1969

Kharrāz, Abū Saʿīd al-. *The Book of Truthfulness (Kitab aṣ-Ṣidq)*. Ed. (Arabic text) and trans. A. J. Arberry. Oxford: Oxford UP, 1937.

Kubrā, Najm ad-Dīn. "Traités mineurs." Ed. M. Molé. *AI* 4 (1963): 1–78.

Makkī, Abū Ṭālib al-. *Qūt al-qulūb fi muʿāmalāt al-maḥbūb*. 2 vols. Beirut: Dār al-Kutub al-ʿIlmīya, 1997.

Massignon, Louis, ed. *Recueil de textes inédits concernant l'histoire de la mystique en pays d'Islam*. Paris: Paul Geuthner, 1929.

Muḥāsibī, al-Ḥārith al-. *Kitāb ar-ri'āya li ḥuqūq Allāh*. Ed. 'Abd al-Qādir Aḥmad 'Aṭā'. Cairo: Dār al-Kutub al-Ḥadītha, 1970.

Munāwī, 'Abd ar-Ra'ūf al-. *Al-kawākib ad-durrīya tarājim as-sādāt aṣ-ṣūfīya*. Ed. 'Abd al-Ḥamīd Ṣālih Ḥimdān. 4 vols in 2. Cairo: al-Maktabat al-Azharīya, 1994.

Nasafī, 'Abd Allah ibn Aḥmad an-. *Le livre de l'homme parfait (Kitāb al-insān al-kāmil) recueil de traités de soufisme en persan*. Ed. Marijan Molé. Teheran: Département d'iranologie de l'Institut franco-iranien, 1962.

Niffarī, Muḥammad ibn 'Abd al-Jabbār an-. *The Mawāqif and Mukhātabāt*. Trans. A. J. Arberry. London: Luzac, 1935.

Nūrī, Abū 'l-H asan. "Risālat Maqāmāt al-Qulūb." Ed. Paul Nwyia. *Mélanges de l'Université Saint-Joseph* 44 (1968): 129–43.

Nwyia, Paul, ed. "Textes mystiques inèdits d'Abū 'l-Ḥasan al-Nūrī." *Mélanges de l'Université Saint-Joseph* 44 (1968): 115–54.

——. *Trois oeuvres inédites de mystiques musulmanes*. Beirut: Imp. Catholique, 1973.

Qushayrī, 'Abd al-Karīm al-. *Risāla fī 't-taṣawwuf*. Beirut: Dār al-Kutub al-'Ilmīya 1998.

Rūmī, Mawlānā Jalāl ad-Dīn. *Mathnawī-i Ma'nawī*. Ed. and trans. R. A. Nicholson, with Commentary. 8 vols. Gibb Memorial Series. London: Luzac, 1925–40.

——. *Maktūbāt*. Ed. Yusuf Jamshidpur and Ghulamhusayn Amin. Tehran 1335/1956.

——. *Fīhi Ma Fīhi*. Ed. B. Furuzanfar. Tehran, 1338/1959. Trans. A. J. Arberry as *Discourses of Rumi*. New York: Samuel Weiser, 1972.

——. *Kulliyāti Diwāni Shamsi Tabrīzī*. Ed. B. Furuzanfar. Tehran, 1351/1970.

Rūzbihīn Baqlī. *Commentaire sur les paradoxes des soufis*. Ed. Henry Corbin. Paris: Adrien-Maisonneuve, 1966.

——. *Quatre traités inédits de Rūzbehān Baqlī Shīrāzī: textes arabes avec un commentaire*. Ed. P. Ballanfat. Teheran: Institut français de récherche en Iran, 1998.

Sarrāj, Abū Naṣr as-. *Kitāb al-luma' fi 't-taṣawwuf*. Ed. R. A. Nicholson. London: Luzac, Gibb Memorial Series, no. 22, 1914.

Ṣāfī ad-Dīn ibn Abī 'l-Manṣūr ibn Ẓafīr. *La Risāla de Ṣāfī ad-Dīn ibn Abī 'l-Manṣūr ibn Ẓafīr: Biographies des maîtres spirituels connus par un cheikh égyptien*. Ed. and trans. D. Gril. Cairo: Institut Français d'Archéologie Orientale, 1986.

Sarrāf, Morteẓa, ed. *Traités des compagnons-chevaliers, Rasā'il-e Javānmardān: recueil de sept Fotowwat-Nâmeh*. Teheran/Paris: Departement

d'iranologie de l'Institut franco-iranien de recherché/Librairie d'Amerique et d'Orient, 1973.
Sīdī Shaykh. *Al-Yaqouta: poème mystique de Sidi Cheikh (1533–1616). Essai d'édition critique et étude du texte selon la tradition soufie*. Ed. Milad Aissa. Alger: Entreprise nationale du livre, 1986.
Suhrawardī, Abū Ḥafṣ 'Umar as-. *'Awārif al-Ma'ārif*. Beirut: al-Kitāb al-'Arabī, 1983.
Sulamī, 'Abd ar-Raḥmān. *Ṭabaqāt aṣ-Ṣūfī ya*. Ed. J. Pedersen. Leiden: Brill, 1960.
Vāhidī. *Vāhidī's Menākib-i Hvoca-i Cihan ve Netice-i Can: Critical Edition and Analysis*. Ed. Ahmet T. Karamustafa. Cambridge, Mass.: Harvard U, Department of Near Eastern Languages and Civilizations, 1993.
Zarrūq, Aḥmad. *Sharḥ ḥikam Ibn 'Aṭā' Allāh*. Eds. 'Abd al-Ḥalīm Maḥmūd and Maḥmūd ibn Sharīf. Cairo: Bulaq, 1969.
———. *Qawā'id al-taṣawwuf*. Ed. Muḥammad Zuhrī Najjār, 2nd ed. Cairo, 1976.

B. Translations: Individual Authors/Texts

'Abd al-Qādir al-Jazā'irī, Amīr. *The Spiritual Writings of Amir 'Abd al-Kader*. Trans. Michel Chodkiewicz. Albany: SUNY, 1995. Original French translation, *Ecrits spirituelles*. Paris: Éditions du Seuil, 1982.
———. *Le livre des haltes (Kitāb al-mawāqif)*. Trans. Michel Lagarde. Leiden: Brill, 2000.
'Abd al-Qādir al-Jīlānī. *The Endowment of Grace and the Spread of Divine Mercy*. Trans. M. Al-Akili. Philadelphia: Pearl, 1990.
———. *Revelations of the Unseen*. Trans. M. Holland. Houston: Al-Baz, 1992.
———. *Utterances of Shaykh 'Abd al-Qadir al-Jilani*. Trans. M. Holland. Houston: Al-Baz, 1992.
———. *The Secret of Secrets*. Trans. Shaykh Tosun Bayrak. Cambridge: Islamic Texts Society, 1992.
———. *The Sublime Revelation*. Trans. M. Holland. Fort Lauderdale, Fla.: Al-Baz, 1993.
———. *Sufficient Provision for Seekers of the Path of the Truth*. Trans. M. Holland. 5 vols. Hollywood, Fla.: Al-Baz, 1995–97.
———. *Fifteen Letters*. Trans. M. Holland. Hollywood, Fla.: Al-Baz, 1997.
———. *The Sublime Revelation*. Trans. M. Holland. Fort Lauderdale, Fla.: Al-Baz, 1998.
———. *The Book of the Secret of Secrets and the Manifestation of Lights*. Trans. M. Holland. Fort Lauderdale, Fla.: Al-Baz, 2000.
Abū Madyan. "I Seek God's Pardon." Trans. R. Austin. *Studies in Comparative Religion* 7:2 (1973): 91–94.

——. *The Way of Abu Madyan*. Trans. Vincent Cornell. Cambridge: Islamic Texts, 1996.

Abū Yazīd al-Bisṭāmī. *Les dits de Bistami: shatahāt*. Trans. Abdelwahab Meddeb. Paris: Fayard, 1989.

Aflākī, Shams ad-Dīn al-. *Legends of the Sufis*. 3rd rev. ed. Trans. James W. Redhouse. London: Theosophical Publishing, 1976 [1881].

——. *The Feats of the Knowers of God: Manaqeb al-Arefin*. Trans. John O'Kane. Leiden: Brill, 2003.

Anonymous (Malay). *Hikayat Sultan Ibrahim ibn Adham*. Trans. Russell Jones. Lanham, Md.: UP of America, 1985.

Anṣārī, Khwāja 'Abd Allāh. *Les étapes des itinérants vers Dieu*. Trans. Serge de Beaureceuil. Le Caire: l'Institut français d'archéologie orientale, 1962.

——. *Intimate Conversations*. Trans. W. M. Thackston. New York: Paulist, 1978.

——. *Sad Maidan: A Hundred Fields Between Man and God*. Trans. Munir A. Mughal. Lahore: Islamic Book Foundation, 1983.

——. *Chemin de Dieu: trois traités*. Trans. Serge de Beaureceuil. Paris: Sindbad, 1985.

——. *Cris du cœur (Munājāt)*. Trans. Serge de Beaureceuil. Paris: Sindbad, 1988.

——. *Abdullah Ansari of Herat (1006–1089): An Early Sufi Master*. Trans. A. G. Ravan Farhadi. Surrey: Curzon, 1994.

'Aṭṭār, Farīd ad-Dīn. *Muslim Saints and Mystics*. Trans. A. J. Arberry. London: Routledge and Kegan Paul, 1966.

——. *The Ilahiname*. Trans. J. A. Boyle. Manchester: Manchester UP, 1976.

——. *The Conference of the Birds*. Trans. Afkham Darbandi and Dick Davis. Harmondsworth: Penguin, 1984.

——. *Memorial of God's Friends*. Trans. P. Losensky. Mahwah, N.J.: Paulist, 2005.

'Ayn al-Quḍāt al-Hamadhānī. *A Sufi Martyr: The Apologia of 'Ain al-Qudat al-Hamadhani*. Trans. A. J. Arberry. London: Allen and Unwin, 1969.

——. *Les tentations métaphysiques (Tamhidāt)*. Trans. C. Tortel. Paris: Les Deux Océans, 1992.

Bābā Ṭāhir. *The Laments of Baba Tahir, Being the Rubā'iyāt of Baba Tahir Hamadani*. Ed. and trans. E. H. Allen and E. C. Brendon. London: B. Quaritch, 1902.

——. *Poems of a Persian Sufi*. Trans. A. J. Arberry. Cambridge: Cambridge UP, 1937.

Bahā' ad-Dīn Walad al-Balkhī. *Ma'ārif*. Trans. A. J. Arberry. In *Aspects of Islamic Civilization* (Arberry). Ann Arbor: U of Michigan P, 1967.

Bāyazīd al-Bisṭāmī. "Encounters with God." Trans. A. J. Arberry. In *Aspects of Islamic Civilization* (Arberry). Ann Arbor: U of Michigan P, 1967.

Darqāwī, al-ʻArabī ad-. *Letters of a Sufi Master*. Trans. T. Burckhardt. Bedfont, England: Perennial Books, 1961.

Daylamī, Abū al-Hasan ad-. *Le traité d'amour mystique d'al-Daylami*. Trans. Jean Claude Vadet. Genoa: Droz/Champion, 1980.

Dimsashqī, Arslan ibn Yaʻqūb ad-. *Djihad et contemplation: vie et enseignement d'un soufi au temps des croisades*. Trans. Eric Geoffroy. Paris: Dervy, 1997.

Elahi, M., trans. *Couplets of Baba Farid*. Lahore: Majlis Shah Hussain, 1967.

Ernst, Carl W., trans. "Lives of Sufi Saints." In *The Religions of South Asia*. Ed. Donald S. Lopez. Princeton: Princeton UP, 1995. 495–506.

Fadlullah, Muhammad ibn. *The Gift Addressed to the Spirit of the Prophet*. Trans. A. H. Johns. Canberra: Australian National University, 1965.

Fanṣūrī, Hamzah. *The Poems of Hamzah Fansuri*. Ed. and trans. G. W. J. Drewes and L. F. Brakel. Dordrecht, Netherlands: Foris, 1986.

Ghazālī, Abū Ḥāmid al-. "Emotional Religion in Islam as Affected by Music and Singing." *JRAS* (1901): 195–252, 705–48; (1902):1–28.

——. *Die Streitschrift gegen die Ibahija*. Trans. Otto Pretzl. Munich: Verlag der Bayerischen Akademie der Wissenschaften, C. H. Beck, 1933.

——. *Al-Gazzali's Buch vom Gottvertrauen: Das 35 Buch des Ihya' ʻulum ad-din*. Trans. Hans Wehr. Halle a. S.: Max Niemeyer, 1940.

——. *O Disciple*. Trans. G. H. Scherer. Beirut: Catholic, 1951.

——. *Worship in Islam*. Trans. E. W. Calverley. London: Allen and Unwin, 1957.

——. *The Book of Knowledge*. Trans. Nabih Amin Faris. 2nd rev. ed. Lahore: Sh. Muhammad Ashraf, 1962.

——. *Book XX of the Ihya'*. Trans. L. Zolondek. Leiden: Brill, 1963.

——. *Al-Ghazali's Book of Fear and Hope*. Trans. W. McKane. Leiden: Brill, 1965.

——. *Al-Ghazali's Book of Fear and Hope*. Trans. W. McKane. Leiden: Brill, 1965.

——. *Ghazali on Prayer*. Trans. Kojiro Nakamura. Tokyo: University of Tokyo, 1973.

——. *The Letters of Al-Ghazali*. Trans. A. Qayyum. Lahore: Islamic Publications, 1976.

——. *Freedom and Fulfillment*. Trans. Richard McCarthy (of *Munqidh min ad-dalal* and selections of five other works). Boston: Twayne, 1981.

——. *Inner Dimensions of Islamic Worship*. Trans. M. Holland. Leicester: Islamic Foundation, 1983.

——. *Muhammad al-Gazzalis Lehre von den Stufen zur Gottesliebe: die Bücher 31–36 seines Hauptwerkes*. Trans. Richard Gramlich. Wiesbaden: F. Steiner, 1984.

——. *The Remembrance of Death and the Afterlife*. Trans. T. J. Winter. Cambridge: Islamic Texts Society, 1989.

——. *The Alchemy of Happiness*. Trans. C. Field, rev. E. Daniel. Armonk, NY: M. E. Sharpe, 1991.

——. *The Ninety-Nine Beautiful Names of God*. Trans. David Burrell and Nazih Daher. Cambridge: Islamic Texts Society, 1992

——. *Disciplining the Soul and Breaking the Two Desires*. Trans. T. J. Winter. Cambridge: Islamic Texts Society, 1995.

——. *Islamische Ethik nach den Originalquellen übersetzt und erläutert*. Trans. Hans Bauer. Hildesheim: Olms, 2000.

——. "Lightning Flashes Refuting Those Who Repudiate Listening to Music." In *Tracts on Listening to Music*. Ed. and trans. J. Robson. London: Luzac 1938.

Ghazali, Ahmad al-. *Sawanih: Inspirations from the World of Pure Spirits*. Trans. N. Pourjavady. London: KPI, 1986.

Gramlich, Richard, trans. *Die Lebensweise der Könige = Adab al-muluk: ein Handbuch zur islamischen Mystik*. [Marburg]/Stuttgart: DMG/Steiner, 1993.

Ḥāfiẓ. *The Divan of Hâfez: A Bilingual Text Persian-English*. Trans. Reza Saberi. UP of America, 2002.

Ḥallāj. *The "Tawasin" of Mansur al-Hallaj*. Trans. Aisha Abd ar-Rahman at-Tarjumana. Berkeley, Calif.: Diwan, 1974.

Ḥasan, Gul. *Tadhkira Ghauthiya—Solomon's Ring: The Life and Teachings of a Sufi Master*. Trans. and intro. Hasan Askari. Walnut Creek, N.Y.: Altamira, 1998.

Heer, Nicholas, trans. "A Sufi Psychological Treatise." *MW* 51 (1961): 25–36, 83–91, 163–72, 244–58.

Hujwīrī, 'Alī ibn 'Uthmān al-. *The Kashf al-Mahjub, the Oldest Persian Treatise on Sufism*. Trans. R. A. Nicholson. London: Luzac, repr. 1976. Reissued as *Revelation of the Mystery: Kashf al-mahjub*. Accord, N.Y.: Pir, 1999.

Ibn 'Abbād. *Letters on the Sufi Path*. Trans. J. Renard. New York: Paulist, 1986.

Ibn 'Ajība, Ahmad. "L'Autobiographie (*fahrasa*) du soufi marocain Aḥmad ibn 'Ajība." Ed. and trans. Jean-Louis Michon. Parts 1–4 in *Arabica* 15 (1968) 225–69; 16 (1969) 25–64, 113–54, 225–68.

——. *Le Soufi Marocain Ahmad Ibn 'Ajiba (1746–1809) et son Mi'raj*. Trans. Jean-Louis Michon. Paris: J. Vrin, 1973.

Ibn 'Arabī. *Sufis of Andalusia*. Trans. R. W. J. Austin. London: Allen and Unwin, 1971.

——. *The Bezels of Wisdom*. Trans. R. W. J. Austin. New York: Paulist, 1980.

——. *Journey to the Lord of Power*. Trans. R. Harris. Rochester, Vt.: Inner Traditions, 1981.

——. *La profession de foi = Tadhkirat al-Khawāçç wa 'aqīdat ahl al-ikhtiçāç*. Trans. Roger Deladrière. Paris: Sindbad, 1985.

——. *Traité de l'amour*. Trans. Maurice Gloton. Paris: A. Michel, 1986.

——. *The Sufi Path of Knowledge*. Trans. W. C. Chittick. Albany: SUNY, 1989.

——. *What the Seeker Needs*. Trans. T. Bayrak and R. Harris. Putney, Vt.: Threshold, 1992.

——. *La parure des abdâl = Hilyatu-l-abdâl*. Trans. M. Vâlsan. Paris: Les éditions de l'œuvre, 1992.

——. *Les illuminations de La Mecque = Al-futūhāt al-Makkiyya*. Trans. Michel Chodkiewicz. Paris: Albin Michel, 1997.

——. *Stations of Desire: Love elegies from Ibn 'Arabi and new poems*. Trans. Michael Sells. Jerusalem: Ibis, 2000.

——. *Le livre de la filiation spirituelle*. Trans. C. Addas. Marrakech: Al Quobba Zarqua, 2000.

——. *Le livre des théophanies d'Ibn Arabî*. Trans. Stéphane Ruspoli. Paris: Cerf, 2000.

——. "Instructions to a Postulant." Trans. Arthur Jeffrey. In *A Reader on Islam* (Jeffrey). The Hague: Mouton, 1962.

Ibn al-'Arīf, Ahmad. *Mahasin al-Majalis*. Trans. W. Elliott and A. K. Abdulla. England: Avebury Publishing, 1980.

Ibn 'Aṭā' Allāh. *Sufi Aphorisms*. Trans. V. Danner. Leiden: Brill, 1973; New York: Paulist, 1978.

——. *The Book of Wisdom*. Trans. V. Danner. Mahwah, N.J.: Paulist, 1978.

——. *The Key to Salvation: A Sufi Manual of Invocation*. Trans. Mary Ann Koury Donner. Cambridge: Islamic Texts Society, 1996.

Ibn al-Farid, 'Umar. *The Poem of the Way*. Tr. A. Arberry. London: Emery Walker, 1952.

——. *The Mystical Poems of Ibn al-Farid*. 2 vols. Trans. A. J. Arberry. London: Emery Walker, 1952–56.

——. *'Umar Ibn al-Farid: Sufi Verse, Saintly Life*. Ed. and trans. Th. Emil Homerin. New York: Paulist, 2001.

Ibn Idrīs, Aḥmad. "Two Biographies of Ahmad ibn Idris al-Fasi, 1760–1837." Trans. John O. Voll. *International Journal of African Historical Studies* 6 (1973): 633–46.

——. *The Exoteric Ahmad Ibn Idris: A Sufi's Critique on the Madhahib and the Wahhabis*. Ed. and trans. B. Radtke et al. Leiden: Brill, 2000.

Ibn-i Munawwar. *Secrets of God's Mystical Oneness*. Trans. J. O'Kane. Costa Mesa, Calif.: Mazda, 1992.

Ibn as-Sabbāgh. *The Mystical Teachings of al-Shadhili*. Trans. E. H. Douglas. Albany: SUNY, 1993.

Ibn Sīnā. *Traités Mystiques d'Avicenne*. Trans. (partial) August Mehren. Amsterdam: APA-Philo, 1889–99, repr. 1979.

Ibn az-Zayyāt, Yūsuf ibn Yaḥyā. *Regard sur le temps des soufis: vie des saints du sud Marocain des Ve, VIe, VIIe, siécles de l'hégire*. Trans. Ahmad Tawfiq. Casablanca: [S.l.] EDDIF; UNESCO, 1995.

‘Irāqī, Fakhr ad-Dīn. *The Book of the Lovers: ‘Ushshaqnama*. Ed. and trans. A. J. Arberry. Oxford: Oxford UP, 1939.

———. *Divine Flashes*. Trans. W. Chittick and P. Wilson. Mahwah, N.J.: Paulist, 1982.

Isfarāyinī, Nūr al-Dīn ‘Abd al-Raḥmān-i. *Le révélateur des mystères = Kāshif al-Asrār*. Trans. Hermann Landolt. Lagrasse: Verdier, 1986.

Jāmī ‘Abd ar-Raḥmān. *Vie des soufis: ou, Les Haleines de la familiarité*. Trans. A. I. Silvestre de Sacy. Paris: Éditions orientales, 1977.

———. *Lawa’ih: A Treatise on Sufism*. Trans. and ed. E. H. Whinfield and M. M. Kazwini. London: Theosophical Publishing House, 1978.

———. *The Precious Pearl*. Trans. Nicholas Heer. Albany: SUNY, 1979.

———. *Les jaillissements de lumière = Lavâyeh*. Trans. R.Yann. Paris: Deux Océans, 1982.

Jīlī, ‘Abd al-Karīm al-. *De l’homme universel: extraits du livre al-Insān al-Kāmil*. Trans. Titus Burckhardt. Alger/Lyon: Messerschmitt/P. Derain, 1953/1952.

Junayd, Abū al-Qāsim al-. *The Life, Personality and Writings of al-Junayd*. Trans. A. H. Abdel Kader. London: Luzac, 1976.

———. *Enseignement spirituel: traités, lettres, oraisons et sentences*. Trans. R. Deladrière. Paris: Sindbad, 1983.

Kalābādhī, Abū Bakr al-. *The Doctrine of the Sufis*. Trans. A. J. Arberry. Cambridge: Cambridge UP, 1935, repr. 1977.

Kirmānī, Awḥād ad-Dīn. *Heart’s Witness*. Trans. B. M. Weischer and P. L. Wilson. Tehran: Imperial Iranian Academy of Philosophy, 1978.

Ma Fu-chu, “The Three-Character Rhymed Classic on the Ka‘bah.” Trans. J. Peter Hobson. *Studies in Comparative Religion* 14 (1980): 181–94.

Makkī, Abū Ṭālib al-. *Die Nahrung der Herzen*. Trans. Richard Gramlich. 4 vols. Stuttgart: Franz Steiner, 1992–95.

Manīrī, Sharaf ad-Dīn. *Hundred Letters*. Trans. P. Jackson. Mahwah, N.J.: Paulist, 1980.

———. *Letters from a Sufi Teacher: Shaikh Sharfuddin Maneri or Makhdum ul-Mulk*. Trans. Baijnath Singh. New York: Samuel Weiser, 1908–1980.

———. *Khwan-i Pur Ni‘mat: A Table Laden with Good Things*. Trans. Paul Jackson. Delhi: Idarah-i Adabiyat-i Delli, 1986.

Muḥāsibī, al-Ḥārith ibn Asad al-. *Une vision humaine des fins dernières: le Kitab al-tawahhum d’al Muhasibi*. Trans. André Roman. Paris: Klincksieck, 1978.

Munāwī, ‘Abd ar-Ra’ūf al-. *Les femmes soufies*. Trans. Nelly Amri and Laroussi Amri. St. Jean-de-Bray, France: Éditions Dangles, 1992.

Nābulusī, ‘Abd al-Ghanī ibn Ismā‘īl an-. *L’éloge du vin = Al khamriya: poème mystique de ‘Omar Ibn Al Faridh et son commentaire par Abdalghani An Nâbolosi*. Trans. Emile Dermenghem. Paris: Véga, 2002.

Niffarī, Muhammad ibn 'Abd al-Jabbār an-. *The Mawaqif and Mukhatabat*. Trans. A. J. Arberry. London: Luzac, 1935.

Niẓām ad-Dīn Awliyā'. *Nizam ad-Din Awliya: Morals for the Heart*. Trans. Bruce B. Lawrence. Mahwah, N.J.: Paulist, 1992.

Qāshānī, 'Abd ar-Razzāq al-. *A Glossary of Sufi Technical Terms*. Trans. Nabil Safwat. London: Octagon, 1991.

Qushayrī, Abū 'l-Qāsim al-. *Al-Kuschairîs Darstellung des Sûfîtums mit Übersetzungs-Beilage und Indices*. Trans. Richard Hartmann. Berlin: Mayer & Müller, 1914.

———. *Das Sendschreiben al-Qushayris über das Sufitum*. Trans. Richard Gramlich. Wiesbaden: Franz Steiner, 1989.

———. *Principles of Sufism*. Trans. B. von Schlegell. Berkeley, Calif.: Mizan, 1992.

———. *Risalah: Principles of Sufism*. Trans. R. Harris. ABC International Group, 2001.

Rābi'a al-'Adawīya. *Doorkeeper of the Heart: Versions of Rabia*. Trans. Charles Upton. Putney, Vt.: Threshold, 1988.

Rāzī, Najm ad-Dīn Dāyā. *The Path of God's Bondsmen from Origin to Return: A Sufi Compendium*. Delmar, N.Y.: Caravan, 1982.

Rūmī, Jalāl ad-Dīn. *The Mathnawi of Jalal uddin Rumi (Spiritual Couplets)*. Trans. R. A. Nicholson. 8 vols. London: Luzac, 1925–40.

———. *The Ruba'iyat of Jalaluddin Rumi*. Trans. A. J. Arberry. London: E. Walker, 1949.

———. *Mystical Poems of Rumi*. Trans. A. J. Arberry. Chicago: U of Chicago P, 1968.

———. *Divani Shamsi Tabriz*. Trans. and ed. R. A. Nicholson. San Francisco: Rainbow Bridge, 1973.

———. *Mystical Poems of Rumi 2*. Trans. A. J. Arberry. Chicago: U of Chicago P, 1979.

———. *Vierzeiler*. Trans. Gisela Wendt. Amsterdam: Castrum Peregrini Presse, 1981.

———. *The Sufi Path of Love*. Trans. William C. Chittick. Albany: SUNY, 1983.

———. *Signs of the Unseen: Discourses of Jalaluddin Rumi*. Trans. W. M. Thackston, Jr. Putney, Vt.: Threshold, 1994.

———. *Nie ist wer liebt allein: mystische Liebeslieder aus dem Diwan-i Šams von Maulana Galaluddin Rumi*. Trans. Uto von Melzer, Vincensz Rosenzweig et al. Graz: Leykam, 1994.

———. *Von Allem und vom Einen: fihi ma fihi*. Trans. A. Schimmel. München: E. Diederichs, 1995.

———. *Mondenschöner, schlafe nicht: Ruba'iyat: 102 mystische Vierzeiler*. Trans. Nosratollah Rastegar, Monika Hutterstrasser et al. Graz: Leykam, 1999.

Rūzbihān Baqlī. *Le dévoilement des secrets et les apparitions des lumières: journal spirituel du maître de Shîrâz*. Paul Ballanfat. Paris: Éditions du Seuil, 1996.

——. *The Unveiling of Secrets: Diary of a Sufi Master*. Trans. Carl W. Ernst. Chapel Hill, N.C.: Parvardigar, 1997.

——. *Le traité de l'Esprit saint de Rūzbehān de Shīrāz: étude préliminaire, traduction annotée suivies d'un commentaire de son "Lexique du Soufisme."* Trans. S. Ruspoli. Paris: Cerf, 2001.

Sa'dī. *Kings and Beggars: The first two chapters of Sa'di's Gulistan*. Trans. A. J. Arberry. London: Luzac, 1962.

Sanā'ī, Abū 'l-Majd Ḥakīm. *The Enclosed Garden of the Truth*. Trans. Major J. Stephenson. New York: Samuel Weiser, 1972.

——. *The Walled Garden of Truth*. Trans. D. L. Pendlebury. London: Octagon, 1974.

Sarrāj, Abū Naṣr as-. *Schlaglichter über das Sufitum*. Trans. Richard Gramlich. Stuttgart: Franz Steiner Verlag, 1990.

Seh Bari. *The Admonitions of Seh Bari*. Trans. and ed. G. W. J. Drewes. The Hague: Martinus Nijhoff, 1969.

Shādhilī, Abū 'l-Ḥasan ash-. "Prayers of al-Shadhili." Trans. E. H. Douglas. In *Medieval and Middle Eastern Studies in Honor of A. S. Atiyah*. Leiden: Brill, 1972. 106–21.

Shāh Walī Allāh Dihlawī. *Sufism and the Islamic Tradition: The Lamahat and Sata'at of Shah Waliullah*. Trans. G. N. Jalbani. London: Octagon, 1980.

——. *The Conclusive Argument from God: Shah Wali-ullah of Delhi's Hujjat Allah al-Baligha*. Trans. Marcia Hermansen. Leiden: Brill, 1996.

Shams-i Tabrīzī. *Me and Rumi: The Autobiography of Shems-i Tabrizi* [*Maqālāt*]. Trans. W. Chittick. Louisville, Ky.: Fons Vitae, 2004.

Sha'rānī, 'Abd al-Wahhāb ibn Aḥmad. *Vite e detti di santi musulmani*. Trans. Virginia Vacca. Turin: Unione Tipografico-Editrice Torinese, 1968.

——. *Il libro dei doni (Kitāb laṭā'if al-minan wa 'l-akhlāq)*. Trans. Virginia Vacca. Naples: Isitituto orientale di Napoli, 1972.

Suhrawardī, Abū Ḥafṣ 'Umar as-. *Die Gaben der Erkenntnisse*. Trans. Richard Gramlich. Wiesbaden: Franz Steiner, 1978.

Suhrawardī, Abū Najīb as-. *A Sufi Rule for Novices*. Trans. Menachem Milson. Cambridge, Mass.: Harvard UP, 1975.

Suhrawardī, Shihāb ad-Dīn Yaḥyā as-. *L'archange empourpré: quinze traités et récits mystiques*. Trans. Henry Corbin. Paris: Fayard, 1976.

——. *The Mystical and Visionary Treatises of Suhrawardi*. Trans. Wheeler M. Thackston, Jr. London: Octagon, 1982.

Sulamī, 'Abd al-Raḥmān as-. *The Book of Sufi Chivalry: Lessons to a Son of the Moment*. Trans. Sheikh Tosun Bayrak. New York: Inner Traditions International, 1983.

Sulṭān Bāhū. *Death Before Dying: The Sufi Poems of Sultan Bahu*. Trans. Jamal J. Elias. Berkeley: U of California P, 1998.

Tirmidhī, al-Ḥakīm at-. *Drei Schriften des Theosophen von Tirmid: Das Buch vom Leben der Gottesfreunde, Ein Antwortschreiben nach Sarahs, Ein Antwortschreiben nach Rayy*. Trans. Bernd Radtke. Beirut: In Kommission bei F. Steiner, 1992.

———. *The Concept of Sainthood in Early Islamic Mysticism: Two Works by al-Hakīm al-Tirmidhī*. Trans. B. Radtke and J. O'Kane. London: Curzon, 1996.

———. *Présentation et traduction annotée de Kitab ma'rifat al-'asrar (le livre de la connaissance des secrets spirituels)*. Trans. Saad Ellah Boughaba. Lille: A.N.R.T., Université de Lille III, 2000.

Ṭūsī, Naṣīr ad-Dīn. *Contemplation and Action: The Autobiography of a Muslim Scholar*. Trans. S. J. Hosseini Badakhchani. New York: St. Martin's/I. B. Tauris, 1999.

'Umar, al-Hājj. "An Introduction to the Tijani Path: Being an Annotated Translation of the Chapter Headings of the *Kitab al-Rimah* of al-Hajj Umar." Trans. John O. Hunwick. *Islam et Sociétés au sud du Sahara* 6 (1992): 17–32.

Watt, W. M., trans. "The Short Creed of as-Sanūsī." In *A. Schimmel Festschrift*. Ed. M. E. Subtelny. *JTS* 18 (1994): 315–21.

Weischer, B. M. "Mystical Quatrains of Awhaddin Kirmani." In *A. Schimmel Festschrift*. Ed. M. E. Subtelny. *JTS* 18 (1994): 323–28.

C. Translations: Anthologized or Excerpted

Atabay, C. *Die Wörte der Ameisen: persische Weisheiten*. Frankfurt/Main: Insel, 1996.

Chittick, William C., trans. *Faith and Practice of Islam: Three Thirteenth-Century Sufi Texts*. Albany: SUNY, 1992.

Cooperson, Michael, trans. "The Autobiography of al-Ḥakīm al-Tirmidhī." In *Interpreting the Self*. Ed. Dwight F. Reynolds. Berkeley: U of California P, 2001.

Drewes, G. W. J., ed. and trans. *Directions for Travellers on the Mystic Path*. The Hague: Martinus Nijhoff, 1977.

Elias, Jamal, trans. "The Autobiography of 'Alā' al-Dawla al-Simnānī." In *Interpreting the Self*. Ed. Dwight F. Reynolds. Berkeley: U of California P, 2001.

Ernst, Carl W., ed. and trans. *Teachings of Sufism*. Boston: Shambhala, 1999.

Gramlich, Richard, trans. *Islamische Mystik: Sufische Texte aus zehn Jahrhunderten*. Stuttgart: W. Kohlhammer, 1992.

Heer, N. trans. "Sufi Psychological Treatise." *MW* 5 (1961): 25–36, 83–91, 163–72, 244–58.

Homerin, Th. Emil. "Ibn Taymiya's *Al-ṣūfīya wa-al-fuqarā'* (Sufis and Mendicants)." *Arabica* 32:2 (1985): 219–44.

Husain Azad, Tabrizi, ed. *La roseraie du savoir: quatrains mystiques tirés des meilleurs auteurs persans traduits et annotées*. Leiden: Brill, 1937.

Lings, M., trans. *Sufi Poems: A Medieval Anthology*. Cambridge: Islamic Texts, 2002.

Moreno, Martino M. *Antologia della mistica arabo-persiana*. Bari: G. Laterza, 1951.

Murata, Sachiko, trans. *Chinese Gleams of Sufi Light*. Albany: SUNY, 2000.

Nicholson, R. A. "An Early Arabic Version of the *Mi'raj* of Abu Yazid al-Bistami." *Islamica* 2 (1926): 402–15.

Pendlebury, David, trans. *Four Sufi Classics*. London: Octagon, 1980.

Radtke, Bernd, trans. *Drei Schriften des Theosophen vin Tirmidh: Zweiter Teil: Ubersetzung und Kommentar*. Stuttgart: Steiner, 1996.

Radtke, Bernd, R. Sean O'Fahey, and J. O'Kane, trans. "Two Sufi Treatises of Ahmad ibn Idrīs." *Oriens* 35 (1996): 143–78.

Renard, John, ed. *Windows on the House of Islam: Muslim Sources on Spirituality and Religious Life*. Berkeley: U of California P, 1998.

——, ed. and trans. *Knowledge of God in Classical Sufism: Foundations of Islamic Mystical Theology*. Mahwah, N.J.: Paulist, 2004.

Schimmel, Annemarie, trans. *Liebe zu dem Einen: Texte aus der mystischen Tradition des Islam*. Munich: Heyne, 1993.

Sells, Michael, ed. and trans. *Early Islamic Mysticism*. Mahwah, N.J.: Paulist, 1996.

Vitray-Meyerovitch, Eva de, trans. *Anthologie du soufisme*. Paris: Sindbad, 1978.

III. FOCUSED STUDIES

A. Individual Figures and Related Texts

Abrahamov, B. "Al-Ghazāli's Supreme Way to Know God." *SI* 77 (1993): 141–68.

Addas, Claude. *Ibn Arabī et le voyage sans retour*. Paris: Éditions du Seuil, 1996.

Affifi, Abu al-'Ala. *The Mystical Philosophy of Muhyiddin Ibnul-'Arabi*. Cambridge: Cambridge UP, 1939.

Alvi, Sajida S. "Qāzī Sanā' Allāh Pānīpatī, an Eighteenth-Century Indian Ṣūfī-'Ālim." In *Islamic Studies Presented to Charles J. Adams*. Eds. W. Hallaq and D. Little. Leiden: Brill, 1991.

Ammi, Kebir M. *Évocation de Hallaj*. Paris: Presses de la renaissance, 2003.

Ansari, Abdul Haqq. "The Doctrine of the One Actor: Junayd's View of *Tawhid*." *MW* 73 (1983): 33–56.

———. *Sufism and Shari'ah: A Study of Shaykh Ahmad Sirhindi's Effort to Reform Sufism*. Leicester, England: Islamic Foundation, 1986.

Anvar-Chenderoff, Leyli. *Du paradoxe à l'unité l'oeuvre lyrique de Djalal al-Din Rumi, 1207–1273*. Lille: A.N.R.T., Université de Lille III, 2000.

Arberry, A. J. "Ibn Abi 'l-Dunya on Penitence." *JRAS* (1951): 48–63.

Asín Palacios, Miguel. *El místico Murciano Abenarabi: monografías y documentos*. Madrid: Tip.de "Revista de archivos," 1925, 1928.

———. *El Islam cristianizado: estudio del "sufismo" a través de las obras de Abenarabi de Murcia*. Madrid: Editorial Plutarco, 1931.

———. *El místico Abulabás Benalarif de Almería y su "Mahasin al-Machalis."* Madrid: Imp. Sáez Hermanos, 1931.

———. *The Mystical Philosophy of Ibn Masarra and His Followers*. Trans. E. H. Douglas and H. W. Yoder. Leiden: Brill, 1978.

———. *L'islam christianisé: étude sur le soufisme à travers les oeuvres d'Ibn 'Arabī de Murcie*. Paris: Guy Trédaniel, Editions de la Maisnie, 1982.

Asín Palacios, Miguel et al. *Tres estudios sobre pensamiento y mística hispanomusulmanes*. Madrid: Hiperión, 1914, 1992.

Asín Palacios, M., and López Baralt, L. *Šadiles y alumbrados*. Madrid: Hiperión, 1990.

Attas, Sayyid Naguib al-. *The Mysticism of Hamza Fansuri*. Kuala Lumpur: Dewan Bahasa dan Pustaka, 1970.

Aubin, Jean. "Shaykh Ibrahim Zahid Gilani (1218?–1301)." *Turcica* 21–23 (1991): 39–53.

Badeen, Edward. *Auszüge aus 'Ammar al-Bidlisis Bahgat at-ta'ifa und Sawm al-qalb*. Basel: [s.n.], 1978.

Baljon, J. M. S. "Prophetology of Shah Wali Allah." *IS* 9 (1970): 69–80.

———. *A Mystical Interpretation of Prophetic Tales by an Indian Muslim: Shah Wali Allah's Ta'wil al-ahadith*. Leiden: Brill, 1973.

———. *Religion and Thought of Shah Wali Allah Dihlaw*. Leiden: Brill, 1986.

Bannerth, E. "Dhikr et Khalwa d'après Ibn 'Atā Allāh." *MIDEO* (1974): 65–90.

Bawa Muhaiyaddeen, M. R. *The Asma' ul-Husna: Ninety-Nine Beautiful Names*. Philadelphia: Fellowship, 1979.

Bayrakdar, Mehmet. *La philosophie mystique chez Dawud de Kayseri*. Ankara: Éditions Ministère de la Culture, 1990.

Beaurecueil, Serge de. *Khwadja 'Abdullah Ansari (396–481 H./1006–1089); mystique hanbalite*. Beyrouth: Impr. catholique, 1965.

Berger, Lutz. *"Geschieden von allem ausser Gott": Sufik und Welt bei Abu 'Abd ar-Rahman as-Sulami (936–1021)*. Hildesheim: Olms, 1998.

Bosworth, C. E. "An Early Persian Sufi, Shaykh Abū Sa'īd of Mayhanah." In *Logos Islamikos*. Ed. R. Savory and D. A. Agius. Toronto: Pontifical Institute of Medieval Studies, 1984.

Boubakeur, Hamza. *Sidi Cheikh, un soufi algérien*. Paris: Maisonneuve et Larose, 1990.

Böwering, Gerhard. *The Mystical Vision of Existence in Classical Islam: The Qur'anic Hermeneutics of the Sufi Sahl at-Tustari*. Berlin: Walter de Gruyter, 1980.

——. "Major Sources of Sulami's Minor Koran Commentary." *Oriens* 35 (1996): 35–56.

——. "Sulami's Commentary on the Qur'an." In *Islamic Studies Presented to C. J. Adams*. Ed. W. B. Hallaq and D. P. Little. Leiden: Brill, 1991.

——. "Mystical Circles and Colors in Kubra's Philosophical Kaleidoscope." In *Beyond Conventional Constructs*. Ed. G. Irgan. Lahore: Maktaba Jadeed, 1987.

Boye, Ibrahima. *Sayyidi Abdal Qadir Djilâni, imam suprême de la "walaya."* Paris: Publisud, 1990.

Burckhardt, Titus. "Le Sheikh al-'Arabī ad-Darqāwī: Extraits de ses letters." *Études Traditionelles* 394 (1966): 60–80.

——. "Le Sheikh Ad-Darqāqī: Nouveaux extraits des ses letters." *Études Traditionelles* 402–3 (1967): 192–210.

Bürgel, J. Christoph. "The Pious Rogue: A Study in the Meaning of *Qalandar* and *Rend* in the Poetry of Muhammad Iqbal." *Edebiyat* 4 (1979): 43–64.

Burrill, Kathleen R. F. *The Quatrains of Nesimi: Fourteenth Century Turcic Hurufi*. The Hague: Mouton, 1972.

Cahen, Claude. "Baba Ishaq, Baba Ilyas, Hadjdji Bektash et quelques autres." *Turcica* 1 (1969): 53–64.

Cameron, Archibald J. *Abu Dharr al-Ghifari: An Examination of His Image in the Hagiography of Islam*. London: Royal Asiatic Society, 1973.

Cartigny, Johan. *Le Cheikh al-Alawi: témoignages et documents*. Drancy [France]: Éditions Les Amis de l'Islam, 1984.

Casewit, Daoud Stephen. "The Mystical Side of the *Muqaddimah*: Ibn Khaldun's Views on Sufism." *IQ* 29:3 (1985): 172–85.

Chabbi, Jacqueline. "Fuḍayl b. "Iyāḍ, un précurseur du ḥanbalisme (187/803)." *Bulletin d'Études Orientales de l'Institut Français de Damas* 30 (1978): 331–45.

Chelkowski, Peter, ed. *The Scholar and the Saint*. New York: New York UP, 1975.

Chittick, William C. "Mysticism Verses Philosophy in Earlier Islamic History: The al-Tusi, al-Qunawi Correspondence." *RS* (1981): 87–104.

——. "Sadr al-Din Qunawi on the Oneness of Being." *International Philosophical Quarterly* 21 (1981): 171–84.

——. "Five Divine Presences: al-Qunawi to al-Qaysari." *MW* 80:2 (1982): 107–28.

Chodkiewicz, Michel. *Seal of the Saints: Prophethood and Sainthood in the Doctrine of Ibn 'Arabi*. Trans. L. Sherrard. Cambridge: Islamic Texts Society, 1993.

——. *An Ocean Without Shore: Ibn 'Arabi, the Book, and the Law*. Albany: SUNY, 1993.

Corbin, Henry. *Quiétude et inquiétude de l'âme dans le soufisme de Rûzbehân Baqlî de Shîrâz (522/1128–606/1209)*. Zürich: Rhein-Verlag, 1959.

——. *Creative Imagination in the Sufism of Ibn 'Arabi*. Princeton: Princeton UP, 1969.

——. "Mystique et humour chez Sohrawardī, Shaykh al-ishrāq." In *Wisdom of Persia*. Ed. H. Landolt and M. Mohaqqeq. Tehran: McGill University Institute of Islamic Studies, Tehran Branch, 1971.

Cordt, Hartwig. *Die Sitzungen des 'Ala' ad-dawla as-Simnani*. Zurich: Juris, 1977.

Cornell, Vincent J. "The Way of the Axial Intellect: The Islamic Hermetism of Ibn Sab'in." *Journal of the Muhyiddin Ibn 'Arabi Society* 22 (1997): 41–79.

Crussol, Yolande de. *Le rôle de la raison dans la réflexion éthique d'Al-Muhasibi: 'Aql et conversion chez al-Muhasibi (165–243/782–857)*. Paris: Consep, 2002.

Dabashi, Hamid. *Truth and Narrative: The untimely thoughts of 'Ayn al-Qudat al-Hamadhani*. Richmond: Curzon, 1999.

——. *Ayn al-Qudat al-Hamadhani: An Intellectual Portrait*. London: Curzon, 2004.

Dahdal, Naser Musa. *Al-Husayn Ibn Mansur Al-Hallag: vom Missgeschick des "einfachen" Sufi zum Mythos vom Märtyrer Al-Hallag*. Erlangen: [s.n.], 1983.

De Bruijn, J. T. P. "Sanā'ī and the Rise of Persian Mystical Poetry." In *La signification du bas moyenâge dans l'histoire et la culture du monde musulman*. Actes du 8me Congrès de l'Union Européene des Arabisants et Islamisants. Aix-en-Provence: Edisud, 1976. 35–43.

Deladrière, R. "Abū Yazīd Bisṭāmī et enseignement spirituel." *Arabica* 14 (1967): 76–89.

Demeerseman, André. *Nouveau regard sur la voie spirituelle d''Abd al-Qâdir al-Jilânî et sa tradition*. Paris: J. Vrin, 1988.

Diakho, Abu Ilyâss Muhammad. *Les dix règles du soufisme selon Ghazzâli = al-Qawâ'id-l-'ashra.* Beirut: Éditions Al-Bouraq, 1999.

Digby, Simon. "'Abd al-Quddus Gangohi (1456–1537 AD): The Personality and Attitudes of a Medieval Indian Sufi." In *Medieval India: A Miscellany 3*. New York: Asian Publishing House, 1975.

Dindar, B. *Šayh Badr al-Din Mahmud et ses waridat*. Ankara: Ministère de la Culture, 1990.

Douglas, Elmer H. "Al-Shadhili, a North African Sufi, according to Ibn Sabbagh." *MW* 38 (1948): 257–79.

Dreher, Josef. *Das Imamat des islamischen Mystikers Abulqasim Ahmad ibn al-Husain ibn Qasi (gest. 1151): eine Studie zum Selbstverständnis des Autors des "Buchs vom Ausziehen der beiden Sandalen" (Kitab Hal' an-na'lain)*. Bonn: n.p., 1985.

Dumont, Fernand. *La Pensée réligieuse d'Amadou Bamba*. Dakar: Nouvelles Éditions Africaines, 1975.

Dunlop, D. M. "Abu 'l-'Abbas al-Mursi, Spanish Muslim Saint." *MW* 35 (1945): 181–96.

Eich, Thomas. *Abu l-Huda as-Sayyadi: eine Studie zur Instrumentalisierung sufischer Netzwerke und genealogischer Kontroversen. . . .* Berlin: Klaus Schwarz, 2003.

Elāhī, B. *Le chemin de la lumière: la voie de Nūr 'Alī Elāhī*. Paris: A. Michel, 1985.

Elias, Jamal J. *The Throne Carrier of God: The Life and Thought of 'Ala' ad-dawla as-Simnani*. Albany: SUNY, 1995.

——. "A Second Ali: The Making of Sayyid Ali Hamadani in Popular Imagination." *MW* 90:3 (2000): 395–419.

Elmore, Gerald T. *Islamic Sainthood in the Fullness of Time: Ibn al-Arabi's Book of the Fabulous Gryphon*. Leiden: Brill, 1999.

Ernst, Carl. W. "Ruzbihan Baqli on Love as 'Essential Desire.'" In *Gott is Schön und Er liebt die Schönheit/God Is Beautiful and Loves Beauty: Festschrift für A. Schimmel*. Ed. A. Giese and J. C. Bürgel. Bern: Peter Lang, 1994.

——. *Ruzbihan Baqli: Mystical Experience and the Rhetoric of Sainthood in Persian Sufism*. Surrey: Curzon, 1996.

Ess, Josef van. *Die Gedankenwelt des Harit al-Muhasibi*. Bonn: Selbstverlag des Orientalischen Seminars der Universität Bonn, 1961.

Ferhat, Halima. "*As-Sirr al-Maṣūn* de Ṭāhir aṣ-Ṣadafī: un Itinéraire mystique au XIIe siècle." *Al-Qanṭara* 16:2 (1995): 273–88.

Frank, H. *Beit. zur Erkenntniss des Sufismus nach Ibn Haldûn*. Leipzig: Drugulin, 1884.

Friedmann, Yohannan. *Shaykh Ahmad Sirhindi*. Montreal: McGill-Queen's UP, 1971.

Furuzanfar, B. *Aḥādīth-i Mathnawī*. Tehran: Intishārāt-i Dānishgāh-i Tehrān, 1344/1955.

Gayoushi, M. I. "Tirmidhi's Theory of Saints and Sainthood." *IQ* 15 (1971): 17–61.

González, Juan José. *Sobre el abandono de sí mismo: Kitab at- Tanwir fi isqat at-Tadbir; tratado de sufismo šadili*. Madrid: Hiperión, 1994.

Gramlich, Richard. "Abū Sulaymān ad-Dārānī." *Oriens* 33 (1992): 22–85.

——. *Abu l-'Abbas b. 'Ata': Sufi und Koranausleger*. Stuttgart: Deutsche Morgenländische Gesellschaft/Kommissionsverlag, F. Steiner, 1995.

Grinberg, Miguel. *Amante del amor: visiones supremas de un místico sufí del siglo XIII*. Buenos Aires: Longseller, 2002.

Haarman, Ulrich. "Abu Dharr: Muhammad's Revolutionary Companion." *MW* 68 (1978): 285–89 (Review of Cameron).

Halman, T. S., ed. *Yunus Emre and His Mystical Poetry*. Bloomington: Indiana UP, 1981.

Hasrat, Bikrama Jit. *Dara Shikuh: Life and Works*. 2nd ed. Delhi: Munshiram Manoharlal, 1982.

Heath, Peter. "Ibn Sīnā's Journey of the Soul." In *A. Schimmel Festschrift*. Ed. Maria Eva Subtelny. *JTS* 18 (1994): 91–102.

Hickmann, William C. "Who Was Üemmi Kemal?" *Boğazici Üniversitesi Dergisi* 4–5 (1976–77): 57–82.

Hirtenstein, S., and Tiernan, M., eds. *Muhyiddin Ibn'Arabi: A Commemorative Volume*. Shaftesbury, UK: Element Books, 1993.

Homerin, Th. Emil. "Ibn 'Arabi in the People's Assembly." *MEJ* 40 (1986): 462–77.

——. *From Arab Poet to Muslim Saint: Ibn al-Farid, His Verse, and His Shrine*. Columbia: U of South Carolina P, 1994.

Hourani, Albert. "Sufism and Modern Islam: Mevlana Khalid and the Naqshbandi Order." In *The Emergence of the Modern Middle East*. Oxford: Macmillan, 1981.

Huda, Qamar-ul. "Remembrance of the Prophet through a Sufi Text: Shaikh al-Suhrawardi's 'Awarif al-Ma'arif Manual." *JIS* 12:2 (2001): 129–50.

Hussanini, A. S. "Uways al-Qarani and the Uwaysi Sufis." *MW* 57 (1967): 103–13.

Hussaini, Syed Shah K. *Sayyid Muhammad al-Husayni-i Gisudaraz (721/1321–825/1422): On Sufism*. Delhi: Idarah-i Adabiyat-i Delli, 1983.

——. "Shuhud vs. Wujud: A Study of Gisudiraz." *IC* 59 (1985): 323–39.

Ivanow, Wladimir. "A Biography of Shaykh Ahmad-i Jam." *JRAS* (1917): 291–365.

——. "An Isma'ili Interpretation of the Gulshani Raz." *Journal of the Bombay Branch of the Royal Asiatic Society*. NS 8 (1932): 69–78.

Izutsu, Toshihiko. "Mysticism and the Linguistic Problem of Equivocation in the Thought of 'Ayn al-Qudat Hamadani." *SI* 31 (1970)

Jabre, Farid. *La Notion de certitude chez Ghazali*. Paris: J. Vrin, 1958.

——. *La Notion de la* ma'rifa *chez Ghazali*. Beirut: Imprimerie Catholique, 1958.

——. *Essai sur le lexique de Ghazali*. Beirut: Dar el-Machreq, 1970.

Jackson, Paul. "Khair al-Majalis: An Examination." In *Islam in India*, vol. 2. Ed. Christian Troll. Delhi: Vikas Publishing House, 1983. 34–57.

——. *The Way of a Sufi: Sharafuddin Maneri*. Delhi: Idarah-i Adabiyat-i Delli, 1987.

Khouri, R. "Importance et authenticité des texts de *Ḥilyat al-awliyā' wa-ṭabaqāt al-aṣfiya'* d'Abū Nu'aym al-Iṣbahānī." *SI* 46 (1977): 73–113.

Khushaim, Ali Fahmi. *Zarruq the Sufi: A Guide in the Way and A Leader to the Truth*. Tripoli: General Company for Publication, 1976.

King, James Roy. "Jesus and Joseph in Rumi's *Mathnawi*." *MW* 80:2 (1990): 81–95.

Knysh, Aledander. *Ibn 'Arabi in the Later Islamic Tradition*. Albany: SUNY, 1998.

Krishna, L. R., and A. R. Luther. *Sultan Bahu: Sufi Poet of the Punjab*. Lahore: Sh. Mubarak Ali, 1982.

Krupp, Alya. *Studien zum Menaqybname des Abu l-Wafa' Tag al-'Arifin*. Munich: Trofenik, 1976.

Landolt, H. "Die Briefwechsel zwischen Kāshānī und Simnānī." *DI* 50:1 (1973): 29–81.

——. "Le paradoxe de la 'face de Dieu': 'Azīz-e Nasafī (VII/XIII siècle) et la 'monisme ésoterique' de l'Islam." *Studia Iranica* 25:2 (1996): 163–92.

Lewisohn, Leonard. "The Life and Times of Kamāl Khujandī." In *A. Schimmel Festschrift*. Ed. M. E. Subtelny. *JTS* 18 (1994): 163–77.

——. *Beyond Faith and Infidelity: The Sufi Poetry and Teachings of Mahmud Shabistari*. Surrey: Curzon, 1995.

——. "Palasi's Memoir of Shaykh Kujuji, a Persian Sufi Saint of the Thirteenth Century." *JRAS* 6:3 (1996): 346–66.

——. "Sufism and Ismā'īlī Doctrine in the Persian Poetry of Nizārī Quhistānī." *Iran* 41 (2003): 229–51.

Lings, Martin. *A Sufi Saint of the Twentieth Century: Shaikh Ahmad al-'Alawi*. Berkeley: U of California P, 1971.

Lory, Pierre. *Les commentaires ésotériques du Coran d'après 'Abd al Razzâq al-Qâshâni*. Paris: Les Deux Océans, 1980.

Madelung, Wilferd. "Yusuf al-Hamadani and the Naqshbandiyya." *Quaderni di Studi Arabi* 5–6 (1987–8): 499ff.

——. "Naṣīr ad-Dīn Ṭūsī's Ethics Between Philosophy, Shī'ism and Sufism." In *Ethics in Islam*. Ed. R. G. Hovannisian. Malibu, Calif.: Undena, 1985. 85–101.

Mahmud, 'Abd al-Halim. *Al-Mohâsibî: un mystique musulman religieux et moraliste*. Paris: P. Geuthner, 1940.

Makdisi, George. "Ibn Taymiya: A Sufi of the Qadiriya Order." *American Journal of Arabic Studies* 5 (1973): 118–29.

Maldonado R., Alvaro. *Algazel, o, La vida espiritual en el Islam según Abu-Hamid al-Ghazzali de Tus*. Cedar Rapids, Iowa: La Mezquita Madre, 1990.

Martin, D. "Return to the One in Philosophy of Najm ad-Din al-Kubra." In *Neoplatonism and Islamic Tthought*. Ed. P. Morewedge. Albany: SUNY, 1992.

Massignon, Louis. *The Passion of al-Hallaj: Mystic and Martyr of Islam*. Trans. Herbert Mason. 4 vols. Princeton, N.J.: Princeton UP, 1982.

Massri, Angelika al-. *Göttliche Vollkommenheit und die Stellung des Menschen: die Sichtweise 'Abd al-Karim al Gilis auf der Grundlage des "Šarh muškilat al-Futuhat al-makkiya."* Stuttgart: DMG/ Kommissionsverlag, F. Steiner, 1998.

Masud, Muhammad K. "Al-Ḥakīm al-Tirmidhī's *Buduww Sha'n*." *IS* 4 (1965): 315–43.

Mayeur-Jaouen, Catherine. *Al-Sayyid Ahmad al-Badawi: un grand saint de l'islam égyptien*. Cairo: Institut français d'archéologie orientale, 1994.

Meier, F. *Der Geistmensch beim persischen Dichter 'Attar*. Zurich: Rhein-Verlag, 1946.

———. *Die Fawa'ih al-gamal wa-fawatih al-galal des Nagm ad-Din al-Kubra eine Darstellung mystischer Erfahrungen im Islam aus der Zeit um 1200 n. Chr*. Wiesbaden: Steiner, 1957.

———. *Abu Sa'id-i Abu l-Hayr (357–440/967–1049): Wirklichkeit und Legende*. Téhéran/Leiden: Bibliothèque Pahlavi/ Brill, 1976.

———. *Baha-i Walad*. Leiden: Brill, 1989.

Michel, Thomas. "Ibn Taymiyya's *Sharh* on the *Futuh al-ghayb* of 'Abd al-Qadir al-Jilani." *HI* 4:2 (1981): 3–12.

Michon, Jean-Louis. *Le soufi marocain Ahmad ibn 'Ajiba (1746–1809) et son Mi'raj; glossaire de la mystique musulmane*. Paris: J. Vrin, 1973.

Miras, Michel de. *La méthode spirituelle d'un maître du soufisme iranien, Nur 'Ali-Shah, circâ 1748–1798*. Paris: Éditions du Sirac, 1974.

Morris, James W. "Ibn 'Arabi's 'Esotericism': The Problem of Spiritual Authority." *SI* 71 (1990): 37–64.

Morris, Zailan. *Revelation, Intellectual Intuition and Reason in the Philosophy of Mulla Sadra*. Surrey: Curzon, 2001.

Mushir-al-Haq. "Shah 'Abd al-'Aziz al-Dihlawi." *HI* 7:1–2 (1984): 51–96, 77–103.

Nasr, Seyyed Hossein. "Islam and Music: The Views of Ruzbihan Baqli, Patron Saint of Shiraz." *Studies in Comparative Religion* 10 (1976): 37–45.

Nettler, Ronald L. *Sufi Metaphysics and Qur'anic Prophets: Ibn 'Arabi's Thought and Method in the* Fuṣūṣ al-Hikam. Cambridge, Eng.: Islamic Texts, 2003.

Nizami, Khaliq Ahmad. *The Life and Times of Shaikh Farid Ganj-i shakar*. Aligarh, India: Department of History, Muslim University, 1958.

Nwyia, Paul. *Ibn 'Ata' Allah (m. 709/1309) et la naissance de la confrérie shadhilite*. Beirut: Dar al-Machreq, 1972.

Olesen, Niels Henrik. *Culte des saints et pélerinages chez Ibn Taymiyya, 661/1263–728/1328*. Paris: P. Geuthner, 1991.

Ormsby, Eric L. "The Taste of Truth: The Structure of Experience in al-Ghazali's *al-Munqidh min al-Dalal*." In *Islamic Studies Presented to Charles J. Adams*. Ed. W. B. Hallaq and D. P. Little. Leiden: Brill, 1991.

Pierunek, Éve. *Faxr al-din 'Erâqi un représentant du soufisme poétique persan au XIIIe siècle*. Lille: A.N.R.T., Université de Lille III, 2000.

Premare, A.-L. de. *Sîdi 'Abd-er-Rahmân el-Mejdûb: mysticisme populaire, société et pouvoir au Maroc au 16e siècle*. Paris/Rabat: Éditions du CNRS/SMER, 1985.

Radtke, Bernd. *Al-Hakim at-Tirmidi: ein islamischer Theosoph des 3./9. [i.e. 8./9.] Jahrhunderts*. Freiburg: K. Schwarz, 1980.

——. "Tirmidhiana Minora." *Oriens* 34 (1994): 248–60.

——. "Studies on the Sources of the *Kitāb Rimāḥ Ḥizb al-Raḥīm of al-Ḥājj 'Umar*." *Sudanic Africa* 6 (1995): 73–113.

Rahim, A. "Shaykh Akhi Siraj al-Din Uthman, a Bengali Saint." *Journal of the Pakistan Historical Conference* 9 (1961): 23–29.

Random, Michel. *Rumi: la connaissance et le secret*. Paris: Dervy, 1996.

Razavi, Mehdi A. *Suhrawardi and the School of Illumination*. Surrey: Curzon, 1996.

Renard, John. "In the Mirror of Creation: A Muslim Mystic's View of the Individual in the Cosmos." *Horizons* 12:2 (1985): 311–27. (On Rumi)

——. *All the Kings Falcons: Rumi on Prophets and Revelation*. Albany: SUNY, 1994.

Renaud, H. P. "Ibn al-Bannā de Marakech, sūfī." *Hesperis* 25 (1938): 13–42.

Ridgeon, Lloyd. *Aziz Nasafi*. Surrey: Curzon, 1998.

Ritter, Helmut. "Die Aussprüche des Bayezid Bistami." In *Westöstliche Abhandlungen*. Ed. Fritz Meier. Wiesbaden: Harrassowitz, 1954.

——. *Das Meer der Seele: Mensch, Welt und Gott in den Geschichten des Fariduddin 'Attar*. Leiden: Brill, 1978.

Sall, I. *Guide du disciple Tijân aspirant à la perfection*. Beirut: Dar al-Bouraq, 1999.

Santiago Simón, Emilio de. *El polígrafo granadino Ibn al-Jatib y el sufismo*. Granada: Departamento de Historia del Islam de la Universidad, 1983.

Schimmel, A. "Ibn Khafif: An Early Representative of Sufism." *JPHS* 6 (1958): 147–73.

——. *Triumphal Sun: Study of Works of Jalaloddin Rumi*. London: Fine Books, 1978.

———. *I Am Wind, You Are Fire: The Life and Works of Rumi*. Boston: Shambhala, 1992.

Schmidtke, Sabine. *Theologie, Philosophie und Mystik im zwölferschiitischen Islam des 9./15. Jahrhundrets: die Gedankenwelten des Ibn Abi Gumhur al-Ahsa'i (um 838/1434–35-nach 905/1501)*. Leiden: Brill, 2000.

Sells, Michael. "Ibn 'Arabi's Garden Among the Flames: A Reevaluation." *HR* 23:4 (1984): 287–315.

———. "Ibn 'Arabi's Polished Mirror: Perspective Shift and Meaning Event." *SI* 67 (1988): 121–49.

Smith, M. *Al-Muhasibi: Early Mystic of Baghdad*. Amsterdam: Philo repr., 1974.

Sobieroj, Florian. *Ibn Hafif Aš-Širazi und seine Schrift zur Novizenerziehung (Kitab al-Iqtisad)*. Beirut: In Kommission bei Franz Steiner Verlag, 1998.

Sorley, H. T. *Shah Abdul Latif of Bhit: Poetry, Life, Times*. London: Oxford UP, 1966.

Spaulding, Jay. *The Enigmatic Saint: Ahmad ibn Idris and the Idrisi Tradition*. Chicago: Northwestern UP, 1994.

Ṭabāṭabā'ī, Sayyid Muhammad Husayn. *Kernel of the Kernel: A Shī'ī Approach to Sufism*. Albany: SUNY, 2003.

Tafhīmī, S. "Shaykh Sultan Bahu: Life and Persian Works." *JPHS* 28:2 (1980): 133–50.

Takeshita, Masataka. "Continuity and Change in the Tradition of Shirazi Love Mysticism: A Comparison between Daylamī's *'Atf al-Alif* and Rūzbihān Baqlī's *'Abhar al-'Āshiqīn*." *Orient* 23 (1987): 113–31.

———. *Ibn 'Arabī's Theory of the Perfect Man*. Tokyo: Institute for the Study of Languages and Cultures of Asia and Africa, 1987.

Teufel, J. *Eine Lebensbeschreibung des Sheich 'Alī- Hamadānī*. Leiden: Brill, 1962.

Ter Haar, J. G. T. *Follower and Heir of the Prophet: Shaykh Ahmad Sirhindi (1564–1624) as Mystic*. Leiden: Het Oosters Instituut, 1992.

Thorning, Hermann. *Studien zu Bast Madad el-Taufiq; ein Beitrag zur Kenntnis des islamischn Vereinswesens*. Glückstadt: J. J. Augustin, 1913.

Ventura, Alberto, and Caramore, Gabriella. *Il crocifisso dell'islam: Al-Hallaj, storia di un martire del 9. secolo*. Brescia: Morcelliana, 2000.

Vikør, Knut S. "A Sanūsī Treatist on *Jihād*." In *BRISMES Proceedings of the 1991 International Conference on Middle Eastern Studies*. SOAS, 1991. 508–20.

———. *Sufi and Scholar on the Desert Edge: Muhammad b. 'Ali al-Sanusi and his brotherhood.* London: C. Hurst, 1995.

Vikør, Knut S., and R. S. O'Fahey. "Ibn Idris and al-Sanusi: The Teacher and His Student." *Islam et Sociétés au Sud du Sahara* 1:1 (1987): 70–83.

Vitray-Meyerovitch, Eva de. *Rûmî et le soufisme*. Paris: Seuil, 1977.

——. *Mystique et poésie en Islam: Djalâl-ud-Dîn Rûmî et l'ordre des derviches tourneurs*. Paris: Desclée de Brouwer, 1982.
Watt, W. M. "The Short Creed of as-Sanūsī." In *A. Schimmel Festschrift*. Ed. M. E. Subtelny. *JTS* 18 (1994): 315–21.
Willis, John Ralph. *In the Path of Allah: The Passion of al-Hajj 'Umar, an Essay into the Nature of Charisma in Islam*. London: F. Cass, 1989.
Zarcone, Thierry. *Mystiques, philosophes, et francs-maçons en Islam: Riza Tevfik, penseur Ottoman, du soufisme à la confrérie*. Paris: Maisonneuve, 1993.
Zayas, R. de. *Ibn 'Arabi ou le Maitre d'amour*. Biarritz: l'Esprit des péninsules, 1998.
Zirke, Heidi. *Ein hagiographisches Zeugnis zur persischen Geschichte aus der Mitte des 14. Jahrhunderts: das achte Kapitel des Safwat as-safa in kritischer Bearbeitung*. Berlin: K. Schwarz, 1987.
Zouanat, Zakia. *Ibn Mashish, maitre d'al-Shadhili*. [Rabat?]: Z. Zouanat, 1998.

B. Thematic Studies and Analyses of Key Concepts

Abrahamov, Binyamin. *Divine Love in Islamic Mysticism: The Teachings of al-Ghazālī and al-Dabbāgh*. London: RoutledgeCurzon, 2003.
Addas, Claude. "Abu Madyan and Ibn 'Arabi." In *Muhyiddin Ibn 'Arabi: A Commemorative Volume*. Ed. S. Hirtenstein and M. Tiernan. Shaftesbury, UK: Element, 1993.
Affifi, A. "The Story of the Prophet's Ascent in Sufi Thought and Literature." *IQ* 2 (1955): 23–29.
Ahmad, M. T. "Who Is a Qalandar?" *Journal of Indian History* 33 (1955): 155–70.
Algar, Hamid. "Reflections of Ibn 'Arabi in the Early Naqshbandi Tradition." *Journal of the Muhyiddin Ibn 'Arabi Society* 10 (1991): 45–66.
Arasteh, Reza. "Psychology of the Sufi Way to Individuation." In *Sufi Studies: East and West*. Ed. L. F. Rushbrook Williams. London: Octagon, 1973.
Asani, Ali, Kamal Abdel-Malek, and Annemarie Schimmel. *Celebrating Muhammad*. Columbia, S.C.: U South Carolina P, 1995.
Auchterlonie, Paul. *Arabic Biographical Dictionaries: A Summary Guide and Bibliography*. Durham, England: Middle East Libraries Committee, 1987.
Awn, Peter. *Satan's Tragedy and Redemption: Iblis in Sufi Psychology*. Leiden: Brill, 1993.
——. "Sexuality and Mysticism: The Islamic Tradition." In *Asceticism*. Ed. V. L. Wimbush and R. Valantasis. New York: Oxford UP, 1995.
Azma, Nazeer el-. "Some Notes on the Impact of the Story of the *mi'raj* on Sufi Literature." *MW* 63 (1973): 93–104.
Böwering, Gerhard. "Sufi Hermeneutics in Medieval Islam." *REI* 57 (1989): 255–70.

——. "The Light Verse: Text and Sufi Interpretation."*Oriens* 36 (2001): 113–44.

——. "The Scriptural 'Senses' in Medieval Sufi Qur'an Exegesis." In *With Reverence for the Word*. Ed. Jane D. McAuliffe. Oxford: Oxford UP, 2003.

Bürgel, J. Christoph. "Love, Lust, and Longing: Eroticism in Early Islam." In *Society and the Sexes*. Ed. A. Sayyid-Marsot. Malibu: U of California P, 1979.

Chambert-Loir, Henri. *Le culte des saints dans le monde musulman*. Paris: Ecôle Francaise d'Extrême Orient, 1995.

Chittick, William C. "The Perfect Man as the Prototype of the Self in the Sufism of Jami." *SI* 49 (1979): 135–57.

Cooperson, Michael. "Ibn Hanbal and Bishr al-Hafi: A Case Study in Biographical Traditions." *SI* 86:2 (1997): 71–101.

Corbin, Henri. "Visionary Dream in Islamic Spirituality." In *Dream and Human Societies*. Ed. G. E. von Gruenebaum and R. Caillois. Berkeley: U of California P, 1966.

——. *The Man of Light in Iranian Sufism*. Trans. Nancy Pearson. Boulder, Colo.: Shambhala Publications, 1978.

Cornell, Vincent J. "The Sufi as Social Critic: The *Alfiyya* of 'Abdallah al-Habti." In *Sufism in Practice*. Ed. Carl W. Ernst. Princeton: Princeton UP, forthcoming.

Cruise O'Brien, Donal B., and Christian Coulon, eds. *Charisma and Brotherhood in African Islam*. Oxford: Clarendon, 1988.

Daiber, Hans. "Sharing Religious Experience as a Problem in Early Islamic Mysticism." In *On Sharing Religious Experience*. Ed. J. D. Gort, et al. Amsterdam, 1992.

Dankoff, Robert. "Baraq and Buraq." *Central Asiatic Journal* 15 (1971): 102–17.

De Jong, F. "The Cairene *Ziyara* Days: A Contribution to the Study of Saint Veneration in Islam." *WI* 17 (1976–77): 26–43.

——, ed. *Shi'a Islam, Sects, and Sufism*. Utrecth: Houtsma Stichting, 1992.

Denny, Frederick M. "God's Friends: The Sanctity of Persons in Islam." In *Sainthood*. Ed. R. Kieckhefer. Berkeley: U of California P, 1988.

Dols, M. *Majnun: Madman in Medieval Islamic Society*. New York: Oxford UP, 1992.

Elad, Amikam. *Medieval Jerusalem and Islamic Worship: Holy Places, Ceremonies, Pilgrimage*. Leiden: Brill, 1995.

Ernst, Carl W. "Esoteric and Mystical Aspects of Religious Knowledge in Sufism." *Journal of Religious Studies* 12 (1984): 93–100.

——. *Words of Ecstasy in Sufism*. Albany: SUNY, 1985.

——. "From Hagiography to Martyrology: Conflicting Testimonies to a Sufi Martyr of the Delhi Sultanate." *HR* 24 (1985): 308–27.

——. "Textual Formation of Oral Teachings in Early Chishti Sufism." In *Texts and Contexts*. Ed. J. Timm. Albany: SUNY, 1991. 271–97.

——. "Mystical Language and the Teaching Context in the Early Lexicons of Sufism." In *Mysticism and Language*. Ed. S. Katz. Oxford: Oxford UP, 1992.

Ewing, Katherine P. *Arguing Sainthood: Modernity, Psychoanalysis, and Islam*. Durham, N.C.: Duke UP, 1997.

Farah, Caesar. "Social Implications of a Sufi diciple's etiquette." In *VIth Congress of Arabic and Islamic Studies*. Ed. F. Rundgren. Leiden: Brill, 1972.

Frembgen, Jürgen. *Derwische: gelebter Sufismus, wandernde Mystiker und Asketen im islamischen Orient*. Köln: DuMont, 1993.

Gardet, Louis. *La langue arabe et l'analyse des "états spirituels"; contribution à l'etude du lexique sufi*. Damas: Institut Francais, 1957.

Gellner, E. "Doctor and Saint." In *Islam in Tribal Societies, from the Atlas to the Indus*. Ed. A. S. Ahmed and D. M. Hart. London: Routledge & Kegan Paul, 1984.

Ghaffary, Emir Nosrateddine. *L'être-parfait de la gnose persane*. [Paris]/Nanterre: Académie européenne du livre/Diffusion Bageca, 1990.

Gibb, H. A. R. "Islamic Biographical Literature." In *Historians of the Middle East*. Ed. Bernard Lewis and P. M. Holt. Oxford: Oxford UP, 1962.

Goldman, Shalom. *The Wiles of Women/The Wiles of Men: Joseph and Potiphar's Wife in Ancient Near Eastern, Jewish, and Islamic Folklore*. Albany: SUNY, 1995.

Goldziher, Ignaz. "The Veneration of Saints in Islam." In *Muslim Studies*. 2 vols. Trans. C. R. Barber and S. M. Stern. Albany: SUNY, 1971. 275–341.

——. "Asceticism and Sufism." In *Introduction to Islamic Theology and Law*. Trans. Andras Hamori and Ruth Hamori. Princeton: Princeton UP, 1981.

Gramlich, Richard. *Die Wunder der Freunde Gottes*. Stuttgart: Steiner, 1987.

——. *Alte Vorbilder des Sufitums*. Wiesbaden: Harrassowitz, 1995.

——. *Weltverzicht: Grundlagen . . . islamischer Askese*. Wiesbaden: Harrassowitz, 1997.

——. *Der eine Gott: Grundzüge der Mystik des islamischen Monotheismus*. Wiesbaden: Harrassowitz, 1998.

Gribetz, A. "The sama' controversy: Sufi vs. legalist." *SI* 74 (1991): 43–62.

Haas, William S. "The Zikr of the Rahmanija-Order in Algeria: A Psycho-Physiological Analysis." *MW* 33 (1943): 16–28.

Hakim, Su'ad, and Pablo Beneito. *Las contemplaciones de los misterios*. Murcia: Consejería de Cultura y Educación, Dirección General de Cultura, 1994.

Hamad, Bushra. "History and Biography." *Arabica* 45 (1998): 215–32.

Heine, Peter. *Mystik und radikaler Islam*. Berlin: Das Arabische Buch, 1987.

Hermansen, Marcia. "Citing the Sights of the Holy Sites: Visionary Pilgrimage Narratives of Pre-Modern South Asian Sufis." In *The Shaping of an Ameri-*

can Islamic Discourse. Ed. E. Waugh and F. Denny. Atlanta: Scholars, 1998. 189–214.

Hiskett, Mervin. "The 'Song of the Shehy's Miracles': A Hausa Hagiography from Sokoto." *African Language Studies* 12 (1971): 71–107.

Huda, Qamar-ul. "Reflections on Muslim Ascetics and Mystics: Sufi Theories on Annihilation and Subsistence." *Jusur* 12 (1996): 17–35.

——. "Celebrating Death and Engaging in Texts at Data Ganj Bakhsh's Death-Festival '*Urs*." *MW* 90:3–4 (2000): 377–94.

——. "Khwaja Mu'in ad-Din Chishti's Death Festival: Competing Authorities over Sacred Space." *Journal of Ritual Studies* 17:1 (2003): 22–43.

——. "The Light beyond the Shore in the Theology of Proper Sufi Moral Conduct—*Adab*." *JAAR* 72:2 (2004): 461–84.

Hurvitz, Nimrod. "Biographies and Mild Asceticism: A Study of the Islamic Moral Imagination." *SI* 85:1 (1997): 41–65.

Jerrahi, Muzaffer Ozak. *The Unveiling of Love: Sufism and the Remembrance of God*. New York: Inner Traditions International, 1981.

Kafadar, Cemal. "Self and Others: The Diary of a Dervish in Seventeenth Century Istanbul and First-Person Narratives in Ottoman Literature." *SI* 69 (1989): 121–50.

Kahale, J. E. *Le soufisme et ses grands maîtres*. Châtenay-Malabry: Alteredit, 2001.

——. *Le soufisme et l'amour divin*. Châtenay-Malabry: Alteredit, 2002.

Karamustafa, Ahmet T. "The Antinomian Dervish as Model Saint." In *Modes de transmission de la culture religieuse en Islam*. Ed. Hassan Elboudrari. Cairo: Institue Francais d'Archaeologie Orientale, 1993.

Katz, Jonathan G. "The Worldly Pursuits of a Would-Be Wali: Muhammad al-Zawawi al-Bija'i (d. 882/1477)." *Al-Qantara* 12 (1991): 497–521.

——. "Shaykh Ahmad's Dream: 19th C. Eschatological Vision." *SI* 79 (1994): 157–80.

——. *Dreams, Sufism and Sainthood: The Visionary Career of Muhammad al-Zawawi*. Leiden: Brill, 1996.

Kazem-Zadeh Iranshahr, Hoseyn. *Die Lehre des Mystisch-esoterischen Schule*. Winterthur: Verlag "Weltharmonie," 1956.

Khalidi, Tarif. "Islamic Biographical Dictionaries: A Preliminary Assessment." *MW* 63 (1973): 53–65.

Kinberg, Leah. "What Is Meant by *Zuhd*?" *SI* 61 (1985): 27–44.

——. "Compromise of Commerce: A Study of Early Traditions concerning Poverty and Wealth." *DI* 66 (1989): 193–212.

Kister, M. J. "The Interpretation of Dreams: An Unknown Manuscript of Ibn Qurayba's 'Ibarat al-Ru'ya.'" *Israel Oriental Studies* 4 (1974): 67–103.

Klappstein, Paul. *Vier türkestanische Heilige: ein Beitrag zum Verständnis der islamischen Mystik*. Berlin: Mayer & Müller, 1919.

Knappert, Jan. "Miiraji, the Swahili Legend of Mohammed's Ascension." *Swahili* 36 (1966): 105–56.

———. *Islamic Legends: Histories of the Heroes, Saints, and Prophets.* 2 vols. Leiden: Brill, 1985.

Knysh, Alexander. *Ibn 'Arabi and the Later Islamic Tradition: The Making of a Polemical Image in Medieval Islam*. Albany: SUNY, 1998.

Krenkow, F. "The Appearance of the Prophet in Dreams." *JRAS* (1912): 77–99.

Lawrence, Brother. *The Kitchen Saint and the Heritage of Islam*. San Jose, Calif.: Pickwick Publications, 1989.

Lawrence, Bruce B. "The Early Chishti Approach to Sama'." In *Islamic Society and Culture*. Ed. Milton Israel and N. K. Wagle. New Delhi: Manohar, 1983.

LeCerf, Jean. "The Dream in Popular Culture: Arab and Islamic." In *The Dream and Human Society*. Ed. G. E. von Grunebaum and R. Caillois. Berkeley: U of California P, 1966.

Mackeen, A. M. Mohamed. "The Sufi-Qawm Movement." *MW* 53 (1963): 212–25.

Madelung, Wilferd. "Ibn Abī Gumhūr al-Ahsā'i's synthesis of *kalām*, philosophy and Sufism." *La Signification du Bas Moyên Age dans l'histoire de la culture du monde musulman*. Aix-en-Provence: Edisud, 1978.

Makdisi, George. "The Hanbali School and Sufism." *Boletin de la Asociacion Espagnola de Orientalistas* 15 (1979): 115–26.

Makowski, Stefan. *Allahs trunkene Poeten*. Zurich: Benziger, 1997.

Massignon, Louis. *Essay on the Origins of the Technical Language of Islamic Mysticism*. Trans. Benjamin Clark. Notre Dame, Ind.: U of Notre Dame P, 1994.

Melchert, C. "The Transiton from Asceticism to Mysticism at the Middle of the Ninth Century C.E." *SI* 83:1 (1996): 51–70.

Miller, Lloyd, ed. *Sufi Sects, Saints, and Shrines*. Salt Lake City, Utah: Society for Islamic and Eastern Mysticism, 1978.

Morewedge, P. "Sufism, Neoplatonism, and Zaehner's Theistic Theory of Mysticism." In *Islamic Philosophy and Mysticism*. Ed. P. Morewedge. New York: Caravan, 1981.

Morris, James W. "The Spiritual Ascension: Ibn 'Arabi and the Miraj." *JAOS*, part 1, 107:4 (1987): 629–52; part 2, 108:1 (1988): 63–77.

Mojaddedi, Jawid A. *The Biographical Tradition in Sufism: The Tabaqat Genre from al-Sulami to Jami*. Surrey: Curzon, 2001.

Muhaiyaddeen, M. R. Bawa. *Why Can't I See the Angels: Questions to a Sufi Saint*. Overbrook, Pa.: Fellowship, 2002.

Murtazavi, Jamshid, and Eva de Vitray-Meyerovitch. *Le secret de l'unité dans l'ésotérisme iranien*. Paris: Dervy, 1988.

Murtazavi, Jamshid. *Symbolisme des contes et mystique persane*. Paris: J. C. Lattès, 1988.

——. *Soufisme et psychologie*. Monaco: Éditions du Rocher, 1989.

——. *L'autre face de la pensée musulmane*. Monaco: Éditions du Rocher, 1997.

Nasr, Seyyed H. "Shi'ism and Sufism." In *Shi'ism: Doctrines, Thought, and Spirituality*. Eds. S. H. Nasr, H. Dabashi, and S. V. R. Nasr. Albany: SUNY, 1988.

Netton, Ian R. *Sufi Ritual: The Parallel Universe*. Surrey: Curzon, 2000.

Nicholson, R. A. *The Idea of Personality in Sufism*. Cambridge: Cambridge UP, 1923.

Nurbakhsh, Javad. *Jesus in the Eyes of the Sufis*. London: Khaniqahi Nimatullahi, 1983.

Nurbakhsh, Javad, and Bernhard Meyer. *Die psychologie des Sufismus = Del wa nafs*. Cologne: Khaniqahi-Nimatullahi/Verlag Kaveh Dalir Azar, 1995.

Nwyia, Paul. *Exégèse coranique et langage mystique*. Beirut: Dar al-Machreq, 1970.

Ohtsuka, K. "Toward Typology of Benefit-Granting in Islam." *Orient* 24 (1988): 141–52.

Olsson, Tord, et al., eds. *Alevi Identity: Cultural, Religious and Social Perspectives*. Stockholm: Swedish Research Institute in Istanbul. Richmond, Surrey: Curzon, 1998.

Qadi, Wadad al-. "Biographical Dictionaries: Inner Structure and Cultural Significance." In *The Book in the Islamic World*. Ed. George N. Atiyeh. Albany: SUNY, 1995.

Radtke, Bernd. "Iranian and Gnostic Elements in Early *tasawwuf* Observations Concerning the *Umm al-kitāb*." In *Proceedings of the First European Conference of Iranian Studies*. Part 2, *Middle and New Iranian Studies*. Ed. G. Gnoli and A. Panaino. Rome: Istituto Italiano per il Medio ed Estremo Oriente, 1990.

——. "Neo-Sufism Reconsidered." *DI* 70 (1993): 52–87.

——. "Ijtihad and Neo-Sufism." *Asiatische Studien* 48:3 (1994): 909–21.

Radtke, Bernd, and John O'Kane. *The Concept of Sainthood in Early Islamic Mysticism*. Surrey: Curzon, 1996.

Rahman, F. "Dream, Imagination, 'Alam al-Mithal." In *Dream and Human Societies*. Ed. G. von Grunebaum and R. Caillois. Berkeley: U of California P, 1966.

Reinert, B. *Die Lehre vom tawakkul in der klassischen Sufik*. Berlin: de Gruyter, 1968.

Renard, J. "*Al-jihad al-akbar*: A Theme in Islamic Spirituality." *MW* 77 (1988): 225–42.

Robinson, Francis. "Religious Change and the Self in Muslim South-Asia Since 1800." *South Asia* 20:1 (1997): 1–15.

Rosenthal, Franz. "Die Islamische Autobiographie." *Studia Arabica* 1 (1937): 1–40.

———. "I am You—Individual Piety and Society in Islam." In *Individualism and Conformity in Classical Islam*. Ed. A. Banani and S. Vryonis. Wiesbaden: Harrassowitz, 1977.

———. *"Sweeter than Hope": Complaint and Hope in Medieval Islam*. Leiden: Brill, 1983.

Safi, Omid. "Did the Two Oceans Meet? Connections and Disconections between Ibn al-ʻArabī and Rūmī." *Journal of the Muhyiddin Ibn ʻArabi Society* 26 (1999): 55–88.

Sanneh, Lamin. "Saints and Virtue in African Islam: An Historical Approach." In *Saints and Virtues*. Ed. J. S. Hawley. Berkeley: U of California P, 1987.

Scattolin, Giuseppe P. *Esperienze mistiche nell' Islam*. Bologne: Editrice Missionaria Italiana, 1994.

Schimmel, Annemarie. "The Veneration of the Prophet as Reflected in Sindhi Poetry." In *The Saviour God*. Ed. S. G. Brandon. Manchester: Manchester UP, 1963.

———. "Some Glimpses of Religious Life in Egypt during the Later Mamluk Period." *IS* 4 (1965): 353–92.

———. "Eros—Heavenly and Not So Heavenly—in Sufi Literature and Life." In *Society and Sexes in Medieval Islam*. Ed. Afaf L. S. Marsot. Malibu: U of California P, 1979.

———. *And Muhammad Is His Messenger: The Veneration of the Prophet in Islamic Piety*. Chapel Hill: U of North Carolina P, 1985.

———. *Garten der Erkenntnis: das Buch der vierzig Sufi-Meister*. Düsseldorf: E. Diederichs, 1985.

Schwerin, K. G. "Saint Worship in Islam: The Legend of the Martyr Salar Masud Ghazi." In *Ritual and Religion among Muslims of the Sub-Continent*." Ed. I. Ahmad. Lahore: Vanguard, 1985.

Sells, Michael. "Bewildered Tongue: The Semantics of Mystical Union in Islam." In *Mystical Union and Monotheistic Faith*. Ed. M. Idel and B. McGinn. New York: Macmillan, 1989.

———. "Heart-Secret, Intimacy, Awe in Formative Sufism." In *Shaping American Islamic Discourse*. Ed. E. Waugh and F. Denny. Atlanta: Scholars, 1998.

Shaibi, Kamil al-. *Sufism and Shiʻism*. Surbiton, Surrey: LAAM, 1991.

Sirriyeh, Elisabeth. *Sufis and Anti-Sufis: Rethinking and Rejection of Sufism in the Modern World*. Surrey: Curzon, 1998.

Smith, Grace M., and Carl W. Ernst, eds. *Manifestations of Sainthood in Islam*. Istanbul: Isis, 1993.

Steffân, Steff. *Das erleuchtete Herz des Islam: die Sufi-Mystik der Erkenntnis und Liebe*. Berlin: Altis-Verlag, 1993.

Takeshita, Masataka. *Ibn 'Arabi's Theory of the Perfect Man and Its Place in the History of Islamic Thought*. Tokyo: Institute for Cultures of Asia and Africa, 1987.

Tall, Amadou. *Niche des secrets: recueil d'arcanes mystiques dans la tradition soufie (islamique)*. Dakar: Librairie islamique, 1995.

Taylor, Christopher S. *In the Vicinity of the Righteous: Ziyara and the Veneration of Muslim Saints in Late Medieval Egypt*. Leiden: Brill, 1999.

Triaud, Jean-Louis. "Khalwa and the Career of Sainthood." In *Charisma and Brotherhood in African Islam*. Ed. C. Coulon and D. C. O'Brien. Oxford: OUP, 1988.

Triki, A. *Neoplatonisme et aspect mystique de la création de l'univers dans la philosophie des Ihwan*. Lille: Université de Lille III, 1974.

Valiuddin, Mir. *Contemplative Disciplines in Sufism*. London: East-West, 1980.

Ventura, Alberto. *La métaphysique de l'ésotérisme islamique dans le traité "Lumière sur les choses difficiles à percer."* Milan: Archè, 1978.

Vett, Carl. *Dervish Diary*. Trans. E. W. Hathaway. Los Angeles: K. Mogensen, 1953.

Vitray-Meyerovitch, Eva de, and F. Skali. *Jésus dans la tradition soufie*. Le Plan d'Aups, Saint-Zacharie [France]: Editions de l'Ouvert, 1985.

Waugh, E. H. "The Popular Muhammad." In *Approaches to Islam in Religious Studies*. Ed. R. C. Martin. Tucson: U of Arizona P, 1985.

Werbner, Pnina. "Powerful Knowledge in a Global Sufi Cult." In *The Pursuit of Cerntainty*. Ed. Wendy James. London: Routledge, 1995.

———. *Pilgrims of Love: The Anthropology of a Global Sufi Cult*. Bloomington: Indiana UP, 2003.

Wilson, Stephen, ed. *Saints and their Cults*. Cambridge: Cambridge UP, 1983.

Zarcone, Thierry, Ekrem Isin, and Arthur Buehler, eds. *Saints and Heroes on the Silk Road*. Vol. 3, *Journal of the History of Sufism*. Paris: Maisonneuve, 2001.

———. *Sufi Dance*. Vol. 4, *Journal of the History of Sufism*. Paris: Maisonneuve, 2003.

IV. HISTORICAL STUDIES BY GEOGRAPHICAL REGION

A. Africa: East

Andrzejewski, B. W. "Sheikh Hussen of Bali in Galla Oral Traditions." In *IV Congresso Int. di Studi Etiopici*. Rome: Accademia Nazionale dei Lincei, 1974.

Bang, Anne K. *Sufis and Scholars of the Sea: Family Networks in East Africa, 1860–1925*. Surrey, Eng.: Curzon, 2003.

Burke, O. M. *Among the Dervishes: Travels in Asia and Africa*. New York: Dutton, 1975.

Daly, M. W., ed. *Al-Majdhubiyya and Al-Mikashifiyya: Two Sufi Tariqas in the Sudan*. Khartoum: U of Khartoum P, 1985.

Karrar, A. S. *The Sufi Brotherhoods in the Sudan*. Evanston, Ill.: Northwestern UP, 1992.

Karsani, Awad al-Sid al. "Beyond Sufism: the Case of Millennial Islam in Sudan." In *Muslim Identity and Social Change in Sub-Saharan Africa*. Ed. L. Brenner. Bloomington: Indiana UP, 1993.

Lewis, I. M. "Sufism in Somaliland: A Study in Tribal Islam." In *Islam in Tribal Societies*. Ed. A. S. Ahmed and D. M. Hart. London: Oxford UP, 1984.

——. *Saints and Somalis*. Lawrenceville, N.J.: Red Sea, 1998.

McHugh, Neil. *Holy Men of the Blue Nile*. Evanston: Northwestern UP, 1994.

Nimtz, August. *Islam and Politics in East Africa: The Sufi Order in Tanzania*. Minneapolis: U of Minnesota P, 1980.

Nimtz, A. "The Qadiriyya and Political Change." In *Islamic and Middle Eastern Societies*. Ed. R. Olson with S. al-Ani. Brattleboro, Vt.: Amana Books, 1987.

O'Fahey, R. S. "Islamic Hegemonies in the Sudan: Sufism, Mahdism, and Islamism." In *Muslim Identity and Social Change in Sub-Saharan Africa*. Ed. L. Brenner. Bloomington: Indiana UP, 1993.

Robinson, D. *Holy War of 'Umar Tal: The Western Sudan. . . .* Oxford: Oxford UP, 1985.

Shahi, Ahmed al-. "A Noah's Ark: The Continuity of the Khatmiya Order in Northern Sudan." *Bulletin, British Society for Middle Eastern Studies* 8:1 (1981): 13–29.

Vikør, Knut S. "Sufi Brotherhoods in Africa." In *The History of Islam in Africa*. Ed. N. Levtzion and R. L. Pouwels. Athens: Ohio UP, 2000.

Voll, John O. *A History of the Khatmiyya Tariqah in the Sudan*. 2 vols. Ann Arbor: U of Michigan P, 1978.

Warburg, G. "Religious Policy in the Northern Sudan: 'Ulamā' and Sufism, 1899–1918." *Asian and African Studies (Jerusalem)* 7 (1971): 89–119.

Werbner, Pnina, and Helene Basu, eds. *Embodying Charisma: Modernity, Locality, and Performance of Emotion in Sufi Cults*. London: Routledge, 1998.

Westerlund, David, and Eva Evers Rosander, eds. *African Islam and Islam in Africa: Encounters between Sufis and Islamists*. London: Hurst & Co., 1997.

Willis, C. A. "Religious Confraternities of the Sudan." *Sudan Notes and Records* 4:4 (1921): 175–94.

B. Africa: West and South

Batran, A. A. "A Contribution to the Biography of Shaikh Muhammad Ibn 'Abd al-Karim Ibn Muhammad al-Maghili." *Journal of African History* 14:3 (1973): 381–94.

——. "The Kunta, Sidi al-Mukhtar al-Kunti, and the Office of *Shaykh al-Tariqah al-Qadiriyyah*." In *Studies in West African Islamic History*. Ed. R. Willis. London: F. Cass, 1979.

Behrman, Lucy C. *Muslim Brotherhoods and Politics in Senegal*. Cambridge, Mass.: Harvard UP, 1970.

Brenner, Louis. *West African Sufi: Cerno Bokar Saalif Taal*. London: C. Hurst, 1984.

Cruise O'Brien, Donal B. *The Mourides of Senegal*. Oxford: Oxford UP, 1971.

——. "A Versatile Charisma: The Mouride Brotherhood 1967–1975." *Archives européennes de sociologie* 18 (1977): 84–106.

Dumont, Fernand. *La Pensée réligieuse d'Amadou Bamba*. Dakar: Nouvelles Éditions Africaines, 1975.

Evans-Pritchard, E. E. *The Sanusi of Cyrenaica*. Oxford: Oxford UP, 1949.

Faure, A. "Le Tasawwuf et l'école ascétique marocaine des XIe–XIIe–XIIIe siècles de l'ère chrètienne." *Mélanges Louis Massignon*. Damascus, 1957, vol. 2, 119–32.

Hiskett, Mervyn. "The 'Song of the Shehu's Miracles': A Hausa Hagiography from Sokoto." *African Language Studies* 12 (1971): 71–107.

Loimeier, R. *Islamische Erneuerung und politischer Wandel in Nordnigeria: die Auseinandersetzungen zwischen den Sufi-Bruderschaften und ihren Gegnern*. Münster: Lit, 1993.

Martin, B. *Muslim Brotherhoods in 19th century Africa*. Cambridge: Cambridge UP, 1976.

Minna, Mahmud. "Bello and the Tijaniyya: Some Light about the Conversion Controversy." *Kano Studies* NS 2:3 (1982–85): 1–18.

Mohammed, A. R. "The Influence of the Niass Tijaniyya in the Niger-Benue Confluence Area of Nigeria." In *Muslim Identity and Social Change in Sub-Saharan Africa*. Ed. L. Brenner. Bloomington: Indiana UP, 1993.

Norris, H. T. *Sufi Mystics of the Niger Desert*. Oxford: Clarendon, 1990.

O'Fahey, R. Sean, and J. L. Spaulding. "Hashim and the Musabba'at." *BSOAS* 35:2 (1972): 316–33.

Paden, John D. *Ahmadu Bello: The Sardauna of Sokoto*. London: Hodder and Stoughton, 1986. (Bibliographical essay on role of Qadiriyya order 729–60.)

Piga, Adriana. *Dakar e gli ordini sufi: Senegal contemporaneo*. Rome: Bagatto, 2000.

Quadri, Y. A. "Qadiriyyah and Tijaniyyah Relations in Nigeria in the 20th Century." *Orita* 16:1 (1984): 15–30.

———. "A Study of the Izalah: A Contemporary Anti-Sufi Organisation in Nigeria." *Orita* 17:2 (1985): 95–108.

Robinson, David. "Beyond Resistance and Collaboration: Amadu Bamba and the Murids of Senegal." *Journal of Religion in Africa* 21 (1991): 149–71.

Sanneh, Lamin. *The Jakhanke: The History of an Islamic Clerical People of Senegambia*. London: International African Institute, 1979.

———. "Tcherno Aliou, the *wali* of Goumba." In *Rural and Urban Islam in West Africa*. Eds. N. Levtzion and H. J. Fisher. Boulder, Colo.: Lynne Rienner, 1987.

Umar, M. S. "Changing Islamic Identity in Nigeria . . .: From Sufism to Anti-Sufism." In *Muslim Identity and Social Change in Sub-Saharan Africa*. Ed. L. Brenner. Bloomington: Indiana UP, 1993.

Ziadeh, N. A. *Sanusiya: Study of a Revivalist Movement*. Leiden: Brill, 1958, repr. 1983.

C. America and Western Europe

Garfinkel, Perry. "Sufis on Shaker Foundations." *New Age Journal* 2:5 (1976): 41–49.

Geaves, Ron. *The Sufis of Britain*. Cardiff: Cardiff Academic, 2000.

Hermansen, Marcia. "In the Garden of American Sufi Movements." In *New Trends and Movements within the World of Islam*. Ed. P. Clark. London: Luzac, 1998.

———. "Hybrid Identity Formations in Muslim America: The Case of American Sufi Movements." *MW* 90:1–2 (2000): 158–97.

Jironet, K. *The Image of Spiritual Liberty in the Sufi Movement Following Hazrat Inayat Khan*. Louvain: Peeters, 2002.

Koese, Ali. "Conversion through Sufism." In his *Conversion to Islam: A Study of Native British Converts*. London: KPI, 1996.

Köszegi, Michael. "The Sufi Order in the West: Sufism's Encounter with the New Age." In *Islam in North America: A Sourcebook*. Ed. J. G. Melton and M. Köszegi. New York: Garland, 1992.

———. "Sufism in North America: A Bibliography." In *Islam in North America: A Sourcebook*. Ed. J. G. Melton and M. Köszegi. New York: Garland, 1992.

Radtke, Bernd. "Erleuchtung und Afklärung: Islamische Mystik und europäischer Rationalismus." *WI* 34 (1994): 48–66.

Trix, F. "Bektashi Tekke and the Sunni Mosque of Albanian Muslims in America." In *Muslim Communities in North America*. Ed. Y. Haddad and J. Smith. Albany: SUNY, 1994.

Webb, Gisela. "Tradition and Innovation in Contemporary American Islamic Spirituality: The Bawa Muhaiyaddeen Fellowship." In *Muslim Communities in North America*. Ed. Y. Haddad and J. Smith. Albany: SUNY, 1994.

——. "Sufism in America." In *America's Alternative Religions*. Ed. Tim Miller. Albany: SUNY, 1995.

Westerlund, David, ed. *Sufism in Europe and North America*. London: RoutledgeCurzon, 2004.

Zein, Amira el-. "Spiritual Consumption in the United States: The Rumi Phenomenon." *Islam and Christian–Muslim Relations* 11:1 (2000): 71–85.

D. Caucasus, Central Asia, and China

Algar, Hamid. "Shaykh Zaynullah Rasulev: Naqshbandi of the Volga-Urals Region." In *Muslims in Central Asia*. Ed. Jo-Ann Gross. Durham, N.C.: Duke UP, 1992.

Babadzanov, Baxtiyor. "On the History of the Naqshbandiya Mugaddidiya in Central Mawara'annahr in the Late 18th and Early 19th Centuries." In *Muslim Culture in Russia and Central Asia from the 18th to the 20th centuries*. Ed. M. Kemper, A. von Kügelgen, and D. Yermakov. 3 vols. Berlin: Schwarz, 1996, 1998, 2000.

Baldick, J. *Imaginary Muslims: Uwaysi Sufis of Central Asia*. London: I. B. Tauris, 1993.

Bennigsen, Alexandre A. "Muslim Conservative Opposition to the Soviet Regime: The Sufi Brotherhoods in the North Caucasus." In *Soviet Nationality Policies and Practices*. Ed. J. R. Azrael. New York: Praeger, 1978.

——. "The Qadiriyah (Kunta-Hajji) Tariqah in North-East Caucasus: 1850–1987." *IC* 52:2–3 (April–July 1988): 63–78.

Bennigsen, Alexandre A., and C. Lemercier-Quelquejay. "Lieux saints et Sufisme au Caucase." *Turcica* 15 (1983): 179–99.

Bennigsen, Alexandre A., and S. E. Wimbush. *Mystics and Commissars: Sufism in the Soviet Union*. Berkeley: U of California P, 1985.

Bodroglietti, A. J. E. "The Impact of Ahmad Yasavi's Teaching on the Cultural and Political Life of the Turks of Central Asia." In *Türk Dili Arastirmalari Yilligi Belleten 1987*. Ankara: Türk Tarih Hurumu Basimevi, 1992.

——. "Yasavi Ideology in Muhammad Shaybani Khan's Vision of an Uzbek Islamic Empire." In *A. Schimmel Frestschrift*. Ed. M. Subtelny. *JTS* 18 (1994): 41–57.

DeWeese, Devin. "Eclipse of the Kubraviyah in Central Asia." *IrS* 21:1–2 (1988): 45–83.

——. *An "Uwaysi" Sufi in Timurid Mawarannahr*. Bloomington, Ind.: Research Institute for Inner Asian Studies, 1993.

——. "A Neglected Source on Central Asian History: The 17th-Century Yasavi Hagiography *Manaqib al-akhyar*." In *Essays on Uzbek History, Culture, and Language*. Ed. D. Sinor and B. A. Nazarov. Uralic and Altaic Series, vol. 156. Bloomington, Ind.: RIFIAS, 1993.

——. "The Descendants of Sayyid Ata and the Rank of *Naqib* in Central Asia." *JAOS* 115 (1995): 612–34.

——. "The *Tadhkira-Bughra-khan* and the 'Uvaysi' Sufis of Central Asia: Notes in Review of *Imaginary Muslims*." *Central Asiatic Journal* 40 (1996): 87–127.

——. "Yasavi Shaykhs in the Timurid Era." In *Oriente Moderno* NS 15 (1996): 173–88.

——. "The *Meshā'ikh-i Turk* and the *Khojagān*: Rethinking the Links between the Yasavī and Naqshbandī Sufi Traditions." *JIS* 7:2 (1996): 180–207.

Fletcher, Joseph F. "Central Asian Sufism and Ma Ming-hsin's New Teaching." *Proceedings of the Fourth East Asian Atlantic Conference*. Ed. Ch'en Chieh-hsien. Taibei: National Taiwan University, 1975.

——. "The Naqshbandiyya and the *Dhikr-i Arra*." *JTS* 1 (1977): 113–19.

——. "The Taylor-Pickens Letters on the Jahri Branch of the Naqshbandiyya in China." Ed. Jonathan N. Lipman. *Central and Inner Asian Studies* 3 (1989): 1–35.

——. "Naqshbandiyya in Northwest China." In *Studies on Chinese and Islamic Inner Asia*. Ed. B. F. Manz. Aldershot, UK, and Brookfield, Vt.: Variorum, 1995.

Gladney, Dru C. "Muslim Tombs and Ethnic Folklore." *JAS* 46:3 (1987): 495–532.

——. "Sufi Communities and National Networks." In his *Muslim Chinese: Ethnic Nationalism in the People's Republic*. Cambridge: Harvard UP, 1991.

——. "The Hui, Islam, and the State: A Sufi Community in China's Northwest Corner." In *Muslims in Central Asia: Expressions of Identity and Change*. Ed. Jo-Ann Gross. Durham, N.C.: Duke UP, 1992.

Jin Yijiu. "The System of *menhuan* in China: An Influence of Sufism on Chinese Muslims." *Ming Studies* 19 (1984): 34–45.

Kemper, Michael. *Sufis und Gelehrte in Tatarien und Baschkirien, 1789–1889: der islamische Diskurs unter russischer Herrschaft*. Berlin: K. Schwarz, 1998.

Leslie, Donald, and M. Wassel. "Arabic and Persian Sources Used by Liu Chih." *Central Asiatic Journal* 26 (1982): 78–104.

Lipman, Jonathan N. "Sufi Muslim Lineages and Elite Formation in Modern China." In *The Legacy of Islam in China*. Ed. Dru C. Gladney. Cambridge: Harvard UP, 1989.

Ma Tong. "China's Islamic Saintly Lineages and the Muslims of the Northwest." In *The Legacy of Islam in China*. Ed. Dru C. Gladney. Cambridge: Harvard UP, 1989.

McChesney, Robert. *Waqf in Central Asia: Four Hundred Years of the History of a Muslim Shrine, 1480–1889*. Princeton, N.J.: Princeton UP, 1991.

Melikoff, Irene. "Ahmed Yesevi and Turkic Popular Islam." *Utrecht Papers on Central Asia* 2 (1989): 83–94.

Murata, Sachiko. *Chinese Gleams of Sufi Light*. Albany: SUNY, 2000.

Öztürk, Yaşar Nuri. *The Eye of the Heart: An Introduction to Sufism and the Tariqats of Anatolia and the Balkans*. Istanbul: Redhouse, 1988.

Poliakova, E. A. "Some Problems of Sufi Studies." In *Utrecht Papers on Central Asia*. Eds. Mark van Damme and Hendrik Beschoten. Utrecht: U of Utrecht P, 1987.

Radtke, Bernd. "Theologen und Mystiker in Hurasan und Transoxanien." *ZDMG* 136 (1986): 536–69.

Roi, Y. "The Sufi Orders and the Sects." In his *Islam and the Soviet Union*. New York: Columbia UP, 2000.

Subtelny, Maria Eva. "The Cult of Holy Places: Religious Practices among Soviet Muslims." *MEJ* 43 (1989): 593–604.

Toğan, Isenbike. "Islam in a Changing Society: The Khojas of Eastern Turkistan." In *Muslims in Central Asia*. Ed. Jo-Ann Gross. Durham, N.C.: Duke UP, 1992.

Tripper, J. "Islamische Gruppe und Graberkult in Nordwest China." *WI* 7 (1961): 142–71.

Van Bruinessen, Martin. "Haji Bektash, Sultan Sahak, Shah Mina Sahib and Various Avatars of a Running Wall." *Turcica* 21:3 (1991): 55–69.

Yang, Hongxun. "A Preliminary Discussion on the Building Year of Quanzhou Holy Tomb and the Authenticity of Its Legend. In *The Islamic Historic Relics in Quanzhou*. Ed. Committee for Protecting Islamic Historic Relics. Quanzhou: Fujian People's Publishing House, 1985.

Yang, Mohammad Usian Huaizhong. "Sufism among the Muslims of Gansu, Ningxia, and Qinghai." In *Minority Nationalities of China*. Ed. C. Li and D. C. Gladney. Amsterdam: Mouton, forthcoming.

Zarcone, Thierry. "Political Sufism and the Emirate of Kashgaria (End of the 19th C.)." In *Muslim Culture in Russia and Central Asia from the 18th to the Early 20th Centuries*. Ed. Anke von Kügelgen et al. Berlin: K. Schwarz, 1998.

——. "Sufi Movements: Search for Identity and Islamic Resurgence." In *Central Asia: Emerging New Order*. Ed. K. Warikoo. Delhi: Haranand, 1995.

E. Egypt and the Arab Middle East (Arabian Peninsula)

Abu-Rabi‘, Ibrahim. "Al-Azhar Sufism in Modern Egypt." *IQ* 32:4 (1988): 207–34.

Bannerth, E. "La Khalwatiyya en Égypte." *MIDEOC* 8 (1964–6): 1–74.

Biegmann, Nicholaas H. *Egypt: Moulids, Saints, Sufis*. The Hague: Swartz/SDU, 1990.

De Jong, F. "Aspects of Political Involvement of Sufi Orders in Twentieth Century Egypt (1907–1970)—An Explanatory Stocktaking." In *Islam, Nationalism, and Radicalism in Egypt and the Sudan*. Ed. G. R. Warburg and U. M. Kupferschmidt. New York: Praeger Special Studies, 1983.

Garcin, Jean-Claude. "Deux saints populaires du Caire au début du XVIe siècle." *Bulletin d'études orientales* 29 (1977): 131–43.

Garcin, J. C. "Histoire et hagiographie de l'Égypte musulmane . . . [c. 1500]." In *Hommages à la mémoire de Serge Sauneron 1927–1976: Égypte post-pharaonique*. Cairo: Institut Francais d'Archéologie Orientale, 1979. 2:287–316.

Geoffroy, Éric. *Le soufisme en Egypte et en Syrie sous les derniers Mamelouks et les premiers Ottomans*. Damascus: IFEAD, 1995.

Gilsenan, Michael. *Saint and Sufi in Modern Egypt*. Oxford: Clarendon, 1973.

Hoffman, Valerie. *Sufism, Mystics and Saints in Modern Egypt*. Columbia: U of South Carolina P, 1995.

Johansen, Julian. *Sufism and Islamic Reform in Egypt*. Oxford: Oxford UP, 1996.

McGregor, Richard. *Sanctity and Mysticism in Medieval Egypt: The Wafa Sufi Order and the Legacy of Ibn 'Arabī*. Albany: SUNY, 2004.

Melchert, C. "The Adversaries of Aḥmad ibn Ḥanbal." *Arabica* 44 (1997): 242–44.

O'Fahey, R. Sean. "Games, Dancing and Handclapping: A Sufi Controversy in South Arabia." In *The Middle East: Unity and Diversity*. Ed. H. Palva and K. Vikør. Copenhagen: NIAS Books, 1993.

Peters, Rudolph. "The Battered Dervishes of Bab Zuwayla." In *Eighteenth-Century Renewal and Reform in Islam*. Ed. N. Levtzion and John O. Voll. New York: Syracuse UP, 1987.

Reeves, Edward B. *The Hidden Government: Ritual, Clientelism, and Legitimation in Northern Egypt*. Salt Lake City: U of Utah P, 1990. (Mawlid of A. Badawi.)

Voll, John O. "Hadith Scholars and Tariqah: An Ulema Group in the 18th century Haramayn. . . ." *Journal of Asian and African Studies* 15:3–4 (1980): 264–73.

Weismann, Itzchak. *Taste of Modernity: Sufism and Salafiyya in Late Ottoman Damascus*. Leiden: Brill, 2001.

F. Iran and Afghanistan

Amitai-Preiss, Reuven. "Sufis and Shamans: Some Remarks on the Islamization of the Mongols in the Ilkhanate." *Journal of the Economic and Social History of the Orient* 42:1 (1999): 27–46.

Arjomand, S. A. "Religious Extremism (*Ghluww*), Sufism and Sunnism in Safavid Iran (1501–1722)." *JAS* 15:1 (1981): 1–35.

Aubin, Jean. "Un santon quhistānī de l'époque timouride." *REI* 35 (1967): 185–216.

Bayat, M. *Mysticism and Dissent: . . . in Qajar Iran*. Syracuse, N.Y.: Syracuse UP, 1982.

Burke, E. "Emergence of Neo-Sufism in the 18th Century." In *Islam, Politics and Social Movements*. Ed. E. Burke and I. Lapidus. Berkeley: U of California P, 1988.

Chabbi, J. "Remarques sur le dévelopment historique des mouvements ascètiques et mystiques au Hurasan." *SI* 46 (1977): 5–71.

Chabbi, J. "Réflexions sur le soufisme iranien primitif." *Journal Asiatique* 266:1–2 (1978): 37–55.

Elāhī, B. *La voie de la perfection: . . . maître kurde en Iran*. Paris: Albin Michel, 1982.

Glunz, M. "Sufism, Shi'ism, Poetry in Fifteenth-Century Iran: Ghazals of Asiri-Lahiji." In *Timurid Art and Culture*. Ed. L. Golombek and M. Subtelny. Leiden: Brill, 1992.

Landolt, H. "Two Types of Mystical Thought in Muslim Iran: An Essay on Suhrawardi Shayk al-Ishraq and 'Aynulquzat-i Hamadani." *MW* 68:3 (1978): 187–204.

Lewisohn, Leonard. "An Introduction to the History of Modern Persian Sufism, I: The Ni'matullahi Order." *BSOAS* 61:3 (1998): 437–64.

——. "Introduction to the History of Modern Persian Sufism, II: A Socio-Cultural Profile of Sufism from Dhahabi revival to present day." *BSOAS* 62:1 (1999): 36–59.

Lewisohn, Leonard, and David Morgan, eds. *The Heritage of Sufism, I: Classical Persian Sufism from its Origins to Rumi (700–1300)*. 2nd ed. Oxford: Oneworld, 1999.

——. *The Heritage of Sufism, II: The Legacy of Medieval Persian Sufism (1150–1500)*. 2nd ed. Oxford: Oneworld, 1999.

——. *The Heritage of Sufism, III: Late Classical Persianate Sufism (1501–1750)*. 2nd ed. Oxford: Oneworld, 1999.

Massignon, L. "Salman Pak and Spiritual Beginnings of Iranian Sufism." In *Testimonies and Reflections*. Ed. and trans. H. Mason. Notre Dame: Notre Dame UP, 1989.

Madelung, Wilferd. "Sufism and the Khurramiyya." In his *Religious Trends in Early Islamic Iran*. Albany: SUNY, 1988.

Mazzaoui, Michel M. *The Origins of the Safawids: Shi'ism, Sufism, and the Ghulat*. Wiesbaden: Steiner, 1972.

Miller, W. M. "Shi'ah Mysticism: the Sufis of Gunabad." *MW* 13 (1933): 336–53.

Mirjafari, H. "Haydari-Ni'mati Conflicts in Iran." Trans. J. Perry. *IrS* 15 (1979): 135–62.

Nasr, S. H. "Spiritual Movements, Philosophy and Theology in the Safavid Period." *The Cambridge History of Iran*. Vol. 5. Cambridge: Cambridge UP, 1986. 656–97.

Newman, Andrew. "Sufism and Anti-Sufism in Safavid Iran: Authorship of the *Ḥadīqat al-Shī'a* Revisited." *Iran* 37 (1999): 95–108.

Pourjavady, Nasrollah, and P. L. Wilson. *Kings of Love: The History and Poetry of the Ni'matullahi Sufi Order in Iran*. Tehran: Imperial Iranian Academy, 1978.

Roy, Olivier. "Sufism in Afghan Resistance." *Central Asian Survey* 4:2 (1983): 61–79.

Takeshita, M. "Continuity and Change in the Tradition of Shirazi Love Mysticism." *Orient* 23 (1987): 113–31.

Utas, Bo. "Scholars, Saints, and Sufis in Modern Afghanistan." In *The Tragedy of Afghanistan*. Eds. B. Huldt and E. Jansson. London: Croom Helm, 1988.

Van den Bos, Mathijs. *Mystic Regimes: Sufism and the State in Iran from the Late Qajar Era to the Islamic Republic*. Leiden: Brill, 2002.

Wieland, Almut. *Islamische Mystik in Afghanistan*. Stuttgart: F. Steiner, 1998.

G. North Africa and Spain

Addas, Claude. "Andalusi Mysticism and the Rise of Ibn 'Arabi." In *The Legacy of Muslim Spain*. Ed. S. K. Jayyusi. Leiden: Brill, 1994.

Akhmisse, Mustapha. *Rites et secrets des marabouts à Casablanca*. Casablanca: S.E.D.I.M., 1984.

———. *Rites et secrets guérisseurs des marabouts de Casablanca*. Casablanca: Imprimerie Kortoba, 1999.

Bachrouch, Taoufik. *Les élites tunisiennes du pouvoir et de la dévotion: contribution à l'étude des groupes sociaux dominants, 1782–1881*. Tunis: U de Tunis, 1989.

Beck, H. L. *L'image d'Idris II, ses descendants de Fas et la politique sharifienne des sultans marinides, 656–869/1258–1465*. Leiden: Brill, 1989.

Ben Driss, Karim. *Sidi Hamza al-Qâdiri Boudchich: le renouveau du soufisme (au Maroc)*. Beirut/Milan: Albouraq; Archè, 2002.

Bin-'Abd Allah, 'Abd al-'Aziz. *Le soufisme afro-maghrebin aux XIXe et XXe siècles*. [Rabat?]: Captours, 1995.

Brett, M. "Arabs, Berbers and Holy Men in Southern Ifriqiya 650–750 H/1250–1350 AD." *Cahiers de Tunisie* 29:3–4/117–18 (1981): 533–59.

Brown, K. "Discrediting of Sufi Movement in Tunisia." In *Islamic Dilemmas, Reformers, Nationalists and Industrialization*. Ed. E. Gellner. Berlin: de Gruyter, 1985.

Chlyeh, Abdelhafid. *Les Gnaoua du Maroc: itinéraires initiatiques, transe et possession*. Grenoble: Pensée Sauvage, 1999.

———. *L'Univers des Gnaoua*. Grenoble: Pensée Sauvage/Le Fennec, 1999.

Clancy-Smith, Julia. "Saints, Mahdis, and Arms: 19th c. N. Africa." In *Islam, Politics, and Social Movements*. Ed. E. Burke and I. Lapidus. Berkeley: U of California P, 1988.

———. "Between Cairo and the Algerian Kabylia: Rahmaniyya *tariqa*." In *Muslim Travellers*. Ed. D. Eickelman and J. Piscatori. Berkeley: U of California P, 1990.

Colonna, Fanny. "Transformation of a Saintly Lineage in the Northwest Aurès Mountains (Algeria): 19th and 20th Centuries." In *Islam, Politics, and Social Movements*. Eds. E. Burke and I. Lapidus. Berkeley: U of California P, 1988.

Cornell, Vincent. "The Logic of Analogy and the Role of the Sufi Shaykh in Post-Marinid Morocco." *IJMES* 15 (1983): 67–93.

———. "Ribat Tit-n-Fitr and Origins of Moroccan Maraboutism." *IS* 27:1 (1988): 23–36.

———. "Socioeconomic Dimensions of Reconquista and Jihad in Morocco." *IJMES* 22 (1990): 379–418.

———. "Mystical Doctrine and Political Action in Moroccan Sufism: The Role of the Exemplar in the *Tariqa al-Jazuliyya*." *Al-Qantara* 13 (1992): 205–36.

———. "Ḥayy in the Land of Absāl: Ibn Ṭufayl and Sufism in the Western Maghrib during the Muwaḥḥid Era." In *The World of Ibn Ṭufayl: Interdisciplinary Perspectives on Ḥayy ibn Yaqẓān*. Ed. L. I. Conrad. Leiden: Brill, 1996.

———. *Realm of the Saint: Power and Authority in Morocco*. Austin: U of Texas P, 1998.

Crapanzano, V. *Hamadsha: Study in Moroccan Ethnopsychiatry*. Berkeley: U of California P, 1972.

Dermenghem, Émile. *Le Culte des saints dans l'Islam maghrébin*, 8th ed. Paris: Gaillimard, 1954.

Eickelman, Dale F. *Moroccan Islam: . . . Pilgrimage Center*. Austin: U Texas P, 1976.

Ensel, Remco. *Saints and Servants in Southern Morocco*. Leiden: Brill, 1999.

Ferkhat, Halima, and Hamid Trika. "Hagiographie et religion au Maroc mediéval." *Hesperis Tamuda* 24 (1986, Fasc. uniq.): 17–51.

Fierro, Maribel. "The Polemic about the *karamat al-awliya'* and the Development of Sufism in al-Andalus (4th–10th/5th–11th Centuries)." *BSOAS* 55 (1992): 236–49.

García-Arenal, Mercedes. "*Mahdī, Murābiṭ, Sharīf*: l'Avènement de la dynastie sa'dienne." *SI* 71 (1990): 77–114.

———. "Sainteté et pouvoir dynastique au Maroc: la Résistance de Fès au Sa'diens." *Annales: ESC* (1990): 1019–42.

Gellner, Ernest. "Sanctity, Puritanism, Secularisation and Nationalism in North Africa. A Study." *Archives de Sociologie des Religions* 15 (1963): 71–87.
———. *Saints of the Atlas*. Chicago: U of Chicago P, 1969.
Hell, B. *Le tourbillon des génies: au Maroc avec les Gnawa*. Paris: Flammarion, 2002.
O'Fahey, R. S. *Enigmatic Saint: Ahmad Ibn Idris*. Evanston, Ill.: Northwestern UP, 1990.
Jenkins, R. G. "The Evolution of Religious Brothers in North and Northwest Africa, 1523–1900." In *Studies in West African Islamic History* 1 (1979): 40–77.
Joffé, George. "The Zawiya of Wazzan" In *Tribe and State*. Eds. E. G. H. Joffé and C. R. Pennel. Cambridgeshire: Middle East and North Africa Studies P, 1991.
Katz, Jonathan G. "Visionary Experience, Autobiography, and Sainthood in North African Islam." *Princeton Papers in Near Eastern Studies* 1 (1992): 85–118.
Kisaichi, M. "Sufi Saints in 12th Century Maghrib Society: Ribat and Rabita." In *Urbanism and Islam*. 5 vols. Vol. 4. *Proceedings of the International Conference on Urbanism in Islam*. Tokyo: Middle Eastern Culture Center in Japan, 1989.
Lagardère, V. "La Tarīqa et la révolte des Murīdūn en 539H/1144 en Andalus." *Revue de l'Occident Musulman et de la Méditeranée* 35 (1983): 157–70.
Lang, Hubert. *Der Heiligenkult in Marokko: Formen und Funktionen der Wallfahrten*. Passau: Passavia Universitätsverlag, 1992.
Loimeier, Roman. *Säkularer Staat und islamische Gesellschaft: die Beziehungen zwischen Staat, Sufi-Brüderschaften und islamischer Reformbewegung in Senegal im 20. Jahrhundert*. Münster: Lit, 2001.
Mackeen, A. M. M. "The Early History of Sufism in the Maghrib Prior to Al-Shadhili (d. 656/1258)." *JAOS* 91 (1971): 398–408.
———. "The Rise of al-Shadhili (d. 656/1258)." *JAOS* 91 (1971): 477–86.
Mansour, Mohamed, el-. "Sharifian Sufism: The Religious and Social Practice of the Wazzani Zawiya." In *Tribe and State*. Eds. E. G. H. Joffé and C. R. Pennel. Cambridgeshire: Middle East and North Africa Studies P, 1991.
Marin, M. "The Early Development of *zuhd* in al-Andalus." In *Shi'a Islam, Sects and Sufism*. Ed. F. De Jong. Utrecht: Houtsma Stichting, 1992.
Mbacké, Khadim. *Soufisme et confréries religieuses au Sénégal*. Dakar: Presses de l'Impr. Saint-Paul, 1995.
Neveu, E. de. *Les Khouan: Ordres religieux chez les Musulmans d'Algérie*. Paris, 1845.
Nwyia, Paul. "Notes sur quelques fragments inédits de la correspondence d'Ibn al-'Arīf avec Ibn Barrajan." *Hesperis* 43:1 (1956).

Temesani, A. K. "The Jbala Region: Makhzan, Bandits and Saints." In *Tribe and State*. Eds. E. G. H. Joffé and C. R. Pennel. Cambridgeshire: Middle East and North Africa Studies P, 1991.

Topper, Uwe. *Sufis und Heilige im Maghreb*. München: E. Diederichs, 1991.

Touati, Houari. "La Mémoire de la sainteté dans le Maghreb du XVIIe siècle." *SI* 76 (1992): 41–52.

——. *Entre Dieu et les hommes: lettres, saints et sorciers au Maghreb: 17ème siècle*. Paris: Éditions de l'Ecôle des hautes études en sciences sociales, 1994.

H. South Asia

Ahmed, A. "The Sufi and the Sultan in Pre-Mughal Muslim India." *DI* 38 (1962): 142–53.

Andreyev, Sergei. *Sufi Illuminati: The Rawshani Movement in Muslim Mysticism, Society, and Politics*. London: Curzon, 2000.

Ansari, S. F. D. *Sufi Saints and State Power*. Cambridge: Cambridge UP, 1992.

Askari, Syed Hasan. "A 15th Century Shattari Sufi Saint of North Bihar." *Journal of the Bihar and Orissa Research Society* 37 (1951): 66–82.

Bayly, Susan. *Saints, Goddesses and Kings: Muslims and Christians in South Indian Society, 1700–1900*. Cambridge: Cambridge UP, 1989.

Begg, W. D. *The Big Five of India in Sufism*. Ajmer: W. D. Begg, 1972.

Chittick, William C. "Notes on Ibn 'Arabi's Influence in India." *MW* 82 (1992): 218–41.

Currie, P. M. *Shrine and Cult of Mu'in al-Din Chishti of Ajmer*. Delhi: Oxford UP, 1989.

Dahnhardt, Thomas. *Change and Continuity in Indian Sufism: Naqshbandi-Mujaddidi Branch in the Hindu Environment*. New Delhi: D. K. Printworld, 2002.

Digby, Simon. "Abd al-Quddus Gangohi (1456–1537): The Personality and Attitudes of a Medieval Indian Sufi." *Medieval India—A Miscellany* 3 (1975): 1–66.

——. "Sufi Shaykh as a Source of Authority in Medieval India." In *Islam et Société en Asie du Sud*. Ed. M. Gaborieau. Paris: L'École des Hautes Études, 1986. 57–77.

Eaton, Richard M. "The Court and the Dargah in the Seventeenth Century Deccan." *Indian Economic and Social History Review* 10:1 (1973): 50–63.

——. *Sufis of Bijapur (1300–1700)*. Princeton, N.J.: Princeton UP, 1978.

Einzmann, H. *Ziarat und Pir-e-Muridi: Golra Sharif, Nurpur Shahan und Pir Baba*. Stuttgart: Steiner Verlag Wiesbaden, 1988.

Ernst, Carl. W. "From Hagiography to Martyrology: Conflicting Testimonies to a Sufi Martyr of the Delhi Sultanate." *HR* 24 (1985): 308–27.

——. *Eternal Garden: Mysticism . . . South Asian Sufi Center*. Albany: SUNY, 1992.

Ewing, Katherine. "Sufis and Adepts: Islamic and Hindu Sources of Spiritual Power among Punjabi Muslims and Christian Sweepers." In *Anthropology in Pakistan*. Ed. S. Pastner and L. Flam. Ithaca: Cornell UP, 1982.

——. "Politics of Sufism: Redefining the Saints of Pakistan." *JAS* 42:2 (1983): 251–68.

——. "Sufi as Saint, Curer, and Exorcist in Modern Pakistan." In *South Asian Systems of Healing*. Ed. E. Valentine Daniel and Judy F. Pugh. Leiden: Brill, 1984.

——. "Malangs of the Punjab: Intoxication or Adab as the Path to God?" In *Moral Conduct and Authority*. Ed. B. Metcalf. Berkeley: U of California P, 1984.

——. "The Dream of Spiritual Initiation and the Organization of Self Representations among Pakistani Sufis." *American Ethnologist* 17 (1990): 56–75.

——. "Dreams from a Saint: Anthropological Atheism and the Temptation to Believe." *American Anthropologist* 96 (1994): 571–83.

Gaborieau, Marc. "Cult of the Saints among Muslims of Nepal and Northern India." In *Saints and Their Cults*. Ed. S. Wilson. Cambridge: Cambridge UP, 1983.

——. "A Nineteenth-Century Indian 'Wahhabi' Tract against Cult of Muslim Saints." In *Muslim Shrines in India*. Ed. Christian W. Troll. Delhi: Oxford UP, 1989.

——. "The Description of Sufism in the First Manifesto of the Indian Wahhabis." In *The Making of Indo-Persian Culture*. Ed. M. Alam, F. Delvoye, and M. Gaborieau. Delhi: Manohar, 2000.

Habib, M. "Chishti Mystics Records of the Sultanate Period." *Medieval India Quarterly* 1 (1950): 1–42.

Halim, A. "Mystics and Mystical Movements of the Saiyyad-Lodi Period: 1414 A.D. to 1526 A.D." *Journal of the Asiatic Society of Pakistan* 8 (1963): 71–108.

Haq, M. E. *A History of Sufism in Bengal*. Dacca: Asiatic Society of Bangladesh, 1975.

Haq, M. M. "Shah Badi' al-din Madar and his Tariqah in Bengal." *Journal of the Asiatic Society of Pakistan* 12 (1967): 95–110.

Husain, S. Iftikhar. "A Nineteenth Century Saint (Haji Sayyad Shah Waris Ali)." *Journal of the United Provinces Historical Society* 3 (1923–24): 123–45.

Jackson, Paul. "Mystical Dimensions." In his *The Muslims of India*. Bangalore: Theological Publications in India, 1988.

Khan, Ghulam Mustafa. "The Naqshbandi Saints of Sind." *Journal of the Research Society of Pakistan* 13:2 (1976): 19–47.

Kokan, Muhammad Yousuf. "Sufi Presence in South India." In *Islam in India*, vol. 2. Ed. Christian W. Troll. Delhi: Vikas Publishing, 1983.

Kunhali, V. "Sufi Saints of Malabar." In *Bias in Indian Historiography*. Ed. S. Devahuti. Dehli: D.K. 1980.

Lawrence, Bruce B., ed. *The Rose and the Rock: Mystical and Rational Elements in the Intellectual History of South Asian Islam*. Durham, N.C.: Duke UP, 1979.

——. *Notes from a Distant Flute: Sufi Literature in Pre-Mughal India*. Tehran: Imperian Iranian Academy of Philosophy, 1978.

——. "The Chishtiyya of Sultanate India: A Case Study of Biographical Complexities in South Asian Islam." In *Charisma and Sacred Biography*. Ed. M. Williams. Chico, Calif.: Scholars, 1982.

——. "The Early Chishti Aproach to Sama'." In *Sacred Sound: Music in Religious Thought and Practice*. Ed. J. Irwin. Chico, Calif.: Scholars, 1983.

——. "Early Indo-Muslim Saints and Conversion." In *Islam in Asia.* Vol. 1, *South Asia*. Ed. Y. Friedmann. Boulder, Colo.: Westview, 1984.

——. "Biography and the 17th-Century Qadiriyya of North India." In *Islam and Indian Regions*. Ed. A. Dallapiccola and S. Z. Lallemant. Stuttgart: Steiner Verlag, 1993.

Lewis, P. *Pirs, Shrines and Pakistani Islam*. Rawalpindi: Christian Study Centre, 1985.

Liebeskind, Claudia. *Piety on Its Knees: Three Sufi Traditions in South Asia in Modern Times*. Delhi: Oxford UP, 1998.

Mattoo, 'Abdul Majid. "The Nurbakhshis of Kashmir." In *Islam in India*, vol. 2. Ed. Christian W. Troll. Delhi: Vikas, 1983.

Mayer, Adrian C. "Pir and Murshid: An Aspect of Religious Leadership in West Pakistan." *MES* 3 (1967): 160–69.

McDaniel, J. *The Madness of Saints*. Chicago: U of Chicago P, 1989.

Michaud, R. and S. Michaud. *Derviches du Hind et du Sind*. Paris: Phébus, 1991.

Nizami, Khaliq Ahmad. "Sufi Movement in the Deccan." In *History of Medieval Deccan (1295–1724)*. Ed. H. K. Sherwani and P. M. Joshi. Chanchalguda: Government of Andhra Pradesh, 1973–74.

——. "Historical Significance of Malfuz Literature of Medieval India." In *On History and Historians of Medieval India*. Delhi: Munshiram Manoharlal, 1982.

——. "Impact of Sūfī Saints on Indian Society and Culture." *IC* 58 (1984): 31–54.

——. *Life/Times of Shaikh Nasir-u'd-din Chiragh-i Delhi*. Delhi: Idarah-i Delli, 1991.

Pastner, S. L. "Feuding with the Spirit among the Zikri Baluch: The Saint as Champion of the Despised." In *Islam in Tribal Societies, from the Atlas to the Indus.* Ed. A. S. Ahmed and D. M. Hart. London: Routledge & Kegan Paul, 1984.

Rafiqi, Abdul Qaiyum. *Sufism in Kashmir from the Fourteenth to the Sixteenth Century*. Varanasi: Bharatiya Publishing House, 1972.

Rahim, A. "Saints in Bengal: Jalal al-Din Tabrezi and Shah Jalal." *JPHS* 7 (1960): 206–26.

Rashid, A. "Some Chishti Saints of Bengal." *Proceedings of the Pakistan Historical Conference* 2 (1952): 207–16.

Rasool, Ghulam. *Chishti Nizami Sufi Order of Bengal till mid 15th Century and Its Socio-religious Contribution*. Delhi: Idarah-i Adabiyat-i Delli, 1990.

Rizvi, A. A. *A History of Sufism in India*. 2 vols. Delhi: Munshiram Manoharlal, 1983.

Robinson, Francis. "Problems in the History of the Farangi Mahall Family of Learned and Holy Men." In *Oxford University Papers on India*. Ed. N. J. Allen et al. Delhi: Oxford UP, 1987.

Schimmel, Annemarie. *Pain and Grace: A Study of Two Mystical Writers of Eighteenth-Century Muslim India*. Leiden: Brill, 1976.

Siddiqi, Iqtidar Husain. "A New Look at Deccani Sufism." In *Islam in India*, vol. 2. Ed. Christian W. Troll. Delhi: Vikas, 1983.

———. "Resurgence of Chishti Silsila in the Sultanate of Delhi . . . 1451–1526." In *Islam in India*, vol. 2. Ed. Christian W. Troll. Delhi: Vikas, 1983.

Siddiqi, Muhammad Suleman. *The Bahmani Sufis*. Delhi: Idarah-i Adabiyat-i Delli, 1989.

Vahiduddin, Syed. "Shah Waliullah and Shah 'Abd al-'Aziz Critically Reconsidered." In *Islam in India*, vol. 2. Ed. Christian W. Troll. Delhi: Vikas, 1983.

I. Southeast Asia

Archer, R. L. "Muhammadan Mysticism in Sumatra." *JMBRAS* 15:2 (1937).

Attas, Syed Naguib al-. *Some Aspects of Sufism as Understood and Practiced Among the Malays*. Singapore: Malaysian Sociological Research Institute, 1963.

Attas, Syed Naguib al-. *Raniri and the Wujudiyya of Seventeenth Century Acheh*. Singapore: MBRAS/Malaysia Printers, 1966.

Azra, A. "Education, Law, Mysticism." In *Islamic Civilization in the Malay World*. Ed. M. T. Osman. Kuala Lumpur: Dewan Bahasa dan Pustaka, 1997.

Bousfield, John. "Adventures and Misadventures of the New Sufis: Islamic Spiritual Groups in Contemporary Malaysia." *Sojourn* 8:2 (1993): 328–44.

Bowen, John. "Islamic Transformations: From Sufi Doctrine to Ritual Practice in Gayo Culture." In *Indonesian Religions in Transition*. Ed. R. S. Kipp and S. Rodgers. Tucson: U of Arizona P, 1987.

Chambert-Loir, Henri, and Anthony Reid, eds. *The Potent Dead: Ancestors, Saints and Heroes in Contemporary Indonesia*. Honolulu: U of Hawaii P, 2002.

Drewes, G. W. J. "Javanese Poems Dealing with or Attributed to the Saint of Bonan." *Bijdragen Kon. Institut* 124 (1968): 209–40.

Fox, James J. "Ziarah Visits to the Tombs of the Wali, the Founders of Islam on Java." In *Islam in the Indonesian Social Context*. Ed. M. C. Ricklefs. Clayton, Australia: Centre of Southeast Asian Studies, Monash University, 1991.

Johns, Anthony H. "Aspects of Sufi Thought in India and Indonesia in the First Half of the 17th Century." *JMBRAS* 27 (1955): 70–77.

———. "Malay Sufism." *JMBRAS* 30 (1957): 1–108.

———. "Muslim Mystics and Historical Writing." In *Historians of South-East Asia*. Ed. D. G. E. Hall. London: Oxford UP, 1961.

———. "Sufism as a Category in Indonesian Literature and History." *Journal of Southeast Asian History* 2 (1961): 10–23.

———. "Friend in Grace: Ibrahim Kurani and 'Abd al-Ra'uf al-Singkeli." In *Spectrum*. Ed. S. Udin. Jakarta: Dian Rakyat, 1978.

Kraus, Werner, and Moeslim Abdurrahman. *Islamische mystische Brüderschaften im heutigen Indonesien*. Hamburg: Institut für Asienkunde, 1990.

Stange, Paul. "Legitimate Mysticism in Indonesia." *Review of Indonesian and Malaysian Studies* 20:2 (1986): 76–117.

Van Bruinessen, Martin. "The Origins of the Naqshbandi Order in Indonesia." *DI* 67:1 (1990): 150–79.

———. "The Origin and Development of Sufi Orders (Tarkeat) in Southeast Asia." *Studia Islamika: Indonesian Journal for Islamic Studies* 1:1 (1994): 1–23.

———. "Tarekat and *tarekat* Teachers in Madurese Society." In *Across Madura Strait*. Ed. K. van Dijk, H. de Jonge, and E. Touwen-Bouwsma. Leiden: Brill, 1995. 91–117.

Winstedt, R. O. "Some Malay Mystics, Heretical, Orthodox." *JMBRAS* 7 (1923): 312–18.

———. *The Malay Magician Being a Shaman, Shaiva and Sufi*. London: Routledge, 1951.

Woodward, Mark R. *Islam in Java: Normative Piety and Mysticism in the Sultanate of Yogyakarta*. Tucson: U of Arizona P, 1989.

Zulkifli. *Sufism in Java: The Role of the Pesantren in the Maintenance of Sufism in Java*. Leiden: INIS, 2002.

J. Turkey and the Balkans

Abu-Manneh, Butros. "The Naqshbandiyya-Mujaddidiyya in the Ottoman Lands in the Early 19th Century." *WI* 22 (1982–84): 14ff.

———. "Shaykh Ahmad Ziyauddin el-Gumushanevi and Ziya'i Khalid suborder." In *Shi'a Islam, Sects and Sufism*. Ed. F. de Jong. Utrecht: Houtsma Stichting, 1992.

Arnakis, G. G. "Futuwwa traditions in the Ottoman Empire, Akhis, Bektashi Dervishes, and Craftsmen." *JNES* 12:4 (1953): 232–47.

Ayata, Sencer. "Traditional Sufi Orders on the Periphery." In *Islam in Modern Turkey*. Ed. R. Tapper. London: I. B. Tauris, 1991.

Clayer, Nathalie. *Mystique, état et société: les Halvetis dans l'aire balkanique de la fin du Xe siècle à nos jours*. Leiden: Brill, 1994.

De Jong, Frederick. "Notes on Islamic Mystical Brotherhoods in Northeast Bulgaria." *DI* 63:2 (1986): 303–8.

Faroqhi, Suraiya. *Peasants, Dervishes and Traders in the Ottoman Empire*. London: Variorum Reprints, 1986.

Feldman, Walter. "Mysticism, Didacticism and Authority in the Liturgical Poetry of the Halveti Dervishes of Istanbul." *Edebiyat* NS 4 (1993): 243–65.

Filipovic, M. S. "The Bektashi in the District of Strumica." *Man* 54 (1954): 10–13.

Flemming, B. "Glimpses of Turkish Saints: Another Look at Lam'i and Ottoman Biographies." In *A. Schimmel Festschrift*. Ed. M. Subtelny. *JTS* 18 (1994): 59–73.

Garnett, L. *The Dervishes of Turkey*. London: Octagon, 1990.

Kehl-Bodrogi, Krisztina. *Die Kizilbas/Aleviten: Untersuchungen über eine esoterische Glaubensgemeinschaft in Anatolien*. Berlin: K. Schwarz, 1988.

Lipa-Lacarrière, Sylvia, Sabrina Michaud, and Roland Michaud. *Paroles soufies des derviches anatoliens*. Paris: Albin Michel, 1996.

Mardin, Şerif. "The Nakşibendi Order in Turkish History." In *Islam in Modern Turkey*. Ed. Richard Tapper. London: I. B. Tauris, 1991.

Mašulovic-Marsol, L. *Les Rifâ'îs de Skopje*. Istanbul: Éditions Isis, 1992.

Mélikoff, Irène. *Sur les traces du soufisme turc: recherches sur l'Islam populaire en Anatolie*. Istanbul: Éditions Isis, 1992.

———. *Hadji Bektach: un mythe et ses avatars: genèse et évolution du soufisme populaire en Turquie*. Leiden: Brill, 1998.

———. *Au banquet des quarante: exploration au cœur du Bektachisme-Alevisme*. Istanbul: Éditions Isis, 2001.

Norris, H. T. "Twentieth-century Men of Letters among the Albanian Kosovan Sufis." *Sufi* (Winter 1990–1): 22–24.

———. "Sufi Movements and Orders in the Balkans. . . ." In his *Islam in the Balkans*. Columbia, S.C.: U of South Carolina P, 1993.

———. *Popular Sufism of Eastern Europe: Sufi Brotherhoods and the Dialogue with Christianity and 'Heterodoxy.'* New York: RoutledgeCurzon, forthcoming.

Norton, J. D. "Bektashis in Turkey." In *Islam in the Modern World*. Ed. Denis MacEoin and Ahmad al-Shahi. London: Croom Helm, 1983.

Ocak, Ahmet Yaşar. *La révolte de Baba Resul, ou, La formation de l'hétérodoxie musulmane en Anatolie au XIIIe siècle*. Ankara: Impr. de la Société turque d'histoire, 1989.

Öztürk, Yaşar Nuri. *The Eye of the Heart: An Introduction to Sufism and the Major Tariqats of Anatolia and the Balkans*. Istanbul: Redhouse, 1988.

Popovic, Alexandre. "Les orders mystiques musulmans dans les territories yougoslaves au 18e siècle." *Revue d'Histroire Maghrebin* 14:47–48 (1987): 201–8.

———. "Typologie de la survie d'un ordre mystique musulman en Yougoslavie: le cas des Kadiris de Kosovska Mitrovica." *Quaderni di Studi Arabi* 5–6 (1987–88): 667–78.

———. *Les derviches balkaniques hier et aujourd'hui*. Istanbul: Éditions Isis, 1994.

Rexhebi, Baba. *The Mysticism of Islam and Bektashism*, part 1. Naples: Dragotti, 1984.

Ringgren, Helmer. "The Initiation Ceremony of the Bektashis." *Studies of the History of Religions* 10 (1985): 202–8.

Rizaj, Skender. "The Islamization of the Albanians During the XVth and XVIth Centuries." *Studia Albanica* 2 (1985): 127–31.

Šamić, Jasna. "La mystique musulmane des écrivains yougoslaves (Bosnie)." *Quaderni di Studi Arabi* 5–6 (1987–88): 690–98.

Van Bruinessen, Martin. "Religions Life in Diyarbekir: Religions Learning and the Role of the Tariqats." In *Eviliya Chelebi in Diyarbekir*. Ed. M. Van Bruinessen and H. E. Böschoten. Leiden: Brill, 1988.

Wolper, Ethel Sara. "Khidr, Elwan Çelebi, and the Conversion of Sacred Sanctuaries in Anatolia." *MW* 90:3–4 (2000): 309–22.

———. *Cities and Saints: Sufism and the Transformation of Urban Space in Medieval Anatolia*. Philadelphia: U of Pennsylvania P, 2003.

Yalman, Nur. "Islamic Reform and the Mystic Tradition in Eastern Turkey." *Eurpoean Journal of Sociology* 10 (1969).

Zilfi, Madeleine. "The Kadizadelis: Discordant Revivalism in Seventeenth-Century Istanbul." *JNES* 45 (1986): 251–69.

V. SOCIETY, POLITICS, THE ARTS, AND GENDER

A. Sufi Organizations, Institutions, and Ritual

Abrahamov, Binyamin. "Fakhr al-Dān al-Rāzī's Philosophical Justification for Visiting Tombs." *Al-Masāq: Islam and the Medieval Mediterranean* 11 (1999): 109–20.

Abu Manneh, B. "The Naqshbandiyya-Mujaddidiyya in the Ottoman Lands in the Early 19th Century." *WI* N.S., 22 (1982): 1–36.

Abun-Nasr, J. M. *The Tijaniyya*. London: Oxford UP, 1965.

Akhmisse, M. *Rites et secrets des marabouts à Casablanca*. Casablanca: SEDIM, 1984.

Ali, M. "Sufi Saints in Pakistan: Main Mausoleums." *Pakistan Studies* 1:1 (1981): 101–10.

Algar, Hamid. "Notes on Naqshbandi Tariqat in Bosnia." *WI* NS 13:3–4 (1971): 168–203.

———. "The Naqshbandi Order: A Preliminary Survey of Its History and Significance." *SI* 44 (1976): 123–52.

———. "Silent and Vocal *dhikr* in the Nawshbandī Order." *Akten des VII Kongresses für Arabistik/Islamwissenschaft*. Göttingen: Vandenhoeck & Ruprecht, 1976.

———. "Der Nakşibendi-Orden in der republikanischen Türkei." In *Islam und Politik in der Türkei*. Eds. J. Blaschke and M. van Bruinesen. Berlin: Edition Parabolis, 1984.

Ali-Shah, Omar. *Un apprentissage du soufisme: Les règles ou secrets de l'ordre Naqshbandi*. Paris: G. Trédaniel, 2001.

Alvi, S. "The *Mujaddid* and *Tajdīd* Traditions in the Indian Subcontinent: An Historical Overview." In *A. Schimmel Festschrift*. Ed. M. Subtelny. *JTS* 18 (1994): 1–15.

Babayan, Kathryn. "Sufis, Dervishes and Mullahs: Spiritual and Temporal Dominion in 17th c. Iran." In *Safavid Persia*. Ed. C. Melville. London: I. B. Tauris, 1996.

Bashir, Shahzad. *Messianic Hopes and Mystical Visions: The Nūrbakhshīya between Medieval and Modern Islam*. Columbia: U of South Carolina P, 2003.

Batran, Aziz A. *The Qadiryya Brotherhood in West Africa and the Western Sahara: . . . al-Mukhtar al-Kunti*. Rabat: Publications de l'Institut des études africaines, 2001.

Bernard, J., and B. Duboy. *Mehdi: l'initiation d"un soufi*. Monaco: Éd. du Rocher, 1994.

Bilgrami, R. "The Ajmer Wakf under the Mughals." *IC* 52 (1978): 97–103.

Bingsbergen, W. M. J. van. "The Cult of Saints in North-Western Tunisia." In *Islamic Dilemmas*. Ed. E. Gellner. Berlin: Mouton, 1985.

Birge, J. *Bektashi Order of Dervishes*. Hartford, Conn.: Hartford Seminary, 1937.

Bodrogligeti, A. J. "Yasavi Ideology in Muhammad Shaybanī Khān's Vision of Uzbek Empire." In *A. Schimmel Festschrift*. Ed. M. Subtelny. *JTS* 18 (1994): 41–57.

Böwering, G. "Adab Literature of Classical Sufism: Ansari's Code of Conduct." In *Moral Conduct and Authority*. Ed. Barbara Metcalf. Berkeley: U of California P, 1984.

Boubrik, Rahal. *Saints et société en Islam: la confrérie ouest saharienne Fâdiliyya*. Paris: CNRS Éditions, 1999.

Buehler, Arthur F. *Sufi Heirs of the Prophet: The Indian Naqshbandiyya and the Rise of the Mediating Sufi Shaykh*. Columbia: U of South Carolina P, 1998.

Brunel, René. *Le monachisme errant dans l'islam: Sidi Heddi et les Heddawa*. Paris: Maisonneuve et Larose, 2001.

Castel, G., and 'Abdel Latif el-Waquil. "Mausolée du Cheikh Hamūda à Balāt (oasis de Dakhla)." *AI* 20 (1984): 183–96.

Chih, R. *Le soufisme au quotidien: confréries d'Egypte. . . .* Arles: Sindbad, 2000.

Chlyeh, Abdelhafid. *La transe*. Rabat: Marsam, 2000.

Clayer, Nathalie, and Alexandre Popovic. *Melâmis-Bayrâmis: études sur trois mouvements mystiques musulmans*. Istanbul: Éditions Isis, 1998.

Dale, Stephen F., and Alam Payind. "The Ahrari Waqf in Kabul in the Year 1546 and the Mughul Naqshbandiyyah." *JAOS* 119:2 (1999): 218–32.

Danziger, Raphael. *Abd al-Qadir and the Algerians*. New York: Homes & Meier, 1977.

De Jong, F. "Turuq and Turuq-Opposition in 20th Century Egypt." In *Proceedings of the VIth Congress of Arabic and Islamic Studies*. Leiden: Brill, 1975.

———. *Turuq and Turuq-linked Institutions in 19th C. Egypt*. Leiden: Brill, 1978.

———. "*Takiya* of 'Abd Allah al-Maghawiri in Cairo." *Turcica* 13 (1981): 242–60.

———. "Mustafa Kamal al-Bakri (1688–1749): Revival and Reform in the Khalwatiyya Tradition." In *Eighteenth Century Renewal and Reform in Islam*. Ed. Nehemiah Levtzion and John O. Voll. Syracuse, N.Y.: Syracuse UP, 1987.

DeWeese, Devin. "The *Masha'ikh-i Turk* and the *Khojagan*: Rethinking the Links between the Yasawi and Naqshbandi Sufi Traditions." *JIS* 7 (1996): 180–207.

Digby, Simon. "Qalandars and Related Groups: Social Deviance in the Religious Life of the Delhi Sultanate of the 13th and 14th Centuries." In *Islam in South Asia*, vol. 1. Ed. Y. Friedmann. Jerusalem: Magnes/Hebrew U, 1984.

———. "*Tabarrukat* and Succession among the Great Chishti Shaykhs." In *Delhi Through the Ages*. Ed. R. E. Frykenberg. Delhi: Oxford UP, 1986.

———. "The Sufi Shaykh and the Sultan: A Conflict of Claims to Authority in Medieval India." *Iran* 28 (1990): 71–81.

———. *Sufis and Soldiers in Aurangzeb's Deccan: Malfuzat-i Naqshbandiyya*. Oxford: Oxford UP, 2001.

Drague, C. *Esquisse d'histoire religieuse du Maroc: confréries et zaouias*. Paris: J. Vrin, 1951.

Eaton, Richard M. "Court of Man, Court of God: Local Perceptions of the Shrine of Bābā Farīd, Pakpattan, Punjab." *Contributions to Asian Studies* 17 (1982): 44–61.

——. "Political and Religious Authority of the Shrine of Baba Farid in Pakpatan, Punjab." In *Moral Conduct and Authority*. Ed. B. Metcalf. Berkeley: U of California P, 1984.

Ernst, Carl W., and Bruce B. Lawrence. *Sufi Martyrs of Love: The Chishti Order in South Asia and Beyond*. New York: Palgrave, 2003.

Farah, C. E. "Rules Governing Shaykh-Murshid's Conduct." *Numen* 21:2 (1974): 81–96.

Faroqhi, Suraiya. "Vakif Administration in Sixteenth Century Konya." *Journal of the Economic and Social History of the Orient* 17 (1979): 145–72.

——. *Der Bektaschi-Orden in Anatolien*. Vienna: Verlag des Instituts für Orientalistik der Universität Wien, 1981.

——. "Seyyed Gazi Revisited: The Foundation as Seen through Sixteenth Century Documents." *Turcica* 13 (1981): 90–122.

Fernandes, Leonor. "The Zawiya in Cairo." *AI* 18 (1982): 116–121.

——. "Aspects of the *Zāwiya* in Egypt/Eve of Ottoman Conquest." *AI* 19 (1983): 9–17.

——. "The Foundation of Baybars al-Jashankir: Its Waqf, History and Architecture." *Muqarnas* 4 (1987): 21–42.

——. *The Evolution of a Sufi Institution in Mamluk Egypt: The Khanqah*. Berlin: Klaus Swarz Verlag, 1988.

Gaborieau, Marc, A. Popovic, and T. Zarcone, eds. *Naqshbandis: Historical Development and Present Situation of a Muslim Mystical Order*. Istanbul: Éditions Isis, 1990.

Gilmartin, David. "Shrines, Succession, and Sources of Moral Authority." In *Moral Authority and Conduct*. Ed. B. Metcalf. Berkeley: U of California P, 1984.

Gramlich, R. *Die schiitischen Derwischorden Persiens*. Wiesbaden: Steiner, 1965–81.

Gross, Jo-Ann. "The Economic Status of a Timurid Sufi Shaykh: A Matter of Conflict or Perception?" *IrS* 21 (1988): 84–105.

Habibis, D. "Change and Continuity: A Sufi Order in Contemporary Lebanon." *Social Analysis* 31 (1992): 44–78.

Hamada, Masami. "Islamic Saints and their Mausolea." *Acta Asiatica (Supplement): Bulletin of the Institute of Eastern Culture (Tokyo)* 34 (1978): 79–105.

Haq, M. M. "The Shuttari Order of Sufism in India and Its Exponents in Bengal and Bihar." *Journal of the Asiatic Society of Pakistan* 16 (1971): 167–75.

Holbrook, V. R. "Ibn 'Arabi and Ottoman Dervish Traditions: The Melāmī Supra-Order." *Journal of Muhyiddin Ibn 'Arabi Soc.* 9 (1991): 18–35; 12 (1992): 15–33.

Homerin, Th. Emil. "The Domed Shrine of Ibn al-Farid." *AI* 25–26 (1989–90): 125–30.

——. "Saving Muslim Souls: The Khanqah and the Sufi Duty in Mamluk Lands." *Mamluk Studies Review* 3 (1999): 59–83.

Hourani, A. "Shaykh Khalid and the Naqshbandi Order." In *Islamic Philosophy/Classical Tradition*. Ed. S. Stern, A. Hourani, and V. Brown. Oxford: Cassirer, 1972.

Huart, C. L. "Les Derviches Bektachis." *Revue du Monde Musulman* 9 (1909): 235–46.

Huda, Qamar-ul. *Striving for Divine Union: Spiritual Exercises for Suhrawardī sūfīs*. New York: RoutledgeCurzon, 2003.

Humoudi, Salah el-Tigani. "The Arab and Islamic Origins of the Tomb and Sacred Enclave in the Sudan." *Sudan Notes and Records* 58 (1977): 107–16.

Islam, Riazul. "Ideas on *Kasb* in South Asian Sufism." *Indian Historical Review* 17 (1991): 90–121.

——. "A Comparative Study of the Treatment of *Futuh* in the Principal Chishti Records." *JPHS* 40 (1992): 91–96.

——. "Sufism and Economy." *Indian Historical Review* 19 (1992): 31–58.

Jackson, Paul. "A History of the Chishti Shaykhs." In *Islam in India*, vol. 2. Ed. Christian W. Troll. Delhi: Vikas, 1983.

Jafri, S., and H. Zaheer. "Landed Properties of a Sufi Establishment." *Proceedings from the Indian History Congress* 1986.

Jarring, Gunnar. "Dervish and Qalandar: Texts from Kashgar Edited and Translated with Notes and Glossary." *Scripta Minora Regiae Societatis Humaniorum Literarum Lundensis* (1985–86): 2, 18–27.

Jeffrey, Patricia. "Creating a Scene: The Disruption of Ceremonial in a Sufi Shrine." In *Ritual and Religion among Muslims of the Sufi Sub-continent*. Ed. I. Ahmad. Lahore: Vanguard, 1985.

Karamustafa, Ahmet T. "*Kalenders, Abdals, Hayderis*: The Formation of the *Bektashiye* in the Sixteenth Century." In *Suleyman the Second and His Time*. Ed. H. Inalcik and C. Kafadar. Istanbul: Isis, 1993.

——. *God's Unruly Friends: Dervish Groups in the Islamic Later Middle Period, 1200–1500*. Salt Lake City: U of Utah P, 1994.

Kissling, H. J. "Aus der Geschichte des Chalvetijje-Ordens." *ZDMG* (1953): 233–89.

Kreiser, K. "Medresen und Derwischkonvente in Istanbul." In *Economies et sociétés dans l'Empire Ottoman*. Ed. J.-L. Bacque-Grammont and P. Dumont. Paris: Fayard, 1983.

——. "Dervischsheiche als Publizisten—Ein Blick in die Türkische religiöse Presse zwischen 1890 und 1925." *ZDMG* Suppl. 6 (1985): 333–41.

——. *Istanbul und das Osmanische Reich: Städte, Bauten, Inschriften Derwische und ihre Konvente*. Istanbul: Isis, 1995.

Kurin, R. "Structure of Blessedness at Muslim Shrine/Pakistan." *MES* 19 (1983): 312–25.

Landau-Tasseron, Ella. "The Cyclical Reform: A Study of the *Mujaddidi* Tradition." *SI* 70 (1989): 79–117.

Lawrence, Bruce B. "The Early Chishti Approach to Sama." In *Islamic Society and Culture*. Ed. M. Israel and N. K. Wagle. Delhi: Manohar, 1983.

Lehmann, Fritz. "The Sufi Khanqahs in Modern Bihar." In *Islam in South Asia*, vol. 1, *South Asia*. Ed. Y. Friedmann. Jerusalem: Magnes/Hebrew U, 1984.

Lewis, P. J. "Pirs, Shrines, and Pakistani Islam." *Al-Mushir* 26 (1984): 1–22.

———. "The Shrine Cult in Historical Perspective." *Al-Mushir* 26 (1984): 54–74.

Little, Donald. "Nature of Khanqahs, Ribats, Zawiyas under Mamluke." *Islamic Studies . . . Charles J. Adams*. Ed. W. Hallaq and D. Little. Leiden: Brill, 1991.

Mala, S. Babs. "The Sufi Convent and Its Social Significance in the Medieval Period of Islam." *IC* 51 (1977): 31–52.

Malamud, Margaret. "Sufi Organizations and Structures of Authority in Medieval Nishapur." *IJMES* 26 (1994): 427–442.

Marcus, M. A. "'The Saint Has Been Stolen': Sanctity and Social Change in a Tribe of Eastern Morocco." *American Ethnologist* 12 (1985): 455–67.

Martin, Bradford G. "Notes sur l'origine de la *tariqa* des Tigāniyya, et sur les débuts d'al-Hagg 'Umar." *REI* 37:2 (1969): 267–90.

———. *Muslim Brotherhoods in 19th Century Africa*. Cambridge: Cambridge UP, 1976.

———. "A Short History of the Khalwati Order of Dervishes." In *Scholars, Saints and Sufis*. Ed. N. Keddie. Berkeley: U of California P, 1972.

Marx, E. "Tribal Pilgrimages to Saints' Tombs in South Sinai." In *Islamic Dilemmas.* Ed. Ernest Gellner. Berlin: Mouton, 1985.

Mazzaoui, Michel M. *The Origins of the Safawids: Shi'ism, Sufism and the Ghulat*. Wiesbaden: Franz Steiner Verlag, 1972.

Moini, S. L. H. "Rituals and Customary Practices at the Dargah of Ajmer." In *Muslim Shrines in India*. Ed. Christian Troll. Delhi: Oxford UP, 1989.

Morton, Alexander H. "The Ardebil Shrine in the Reign of Tahmasp I." *Iran*, part 1–12 (1974): 31–64; part 2–13 (1975): 39–58.

Mostafa, Salih. *Kloster und Mausoleum des Faraj ibn Barquq in Kairo*. Cairo: Abhandlungen des Deutschen Archäologishchen Institut, 1968.

Mostafa, Salih, and Felicitas Jaritz. *Madrasa, Hanqah und Mausoleum des Barquq in Kairo*. Glückstadt: J. J. Augustin, 1982.

Nabi Khan, A. "Tomb of Baba Farid Ganj-i-Shakar/Pakpatan." *JPHS* 27 (1979): 140–53.

Nizami, Khaliq Ahmad. "Early Indo-Muslim Mystics and Their Attitude towards the State." *IC* 22 (1948): 387–98; 23 (1949): 13–21, 162–70, 312–24; 24 (1950): 60–71.

———. "The Shattari Saints and Their Attitude towards the State." *Medieval India Quarterly* 3 (1950): 56–70.

———. "Some Aspects of Khanqah Life in Medieval India." *SI* 8 (1957): 51–70.

———. "The Suhrawardi Silsilah and Its Influence on Medieval Indian Politics." *Medieval Indian Quarterly* 3 (1957): 109–49.

———. "Naqshbandi Influence on Mughal Rulers and Politics." *IC* 39 (1965): 41–52.

———. "Socio-Religious Movements in Indian Islam (1763–1898). In *India and Contemporary Islam*. Simla: Indian Institute for Advanced Study, 1971.

Norris, H. T. "À la recherche de Sīdī Mahmūd al-Baghdādī: Silsila of the Mahmūdiyya Tarīqa in the 'Qudwa.'" *Islam et Sociétés au Sud du Sahara* 3 (1989): 128–58.

Nurbakhsh, Javad. "The Rules and Manners of the Khanaqah." In his *In the Tavern of Ruin*. New York: Khaniqahi Nimatullahi, 1975.

———. *Masters of the Path: A History of the Masters of the Nimatullahi Sufi Order*. New York: Khaniqahi Nimatullahi, 1980.

Ocak, Ahmet Yaşar. "Quelques remarques sur le role des derviches kalenderis dans les mouvements populaires et les activités anarchiques aux XVe et XVIe siècles dans l'empire Ottoman." *Osmanlī Araşīrmalarī* 3 (1982): 69–80.

Pâques, Viviana. *La religion des esclaves: recherches sur la confrérie marocaine des Gnawa*. Bergamo, Italy: Moretti & Vitali, 1991.

Piga, Adriana. *Dakar et les ordres soufis: processus socioculturels et développement urbain au Sénégal contemporain*. Paris: Harmattan, 2002.

Pinto, D. *Piri-Muridi Relationship: Nizamuddin Dargah*. Delhi: Manohar, 1995.

Pfleiderer, B. "Mira Datar Dargah: The Psychiatry of a Muslim Shrine." In *Ritual and Religion among Muslims in India.* Ed. I. Ahmad. Delhi: Manohar, 1981. 193–233.

Popovic, Alexandre. *Un ordre de derviches en terre d'Europe: la Rifâ'iyya*. Lausanne: Age d'homme, 1993.

Popovic, Alexandre, and Gilles Veinstein, eds. *Les Ordres mystiques dans l'Islam: cheminements et situation actuelle*. Paris: Éd. de l'Ecôle des hautes études, 1986.

———. *Bektachiyya*. Istanbul: Isis, 1995.

Salim, M. "The Attitude of Chishti Saints towards Political Power." *Proceedings of the Pakistan Historical Conference* 2 (1952): 225–29.

Savadogo, Boukary. *Confrérie et pouvoirs: la Tijaniyya Hamawiyya en Afrique occidentale, 1909–1965*. Doctoral dissertation. Provence: U of Provence. 1998.

Sirriya, Elizabeth. "*Ziyārāt* of Syria in a *Riḥla* of 'Abd al-Ghanī al-Nābulusī (1050/1641–1143–1731)." *JRAS* (1979): 109–22.

Subhan, John A. *Sufism: Its Saints and Shrines.* New York: S. Weiser, 1970.
Subtelny, Maria Eva. "The Cult of Holy Places: Religious Practices among Soviet Muslims." *MEJ* 43:4 (1989): 593–604.
Taysi, M. S., Efendi Zâkir Sükrî, and Klaus Kreiser. *Die Istanbuler Derwisch-Konvente und ihre Scheiche (Mecmu'a-i tekaya).* Freiburg im Breisgau: Schwarz, 1980.
Trimingham, J. Spencer. *The Sufi Orders in Islam.* New York: Oxford UP, 1971.
Troll, Christian, ed. *Muslim Shrines in India.* Delhi: Oxford UP, 1989.
Utas, Bo. "Notes on Afghan Sufi Orders and Khanaqahs." *Afghanistan Journal* 7:2 (1980): 60–67.
Vadet, Jean-Claude. *La Futuwwa: morale professionnelle ou morale mystique.* Paris: Revue des Études Islamiques, 1985.
Van Bruinessen, Martin. "The Origins and Development of the Naqshbandi Order in Indonesia." *DI* 57 (1990): 150–79.
Vikør, Knut S. *Sources for Sanusi Studies.* Bergen, Norway: U of Bergen, 1996.
Voll, John O. "Hadith Scholars and *tariqahs*." *Journal of Asian and African Studies* 15:3–4 (1980): 264–73.
———. "Traditional and Conservative Orders." *Annals of the American Academy of Political and Social Science* 524 (1992): 66–78.
Weigert, Gideon. "The Khalwatiya in Egypt in the Eighteenth Century: A Nucleus for Islamic Revival." *Bulletin of the Israel Academic Centre, Cairo* 19 (1994).
Weingrod, Alex. "Saints and Shrines, Politics and Culture." In *Muslim Travellers.* Ed. Dale Eickelman and James Piscatori. Berkeley: U of California P, 1990.
Welte, Frank Maurice, and Jordi Aguadé. *Die Lieder der Gnawa aus Meknes.* Marburg: Diagonal-Verlag, 1996.
Werbner, Pnina. "Murids of the Saints: Occupational Guilds and Redemptive Sociality." In *Muslim Traditions and Modern Techniques of Power*, vol. 3. Ed. A. Salvatore. New Brunswick: Lit Verlag & Transaction, 2001.
Zarcone, Thierry. *Secret et sociétés secrètes en islam: Turquie, Iran et Asie centrale, XIXe–XXe siècles.* Milan: Archè, 2002.
Zarcone, Thierry, Ekrem Isin, and Arthur Buehler, eds. *The Qadiriya Order.* Vol. 1–2 of the annual *Journal of the History of Sufism.* Paris: Maisonneuve, 2000.

B. Sufism and Literature

Andrzejewski, B. W. "Allusive Diction in Galla Hymns in Praise of Sheikh Hussein of Bale." *African Language Studies* 13 (1972): 1–31.
Asani, Ali S. "Amir Khusrau's Poetry in Indic Languages." *IC* (1988): 50–62.

——. "Sufi Poetry in the Folk Tradition of Indo-Pakistan." *Religion and Literature* 20:1 (1988): 81–96.

Askari, S. H. "Malfuzats and Maktubats of Hazrat Sharfuddin Yahya Maneri." *Journal of the Bihar Research Society* 34 (1948).

Banuazizi, Ali. *Iranian Nationality and the Persian Language 900–1900: The Roles of Court, Religion and Sufism in Persian Prose Writing*. Washington, D.C.: Mage, 1992.

Bausani, A. "About a Curious Mystical Language." *East and West* 4:4 (1958): 234–48.

Boullata, Issa. "Verbal Arabesque and Mystical Union: A Study of Ibn al-Farid's *Al-Ta'iyya Al-Kubra*." *Arab Studies Quarterly* 3 (1981): 152–69.

De Bruijn, J. T. P. *Of Piety and Poetry: The Interaction of Religion and Literature in the Life and Works of Hakim Sana'i of Ghazna*. Leiden: Brill, 1983.

——. *Persian Sufi Poetry: An Introduction to the Mystical Use of Classical Persian Poems*. Surrey: Curzon, 1997.

Deol, J. S. "Acceptable Poetry: Muqbil's Mystical *Qissah Hir Ranjha*." *International Journal of Punjab Studies* 3:2 (1996): 181–212.

Eaton, Richard M. "Sufi Folk Literature and the Expansion of Indian Islam." *HR* 14:2 (1974): 117–27.

Farah, Caesar E. "The Prose Literature of Sufism." In *Religion, Learning and Science in the 'Abbasid Period*. Ed. M. L. J. Young, J. D. Latham, and R. B. Serjeant. Cambridge: Cambridge UP, 1990.

Farzan, Massud. "Whitman and Sufism: Towards a 'Persian Lesson.'" *American Literature* 4:4 (1976): 572–82.

Glünz, M. "Sufism, Shi'ism, and Poetry in Fifteenth-Century Iran." In *Timurid Art and Culture*. Ed. L. Golombek and M. Subtelny. Leiden: Brill, 1992.

Hafsi, Ibrahim. "Recherches sur le genre *Ṭabaqāt* dans la littérature arabe." *Arabica* 23 (1976): 227–65; 24 (1977): 1–41.

Hamori, Andras. "Ascetic Poetry." In *Cambridge History of Arabic Literature: 'Abbasid Belles Lettres*. Ed. J. Ashtiany et al. Cambridge: Cambrdge UP, 1990.

Holbrook, Victoria. *The Unreadable Shores of Love*. Austin: U of Texas P, 1994.

Hyder, Syed Akbar. "Revisiting Wine and the Goblet in South Asian Martyrdom and Mysticism." *Sufi Illuminations* 3:1 (2002): 14–33.

Islam, R. "Survey in Outline of the Mystic Literature of the Sultanate Period." *JPHS* 3 (1955): 200–208.

Kamada, S. "Nabulusi's Commentary/Ibn al-Farid's *Khamriyya*."*Orient* 18 (1982): 19–40.

Keshavarz, Fatemeh. *Reading Mystical Lyric: The Case of Jalal ad-Din Rumi*. Columbia: U of South Carolina P, 1997.

King, James Roy. "Narrative Conjunction and Disjunction in Rumi's *Mathnawi*." *Journal of Narrative Technique* 19:3 (1989): 276–85.

Knappert, Jan. *Swahili Islamic Poetry*. Leiden: Brill, 1971.

Krishna, L. Rama. *Panjabi Sufi Poets*. Calcutta: Oxford UP, 1938.

Lawrence, Bruce B. "Thematic Antecedents for the Urdu Ghazal in the Sufi Poetry of the Sultanate Period." In *Studies of the Urdu Ghazal and Prose Fiction*. Ed. M. U. Memon. Madison: U of Wisconsin P, 1979.

Lewisohn, Leonard. "Shabestari's Garden of Mysteries: The Aesthetics and Hermeneutics of Sufi Poetry." *Temenos* 10 (1989): 177–207.

——. *Beyond Faith and Infidelity: The Sufi Poetry and Teachings of Mahmud Shabistari*. Surrey: Curzon, 1995.

Lings, Martin. "Mystical Poetry." In *'Abbasid Belles-Lettres*. Ed. Julia Ashtiany et al. Cambridge: Cambridge UP, 1990.

Lubis, Hj. Muhammad Bukhari. *Qaṣīdahs in Honor of the Prophet*. Bangi, Selangor, Malaysia: Penerbit Universiti Kebangsaan Malaysia, 1983.

Matringe, D. "Krsnaite and Nath Elements in the Poetry of the Eighteenth-Century Panjabi Sufi Bullhe Shah." In *Devotional Literature in South Asia*. Ed. R. S. McGregor. Cambridge: Cambridge UP, 1992.

Meisami, Julie S. "Allegorical Gardens in the Persian Poetic Tradition: Nezami, Rumi, Hafez." *IJMES* 17:2 (1985): 229–60.

Norris, H. T. "Albanian Sufi Poets of the Nineteenth and Twentieth Centuries." In his *Islam in the Balkans*. Columbia: U of South Carolina P, 1993.

Pandey, S. M. "Social Relevance of Mystic Poetry—Contribution of Hindi Sufi Poet Maulana Daud." *Journal of Medieval Indian Literature* 1:1 (1977): 28–43.

Rasheed, G. D. "Development of na'tia Poetry/Persian Literature." *IC* 39 (1965): 53–69.

Rineheart, Robin. "Interpretations of the Poetry of Bullhe Shah." *International Journal of Punjab Studies* 3:1 (1996): 44–63.

Sadler, Albert W. "Visit to a Chishti *Qawwālī*." *MW* 53 (1963): 287–92.

Scattolin, Giuseppe. "Al-Farghani's Commentary on Ibn al-Farid's Mystical Poem *Al-Ta'iyyat Al-Kubra*." *MIDEO* 21 (1993): 331–83.

Schimmel, Annemarie. "The Influence of Sufism on Indo-Muslim Poetry." In *Anagogic Qualities of Literature*. Ed. J. P. Strelka. Philadelphia: U of Pennsylvania P, 1971.

——. *As Through a Veil: Mystical Poetry in Islam*. New York: Columbia UP, 1982.

——. *A Two-Colored Brocade*. Chapel Hill: U of North Carolina P, 1992.

Shackle, Christopher. "Styles and Themes in the Siraiki Mystical Poetry of Sind." In *Sind through the Centuries*. Ed. H. Khuhro. Karachi: Oxford UP, 1981.

Singh, Attar. "Sheikh Farid and the Punjabi Poetic Tradition." In *Perspectives on Sheikh Farid*. Ed. G. S. Talib. Patiala: Baba Farid Memorial Society, 1975.
Smith, G. M., trans. *The Poetry of Yunus Emre*. Berkeley: U of California P, 1993.
Sperl, Stefan, and Christopher Shackle, eds. *Qasida Poetry in Islamic Asia and Africa*. 2 vols. Leiden: Brill, 1996.
Ünlü, Hülya. *Das Ghasel des islamischen Orients in der deutschen Dichtung*. New York: P. Lang, 1991.
Usborne, Charles F. *Bullah Shah: Sufi, mystic, and poet of the Punjab*. Lahore: Saadi Punjabi Academy, 1976.
White, C. S. J. "Sufism in Medieval Hindi Literature." *HR* 5:1 (1966): 114–32.
Wilson, Peter Lamborn, and Nasrollah Pourjavady. *The Drunken Universe: An Anthology of Persian Sufi Poetry*. Grand Rapids, Mich.: Phanes, 1987.

C. Sufism, Architecture and the Visual Arts, and Music

Ardalan, Nader, and Laleh Bakhtiar. *The Sense of Unity: The Sufi Tradition in Persian Architecture*. Chicago: U of Chicago P, 1973.
Asani, Ali. "Music and Dance in the Work of Jalal al-Din Rumi." *IC* 60:2 (1986): 41–55.
Baer, Eva. "Aspects of Sufi Influence on Iranian Art." *AIr* 12 (1977): 1–12.
Behrens-Abouseif, Doris, and Leonor Fernandes. "Sufi Architecture in the Early Ottoman Period." *AI* 20 (1984): 103–14.
Behrens-Abouseif, Doris. "Change in Function and Form of Mamluk Religious Institutions." *AI* 21 (1985): 73–93.
Blair, Sheila S. "Sufi Saints and Shrine Architecture in the Early Fourteenth Century." *Muqarnas* 7 (1990): 35–49.
Borrás Gualis, Gonzalo M. *Música en la Aljafería: homenaje a Avempace: Ensemble Ibn 'Arabi, música Sufí*. Zaragoza: Aragón-LCD Prames, 1999.
Bourgeois, J. L. "Afghan Muslim Shrines." *Architectural Review* 168 (1980): 367–69.
Burckhardt, Titus. *Art of Islam: Language and Meaning*. London: World of Islam, 1976.
De Jong, Frederick. "The Iconography of Bektashiism." *Manuscripts of the Middle East,* vol. 4. Leiden: Brill, 1989.
During, Jean. *Musique et extase*. Paris: A. Michel, 1988.
——. *Musique et mystique en Iran*. Paris: Peeters-IFRI, 1989.
Erguner, Kudsi. *La fontaine de la séparation: voyages d'un musicien soufi*. L'Isle-sur-la-Sorgue: Bois d'Orion, 2000.
Ettinghausen, Richard. "Persian Ascension Miniatures of the Fourteenth Century." In *L'Iran nel medioevo*. Rome: Accademia dei Lincei, 1957.

——. "Al-Ghazali on Beauty." In *Art and Thought*. Ed. K. B. Iyer. London: Garland, 1974.

Frembgen, J. W. "Saints in Modern Devotional Poster-Portraits." *Anthropology and Aesthetics RES* 34 (1988): 184–91.

Gaeffke, Peter. "The Garden of Light and the Forest of Darkness in Dakkini Sufi Literature and Painting." *AA* 38 (1987): 224–34.

Golombek, L. *The Timurid Shrine at Gazar Gah*. Toronto: Royal Ontario Museum, 1969.

——. "The Cult of Saints and Shrine Architecture in the Fourteenth Century." In *Near Eastern Numismatics, Iconography, Epigraphy, and History*. Ed. D. Kouymjian. Beirut: American U of Beirut P, 1974.

Graham, Terry. "The Influence of Sufism on Music in Islamic Countries." *Sufi* 1 (1988–89): 22–27.

Grube, Ernst. "The Language of the Birds: The Seventeenth Century Miniatures." *Metropolitan Museum Bulletin* n.s. 25 (1967).

Guerrera, Guido. *Franco Battiato: un sufi e la sua musica*. [Firenze]: Shakespeare and Co. Florentia, 1994.

Hammarlûnd, A., et al., eds. *Sufism, Music and Society in Turkey and the Middle East*. London: Curzon, 2001.

Hillenbrand, Robert. "Political Symbolism in Early Indo-Muslim Architecture: The Case of Ajmir." *Iran* 26 (1988): 105–17.

Hillenbrand, Carol. "Some Aspects of al-Ghazālī's Views on Beauty." In *God Is Beautiful and He Loves Beauty*. Ed. A. Giese and J. C. Bürgel. Bern: Peter Lang, 1994.

Khan, Inayat. *Musik und kosmische Harmonie aus mystischer Sicht*. Heilbronn: Verlag Heilbronn, 1984.

Kiel, M. "The Türbe of Sari Saltık at Babada-Dobrudja." *Güney Doğu Abrupa Araştirmaları Dergisi* 6–7 (1977–78): 205–25.

Klimburg-Salter, Deborah. "A Sufi Theme in Persian Painting: The Divan of Sultan Ahmad Galair." *KO* 11 (1976–77): 43–84.

Krasberg, Ulrike. *Die Ekstasetänzerinnen von Sîdî Mustafa: eine theater-ethnologische Untersuchung*. Berlin: Dietrich Reimer Verlag, 2002.

Lifchez, Raymond, ed. *The Dervish Lodge: Architecture, Art and Sufism in Ottoman Turkey*. Berkeley: U of California P, 1992.

Lu'aybi, Shakir. *Soufisme et art visuel: iconographie du sacré*. Paris: L'Harmattan, 1998.

Lukens, Marie G. "The Language of the Birds: Fifteenth-Century Miniatures." *Bulletin of the Metropolitan Museum of Art* n.s. 25:9 (1967): 317–39.

MacDonald, Duncan Black. "Emotional Religion in Islam as Affected by Music and Singing." *JRAS* (1901–1902): 1–28, 195–252, 705–48.

Melikian-Chirvani, A. S. "The Sufi Strain in the Art of Kashan." *Oriental Art* 12:4 (1966): 258–58.

——. "From Royal Boat to the Beggar's Bowl." *IA* 4 (1991): 3–111.

Michot, Jean, and M. Manbiji. *Musique et danse selon Ibn Taymiyya: le livre du Samāʿ et de la danse (Kit ab al-Samāʿ wa l-Raqs)*. Paris: J. Vrin, 1991.

Miller, Lloyd. "Music, Islam, Mysticism, and Proper Performance." In his *Music and Song in Persia*, chap. 2. Richmond, Surrey: Curzon, 1999.

Milstein, Rachel. "Sufi Elements in Late 15th Century Painting of Herat." In *Studies in Honor of Gaston Wiet*. Ed. M. Rosen-Ayalon. Jerusalem: Hebrew U, 1977.

Nasr, Seyyed Hossein. *Islamic Art and Spirituality*. Albany: SUNY, 1987.

Nürnberger, M., and S. Schmiderer. *Tanzkunst, Ritual und Bühne*. Frankfurt am Main: IKO-Verlag für Interkulturelle Kommunikation, 1996.

Qureshi, Regula Burckhardt. *Sufi Music of India and Pakistan: Sound, Context, and Meaning in Qawwali*. Cambridge: Cambridge UP, 1986.

——. "Exploring Time Cross-culturally: Ideology and Performance of Time in the Sufi 'Qawwali.'" *The Journal of Musicology* 12 (1994): 491–528.

Random, M. *Mawlana Djalâl-ud-Dîn, Rûmî* (Dance). Tunis: Sud-Éditions, 1980.

Roberts, A. F., M. Roberts, G. Armenian, and Ousmane Gueye. *A Saint in the City: Sufi Arts of Urban Senegal*. Berkeley: U of California Museum, 2003.

Schimmel, Annemarie. "Calligraphy and Mysticism." In her *Calligraphy and Islamic Culture*. New York: New York UP, 1984.

Seguy, M.-R. *Miraculous Journey of Mahomet: Miraj Nameh*. New York: Braziller, 1977.

Simpson, M. S. *Sultan Ibrahim Mirza's "Haft Awrang."* New Haven, Conn.: Yale UP, 1997.

Waugh, Earle H. *The Munshidin of Egypt*. Columbia: U of South Carolina P, 1989.

Williams, Caroline. "The Cult of 'Alid Saints in the Fatimid Monuments of Cairo, Part 1: The Mosque of al-Aqmar." *Muqarnas* 1 (1983): 37–52.

——. "The Cult of 'Alid Saints in the Fatimid Monuments of Cairo, Part 2: The Mausolea." *Muqarnas* 3 (1985): 39–60.

D. Women, Gender, and Sufism

Abbas, Shemeem Burney. *The Female Voice in Sufi Ritual*. Austin: U of Texas P, 2003.

Austin, R. W. J. "The Feminine Dimensions in Ibn al-ʿArabi's Thought." *Journal of the Muhyiddin Ibn 'Arabi Society* 2 (1984): 5–14.

Bakhtiar, Laleh. *Sufi Women of America: Angels in the Making*. Chicago: Institute of Traditional Psychoethics and Guidance, 1996.

Beelaert, A. L. F. "The Kaʿba as a Woman: A Topos in Classical Persian Literature." *Persica* 13 (1988–89): 107–23.

Betteridge, Anne H. "Women and Shrines in Shiraz." In *Everyday Life in the Muslim Middle East*. Ed. D. L. Bowen and E. Early. Bloomington: Indiana UP, 1993.

Chodkiewicz, Michel. "Female Sainthood in Islam." *Sufi* 21 (1994): 12–19.

Dialmy, A. *Féminisme soufi*. Casablanca: Afrique orient, 1991.

——. *Féminisme, islamisme, soufisme*. Paris: Publisud, 1997.

Elias, Jamal. "Female and Feminine in Islamic Mysticism." *MW* 78 (1988): 209–24.

Helminski, Camille. *Women of Sufism: A Hidden Treasure*. Boston: Shambhala, 2003.

Hermansen, Marcia. "The Female Hero in the Islamic Religious Tradition." *Annual Review of Women in World Religions* 2 (1992): 111–43.

Hoffman, Valerie. "Devotion to the Prophet and His Family in Egyptian Sufism." *IJMES* 24 (1992): 615–37.

——. "Mysticism and Sexuality in Sufi Thought and Life." *Mystics Quarterly* 18:3 (1992): 82–93.

——. "Women and Sexuality." In her *Sufism, Mystics and Saints in Modern Egypt*. Columbia: U of South Carolina P, 1995.

Kimball, Michelle, and Barbara R. von Schlegell. *Muslim Women throughout the World: A Bibliography*. Boulder, Colo.: Lynne Rienner, 1997.

Lawrence, Bruce B. "Honoring Women through Sexual Abstinence: Lessons from the Practice of . . . Shaykh Nizam ad-Din Awliya." In *Annemarie Schimmel Festschrift*. Ed. M. Subtelny. *JTS* 18 (1994): 149–61.

Lutfi, Huda. "The Feminine Element in Ibn 'Arabi's Mystical Philosophy." *Alif: Journal of Comparative Poetics* 5 (1985): 7–19.

Makowski, Samsam Renate, and Stefan Makowski. *Sufismus für Frauen: Zugänge zur islamischen Mystik*. Zürich: Benziger, 1996.

Malamud, Margaret. "Gender and Spiritual Self-Fashioning: The Master-Disciple Relationship in Classical Sufism." *JAAR* 64:1 (1996): 89–117.

Malti-Douglas, Fedwa. *A Woman and Her Sufis*. Washington, D.C.: Georgetown U Center for Contemporary Arab Studies Occasional Papers, 1995.

——. "Gender and Uses of the Ascetic in an Islamist Text." In *Asceticism*. Ed. V. L. Wimbush and R. Valantasis. New York: Oxford UP, 1995.

Murata, Sachiko. *The Tao of Islam: A Sourcebook on Gender Relationships in Islamic Thought*. Albany: SUNY, 1992.

Nurbakhsh, Javad. *Sufi Women*. New York: Khaniqahi Nimatullahi, 1983; 2nd ed., 1990.

Özelsel, Michaela M. *Forty Days: The Diary of a Traditional Solitary Sufi Retreat*. Brattleboro, Vt.: Threshold, 1996.

Qamar Jahan Begam. *Princess Jahan Ara Begam, Her Life and Works*. Karachi: S. M. Hamid 'Ali, 1991.

Raudvere, Catharina. *The Book and the Roses: Sufi Women, Visibility and Zikr in Contemporary Istanbul*. London: I. B. Tauris, 2003.

Reinhertz, Shakina, et al. *Women Called to the Path of Rumi: The Way of the Whirling Dervish*. Prescott, Ariz.: Hohm, 2001.

Roded, Ruth. *Women in Islamic Biographical Collections: From Ibn Sa'd to Who's Who*. Boulder, Colo.: Lynne Rienner, 1994.

Smith, Margaret. "Woman Saint in Development of Islam." *MW* 17 (1927): 130–38.

———. *Rabi'a the Mystic and Her Fellow Saints in Islam*. Cambridge: Cambridge UP, repr. 1984.

Sulami, Muhammad ibn al Husayn as-. *Early Sufi Women*. Trans. Rkia Cornell. Louisville, Ky.: Fons Vitae, 2000.

Tapper, Nancy. "*Ziyaret*: Gender, Movement, and Exchange in a Turkish Community." In *Muslim Travellers*. Ed. D. Eickelman and J. Piscatori. Berkeley: U of California P, 1990.

Trix, Frances. *Spiritual Discourse: Learning with an Islamic Master*. Philadelphia: U of Pennsylvania P, 1993.

Tweedie, Irina. *Chasm of Fire: A Woman's Experience with the Teachings of a Sufi Master*. New York: HarperCollins, 1993.

Van Gelder, G. J. H. "Rabi'a's Poem on the Two Kinds of Love: A Mystification?" In *Verse and the Fair Sex*. Ed. F. de Jong. Utrecht: Houtsma Stichting, 1993.

Wilcox, Lynn. *Women and the Holy Quran*. San Rafael, Calif.: MTO, 1998.

Yashrutiyyah, al-Sayyidah Fatimah. "Contemplation and Action: The Sufi Way." In *Contemplation and Action in World Religions*. Ed. Y. Ibish and I. Marculescu. Seattle: U of Washington P, 1978.

Yazdani, G. "Jahānārā." *Journal of the Panjab Historical Society* 2 (1914): 152–69.

About the Author

John Renard received a Ph.D. (1978) in Islamic studies from Harvard University's Department of Near Eastern Languages and Civilizations, specializing in medieval religious literature in Arabic and Persian. His dissertation was on the prophetology of the great 13th-century Sufi Jalāl ad-Dīn Rūmī and was later published as *All the King's Falcons: Rūmī on Prophets and Revelation* (SUNY, 1994). He is professor in the Department of Theological Studies at Saint Louis University, where he has taught Islamic studies, history of religion, and comparative theology since 1978. He has previously published 12 books, including *Ibn 'Abbād of Ronda: Letters on the Sufi Path* (Paulist, 1986) and *Knowledge of God in Classical Sufism: Foundations of Islamic Mystical Theology* (Paulist, 2004)—both volumes in the translation series Classics of Western Spirituality; *Seven Doors to Islam: Spirituality and the Religious Life of Muslims* (U of California P, 1996) and its companion anthology, *Windows on the House of Islam: Muslim Sources on Spirituality and Religious Life* (U of California P, 1998); *Islam and the Heroic Image: Themes in Literature and the Visual Arts* (U of South Carolina P, 1993, paperback Mercer UP, 1999); *Understanding the Islamic Experience* (Paulist, 2002), previously published as *In the Footsteps of Muhammad* (Paulist, 1994); volumes on Islam (1998); Hinduism (1999); Buddhism (1999); and Daoism, Confucianism, and Shinto (2002) in the Paulist Press's 101 Questions series; and *The Handy Religion Answer Book* (Visible Ink Press, 2001). His other publications include five dozen articles, book chapters, and review essays; 20 encyclopedia entries; and over 60 book reviews. He plays guitar and mandolin, enjoys music and art of all kinds, and lives with his wife Mary Pat in St. Louis, Missouri.